1983

University of St. Francis
GEN 301.161 U423
Ulloth. Dana Royal.

T4-ALA-738

MASS MEDIA
Past, Present, Future

MASS MEDIA
Past, Present, Future

DANA R. ULLOTH
University of South Carolina

PETER L. KLINGE
Ithaca College

SANDRA EELLS

LIBRARY
College of St. Francis
JOLIET, ILL.

WEST PUBLISHING COMPANY

St. Paul   New York   Los Angeles   San Francisco

Copy Editor: Lynette Lamb Gollmar
Cover Design and Part Opening Art: Brenda Booth
Compositor: TriStar Graphics

Persons depicted on the cover are, in descending order: Johann Gutenberg, Benjamin Franklin, Thomas Edison, Billie Holiday, Clark Gable, Vivian Leigh, Barbara Walters, Walter Cronkite, and Ray Charles.

COPYRIGHT © 1983 By WEST PUBLISHING CO.
50 West Kellogg Boulevard
P.O. Box 3526
St. Paul, Minnesota 55165

All rights reserved

Printed in the United States of America

Library of Congress Cataloging in Publication Data

Ulloth, Dana Royal.
  Mass communications.

  Bibliography: p.
  Includes index.
  1. Mass media—United States. I. Klinge, Peter L.
II. Eells, Sandra. III. Title.
P92.U5U4   1983   001.51′0973   82-20205
ISBN 0-314-69683-0

301.161
2(423

For our families, who encouraged us through endless
research and rewrites.

106,085

CONTENTS

12 REGULATION OF BROADCASTING AND NEWER TECHNOLOGIES   335

PART IV   Audience/Futures   371

13 MEDIA EFFECTS   373

PREFACE

Today we live in an environment of media that continuously expands. Television grew through the development of cable capable of delivering dozens of channels to the home set; magazines grew by creating a wealth of specialized products; books discovered the spin-off—repackaged products from other media; motion pictures found the blockbuster movie; and newspapers produced the national daily. Even direct mail advertising has found new markets. In the Great Depression of the 1930s, radio flourished and made huge sums for its creators and managers. During the recession of the 1980s new communication technologies—computers and cable television—produced the new millionaires. In hard times as in good times, people want to be entertained, and the mass media offer an inexpensive means to that goal. For most people in the United States, the mass media are the primary source of entertainment—broken by occasional church picnics, dinners out, and trips to the live theater. However inadequately, the mass media provide the culture most people experience.

But the mass media are not primarily means for the transmission of culture—they are businesses first. Businesses that are supported by subscribers, advertisers, and endowment. Because the media are businesses, their concerns are the same as every other business—changing markets, strikes, law suits, bankruptcy, competition from other media, and rising costs. Sometimes, perhaps too often, the business worries overshadow the needs to provide a responsible product to the buying public. This competition between commerce and culture has been at the heart of most criticism of the media.

In this book, we will spend less time evaluating the media, and more space reviewing the history, business, regulation, and economics of the mass media. This treatment is based upon the examination of each of three major groups of media separately: Paper and ink media (newspapers, books, and magazines); plastic based media (motion pictures and records); and electronic media (radio, television, cable television, computers, and satellites). Each of the media has individual characteristics that need to be examined independently of other media.

The three media sections start with a "day in the life of" based on a real event in one of the media treated in that section. Students have the opportunity to see how a city newsroom of an afternoon paper works; how a midday network television newscast comes together; and how events transpire on a motion picture set. As is apparent, real people with real concerns produce the newspapers, television programs, and motion pictures we enjoy or dislike. We hope the look inside real events will provide a clear basis for the study of the media.

Throughout your study, you will encounter sidebars and material separated from the main text. These asides provide the opportunity to examine interesting events or people that do not fit the basic narrative. Important dates in media development are highlighted; a look at the lives of media figures becomes possible; and statistical information is tabulated.

The book concludes with an examination of the audience for the mass media and the findings of research regarding audience behavior. Some conclusions of that research have been disturbing, others have been surprising. The final chapter looks back over the book and suggests directions the future might take.

As you read, you might ask yourself how you would produce the media around you—could you do a better job, a different job? If you are considering a career in the media, these are questions you must address. If you plan another career but are a consumer of the media, the questions bear reflection, so that you may make rational judgments about the media around you.

ACKNOWLEDGMENTS

Many people provided assistance or opened doors during the preparation of this book. Some of them gave information available from no other source. While not everyone can be named, the following deserve special mention: Thomas N. McLean, Robert M. Hitt, III, Melissa Mills Herring, John Goyer, Martin E. Appel, Frank Coffey, Claire Carter, Marvin Scott, Richard Frishman, Stanley Quinn, Harry Herrmann, Lee McConkey, and Ed Rice.

The comments of our reviewers and editors were most helpful and had much to do with the final shape of the book. Thanks go to Gary Woodruff, Marta Reynolds, Ronald E. Sutton, Shirley Biagi, Don Jacobs, Haluk Sahin, Beverly Bethune, Barbara Hartung, Rebecca Quarles, Dario Politella, and Robert E. Davis.

MASS MEDIA
Past, Present, Future

PART I

Print/Ink

1

JOURNALISTIC TRADITIONS

A report about an automobile accident or the latest unemployment statistics in your favorite newspaper does not just happen. The stories to be covered must be selected, and once selected, much editing takes place. Decisions about which facts to emphasize, how long to make the story, where to put the final report are made by editors and reporters. The term "gatekeeper" arose to describe the process of using or rejecting stories or story elements. The following report of a day in the life of a real newspaper, the *Columbia* (SC) *Record,* illustrates the process.

April 6, 1982—The Making of *The Columbia Record*

7:30 A.M. A Hardees's steak biscuit half eaten in the left hand. A large cup of coffee on the table and a wire story about the impending Northeast snowstorm flashing on the video display terminal. Martin Mobley, the news editor, takes another bite of the steak biscuit, punches some changes into the weather story and leans back in his padded chair to consider the day's agenda.

Reporters and photographers are just settling into the newsroom, as the city editor, her two assistants, the assistant news editor, and a couple of copy editors get organized. Within minutes the newsroom will be filled with forty-five people. All around the room, twenty-five "tubes," as the video display terminals are called, wait for the day's action. Gone are the noisy typewriters of another era. Gone too are the linotype machines— replaced by four silent computers and the high speed typesetters that all the tubes are hooked up to.

7:35 A.M. "Do you have an item on reapportionment?" Bunny Richardson, the assistant city editor, asks. "On AP wire from Charlotte," another editor replies.

"About South Carolina?"

"Yes, but from Charlotte."

7:45 A.M.   Twelve items on the news budget—a synopsis of stories being considered for the day's newspaper—are gleaming out of the tube. Richardson stares at them, changing a line here or there.

8:02 A.M.   Richardson takes a call, then hangs up. "John Goyer, check Lexington Schools on bus accident in South Congaree." No specific facts are available yet.

8:03 A.M.   The first of two daily budget meetings coordinated by the city editor, Elizabeth Latt. She inquires about the twelve items on the local budget, makes assignments. "What about the garbage story? Has the health department granted a license yet? Check it out." A few laughs, sips on coffee cups, assignments for the day, postponements to another day. Last item: "Eastover is

---

FIGURE 1-1   Flowchart of a Newspaper Story

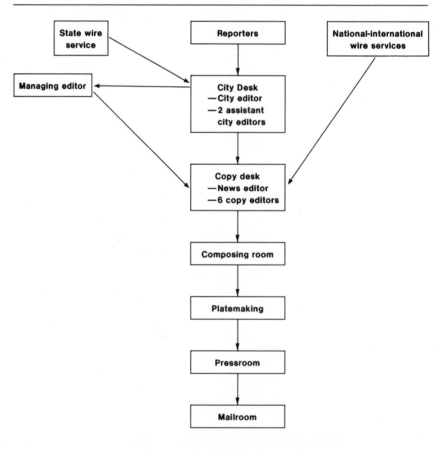

having its annual barbecue roast. They will roast twenty-five pigs. Big thing." Laughter and everyone is gone.

Reporters' assignments include municipal meetings, Special Olympics, school districts, and so on.

8:17 A.M.   Paper copy of first news budget is printed out from computer and distributed to editors and reporters.

Managing editor, Robert Hitt, who came in a few minutes earlier, is on the floor talking to editors and reporters.

8:20 A.M.   Hitt and news editors talk about status of day's stories: Snowstorm descending on the Northeast; something about the Supreme Court; Haig to talk somewhere; private ships carrying troops to Falkland Islands. Several state agencies are meeting this morning, most too late for deadline. A commission meeting about a pink house—evidently it doesn't like the color.

Get local slant on that reapportionment story—call officials who worked on it.

8:30 A.M.   Meeting's over.

9:00 A.M.   Richardson is rewriting some of these stories. She corrects improper tenses, shortens sentences. Early stories are being transferred from city desk to news editor's desk by pushing a button on the tube keyboard.

10:15 A.M.   Latt talks to reporter about story. She checks picture, rejects it. She looks at reapportionment story, suggests changes.

10:20 A.M.   Most reporters are working on stories. The carpeted floor and the soundless tubes leave the room strangely silent except for one reporter pounding on a 1950 Royal perched on a low file cabinet. Copyboy returns with first page of proofs, big photcopied pages of set copy and headlines with blank spaces where the pictures will be. Hitt crossing room with big strides, paper in hand, stops at Richardson's desk. "This remap story is too complicated . . . nobody will understand this last 'graf' (paragraph). Drop it or shorten."

10:30 A.M.   Bus accident story has taken shape in hands of police reporters, Goyer and John Emerson, but questions remain. Where was the school bus going? Need correct name of auto occupants—is one of their names Setzer or Setzler? How many are hurt? Already the two reporters are getting the run-around from school officials—probably they were coached not to talk to the media. Try again or call someone else.

10:33 A.M.   Final budget meeting before today's edition goes to press. Hitt is in charge. Updated news budgets are distributed. Hitt: "What about this armed robbery? Did they get anything besides checks? Money? How much?"

"They don't want the amount mentioned, but it was. . . ."

"Say more than $15,000 in cash and checks or similar."

"What about bus accident?"

"Information still coming in . . . we'll keep on it."

"Run it on the split." (The split is the front page of Section II of the newspaper—a page reserved for metropolitan news.) "Redistricting to go on page 1A (first section)." Give and take: Richardson suggests one story for 1A, Latt recommends inside page, Hitt goes with inside. Add information here. Drop that story. Before long every story has its position or has been dropped. And that winter freeze story makes page 1A —actually it's two stories—one on the Northeast and one on South Carolina.

A story on a woman passing bad checks ends with the woman trying to get charity in Texas because she has no money. Laughter.

11:00 A.M.	Copy deadline only an hour away. Activity has reached a feverish pitch. Copy boy keeps returning with proofs to review. He gets a picture of Margaret Thatcher from the morgue file (file for pictures, etc.), but can't find the right size to fit the space so new picture has to be shot.
11:30 A.M.	More shortening on reapportionment story.
11:45 A.M.	School bus accident story needs more detail. Finally, Goyer gets correct spelling on Setzer. Still doesn't know where bus was going.
11:57 A.M.	City editor reviews accident story. Both Goyer and Emerson call for information. Discovered that the bus belonged to Lexington District I. Bus was en route to schools, but which schools? Five elementary students, one high school student, and driver were on board.
12:08 P.M.	Story transferred to copy desk for headline and final editing.
12:10 P.M.	More information: Story returned to city desk and destinations added—bus was going to Pelion elementary and high schools.
12:15 P.M.	Transferred to composing department where camera-ready copy comes out of the typesetter ready to paste up. Last story of day is finished just 15 minutes after copy deadline. Other pages are already finished.
12:30 P.M.	Final page is pasted up, then production starts. A picture the full size of the newspaper page is taken. This picture is a giant negative of all the type, pictures, headlines, and artwork that will appear on the printed newspaper page. From that negative other workers create a plastic plate like a large rubber stamp with raised surfaces that conform to the pictures, artwork, and type

on the negative. This has already been done for other pages in the paper.

1:01 P.M.   Page 1B—the front of Section II—is fastened to one of the huge press's cylindrical printing surfaces—called a saddle—that is capable of printing several sections and many pages at one time. Actually, there are fifteen press units tied together simultaneously printing different parts of the newspaper, which are fed into a collecting machine that sorts, folds, and cuts the huge sheets into a newspaper.

1:05 P.M.   Ring—a sound not unlike a telephone—and the presses begin to slowly turn. Presspersons examine each page of the newspaper and make ink and alignment adjustments. The presses are running perhaps 150 copies per hour. Pressperson after pressperson calls out that each section is printing correctly.

1:09 P.M.   Slowly the press foreman moves the speed control up— 10,000 copies per hour, 17,000 copies per hour, 26,000 copies per hour, 42,000 copies per hour—now the press is fast enough for the afternoon run.

    Newspapers—hundreds of them—slide smoothly through the printing surfaces into a web of angles as the pages come together in the folder machine. There they are cut before being streamed to the mailroom on a conveyor belt to an automatic counter where the papers are bundled and advertising sections are inserted.

1:57 P.M.   The first trucks leave the plant to be delivered to distributors for newsstands and vending machines, then to carriers for home delivery.

3:00 P.M.   I drop twenty-five cents into the corner vending box, select a newspaper, and read:

"Two Teachers Hurt When Bus, Car Collide."

Every story that finds its way to the pages of the newspapers throughout the world must go through a complex process. Reporters who cover the stories and report their observations submit their results to editors who review, change, or reject the piece. *The Columbia Record* and other newspapers use variations of the pattern shown in figure 1.1, which details the flow of a story through the editorial process from reporting to printing.

When the story reaches the city desk, editors correct style and technical aspects of grammar and make changes designed to create a clearer story. From the city editor the story moves to the news desk where it is combined with stories from the state and national wires. Here, too, the final pages are laid out. Finally, the copy desk makes final corrections before the story is sent to production.

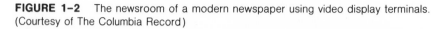

FIGURE 1-2 The newsroom of a modern newspaper using video display terminals. (Courtesy of The Columbia Record)

At each stage along the process the managing editor maintains close contact with developing stories—making changes, choosing story placement, making more changes. Although the managing editor's decisions are final on a story, other editors and reporters may make recommendations.

THE FIRST NEWSPAPERS IN EUROPE

People live in the 1980s surrounded by a vast array of communication media. Besides the older media of television, newspapers, magazines, radio, and billboards, a host of new media have burst upon the scene in the past few years. Computers, video cassettes, satellites, and cable television are well known, but other media have only begun to appear—video disc, two-way cable, big-screen television, electronic newspapers and mail, and electronic games. The media environment is as pervasive as sunlight—feature movies without commercials are even available in hotel rooms. Some hotels even advertise free movies if you stay with them, much as hotels once advertised free swimming pools or other complementary items.

With such an extensive array of communication media, one almost wonders if there was life before the media. Back before television (1950s), mass newspapers (1830s), and the printing press (1450), people had no means of quickly spreading "the word." Yet as far back as the cave people there were reporters, or at least recorders, who charted the events of their day on the walls of caves. Pictures of animals, battles, and even political events found their way to the walls of caves, and eventually, to buildings. The Chinese invented an inexpensive means for making paper around 105 A.D. Centuries later, the Chinese invented movable wood type (1221) and later copper movable type (1445).

In Europe, monks of the Middle Ages painstakingly transcribed books such as the Bible and messengers traveled from manor to manor with the news of the day. But soon a new era was upon the world. Wealthy landowners with many serfs still existed, but a new class of craftspeople and merchants were appearing who needed faster, more accurate news to base their business decisions on. And the new middle class needed a way to advertise its wares and services.

As a new middle class was developing in Europe, so were new universities for the preservation and teaching of human knowledge. Between the years 1200 and 1400 more than fifty European universities were formed. With the rise of these universities came a demand for cheap books and other printed materials. The beautiful and expensive volumes produced by the monks fell far short of meeting the demand for books at a reasonable price.

THE BEGINNINGS OF INFORMATION TRANSFER BY MEDIA

The course humanity took in reaching the modern media so much in evidence today may have started slowly, but has accelerated in recent years. The beginnings followed this pattern:

3500 B.C.–2500 B.C.	First picture language develops, crude paper appears.
200 B.C.	Greeks devise parchment from animal skins.
105 A.D.	Chinese invent inexpensive paper.
1221	Chinese invent movable wood type.
1200–1400	Fifty European universities come into existence, the merchant class grows, and people demand books.
1445	Chinese invent movable copper type.
1450	Johann Gutenberg introduces his new printing press with movable metal type.
1476	William Caxton brings a press to England.
1644	John Milton defends the need for press freedom.
1679	British Parliament refuses to renew the 1662 law regulating printing.

The demand for large numbers of cheap books opened the way for the creation of a new industry—the printing industry. The first European printers used presses modeled after wine presses. Made up of wooden blocks carved with letters and illustrations and pressed onto paper with a screw, these early presses greatly reduced the time required to print books. But the system did have its limitations. After a few hundred impressions the wood type broke, and a new block had to be carved. Carvers had to craft each printing block separately—a long and tedious process.

Johann Gutenberg of Mainz, Germany, solved the problems of wood type by developing metal type. Each letter was cast separately. Then the letters were arranged in a wood frame to compose the words of the page to be printed. After enough pages were printed, the letters could be rearranged into another page and the process continued. Introduced· in 1450, Gutenberg's invention opened the way for some 15 million copies of 35,000 titles to be published by 1500. The era of the book and newspaper was upon the world.[1]

Printing came more slowly to England than to the European continent because England was more agricultural than countries like France and Germany. Yet, when Edward IV became king in 1461, conditions in England changed and William Caxton, a wealthy merchant, was able to bring printing to the island. Caxton already had established a press in Belgium, which he moved to London in 1476. He was eager to print the best secular English literature, including Chaucer

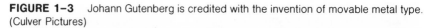

FIGURE 1–3 Johann Gutenberg is credited with the invention of movable metal type. (Culver Pictures)

and Lydgate. In this Caxton differed from his continental counterparts who concentrated on religious literature.[2]

The freedom that Caxton experienced vanished under King Henry VIII when, in about 1531, the first system for printing patents or licenses was initiated. The first royal patent was issued to William Fagues and the patent system was widespread in one form or another until 1695.

THE ENGLISH EXPERIENCE

Sometimes the study of American mass media leads to the conclusion that everything worth happening occurred in the United States. Forces in England were just as alarmed over repressive government as elsewhere. The British Parliament took progressive steps in 1679 by refusing to renew the 1662 law regulating printing. The action opened the way for some 20 papers to get started over the next three years. Moreover, Parliament refused to permit the King to force Catholicism upon the nation. The winds of freedom blew strongly across England, just as they did in the American colonies.

Perhaps the clash that developed in England under the printing patents is best illustrated by the printers John Binkenhead and Marchmont Nedham (1643–1660). Binkenhead, who found favor with the palace, founded a journal whose Latin title was *Court Journal.* Binkenhead accepted the notion that kings and queens ruled by divine right and accorded their every thought free discourse in his journal. No matter what, Binkenhead staunchly supported the official powers.

In contrast, Nedham began a journal whose title might be translated *People's Paper.* As the title suggested, Nedham rejected Binkenhead's views about the absolute power of the monarchy and was constantly at variance with the court. So irked was the crown over Nedham's writing that an office of press censorship was formed—clearly a monument to Nedham's unpopularity with the government.[3]

The conflicts between British journalists and the crown became the standard upon which later conflicts in other countries were to develop. Even the American colonies, and later the United States, had to make decisions on how to treat the press.

In England many writers argued vigorously for press freedom. Among them were William Walwyn, Henry Robinson, and John Milton. In 1644, Milton wrote:

Though all the winds of doctrine were let loose to play upon the earth, so truth be in the field, we do injuriously by licensing and prohibiting to misdoubt her strength. Let her falsehood grapple; whoever knew truth put to the worst in a free and open encounter? Give me liberty to know and to utter and to argue freely according to conscience, above all liberties.

Ironically, that ringing defense of freedom found in *Areopagitica* came from the pen of a man who later was appointed censor for Oliver Cromwell.

Since the conflicts over the role of the press in society began in England, there have been but two (with two variant) views on the role of the press: authoritarian and libertarian.

The diversity represented by Binkenhead—defender of authoritarian rule, and Nedham—defender of a press free to treat all views, reflects the duality of opinion on the role of the journalist to this day. In a small book entitled *Four Theories of the Press,*[4] the two notions on the role of the mass media are given two extensions—the social responsibility and the Soviet-totalitarian views. The first has its roots in the libertarian theory, the second in the authoritarian theory.

AUTHORITARIAN THEORY

Of the four theories, the authoritarian theory has been practiced most widely. Plato was one of the first to idealize the authoritarian theory; he contended that the magistrate was essential to keep society under control. Plato's teacher Socrates also believed that the state must rigidly regulate society.

Other famous thinkers through the centuries also have subscribed to the authoritarian powers of the state. Among them are Machiavelli, Hobbes, Hegel, and Treitschke. All these people held one belief in common—they distrusted the discipline of the common person. Georg Hegel, the German philosopher, is most often credited with the modern theory of authoritarianism. To Hegel, "The State is embodied Morality." Hegel could see no reason for the individual to participate in the state activities—freedom was freedom within the state.

Authoritarian thinking leads to state control of the mass media so that state goals can be promoted, developed, and disseminated. Authoritarian control of the mass media appeared in early England, but it also existed in Mussolini's Italy and Hitler's Germany.

As the famous writer, Dr. Samuel Johnson, reflected:

> Every society has a right to preserve public peace and order, and therefore, has a good right to prohibit the propagation of opinions which have a dangerous tendency. To say the magistrate has this right is using an inadequate word; it is the society for which the magistrate is agent. He may be morally or theologically wrong in restraining the propagation of opinions which he thinks dangerous, but he is politically right.[5]

Johnson's writing spells out the underlying tenet of the authoritarian thinking.

SOVIET COMMUNIST THEORY

Marxism and the development that followed is a philosophy of history—a neat system that includes everything from the role of the worker to the governing system. Included in the total system are attitudes about truth, social and political institutions, and the ability of the Marxist philosophy to make the world better for the masses. A key to the Marxist concept is the belief that unity is paramount; diversity is an anathema. Free and frank discussion, compromise, and criticism are signs of weakness. Freedom in the Soviet Union—probably the best illustration of the Marxist state—only exists within the bounds of what the state has declared to be the truth.

Because the Soviets are so certain that their system holds the greatest promise for improving humanity's lot, defection from the principles of the government is viewed as a significant weakening of progress towards the perfect condition that all citizens deserve. The individual becomes an instrument to improve the condition of the masses so that the condition of the individual may be improved.

In the same way, the mass media become instruments that help develop the perfect state. The mass media, the masses, and the central party all work together for that perfect state. Consequently, the mass media are used by the governing party to promote what they view as the common good of the state. Diversity, conflict, debate, and contrast are eliminated. To allow otherwise would be to permit anarchy and chaos.

While the philosophical underpinnings of the Soviet Communist theory of the mass media differ somewhat from the standard authoritarian theory, the result is the same—party control of the mass media.

The content of mass media, consistent with party philosophy, does not criticize the central doctrine of Communism, but rather focuses on expounding truth as seen by the leaders of the party. Although the news media do not criticize the doctrine of collective government, they may focus attention on a factory not producing its quota, the failures of certain groups within the Soviet system, or the error of dissidents. Indeed, the media are expected to take these "positive" steps to criticize elements that do not live up to party standards. As a result, the media assume a positive role in promoting the truth of the revolutionary proletariat or working class.

Criticism in the Soviet media may be directed against specific officials, agencies, or groups, but it must never question the underlying dogma of the nation. The media may even criticize the way citizens relax, rear their children or engage in other personal activities.

While the Soviet leaders believe they have a media system much freer than the United States' capitalist-controlled media, they have not been tolerant of the underground press that has grown up. People like "Phoenix Group" members Andrei D. Sakharov and Aleksandr I. Solzhenitsyn have become famous outside the Soviet Union for their criticism of fundamental Soviet doctrines—criticisms that have led to the explusion of some Soviet writers from their native land. Yet criticism continues to circulate through mimeographed, handwritten, and typewritten newsletters and small private meetings. From time to time the Soviet Union purges these dissident voices, but with only temporary success.

The Soviets believe their system to be superior to the libertarian and social responsibility theories (discussed next); citizens of the Western world believe their systems to be superior. It may take a few generations to determine which system better satisfies people's needs.

LIBERTARIAN THEORY

Much newer than authoritarian theory, libertarian theory grew out of the state-dominated English publishing system. Seventeenth and eighteenth century British thought culminated in the work of John Milton and John Erskine. In the nineteenth century, John Stuart Mill was to add further dimensions to the libertarian view of the mass media.

Milton advanced the argument for intellectual freedom in the *Areopagitica,* published in 1644. Milton believed that if people were given unlimited access to ideas—good and bad, right and wrong—truth would ultimately emerge. To find truth, people would need freedom to debate all issues. Although Milton believed that some boundaries might be imposed on the freedom of speech and printing, he stopped short of suggesting what they might be.

John Erskine argued more specifically: He said that people should have the right to discuss governments in general, and their own government in particular. Early thinkers believed in libertarian principles because they thought free and frank discussion brought forth truth; the human race could find truth and justice in a kind of marketplace of ideas.

John S. Mill took the libertarian view a step further by observing that people have a right to explore unpopular ideas as long as they do not harm others. The truth or falsehood of the idea is of no consequence.

About individual freedom Mill had much to say:

> If all mankind minus one, were of one opinion, and only one person were of the contrary opinion, mankind would be no more justified in silencing that one person, than he, if he had the power, would be justified in silencing mankind. Were an opinion a personal possession of no value except to the owner; if to be obstructed in the enjoyment of it were simply a private injury, it would make some difference whether the injury was inflicted on a few persons or on many. But the peculiar evil of silencing the expression of an opinion is, that it is robbing the human race; posterity as well as the existing generation; those who dissent

from the opinion, still more than those who hold it. If the opinion is right, they are deprived of the opportunity of exchanging error for truth; if wrong, they lose, what is almost as great a benefit, the clearer preception and livelier impression of truth, produced by its collision with error.[6]

In the United States, the libertarian concepts were taking hold, too. As a president and politician, Thomas Jefferson tried to put his philosophies regarding freedom of the press into practice. Jefferson argued forcefully for the right of the press to criticize, claiming that an administration that could not withstand criticism did not deserve to continue. Out of criticism and favorable commentary the public would make the correct judgment. Jefferson was able to successfully practice his views when his administration was severely criticized.

The British won a Bill of Rights in 1689 while the United States added its own to the constitution after independence in the late 1700s. Both of these documents incorporated the libertarian concepts of individual and press freedoms into the fundamental laws of the two countries.

The big battles of the eighteenth century were over seditious libel—criticism of the government or its officers—and the right to publish government proceedings. Related to these two issues was the notion of "truth as a defense" against libel and a protection for a publisher who reported governmental actions. At John Peter Zenger's 1735 trial for printing some remarks critical of a government official, the "truth as defense" idea was tested. In that celebrated trial, a jury decided that truth was grounds for protecting a printer from legal sanctions. Although the decision was celebrated on both sides of the Atlantic, libertarian principles did not really triumph until the nineteenth century, when a Parliamentary act (1843) was passed in England and a series of court cases was decided and laws were established in the United States.

What emerged during the seventeenth and eighteenth centuries was a debate over the role of time-tested laws versus the rights of the press. Judges such as Lord Mansfield and Chief Justice Blackstone argued against licensing printers, but argued for sanctions against printers who published crime news. Blackstone believed that the press had the right to publish anything it chose—that is, prior restraint should not be imposed on the press—but after publication appropriate legal recourse to punish must exist. "If [the press] publishes what is improper, mischievous, or illegal, [the press] must take the consequences."

Most libertarians do acknowledge some restraints on the news media. In the chapter on print media law, these restraints will be examined in detail. For now a list of the standard limitations will suffice: (1) defamation—the news media are not free to discredit an individual inaccurately; (2) obscene and indecent materials—the media should recognize that at least some segments of the population must be protected from obscene material; and (3) sedition—the media cannot gravely endanger the safety of the state or its citizens.

In one form or another, the libertarian view of the mass media is practiced today in the United States, Canada, and Western Europe. Many emerging countries of Africa and South America also have tried libertarian principles—some with much success.

THE SOCIAL RESPONSIBILITY THEORY

The social responsibility theory is an updated version of the libetarian theory.

In the twentieth century the number of independent newspapers and other forms of mass media has declined and the number of chain owners has increased. With this shift in ownership, the number of diverse media voices has declined to include just a few very powerful media owners. Under the libertarian theory, the mass media are owned by private individuals and corporations and are the voices of those owners who seek to make a profit from their product. As long as many small owners existed, so did the many voices envisioned by Jefferson. Owners were free to promulgate what they wished. But when the diversity of ownership disappeared, libertarians felt that media owners had a social responsibility to see that many different views received exposure in the mass media. In this way they felt diversity would be protected.

Under the social responsibility theory, the mass media must accomplish six tasks: provide debate and information on public affairs; enlighten the public; protect individual rights by being a government "watchdog"; provide an advertising avenue for sellers and buyers; provide entertainment; and develop the sufficient financial security to avoid being influenced by special interests. Obviously, this is a big job for the media.

The social responsibility theory received a huge boost during the 1920s with the growth of radio broadcasting. Left unregulated, broadcasters initially created much confusion as their transmitters settled on the same frequencies. Listeners tried vainly to select clear signals. Because radio station owners appeared incapable of policing themselves and because of the resulting cry for government involvement from broadcasters, educators, and the public, a new law was passed that was designed to impose responsible behavior on the broadcast industry. The law grew out of a belief that listeners as well as broadcasters had a right—the right to receive programs representing a variety of views.

To enforce the provisions of the new law, Congress created the Federal Radio Commission (1927) which later became the Federal Communications Commission (1934). Both agencies kept a watchful eye on the broadcast industry, which of course later included television. Although both commissions have exercised some control over programming, the law specifically forbids censorship—defined in broadcasting as a form of prior restraint that would keep a station from airing a program. Although the government may not prevent a broadcaster from airing a program, nothing prevents the government from taking action after the offensive program has been broadcast.

More than any other media, broadcasters have been required to follow some form of imposed standards. Although print media must refrain from certain communications such as defamation, the primary controls exercised on the print media are public opinion, the threat of regulation, and the writings of critics. The newspaper industry also has its self-imposed canons of ethics.

The film industry decided to show its social responsibility through creating a rating system—G, PG, R and X were the symbols selected to indicate a film's intended audience. This voluntary system defused a movement threatening to impose a law regulating the film industry.

Most communications industries have some form of code proclaiming their industry's intention to serve the public. The Commission on Freedom of the Press, however, has been less than enthusiastic about these. The commission noted that the primary responsibility of the press is to provide "a truthful, comprehensive, and intelligent account of the day's events in a context which gives them meaning."[7]

Although the social responsibility theory applies differently to different media, at its most fundamental level the theory demands that all mass media serve more than the private interests of their owners. Moreover, the theory rejects the notion that the mass media are free from all restraints on their operation. The natures of these restraints are the topics of several chapters.

ADDITIONAL READINGS

Cook, Elizabeth C. *Literary Influences in Colonial Newspapers, 1704–50.* Port Washington, New York: Kenneth Press, 1966.

Elliott, T. H. S. *Masters of English Journalism: A Study of Personal Forces.* London: T. Fisher Unwin, 1911.

Mill, John Stuart. *On Liberty.* Edited by Alburey Castell. New York: F. S. Crofts and Co., 1947.

Olson, Kenneth E. *The History Makers.* Baton Rouge: Louisiana State University Press, 1966.

Patterson, Theodore; Schramm, Wilbur; and Siebert, Fred S. *Four Theories of the Press.* Urbana: University of Illinois Press, 1956.

FOOTNOTES

1. Kenneth E. Olson, *The History Makers* (Baton Rouge: Louisiana State University Press, 1966), p. 100.

2. Ibid., p. 6.

3. T.H.S. Elliott, *Masters of English Journalism: A Study of Personal Forces* (London: T. Fisher Unwin, 1911), pp. 36–40.

4. Theodore Peterson, Wilbur Schramm, and Fred S. Siebert, *Four Theories of the Press* (Urbana: University of Illinois Press, 1966).

5. Ibid., p. 36.

6. John Stuart Mill, *On Liberty,* ed. Alburey Castell (New York: F.S. Crofts and Co., 1947).

7. Peterson, *Four Theories of the Press,* p. 87.

JOURNALISM: THE AMERICAN EXPERIENCE

Joseph Glover, a clergyman of some means in England, brought printing to America. Unhappy with the repressive government of his home-
land, he decided to move to English America. Grover died during the
arduous ocean crossing, but his partner, Stephen Daye, did establish
the first printing press in 1638 at what was to become Harvard College.[1]

Daye printed almanacs, sermons, a catechism, and a few books, but
with little freedom. Both church and state watched him carefully to
insure that nothing dangerous was printed. Sir William Berkeley, governor of Virginia, expressed the antipathy towards printers in America
in remarks he made in 1671:

> But I thank God, we have not free schools nor printing; and I
> hope we shall not have these hundred years. For learning has
> brought disobedience and heresy and sects into the world; and
> printing has divulged them and libels against the government.
> God keep us from both.[2]

NEW ENGLAND NEWSPAPERS

The first newspaper in America lasted one day. As the publisher of the
London *Domestic Intelligence,* Benjamin Harris fought against religious persecution, and had even criticized the king. At the trial that
followed, Harris showed himself to be so aggressive that the Chief Justice observed that the author was the "worst man in the world." After
the conviction, Harris appealed to the judge to send him to any prison

except Newgate, but the request was denied. On September 25, 1690, however, Harris was back in print—in Boston.[3] He had changed little. He was a vigorous advocate of freedom of speech and press. In the first and only edition of *Publick Occurrences Both Foreign and Domestic,* Harris chose to print only those items that "objectively" appeared to be true. The paper was to be issued monthly or more frequently if warranted. But the conservative governor and council in Boston weren't ready for Harris's newspaper and issued a statement that the newspaper was published "without the least Privity or Countenance of Authority" and called for its suppression.[4] On both sides of the Atlantic Harris had shown himself to be a libertarian, a tradition that would become a rallying cry in later years.

Any long-term independent printing in the Massachusetts colony was out of the question. The royal governor issued licenses to print, but for this privilege printers had to agree to print only what was approved by the government. This kind of censorship existed in all of the American colonies during most of the pre-Revolutionary War years.

The second American newspaper was established by John Campbell in 1704 and was titled the Boston *News-Letter.* Campbell used his job as a Boston postmaster and bookseller to glean information for the paper, two-thirds of which came from London. The remainder was primarily sermons and weather and death notices.

MEDIA IN THE COLONIES

1638   Stephen Daye establishes first printing press at the site of the present Harvard University to print almanacs, sermons, and books.

1690   Benjamin Harris publishes the first newspaper in the colonies—*Publick Occurrences Both Foreign and Domestic.* It lasted one issue.

1704   Boston *News-Letter* appears, edited and printed by John Campbell.

1719   William Brooker starts the Boston *Gazette* and James Franklin serves as printer.

1719   Philadelphia gets its first newspaper, *The American Weekly Mercury,* started by William Bradford.

1721   James Franklin and friends start the *New-England Courant* and Benjamin learns of his brother's interest in printing.

1725   The New York *Gazette* starts in New York—that city's first newspaper.

1735   Alexander Hamilton gets his client John Peter Zenger acquitted of a libel charge on basis of truth of statement.

1765   English pass the Stamp Act and impose a tax on paper products including newspapers.

1775   Battles of Lexington and Concord open the Revolutionary War.

BENJAMIN FRANKLIN

Benjamin Franklin was born in Boston January 17, 1705 (or 1706). Very early in life he became an avid reader, apprenticed himself to his brother and tried to get his brother to publish his articles. Benjamin fi-nally succeeded by using a ploy, a pseudonym—"Silence Dogwood." He would place articles under the door of the newspaper office at night.

Source: Mott (1962), p. 19.

When William Brooker took over the Boston Post Office, he wanted control of the *News-Letter* as well, but Campbell refused, whereupon Brooker started the Boston *Gazette* in 1719. The *Gazette* was better written and better printed than its competitor and became one of the most prominent patriot newspapers of the day.

Benjamin Franklin's brother, James, was the *Gazette's* first printer, but he soon turned his attention to contract printing. Then, on August 6, 1721, James Franklin started his own paper, the *New-England Courant.* The purpose of the *Courant,* according to Franklin, was:

> To entertain the Town with the most comical and diverting Incidents of Humane Life, which in so large a Place as Boston, will not fail of universal Exemplification.[5]

The articles brought fame to the weekly paper and stimulated lively debate in Boston.

James and his printer friends at the *Courant* cast themselves at odds with established government and religious policy. This rebellious attitude led displeased governmental officials to call for his arrest (1722) because they felt the newspaper would lead public opinion to oppose the royal governor of Massachusetts. (James did spend a month in prison.)

When James was arrested for supposedly printing libelous information, he was ordered to stop publishing. To circumvent the order James turned the paper publicly over to his brother Benjamin, apparently intending to retain private control.

FIGURE 2–1 Ben Franklin. (Culver Pictures)

PRINTING IN PHILADELPHIA

William Bradford established the first printing press outside New England. A Quaker, Bradford had come to America in 1682 to print pamphlets and books.[6] He was soon accused of printing seditious material, which led to a libel suit. In the trials that followed he successfully defended himself and laid some of the ground work that proved important in the development of freedom of the press. But he never started a newspaper. Bradford's son Thomas started Philadelphia's first newspaper, *The American Weekly Mercury* on December 22, 1719, and soon got into trouble for publishing the "simple hope" that the

General Assembly "will find some effectual remedy to revive the dying credit of the Province and restore to us our former happy circumstances."[7]

This remark got Bradford arrested, but he continued to publish the *Mercury* until his death in 1742. Thereafter Bradford's widow continued publishing either by herself or with the help of others until 1746.

The *Mercury* was the only newspaper in Philadelphia until Samuel Keimer began *The Universal Instructor in all Arts and Sciences: and Pennsylvania Gazette*.[8] But Keimer's paper lacked style and carried little current news.

So Benjamin Franklin, who had arrived in Philadelphia to start his own paper, turned his attention to discrediting the *Universal Instructor* through a series of "Busy Body" articles that appeared in the *Mercury*. Although Keimer's paper might have gone out of business anyway, Franklin's essays undoubtedly sped up its demise. After it failed, Franklin bought the paper and reduced its title to the *Pennsylvania Gazette*.[9]

Franklin's new *Pennsylvania Gazette* developed a lively style. It dispensed with long rambling articles and carried advertising. The Newspaper was so successful it enabled Franklin to start other publishing ventures, and eventually to retire as a wealthy man while still in his forties.

Franklin amassed impressive credentials in the printing world. Besides starting a group of newspapers, he began one of the first magazines in the colonies. His *General Magazine* (1741) appeared the same year that Bradford started the *American Magazine*.[10] Franklin also offered the first foreign language newspaper in 1732.

Franklin had great respect for the task of a printer, as illustrated by his response to a proposed article:

> I have perused your piece, and find it to be scurrilous and defamatory. To determine whether I should publish it or not, I went home in the evening, purchased a two penny loaf at the baker's, and with water from the pump made my supper; I then wrapped myself up in my great coat, and laid down on the floor and slept till morning, when, on another loaf and a mug of water, I made my breakfast. From this regimen I feel no inconvenience whatever. Finding I can live in this manner, I have formed a determination never to prostitute my press to the purposes of corruption, and abuse of this kind for the sake of gaining a more comfortable subsistence.[11]

NEW YORK NEWSPAPERS

The third city to acquire a newspaper was New York City. William Bradford had left Pennsylvania for a time to take up the official printing for New York with a salary paid out of the government treasury. Part of the agreement allowed him to engage in his own private printing. The resulting *New York Gazette* (1725)—an uninteresting collection of old foreign news, reprints of official documents, lists of ships, and some advertising—was hardly up to the standards set by Franklin in Philadelphia.[12]

Then young immigrant John Peter Zenger began New York City's *Weekly Journal* in 1733 and became a crusader. One attack took on the High Sheriff who had apparently prevented some supporters of an opposition candidate for governor from voting. The displeased Royal Governor had Zenger arrested and tried for seditious libel, claiming that his attacks "vilify the high administration."[13]

Zenger went to jail, refused bail or was unable to pay it, and continued to edit his newspaper from jail. In an attempt to secure Zenger's release, his lawyers attacked the credentials of the chief judge, whereupon they were disbarred in New York. This left Zenger without legal counsel. Without anyone else in New York to turn to, Zenger's friends secured the services of an elderly Philadelphia lawyer named Alexander Hamilton.

The government's entire case was based upon a statement appearing in the *Journal* that said the property and liberty of New Yorkers was in jeopardy because of their colonial government. Hamilton admitted in court that Zenger had printed the statement. Once he recovered from his shock, the prosecutor called for an immediate conviction. Hamilton, regaining the court's attention, argued that "the words themselves [must] be libelous, that is false, scandalous, and seditious, or else we are not guilty."[14] Truth, Hamilton said, was a defense against libel. This was a startling departure from precedent, but the jury agreed with Hamilton and returned a verdict of not guilty. Zenger returned to work and edited his newspaper until 1751. But, although the case was heralded on both sides of the Atlantic as very important to printers' freedom, it had little immediate impact on colonial legal and journalistic history.[15]

NEWSPAPERS THROUGHOUT THE COLONIES

Newspapers were established in many other colonies throughout English America during the 1700s. The *Maryland Gazette* was founded in Annapolis in 1727. In Providence there was the *Rhode Island Gazette;* in Virginia the *Virginia Gazette* was established in 1736. Further south, one of Benjamin Franklin's employees established the *South-Carolina Gazette* (1731) in Charleston. James Johnston started printing in Savannah, with the *Georgia Gazette* (1763).

By 1765 most of the colonies had at least one newspaper. These newspapers were divided into two camps: the loyalists who supported the crown, and the patriots who opposed it. This division of newspapers had much to do with organizing public opinion for or against the crown during the Revolutionary War period.

Newspapers were not the only means of reaching the public: pamphlets and newsletters reached them, too. But because both of these media forms were printed by the same individuals who published the newspapers, eighteenth century printers were a central force in leading public opinion.

THE STATE OF PRINTING—1760s

The first papers were small one- or two-sheet formats, but after 1765 the major papers were four pages long and measured about eleven by seventeen inches or ten by fifteen inches. A few of the papers were even six to eight pages long because of advertising demand.

Although the format had changed, many of the papers were still printed with old, worn type and inferior presses. Moreover, paper was in short supply because it had to be imported from England until the first paper was produced in Germantown, Pennsylvania (1690).[16] Even then, early American mills were small and their product was crude.

Most presses used during the eighteenth century were very similar to Gutenberg's press of centuries before. Presses were constructed largely of wood with levers that operated a screw. The screw lowered the printing type to the paper where an impression was made. A good operator could make about 200 impressions an hour.

The Printing Business

During the colonial era and into the eighteenth century, newspapers were published by printers who derived income from many sources. The editor-printer, who was as much entrepreneur as editor, frequently published books and pamphlets, often was a postmaster and sometimes was a retailer. Franklin advertised coffee, soap, wines, patent medicines, spectacles, and other merchandise. To set up a printing press required 75 to 100 pounds, quite a sum at the time.

Circulation for most colonial newspapers ranged from a few hundred to over 1,000, with the average about 600. Yet many more people read newspapers than circulation figures suggest because every copy was passed from hand to hand.

Newspaper readers had to purchase their papers—usually with cash, but sometimes with food or fuel. An extra cost was added when newspapers were sent to subscribers by mail. Subscriptions paid for only a fraction of newspaper costs—advertising provided most revenue. Early colonial newspapers contained less than a page of advertising, but that quickly rose to three to five pages. Early advertisements looked more like classified advertising than like modern display copy. Advertisements rarely exceeded one column width and used small headlines. One of the main topics of advertising was runaways: slaves, bondservants, apprentices, and soldiers. Product advertising offered cure-alls, lotteries, dry goods, rum and wines, and livestock.

The News

Much of the news was two- and three-month-old items from Europe. Because the colonies were founded mostly by Europeans, and most goods were imported from and exported to Europe, the interest was natural. News in Europe, even old news, was very important to the colonists.

Colonial news was scanty. It traveled by sea up and down the coast—a very slow process. Amazingly, colonial news was often just as old as news from Europe.

Printers at this time were redefining what was news. Some of the important stories were the Seven Year War, the War of Austrian Succession, and the crowning of the Georges. Local news included speeches, often printed in their entirety, and political information.[17]

Editorials were rare during the eighteenth century. There was not enough space to accommodate the long rambling arguments popular with writers of the day. And then there was the problem of editorials with points of view contrary to the establishment. Consequently, printers simply avoided editorials. They would often print this type of opinion piece in a pamphlet. Franklin, for instance, advanced his argument for currency reform in a pamphlet.

THE STAMP ACT

Politics became very important to colonial newspapers after 1765—the year the Stamp Act was passed.[18] The act required a tax on all legal documents, official papers, books, and newspapers. To insure that the tax was collected, all printing had to be done on taxed paper.

Printers had to pay a tax that amounted to about 50 percent of the cost of the newspaper. Some of the bolder papers said they would publish without using the stamped paper. Others stopped printing or changed their status to that of a newsletter; newsletters were not taxed.

In defending its decision to continue printing on nonstamped paper, one New York newspaper reported receiving threatening letters. One letter supposedly promised personal damage to the printer if the newspaper was suspended.

The New York *Mercury* proclaimed that "No Stamped Paper [was] to be had"[19] and continued printing on unstamped paper. The *Maryland Gazette* suspended publication for a short time and then published a paper with the proclamation "An Apparition of the late *Maryland Gazette,* which is not dead but Sleepth."[20] In the South some newspapers suspended publication for a much longer time. The furor soon proved successful. So great a failure was the Stamp Act that the British government repealed it March, 1766. The major outcome of the conflict was that the press learned its power.

Then came the Townshend Acts with taxes on tea, paper, wines, oil, glass, lead, and paint. Like the Stamp Act before it, the Townshend Acts were another form of hated taxation, and newspapers were quick to take up the cry against them. Although these taxes were applied uniformly throughout the British Empire, the American colonists wanted freedom from this obligation.

The new laws affected almost everyone and the colonists devised many ways to combat or circumvent them, such as blacklists identifying merchants who sold taxed items. It almost seemed as if England were purposely irritating the colonies. The hated tax laws and the ability of newspapers and pamphlets to crystallize public opinion probably had the most influence in leading to the colonies' ultimate split with England.

NEWSPAPERS BEFORE THE REVOLUTION

During these tempestuous years, Boston was the "hotbed of sedition," and at the center of the controversy was the Boston *Gazette* printed by Benjamin Edes and John Gill. This newspaper was so openly opposed to the crown that Governor Bernard called it "an infamous weekly paper which has swarmed with libels of the most atrocious kind."[21]

At times it appeared that the *Gazette* would be closed down by the crown's representatives, but a Grand Jury refused to indict the newspaper. Later, the Massachusetts House of Representatives followed with its own declaration: "the liberty of the Press is a great Bulwark of the Liberty of the people: It is therefore the incumbent Duty of those who are constituted the Guardians of the People's Rights to defend and maintain it."[22]

The *Gazette* continued its outspoken support of radical causes and reached the unheard of circulation of 2,000. The governor, meanwhile, thought that many of the problems in Massachusetts were caused by its citizens reading the *Gazette* rather than more moderate newspapers. Contributors to the *Gazette* included some of the most important names in the colony: Samuel Adams, John Adams, Joseph Warren, Josiah Quincy, Samuel Cooper, and James Otis. They wrote under pen names as members of the Caucus Club, an organization concerned with focusing political action in Massachusetts.

Another important Boston paper was the *Spy*. Started as a nonpartisan paper, the Spy was soon filled with information about nonimportation agreements, and essays espousing independence. The first issue of the *Spy* came out on March 7, 1771, during a period of intense partisan feeling in the colonies. It was not long before the Boston Council was angry.

One of the higher quality newspapers sympathetic to the crown was James Rivington's *New-York Gazetteer*, started on April 22, 1773. The full name was *Rivington's New-York Gazetteer; or the Connecticut, New-Jersey, Hudson's River, and Quebec Weekly Advertiser*. Rivington's printing office was destroyed by patriots; he rebuilt but continued to have trouble producing his paper because the patriots controlled New York during the American Revolution. Although he was hung in effigy, Rivington struggled on through the war and for some time afterward.

During the Revolutionary War, a complex arrangement of newspapers existed in New York City. Rivington's *Gazetteer* was printed on Wednesday and Saturday; Hugh Gaine's New York *Gazette and Mercury* was printed on Monday; James and Alexander Robertson's *Royal American Gazette* was published on Thursday; and William Lewis's New York *Mercury and General Advertiser* came out on Friday.[23]

It is important to note that Rivington's newspaper was not the only Revolutionary War-era newspaper in the colonies sympathetic to the Tories. But although most major cities had at least one Tory paper, the weight of newspaper sentiment was clearly with the patriots.

Many of the writers of this period were neither printers nor editors. One such writer was Thomas Paine, whose major contribution to the revolution was writing the pamphlet *Common Sense* (1776). Often quoted by the Patriots, the pamphlet was an important element in formulating public opinion in the colonies. Its success is evident by the number of copies that were sold—the truly unheard of quantity of 120,000.

Another of Paine's important contributions was his "Crises" series which was printed in the *Pennsylvania Journal* in December, 1776. The first article started with the words so many schoolchildren have memorized: "These are the times that try men's souls. . . ." The times did trouble many souls because colonists still considered themselves English, but did not want to be second-class British subjects.

THE REVOLUTION AND NEWSPAPERS

On April 19, 1775, the battles of Lexington and Concord began the Revolutionary War. At that time, thirty-seven newspapers were being published. Six and a half years later when the revolution ended, thirty-five newspapers were still being published. Some papers had died but others had taken their place. The size of the papers did not change during the war period. Most papers' layouts consisted of small headlines; a few papers had drawings. When there were graphic illustrations, however, they were usually stock cuts that had been used for advertising. One important change in the format was the reduced size of the type.

Most printers and editors sensed their power. They were increasingly popular with readers. George Washington even contributed worn out tents to paper mills so that there would be enough paper for newsprint. Feeling secure and important, editors allowed editorial comments to creep into news stories.

The public craved news of the war, but the papers lacked any organized news gathering service to obtain it. Most coverage was secured

106,085

LIBRARY
College of St. Francis
JOLIET, ILL.

DAILY PAPERS

Benjamin Towne made the *Pennsylvania Evening Post* a daily on May 30, 1783. The attempt, although short-lived, introduced the innovation of selling newspapers on street corners. The streets of Philadelphia rang with the cry, "All the news for two coppers!"

Philadelphia's second daily was *The Pennsylvania Packet, and Daily Advertiser* (March 1, 1785). It should be pointed out that New York City had a daily that started a week earlier than the *Advertiser,* but it did not last.

Source: Mott (1962), p. 115, 116.

through an exchange of newspapers among printers. Typical of war coverage was this story that appeared in the New York *Gazette* on February 2, 1778:

> The Hartford *Post* tells us, That he saw a Gentleman in Springfield who informed him that (the Gentlemen) saw a letter from an Officer in Gen. Howe's Army to another in Gen. Burgoyne's, giving him to understand, WAR was declared on the sides of France and Spain, against the MIGHTY Kingdom of Britain.

With the close of the revolution, the power and popularity of the press continued to grow. Crown sympathizers ceased publication of their papers. While a few which sympathized with the colonists failed, many new papers sprang up with dramatically different content. On both sides of the Atlantic it was an era of intense political activity, and American newspapers became organs for transmitting political arguments. Some papers were actually started to promote specific political goals. What would be the form of the new constitution? How should the financial debt be handled? What about taxes?

NEWSPAPERS IN A NEW NATION

After the revolution there were those who thought that the United States needed a newspaper that would serve the government's needs. To that end, John Fenno, a new arrival in New York City (then the nation's capital), became the first editor of a national newspaper. *The Gazette of the United States* (April 15, 1789) was almost immediately attacked by Federalist opponents. These opponents threw their support to Philip Freneau's *National Gazette* (October 31, 1791) of Philadelphia and the *General Advertiser* (October 1, 1791) also of Philadelphia, founded by the grandson of Franklin Benjamin Franklin Bache.

Both newspapers were strongly against President Washington. On the day of Washington's retirement, the *General Advertiser* observed:

LIBRARY
College of St. Francis
JOLIET, ILL.

> The man who is the source of all the misfortunes of our country is this day reduced to a level with his fellow-citizens, and is no longer possessed of power to multiply evils upon the United States . . . this day ought to be a JUBILEE in the United States.[24]

Unbridled political attacks on public figures were now common in American newspapers and led to a series of libel suits, many of which were won by the plantiffs. Indeed, by about 1840, newspapers began showing more of a sense of responsibility. But not all papers were political. Many small towns started their own local papers. The *Farmer's Weekly Museum* in Walpole, New Hampshire, gained considerable fame until its demise in 1810.

By 1800, New York City was the commercial, population, and newspaper center of the United States. Eleven papers were published there, most of which, like Noah Webster's The *American Minerva* (1793), were meant for the mercantile class.

NEWSPAPERS AND FREEDOM

Newspapers spread not only to the small towns of the East, but across the Appalachian Mountains into the western frontiers of Kentucky, Ohio, and Michigan. The first newspaper west of the mountains was the Pittsburgh *Gazette* (1786) founded by Joseph Hall and John Scull.

Newspapers grew quickly in postwar years in both number and circulation because of the unprecedented freedom from governmental interference. There wasn't unbridled freedom, however. For a time Massachusetts had a revenue tax on newspapers and other printed materials. Other states used printing contracts and post office positions as leverage and because most printers were so poor, they need those contracts and positions. As states wrote their constitutions, none included provisions guaranteeing press freedom.[25]

Interestingly, the national constitution omitted any mention of freedom of the press. Many thought this was an unwarranted omission and a heated battle for a bill of rights ensued. The Bill of Rights ultimately adopted did include freedom of the press but the wording was vague and questions about the limits of freedom arose almost immediately.

During the summer of 1798, Congress passed the Alien and Sedition Acts, which curbed press activities because anyone convicted of writing, printing, or uttering a "false, scandalous, and malicious" statement against the Congress or the United States could be fined up to $2,000 and sentenced to two years in prison. However, an amendment did provide that the truth of a printed statement could be submitted as evidence at a trial and would be sufficient reason for rejection of a libel suit.[26]

Although some animosity existed between the United States and France at this time, the United States was not formally at war with any

MEDIA IN A NEW NATION

1789 John Fenno starts the first national newspaper in the United States, *The Gazette of the United States*.

1789 The Bill of Rights is added to the Constitution of the United States which provides the framework for press freedoms.

1798 Alien and Sedition Acts abridge some freedoms.

1812 James M. Bradford covers the war for newspapers in a series of letters, marking the emergence of the correspondent idea.

1832 Richard Hoe invents the double cylinder press to speed up the printing process.

1833 Benjamin H. Day introduces the *Daily Sun* as the first one-cent newspaper for the working citizens of New York. Other penny newspapers follow quickly.

1844 Invention of the telegraph foreshadows improved news transmission, but the adoption takes time.

1846 The Charleston (S.C.) *Courier* and the New York *Sun* share the high cost of securing news about the Mexican-American War.

1848 First cooperative news-gathering association, Associated Press of New York, is formed.

1851 New York *Times* founded.

1860–1864 Civil War opens new challenges to war coverage.

1883 Joseph Pulitzer buys the New York *World*, opening the way for yellow journalism. The new era leads to unheard-of circulation figures.

nation. The acts, therefore, were not passed because of wartime necessity. Apparently, thought Jefferson, they were intended to censor the Republican press. Of course, the Republican printers and editors were angry because the Federalist politicians had shown no restraint in their attacks. Ten opposition editors and printers were convicted under the Sedition Act, with juries composed mainly of Federalists.[27]

The main danger of the Sedition Act, however, was that it permitted the court to examine the motives of the printer or editor in determining guilt. Fortunately, the Sedition Act was soon repealed and many of the fined printers got their money back.

With the restoration of press freedom, editorials became more common again and the newspaper editors' major concern became stale news. The news staple during the 1790s was foreign news, which was late, dull, and insipid. The *Pennsylvania Evening Herald* observed that finding good foreign news was like finding "an article or two amidst heaps of trash."[28]

News traveled slowly. Communication depended on the postal system, which did not work well, particularly in bad weather. It often took nine days for a letter to travel from Boston to New York. To compound the problem, there was no stringer system, whereby a local reporter covered a local event and sent it to a larger organization for a fee. Washington's death illustrates the problem. He died on December 14, 1799, but the Alexandria *Times,* the first paper to cover the story, didn't print an announcement until December 16. The *Columbian Centinel* of Boston printed the story nine days after the *Times.*[29]

The system of exchanging papers meant editors had to rely heavily on rumor and unsubstantiated information or on the memories of witnesses or people who had talked to witnesses. Not infrequently the headline "Important—If True" would appear to warn the reader of the news source's dubious credibility. But even with these problems, newspapers were becoming financially secure. Advertising space was increasing so rapidly that some papers could have printed only ads if they had chosen to.

A NEW LITERACY, 1800–1833

The nineteenth century was a period of important growth for newspapers. Literacy was increasing rapidly. People were moving from the farms to the cities to take new jobs created by industrialization. Immigrants, who flocked to United States factory cities, wanted news from abroad because they were now cut off from their families and friends back home. New inventions appeared that sped up the process of printing. The Federal government expanded the postal system and improved its speed of delivery. The postal system provided a free exchange of newspapers among printers and editors. Post riders often delivered newspapers to subscribers, collecting a small service charge.

This healthy climate for newspapers helped their numbers grow from about 200 in 1800 to 1,200 in 1832. The number of dailies did not increase quite so fast,[30] growing in that period from twenty to sixty-five. The growth of newspapers in the United States was greater than that of anywhere else in the world.

Several political factors were involved in the expansion of newspapers. The national capital moved from Philadelphia to Washington, opening up a whole new city to newspapers. Then the opposition, Republican Thomas Jefferson, won the presidency. As outsiders, they knew very well the strength of the Federalist press and how important newspapers were to winning elections. Moreover, there were three philosophical points of view within the party and each wanted its own newspapers. Finally with the Louisiana Purchase, new territory was opened up for settlers and papers.

While the number of papers increased, the quality did not. The mercantile newspapers of an earlier time, although still in existence, were overshadowed by the partisan press. The political press engaged in the most vicious attacks upon their political foes—attacks that were just as often false as true. One of the worst attackers was Harry Croswell who published the nasty-humored *Wasp* in Hudson, New York. Croswell particularly enjoyed defaming Jefferson during his term as president. For example, Croswell printed that Jefferson had paid someone to call "Washington a traitor, a robber, and a perjurer."[31]

At Croswell's trial, the court refused to consider testimony about the truth of his claim, and it convicted him. Alexander Hamilton, however, argued for a new trial on the grounds that editors and printers had to be free to examine people as well as issues because people established the issues. The New York legislature, disapproving of the handling of the trial, passed a new law authorizing the admission of truth as evidence. Even though it still allowed the courts to determine the motives of a printer or editor in printing an accusation, the law became a model for many of the new states when they incorporated the freedom to publish into their constitutions.

The Croswell case was but one of many. Joseph Dennie attacked the concept of democracy in 1805. Although acquitted by a jury, he continued his attacks until he was threatened with further prosecution and finally moderated his views. Another interesting case occurred in what was then the frontier town of Detroit when a newspaper critcized a court for wasting time. The editor was cited for contempt.

An important question began to develop when Nathaniel Rounsavell refused to reveal the source of his information about a secret congressional proceeding. The case opened up an issue that is still disputed. Can reporters be cited for contempt or sent to jail for not revealing their sources?

Fiery times in the courts and on the dueling grounds were regular newspaper happenings in the early 1800s. At least two newspaper printers dueled as the result of attacks carried in their papers. Even the famous duel between Alexander Hamilton and Aaron Burr occurred because of remarks that appeared in the Albany *Register*.[32]

TECHNICAL IMPROVEMENTS

Life for the poor after the revolution was often miserable. For many, the West held the promise of a new life. This attitude led western journalism to be decidedly independent from the eastern variety. This same independence from the East occurred in the South, where some politicians were already suggesting that the South and West might band together and withdraw from the Union.

Although newspapers were springing up all over the nation, circulation was held back because of technical problems: paper was scarce, presses were slow, and distribution was limited by both the roads and the mail. These conditions began to change around 1813. In that year, George Clymer in Philadelphia substituted a series of iron levers for the old screw press, an innovation that speeded up the presses. This invention was quickly superseded by the development of the steam-driven cylinder press. The new press, invented by Frederick Koenig and improved by David Napier, cost approximately $4,000, but it could print about 2,000 papers per hour in 1825. Soon Richard Hoe had invented the double cylinder press, a development that made it possible to print 4,000 papers per hour by 1832.[33]

Improvements in paper and ink completed the new mass printing technology. Jacob Johnson developed the mechanics for the large scale manufacture of printing inks in 1804. A few years later, David Bruce invented a new casting machine that improved the production of the casting used for printing the newspaper page (1822). But the new technology cost money. The small independent, issuing a few hundred papers, could not break even. Printing became big business.

Gathering news quickly was still a problem. Samuel Topliff was the first who tried to rectify this, even though he wasn't particularly interested in the newspaper business. He would send fast boats out to foreign ships to bring the information back. A. S. Willington, printer of the Charleston, South Carolina, *Courier,* adapted the fast boat idea to secure news for his newspaper. Of course, this was not really a major improvement in speed. The next developments came during the coverage of the War of 1812 when James M. Bradford, a fighting soldier under Jackson, came close to being the first war correspondent with a series of letters he wrote to his hometown newspaper describing the war. Having an on-the-scene reporter sped things up a little but did not solve the transportation problem. Here is a case in point: Jackson won the Battle of New Orleans in early December but it was not reported in the New York City press until January 8, 1815.[34]

Most news still had to be transmitted by the postal system. As the system expanded across the West and South, the government did institute an express service between the larger cities, but the time involved was still considerable. Getting news from Washington to St. Louis took almost a week—in good weather.

A NEWSPAPER FOR A PENNY, 1833-1860

The mid-century period beginning in 1833 was far from tranquil. Slavery was a major issue in state and federal legislatures and in publications as well. Arthur Tappan, the abolitionist who started the New York *Journal of Commerce*, was wanted by a vigilante committee in Louisiana, which offered $50,000 for his delivery. President Jackson got into the conflict with his annual message of December, 1835, when he recommended severe penalties for anyone who circulated inflammatory

information in the southern states. Editors and printers were confronted with vexing questions: Should they remain silent on the issue to
avoid controversy or worse? Or should they speak out?

Until about 1833 newspapers had been serving largely politicians,
the rich, and the merchant classes at an annual subscription cost of
eight to ten dollars. The poor and laborers had little access to news;
consequently, they had little to do with political debate. But by the
1830s they had moved to the cities and to the West and had learned
how to read. The new class was offered a daily for one cent. The 1,200
newspapers in existence in 1830 grew to 3,000 by 1860.

With the reduction in price for the new audience, journalists began
tailoring their style to popular tastes. This usually meant they emphasized sex and violence. De Tocqueville observed after a trip to the
United States:

> The journalists of the United States are usually placed in a very
> humble position with a scanty education and a vulgar turn of
> mind. . . . The characteristics of the American journalist consist of
> an open and coarse appeal to the passions of the populace. . . .[35]

One of the first newspapers to approach one cent per day was founded by Seba Smith in Portland, Maine, in 1830. The newspaper sold for
four dollars per year and was named the *Daily Courier*. Other newspapers followed in a similar four dollar format, including the Boston *Evening Bulletin*, but most of these first cheap papers were short-lived.

Horace Greeley came to New York at the age of twenty with ten
dollars in his pocket. Greeley moved from job to job until he fell into a
partnership with Dr. H. D. Shepard who wanted to start a penny newspaper. Unlike other dailies, Shepard's was to be sold on the streets by
single copies rather than by annual subscription. The *Morning Post*
was first issued on January 1, 1833. A snowstorm in New York City
prevented many sales the first day, and sales in days to follow did not
pick up. Actually the paper was first sold for two cents, but was reduced to a penny in an attempt to improve sales. The paper still failed.

The first successful attempt at a penny daily was made by Benjamin
H. Day on September 3, 1833, when *The Sun* appeared on the streets
of New York. The paper reached a circulation of 2,000 within two
months and 4,000 in four months. Reductions in printing costs had
made the successful attempt possible; new editorial techniques en-
sured its continued success. One of the paper's new editorial techniques was to cover police court, where George W. Wisner's writing
concentrated on the sensational.[36]

Benjamin Day had learned printing from Samuel Bowles who owned
the Springfield *Republican*. From Springfield, Day went to New York
City where he worked in the offices of two newspapers before deciding to print his own. The first edition differed very little from existing
newspapers except for its cost. But as the newspaper developed, Day
made sure it thoroughly covered the activities of the community. In
explaining its goal the newspaper proclaimed:

The object of this paper is to lay before the public, at a price within the means of every one, all the news of the day, and at the same time offer an advantageous medium for advertisements.[37]

The paper was light, breezy, and readable, concentrating less on political activities than on the more sensational items of interest to the local populace. But as important as his newspaper's style was, Day's marketing plan was just as important. Newsboys were sent to the streets. The newspapers cost the young vendors sixty-seven cents per hundred cash or seventy-five cents on credit. The carrier made twenty-five or thirty-three cents for street sales and some had routes where they charged their customers six cents per week. This marketing plan was so successful that Day was soon selling 10,000 copies a day. Business was so good that Day installed a new Napier press, enlarged the size of the paper, and by mid-1835 had a circulation topping 15,000.

The success of the *Sun* brought competitors. The first was James Gordon Bennett's New York *Herald* on May 6, 1835. Bennett began as a schoolteacher, but became discouraged and tried journalism with the Charleston *Courier*. A little later he moved to New York City where he first tried a two-cent newspaper, the *Globe*, which quickly died. Other unsuccessful ventures followed, and at age forty he was broke and un-

---

POLICE OFFICE NOTES

Margaret Thomas was drunk in the street—said she never would get drunk again "upon her honor." Committed, "upon honor." . . .

Bridget McMunn got drunk and threw a pitcher at Mr. Ellis, of 53 Ludlow St. Bridget said she was the mother of 3 orphans—God bless their dear souls—and if she went to prison they would choke to death for the want of something to eat. Committed. Bill Doty got drunk because he had the horrors so bad he couldn't keep sober. Committed. . . .

Patrick Ludwick was sent up by his wife, who testified that she had supported him for several years in idleness and drunkenness. Abandoning all hopes of a reformation in her husband, she bought him a suit of clothes a fortnight since and told him to go about his business, for she would not live with him any longer. Last night he came home in a state of intoxication, broke into his wife's bedroom, pulled her out of bed, pulled her hair, and stamped on her. She called a watchman and sent him up. Pat exerted all his powers of eloquence in endeavoring to excite his wife's sympathy, but to no purpose. As every sensible woman ought to do who is cursed with a drunken husband, she refused to have anything to do with him here-after—and he was sent to the penitentiary.

The foregoing was typical of the stories appearing under the title of "Police Office" and written by Wisner. The stories evoked wide response from readers.

Source: "Police Court Office" *The Sun*, July 4, 1834.

NEWS AS TRUTH OR FICTION

Not all the news was fact. On June 30, 1835, the *Sun* printed an introductory article about one Sir John Herschel's scientific discoveries. According to the article, he had a telescope that revealed many things about the solar system. Although the article was sketchy, it aroused some interest in scientific circles. A few days later the paper further explained that the telescope gave a view of the moon as good as "the unaided eye commands of terrestrial objects at the distance of one hundred yards." Other articles purported to explain the existence, or lack thereof of life on the moon, the nature of other planets, and the whereabouts of previously unknown planets. Competing newspapers became so excited that many reprinted the articles. At least one delegation of scientists traveled to New York to confer with the writer of the articles. The fiction exploded when Richard Adams Locke, the author of the series, confessed to a reporter for the *Journal of Commerce* that he had dreamed up the whole idea. His disclosure, made while less than sober, was promptly printed in the *Journal of Commerce*. Many newspapers expressed the view that the *Sun* had been unethical, but the public accepted the event in good spirit.

Source: Richard Adams Locke. "Great Astronomical Discoveries." *The Sun*, August 25, 1835, p. 1.

employed. Other papers wouldn't even hire him as a reporter despite his lively, flowery writing style.

With his last $500 Bennett went to the firm that did the mechanical work for the *Sun* and *Transcript* and contracted for one last try. When the *Herald* appeared, it quickly developed a reputation for superior foreign news, good economic analysis, plenty of theatrical chitchat, and lively editorials. In fact, Bennett produced the first financial column—the predecessor of the modern financial page.

Admittedly, Bennett's goals for the *Herald* were a bit idealistic—he thought it would displace the church, the theater, and books in bringing salvation to the world. It's unclear if the paper ever sent anyone to heaven, but it was not long before it was defending a young man accused of killing a prostitute. Each day as the trial progressed, Bennett devoted a large section to the testimony and to evidence that he had dug up. Bennett was convinced that the man had not committed the crime and was determined to prove his innocence. Many other papers reprinted all or part of the *Herald's* reports on the crime. In time the man was acquitted and the *Herald* experienced a great growth in its circulation.

Although Bennett wanted to serve the public good, he was just as interested in making money. After a few months, Bennett decided to raise the price of the paper to two cents. He spelled out his plan to his readers—the higher price would permit him to make the *Herald* the best, most comprehensive newspaper in the nation. He even showed the amount of revenue that he would receive under the new price and how he would spend the money. The promise was carried out. Bennett added a Washington correspondent, improved the foreign news, and hired correspondents for several other American cities. He also added new printing equipment and a fleet of high speed boats to secure news from arriving ships. By 1850, the *Herald* was selling over 30,000 copies daily and by 1860 it had passed the circulation leader, the *Sun*.

Although New York City was the site of the first permanent penny dailies, other cities quickly added their own. George Roberts and William H. Garfield started the Boston *Daily Times* in 1836; the Baltimore *Sun* appeared in 1837; Philadelphia had the *Public Ledger* (1836). Almost everyone could afford six cents a week. Many working men and women began reading newspapers, which increased their political power. They learned what was going on and therefore politicians who wanted to be elected could not afford to ignore them.

The timeliness of the penny press was a major innovation supported by inventions: telegraph, steamship, and railroad. For a time the press did not use the telegraph, which was invented May 1, 1844, because of its high cost. But the Baltimore *American* soon started a rush to obtain the new service when it began using the telegraph to get news from Washington quickly. The first message cost one cent per character, but the price dropped rapidly as the telegraph spread across the country.[38]

THE NEWS SERVICE

Covering the Mexican-American War (1846) brought changes in the methods of reporting. The Charleston, South Carolina, *Courier* and the New York *Sun* shared the high cost of securing battlefield news. The news was sent by fast horses, railroads, and in time the telegraph. At the front, reporters like George W. Kendall, a Yankee printer who had worked with Greeley and others, wrote thorough and accurate accounts of military actions interspersed with human interest stories.[39]

The costs of gathering and transmitting news during the Mexican-American War were so great that newspapers were forced to find new ways of combining forces to reduce costs. One such method was the creation of the Associated Press of New York, forerunner of the modern Associated Press. Formed in May, 1848, at the office of the New York *Sun,* the new association included six member newspapers: *Sun, Herald, Courier and Enquirer, Tribune, Journal of Commerce,* and *Express.* The organization was informal, with no charter or structure until 1856 when Gerald Hallock of the *Journal of Commerce* took charge, and the provisions for sharing and distributing information were spelled out.

POLITICAL NEWSPAPERS

Although the penny press had a lot to do with the character of modern newspapers, they did not dominate journalism in the mid-nineteenth century—political newspapers did. Democrats dominated the national political arena, but the Whigs had more and stronger newspapers. The Whig party came about as a result of anti-Andrew Jackson forces. The National Republicans, the anti-Masons and southern anti-Jackson Democrats merged to create the Whig party; however, the party disintegrated after the repeal of the Missouri Compromise. Two parties survived the realignments—the Democrats and the Republicans—with two minor parties (the Free-Soilers and the Know-Nothing party) hanging on for a time.

Because of their support for the mercantile class, the Whigs had more money. Consequently, they had newspapers in large cities. By contrast, the Democrats were weak in the major cities and had to be supported by public printing contracts. The Whigs led with the *National Intelligencer* of Washington; the *North American* of Philadelphia; and Greeley's *Tribune* and the *Courier and Enquirer* in New York City.

Greeley's approach to newspaper publishing brought important innovations to the business. To speed up the dissemination of news from the state capital in Albany, Greeley had stories typeset en route to New York City on Hudson river steamers. Thus, when the story reached New York City, it could be rushed into print. To set his papers apart from the others, Greeley reduced his use of crime and sex news and advertisements for questionable products like patent medicines. The serious *Tribune* also proclaimed itself a champion of morality, but it still ran murder trials to build circulation.

Greeley, the individual, was very much a champion of the poor and defenseless. He took on a Socialist philosophy by supporting a number of reforms—free land for those moving west, improved railroads so that migrants could reach their destinations, and the abolishment of capital punishment. The 1830s and 1840s were a period during which slavery was hotly debated and Greeley came out as a strong opponent to it.

Greeley's early support of the socialist movement in time gave way to a belief in the Free Soil party and later the Republican party. His frequent involvement in politics helped Greeley to amass considerable political influence by midcentury.

During the 1850s New York City grew rapidly: it had the unheard of population of 500,000. Although many newspapers already existed, Henry J. Raymond, George Jones, and Edward B. Wesley thought there was room for another. Together they raised $100,000 and set up a new company to publish the New York *Daily Times* (September 18, 1851). Raymond was the editor and Jones was the business manager. Their inspiration lay in the fact that the *Tribune* had cleared $60,000 the previous year.[40]

The *Times* (the word Daily was shortly dropped) was well edited and had ample, timely foreign news. It was also popular; within two weeks it had a circulation of 20,000. Success, however, required that the price be raised to two cents. This move lost the paper a third of its circulation, but the owners were in New York City to stay.

Competition was good for the public. Greeley had forced Bennett and the *Herald* to cut down on sensationalism and both had been forced to upgrade their journalistic standards in order to compete with the even higher quality *Times*. Greeley once observed of the *Times's* Raymond that he was one of the ablest and most energetic young writers he had seen.

Raymond joined Greeley as an important abolitionist. In this they were opposed by the *Herald* and the *Sun*. The strong antislavery feelings of Raymond and Greeley brought them into close association with major politicians in the Whig party. This association led them to promote a new political party, the Republicans.

A TIME OF RAPID CHANGE

Railroads and telegraphs covered the nation east of the Mississippi, bringing the nation much closer together. In 1850, there were 10,000 miles of railroad—and that figure was tripled by 1860. More important than the growth of telegraph and railroad were the changing population patterns and the growth of states like Illinois, Minnesota, and Kansas. Cities like Chicago and St. Louis were now among the nation's largest. Illinois became the fourth largest state and Missouri the eighth largest. As the population moved even farther west and southwest, attracted by free land and gold, papers moved right behind them. The western newspapers received much of their news by pony express from the East. The new settlers wanted to hear what was happening back home. The pony express could carry a message from Missouri to California in ten and a half days. When an express rider reached California, a crowd would assemble to celebrate.

The pony express went both ways, of course. And on the return trip

TABLE 2-1 Some Early Newspapers of the Midwest

CITY/STATE	NEWSPAPER	DATE STARTED
Chicago (IL)	*Weekly Democrat*	1833
Green Bay (WI)	*Intelligencer*	1833
Baptist Mission (KS)	*Shawnee Sun*	1835
Dubuque (IA)	*Visitor*	1836
Milwaukee (WI)	*Sentinel*	1837
Chicago (IL)	*Daily Tribune*	1847
St. Paul (MN)	*Minnesota Pioneer*	1849
Belleview (NB)	*Nebraska Palladium*	1854 (moved there)
Sioux Falls (SD)	*Democrat*	1858

Source: Mott (1962), pp. 282–286.

TABLE 2–2   Some Early Newspapers of the Southwest and Far West

CITY/STATE	NEWSPAPER	DATE STARTED
Santa Fe (NM)	*El Crepusclo*	1834
San Felipe (TX)	*Telegraph and Texas Register*	1835
Westville (OK)	*Cherokee Messenger*	1844
Oregon City (OR)	*Oregon Spectator*	1846
Monterey (CA)	*Californian*	1846
Santa Fe (NM)	*Republican*	1847
Salt Lake City (UT)	*Desert News*	1850
Genoa (NV)	*Territorial Enterprise*	1850
Olympia (WA)	*Columbian*	1852
Denver (CO)	*Rocky Mountain News*	1858
Tubao (AZ)	*Arizonian*	1859

Source: Mott (1962), p. 287.

it would bring east the news of the frontier. Some of the most famous newspaper correspondents were sent west to report what was happening. Others, who later became famous in the East, started in western newspaper offices. Mark Twain, for instance, worked for a time at the *Territorial Enterprise* in Genoa, Nevada. The relationship between western and eastern newspapers was further nurtured by Eastern publishers who sent copies of their newspapers west for settlers to read.

Newspapers at mid-century underwent sharp changes in both format and style. Earlier papers had engaged in editorial-style leads filled with the opinions of the editor or writer, but few facts. But by the early 1850s, editorializing had faded from leads. The modern news style, in which important facts were summarized in leads and followed by the who, what, when, and where, began to emerge. Editorial comments, when they were even used in a news story, were reserved for the end of the article.

Like content, newspaper formats changed. More illustrations appeared. Woodcuts were usually small, however, as were the headlines, and were still used to illustrate advertising more than news items. Another format change was the increasing size of the papers. The *Journal of Commerce* became the largest newspaper of the day, measuring about three by five feet.[41] The penny newspapers adopted a much smaller size, about fifteen by twenty-two inches, because they could not afford the larger size. Nevertheless, all papers were printed on larger pages than in the past.

With the disappearance of the editorial news story lead, the editorial page emerged. Greeley was its chief architect. His *Tribune* editorials discussed social, political, economic, and literary topics at a high level. The *Herald* had its editorial page, but it was usually flippant and cynical. At the other extreme was the *Times* with editorials written according to a strict fairness code.

News at mid-century concentrated on national politics, the Mexican-American War, and the gold rush to California. There were lesser stories, but newspapers were showing great sensitivity to large American issues. Foreign news no longer dominated the pages of American newspapers.

The rights of Black citizens had become increasingly important in the small segment of the newspapers (perhaps twenty-five by 1860) devoted to the Black reader. *Freedom's Journal* (1827) was the first such newspaper and was founded by Samuel Cornish and John B. Rushwurn in New York.

Sports news became more a part of American journalism. The first sports newspaper, the *American Turf Register,* started in 1829. A second sports newspaper appeared as the *Spirit of the Times* (1831). And nonsports newspapers were carrying news of important sporting events.

Advertising also became more dominant. Some advertisements took

FIGURE 2–2 A page from an eighteenth century newspaper. Format is typical of newspapers of that era. (Culver Pictures)

up more than one column. One advertisement extended a full seven pages. Most newspapers of the day accepted any and all advertising without any attempt to verify its content or the acceptability of its product. One newspaper, the Boston *Daily Times,* defended the practice:

> Some of our readers complain of the great number of patent medicines advertised in this paper. To this complaint we can only reply that it is for our interest to insert such advertisements as are not indecent or improper in their language, without any inquiry whether the articles advertised are what they purport to be. That is an inquiry for the reader who feels interested in the matter, and not for us to make. It is sufficient for our purpose that the advertisements are paid for . . . One man has as good a right as another to have his wares, his goods, his panaceas, his profession published to the world in a newspaper, provided he pays for it.[42]

Newspapers followed the migration west and strengthened their positions in the major cities. Every class—the mercantile, the penny, and the political—had its own newspaper. Circulation figures were at dramatic heights: The New York *Herald* sold 77,000 copies daily; the New York *Weekly Tribune* sold 200,000 copies weekly; and the New York *Ledger* sold 400,000 copies weekly. These figures are particularly impressive because in 1833, no newspaper had a circulation exceeding 5,000.[43] The reasons for increased circulation are clear. Literacy had increased because of public education, democratic politics had increased interest in political matters, and the U.S. population had increased threefold.

Some of the press freedoms were tested again at mid-century. Sentiment on slavery ran high—so high that writers who dared to express their views faced attacks and censorship. Amos Kendall, once a newspaperman, threatened newspaper freedom as head of the Post Office Department.[44] He approved actions taken by a postmaster in Charleston, South Carolina, who allowed a local committee to sort through the mail to find and burn abolitionist newspapers. Moreover, Kendall urged President Jackson to seek the power to censor inflammatory newspapers. Jackson did try to obtain that power, but he failed. Abolitionist newspapers had as much trouble in the North as in the South; some even had their offices sacked or burned. Yet, for the most part newspapers did not lose any of their constitutional guarantees of the right to publish.

There was trouble with unions, too. Wages were very low for most reporters and laborers associated with papers, and this inequity led to the formation of the National Typographical Union, later known as the International Typographical Union.[45] And besides rising labor costs, there were greater equipment costs because of a newer generation of presses. The cylinder Napier presses began to use steam power to drive their cylinders. In 1847, the Hoe lightning press, in which type was locked onto a rotating cylindrical form, was started up. The new press could produce 8,000 newspapers per hour and was first installed at the Philadelphia *Public Ledger.* But the presses cost $20,000, a price that forced more small papers out of business.

COVERING THE CIVIL WAR, 1860–1865

The first well-covered war in history was the Civil War. Large circulation papers devoted up to a third of their space to it. Northern newspapers sent as many as 150 correspondents to cover every aspect of the war. But the correspondents had many difficulties. For one thing, southern generals often perceived them as spies. R. B. Rhett, editor of the Charleston *Mercury,* told John Bigelow of the New York *Evening Post* that a reporter covering the South Carolina secession convention in 1860 was taking his life in his hands. Nevertheless, at least one reporter gained access, covering the convention for the New York *Times.*

While covering the Battle of Fredericksburg, Henry Villard defied the direct orders of a general who told him not to report the defeat. Villard defied the order by riding impassable roads and tricking a freighter captain into taking him to Washington. When he found the telegraph there was no longer working, he sent news of the defeat to the New York *Tribune* by railroad.

Only one correspondent covered the war in its entirety—Charles Carleton Coffin, who wrote under his middle name for the Boston *Journal.* He worked long hours, nearly starved, and once rode forty miles to research a report. His honest, personable qualities made him a favorite with other correspondents and military officials.

Roadblocks to News Coverage

Although the Civil War was the best covered war up to that time, reporters worked under restrictions like the 57th Article of War. The article threatened imprisonment to anyone providing information to the enemy—directly or indirectly. To clarify the intention of the provision, the War Department forbade anyone from printing information about troop movements or camps. That military generals believed correspondents were doing great harm was apparent from General Sherman's comment upon hearing that three correspondents had just been killed, "Good! Now we shall have news from hell before breakfast." [46]

Various forms of censorship appeared—Washington telegraph lines were censored by State Department officials in 1861 and generals tried to extract agreements of silence from reporters.

Lincoln, like many other politicians, respected the press and its need for freedom, but lost respect for editors like Horace Greeley who frequently criticized administration policies.

Most newspapers retained their freedom to criticize and report the war, but there were exceptions. When Joseph Howard, Jr., of the Brooklyn *Eagle* published a hoax regarding a draft order for 400,000, he found himself in prison for two weeks. Other newspapers that published the "order" also suffered at least some retaliation. On another occasion, the Postmaster General suspended mailing permits for several newspapers that had strongly criticized the war. Among them were the *Journal of Commerce* and the *Daily News.* The *Daily News* also had some of its newspapers confiscated.

Support for the War

Not all papers north of the Mason-Dixon Line supported the war or the way it was handled. The Republican press usually supported the war, but didn't always back Lincoln or his cabinet. Greeley of the Tribune wielded considerable influence in getting Lincoln elected, but later had serious disagreements with the president over cabinet appointments and for a time even opposed the war, claiming that the South should be free to peaceably separate. But Greeley modified his position as the number of people in the North who supported the war increased. When Fort Sumter fell, the *Tribune* went so far as to rebuke Lincoln for not fighting.[47]

The Democratic newspapers were not uniformly disloyal to the Republican war. Many supported it, but were opposed to Lincoln and emancipation. Bennett had early supported the right of the South to revolt, and had denounced Lincoln and his cabinet, but by 1864 he gave the Republican cause his full support.

A third war coverage tactic was practiced by the "copperhead" press, named for a dangerous snake that strikes without warning. Copperheads were for the Confederacy, but appeared to be on the side of the Union. The *Journal of Commerce,* listed some 154 so-called peace papers which were opposed to the war, but it is doubtful that all were Copperheads.[48] The New York *Evening Post* spelled out the Copperhead formula in 1863. Its tactic was to magnify southern victories, strategies, and armies while minimizing northern victories, strategies, and armies. This was not hard to do because there were as many rumors as facts coming from the front.

Border state papers had special difficulties because they were bound to alienate either one side or the other. In Kentucky, the *Journal* influenced the state to stay with the Union, even though the publisher disliked Lincoln personally. Eventually, public pressure reversed the *Journal's* point of view.

During the war Southern papers had difficulty staying in print for three reasons: paper was in short supply because most of it was manufactured in the North; labor was in critically short supply; and military commanders suppressed, destroyed, or censored newspapers. Then, too, much of the war was fought on southern soil forcing many newspapers to flee the invading armies. Such was the case with the Memphis *Appeal.* As the fighting drew closer to Memphis, the *Appeal's* printer packed up his type and press and moved to Hernando, then

Vicksburg, Mississippi. But the northern army continued its advance, so the *Appeal* had to move to Grenada, Mississippi, and then to three successive towns in Alabama, and finally to Georgia before the army put it out of business. Its many moves gave the paper the nickname *Moving Appeal.*[49]

Like those in northern papers, editorial opinions in southern papers covered the gamut of attitudes toward the war. The Charleston *Mercury* openly favored separation. The New Orleans *Bee,* along with other moderate papers, believed that the South should stay in the Union but that it should have certain rights. A few papers were openly critical of Jefferson Davis, the president of the Confederacy, and opposed secession.

RECONSTRUCTION

With the end of the Civil War, newspaper faced new challenges and opportunities.

Charles A. Dana purchased the New York *Sun* in 1868 when the newspaper was suffering financially. Although the paper sold for two cents while others were four, its circulation was faltering largely because of weak editorial content and style. Dana brought a new lively style to the paper and developed human interest stories that were amusing or pathetic. His efforts to increase circulation were successful: Circulation rose from 43,000 in 1868 to 131,000 in 1876, making it the best-selling paper in New York City.[50]

Several weeklies also rose to prominence during the reconstruction period. Among them were two edited by Henry Ward Beecher, the *Independent* and the *Christian Union*. Then there were secular journals such as *Leslie's Weekly* (1855-1922) and *Harper's Weekly* (1857–1916). Leslie's Weekly was filled with woodcut illustrations of murders, prizefights, and other sensational fare. *Harper's Weekly* used more dignified woodcuts.[51]

American news continued to dominate the press. There was coverage of "Black Friday," September 24, 1869, when Wall Street barons James Fisk and Jay Gould tried to gain control of the nation's gold supply. The Chicago fire of 1871 got considerable newspaper coverage. Then there were the newspapers' crusades against groups like the Tweed Ring. William M. Tweed, the Tammany boss (a term referring to a building and a district in New York), engineered a swindle of New York City amounting to some $200 million. He used all kinds of methods to get the money, but one of the most open was when he employed a plasterer to work on the new city court house for $50,000 per day. The plasterer received a total of $2,807,464.06 for his services. The *Times* observed that the plasterer might have at least given the six cents to charity.[52]

Reconstruction also brought changes in news gathering techniques, one of which was exchange agreements between American and En-

sidebar

NEWSPAPER CHAINS

Although single owners acquired multiple newspapers since the days of Benjamin Franklin, the Scripps family were avid collectors. The first Scripps newspaper was started by James E. Scripps in Detroit in 1873 and called the *News*. Soon they owned papers in many sections of the country, including the Cleveland *Press* and the Kentucky *Post*.

glish papers. The telegraph and the trans-Atlantic cable (1866) made it possible to arrange agreements between Associated Press of New York and the telegraph company that greatly improved the transmission of news. But the agreement, a virtual monopoly for the New York City papers, angered the western press. They formed the Western Associated Press, which lasted for four years until an agreement was finally worked out between East and West.

Newspapers had become more independent by about 1870. Although most of them were still associated with a political party, they felt free to deviate from the party line. Politicians began to wonder where their support was. Newspapers added more woodcuts to illustrate news and advertising. The rigid rule of not breaking columns for woodcuts began to disappear, and headlines and woodcuts were spread across two, three, or even more columns. Along with changes in format came a new generation of poetry and humor writers: Artemus Ward, David R. Locke, Bill Arp, Charles B. Lewis, and Mark Twain.

Newspaper independence came through financial security. Some papers' circulations topped 100,000. No longer was newspaper publishing an adjunct to the printing business or at the mercy of political or mercantile support. Publishers had consumers.

THE RISE OF BIG CITY DAILIES

During the 1880s, dailies became complacent. The New York *World's* circulation started to slip, so a young man from St. Louis was able to purchase it for $346,000.[53] Joseph Pulitzer, the son of a rich European family, had come to the United States to develop an army career. Nine months later he left the army as a failure and sought his fortune in St. Louis where he worked at several jobs, including a term as a state senator in the Missouri legislature. In 1878, he bought the bankrupt St. Louis *Dispatch* and combined it with the *Post*. The *Post-Dispatch* was so successful that Pulitzer purchased the New York *World* in 1883.

The *World* underwent several rapid changes after Pulitzer took over as publisher. There was increased attention to human interest, gossip, and scandal stories. Headline size was reduced, but content was more sensational. Woodcuts, when used, seldom exceeded a column in width. Circulation increased from 20,000 to 100,000 by September, 1884. After an evening edition of the *World* was added in 1892, it had a combined circulation of 374,000.[54] The *World* was then the largest circulation newspaper in the United States. Moreover, it had the largest advertising income.

The *World* used at least six strategies to make it successful: A staff of hard driving reporters who combed New York City for news; some of the most successful newspaper crusades of the time, including the story of Nellie Bly's 72-day voyage around the world; an outstanding editorial page; a cheap price; many effective illustrations; and the use of every imaginable method, including contests and stunts, to promote itself.

The *World* was more successful than ethical. Reporters disguised themselves to gain admittance to places as participants rather than as reporters. They were admitted to mental institutions and hospitals as patients, to jails as convicts. They would then write a participant story—a subjective report that illuminated the institutions' many undesirable conditions. Among the reporters who used this technique was Nellie Bly, who became famous for exposing flaws in government, health, and business.

In Chicago Melville E. Stone started the Chicago *Daily News* in 1876, and made the newspaper a lively study of Chicago events. Stone had gotten his start as a newspaper carrier for the *Tribune* and had worked for several Chicago papers before starting his own. The *Daily News* was so successful the *Post and Mail* frequently pirated its news. To prove to Chicago that the *Daily News* was being robbed, Stone published a fictitious story about a famine in Serbia and concluded the article with the following words: "Er us siht la Etsll iws nel lum cmeht." The *Post and Mail* promptly published the entire story, including the final sentence, which was supposedly written in a foreign tongue. Stone quickly pointed out that the sentence spelled backwards referred to the owners of the *Post and Mail*. "The McMullens will steal this sure."[55] Two years later, Stone bought the *Post and Mail*.

Much has been said about city newspapers, but there were many country newspapers in the United States that were wielding power, too. Some of the papers were well supported and had strong impacts on their communities, despite small circulations of perhaps 300 to 3,000.

Papers continued to prosper. The *World,* for example, built its own building in New York City in 1890 at a cost of $2,500,000.[56] In 1870, total newspaper advertising revenue was $20 million. This figure rose to $39 million in 1880 and to $71 million in 1890. Large newspapers were able to command large sums for advertising because of their huge circulations. The *World's* several editions had a combined circulation of 374,741 and the Chicago *Daily News* had a circulation of 243,619. By way of comparison, though, the French newspaper *Le Petit Journal* had a daily circulation of over 750,000 and the *Ladies' Home Journal* magazine was selling about 700,000 copies per issue.

Inventions again accounted for part of the circulation surge. The telephone, invented in 1876, made rapid transmission of information possible. The linotype, which set type faster than any previous method was first used by newspapers in 1886. Then there was the halftone process that revolutionized the printing of photographs.

sidebar

SOME NEWSPAPER FIRSTS

The rapidly growing newspaper industry gave rise to some related enterprises.

1875–1879—First journalism program, Cornell University.

1887—American Newspaper Publisher's Association formed.

1907—First two trade periodicals, *Journalist* and *Editor & Publisher,* merge.

YELLOW JOURNALISM

When William Randolph Hearst purchased the New York *Morning Journal* in 1895, he intended to make his paper the circulation leader. He hired the brightest, most creative reporters from any newspaper he found them at, no matter what the price.

The *Journal* was devoted to campaigns that attracted public attention, such as the free silver campaign of 1896, stories that exploited sex and crime, and stories that were filled with emotion. The term yellow journalism was applied to the sex and crime exploitation stories. Within two years, the *Journal* had passed Pulitzer's *World,* which also followed the yellow journalism tradition. Some reformers wanted to ban both papers because of their preoccupation with sex and violence.

The *Journal* did not limit itself to reporting the news; It became an active participant in it. Said the *Journal,* "While Others Talk, the *Journal* Acts."[57] The paper tried to "scoop" its competition by covering every event faster and reporting them first. As if its daily edition was not enough, Hearst employed Dartmouth graduate Morrill Goddard to develop a unique Sunday edition filled with the unusual in learning, pseudo-scientific fact, and amusing features.

To combat the *Journal*'s incredible circulation gains, Pulitzer employed Albert Brisbane, a socialist friend of Horace Greeley, to take over the Sunday edition of the *World.* Brisbane competed well with the *Journal,* using equally bizarre facts. For Hearst the Spanish-American War became a circulation bonanza—a war that was more a journalist's concoction than reality.

SPANISH-AMERICAN WAR

Hearst used the Spanish-American War to improve circulation. Although Spain had consented to all the points imposed by the United States, Hearst was sure there was going to be a war in Cuba. He sent Frederic Remington there to report the conflict. Upon arriving in Cuba, Remington supposedly sent Hearst a telegram as follows:

Hearst, Journal, New York:

Everything is quiet. There is no trouble here.

There will be no war.

Wish to return. Remington

Not to be stopped, Hearst replied:

Remington, Havana:

Please remain. You furnish the pictures and I'll furnish the war.

W. R. Hearst.

Source: Swanberg, pp. 107, 108.

Hearst pursued the nonexistent war with the story of Evangelina Cisneros, the niece of the president of the insurrectionists, who had been caught, assaulted, and jailed. Hearst described the young woman's plight on the front page for weeks. He solicited letters from prominent women across the United States, making the story such a favorite of the American people that other newspapers picked it up.

When public sentiment peaked, Hearst pulled out his final stop. He sent *Journal* reporter Karl Decker to Cuba to save Cisneros. Decker rented a house adjacent to the prison, removed the iron bars from the prison window, rescued Cisneros and arrived in New York to a gala welcoming party.

It is difficult to say if there would have been a Spanish-American War in 1898 without the inflammatory reporting of the *Journal;* certainly the reports encouraged the war.

Hearst personally took some of his reporters to Cuba to cover the war. At one point Hearst and his reporters captured twenty-six Spanish soldiers. The sensational coverage of the Hearst feat took *Journal* circulation to 1,500,000—and the *World* was not far behind.

Yellow journalism as practiced by Hearst had at least five distinct characteristics: large, bold, headlines that screamed excitement; many pictures; imposters, faked interviews, and other stories designed to add excitement; Sunday supplements filled with superficial stories and comics; and articles that solicited sympathy for the underdog.

Yellow journalism began in 1896 with the *Journal* and *World,* but was quickly adopted by papers across the nation. It is estimated that as many as one third of U.S. newspapers were yellow by 1900.

Yellow journalism, new high speed presses, cheap paper, and good marketing turned newspaper publishing into big business. Gone were the days of one or two people opening and operating a print shop. Some of the early twentieth century newspapers were earning their owners one million dollars annually and had physical plants worth ten million dollars.

Reporters noticed the change. Rollo Ogdon of the New York *Evening Post* observed in 1906: "Large capital in newspapers and their heightened earning power tend to steady them."[58] Other reporters were not so sure the trend was desirable. By 1914 there were 2,250 dailies, 12,500 weeklies, and 600 semi-weeklies.

Not all papers practiced yellow journalism. Adolph S. Ochs, who came from Tennessee to take over *The New York Times,* consistently opposed yellow journalism—at a cost in circulation. When the *Christian Science Monitor* was founded in Boston in 1908, its purpose was to avoid publishing information about crime and disasters, except where they affected the greater human condition.

MUCKRAKERS

Sometimes called the golden age of "muckrakers," the period between 1902 and 1912 found Lincoln Steffens, Upton Sinclair, David Graham Phillips, Ida Tarbell, Ray Stannard Baker, and others writing about corruption in government and business. Theodore Roosevelt gave them the name "muckrakers," which was based on the man with the Muck-rake in *Pilgrim's Progress* who continually looked at the filth on the floor rather than at the celestial crown offered him. Roosevelt,

THE TWENTIETH CENTURY

1902– A group of reporters
1912   search to expose the eco-
       nomic, political, and social
       problems in society and
       find themselves named
       Muckrakers.

1914   *The New York Times*
       called it a "Press Agents
       War," but whatever the ti-
       tle, World War I was start-
       ing.

1917   United States passes the
       Espionage Act.

1929   A depression threatens the
       future of many businesses,
       but newspapers survive.

1941   World War II opens new re-
       porting fronts with many
       reporters allowed to cover
       the war zones. D-Day is
       perhaps the most covered
       event in history.

1945   The war is over.

who had once respected their work, thought the muckrakers were pre-
occupied with the evil in society and failed to acknowledge the good.[59]
The muckrakers took on such institutions as Standard Oil, the U.S.
Senate, unregulated oil, railroads, banking, and insurance.

During the years after the Civil War, business and industry made
great strides and some companies became virtual monopolies in their
industries. The growing web of railroads helped the oil, iron, and steel
industries to grow rapidly and make some people exceedingly
wealthy. The rising wealth of a few citizens stood in contrast to the
increasing poverty of many others. Coupled with the increasing concentration of wealth was rampant inflation—a problem that had so angered Americans in the 1880s that it became known as a bloody decade. By 1901, it was estimated that 1 percent of the population
controlled 54 percent of the wealth. Behind the statistics were persis-
tent rumors that some companies had achieved their wealth through
illegal and questionable means.

Ida Tarbell, a reporter with *McClure's,* had grown up in the oil region of Pennsylvania; consequently, the magazine asked her to do a
series of articles on the rise of John D. Rockefeller's Standard Oil
Company.[60] As much historian as reporter, Tarbell set out to find all
the records of company dealings—a task that took many months and
much research. Her articles appeared in *McClure's* in 1902 and 1903
and resulted in a huge public outcry for reform. Tarbell, now famous
as muckraker, found herself criticized by some and applauded by others. Whatever her reputation, in 1911 the Standard Oil Company was
broken up.

Reporting on her death in 1944, *The New York Times* called Tarbell
the "dean of women authors in this country," but she was more than

that—she reflected the role and significance of the muckrakers in the nation during the first years of the twentieth century. Other reporters took on issues of illegal dealings in other industries such as child labor in textile mills and Tarbell dealt with unfair tariffs. Muckrakers were a product of troubled times and they triggered reform in many places.

A NEW CENTURY

Some of the important turn-of-the-century issues were the Klondike gold rush (1897), and the San Francisco earthquake disaster so brilliantly covered in the *Sun's* article, "The City that Was." There was an increase in foreign news; the press associations all had reporters in foreign centers. And the newspapers became departmentalized: There were sections on women's issues, sports, editorials, and features. The larger size of the papers opened the way for columns like George Ade's "Stories of the Streets and of the Town." And U.S.-based foreign language newspapers abounded: German, French, Yiddish, Italian, Japanese and Polish.

News services were changing, too. Charles A. Dana of the *Sun* set up the Laffan News Bureau under the direction of William M. Laffan to gather news for the *Sun* and others. The service quickly became independent. E. W. Scripps of the Scripps chain decided the family newspapers needed a news service and set up the United Press Associations (shortened to United Press in 1897). United Press quickly acquired a number of subscribing papers, but was excluded from the coast where the Scripps News Service was functioning. Not to be outdone, Hearst started the International News Service in 1909. Later INS would merge with United Press to form UPI.

Women were a big newspaper audience at the turn of the century. Department stores found that newspapers were an effective means of reaching women buyers and mounted large campaigns to reach them. The newspapers added special women's sections to attract women readers. A new breed of women reporters arose, and they did not just report fashions and foods. Fanny B. Ward covered the blowing up of the *Maine* for the New Orleans *Picayune*. Dorothy Dix, Beatrice Fairfax, and Helen Dare all made important contributions to newspaper writing, too.

Larger circulations demanded still more technical advances. The Hoe octuple press (1895) could print 48,000 sixteen-page newspapers in an hour. The double octuple quickly followed; it could print 144,000 newspapers per hour. Electronic motors replaced gas-driven presses. The "fudge" could insert a sheet of late news on a single role of paper into an already set-up press run. Smaller newspapers used the Duplex press, which improved their efficiency. And, color perfecting presses and composing machines made the paper look better or work faster.

WORLD WAR I

Events make news, news sells newspapers. The next major news event was World War I.

The English got the first punch in the propaganda war by cutting the cable that ran from Germany to the United States. Any news about the war, therefore, was filtered through British hands (August 5, 1914). Whether the British had any malicious intent in handling news for American consumption is not known, but it is clear that the new arrangement affected editorial opinion. The New York *Times* called the early days of the war a "press agents war."[61]

To cover the American Expeditionary Force in Europe, reporters had to be accredited by purchasing a $2,000 bond and paying $1,000 for maintenance, but some reporters received the same privileges without accreditation. Accredited reporters could travel as they wished with or without military escorts. Their reports, however, were screened before they were transmitted back to the United States.

Information Control and Censorship

Soon after entering the war, the United States passed the Espionage Act (June 15, 1917). The law called for heavy fines and imprisonment for anyone who "Willfully caused or attempted to cause . . . disloyalty . . . or willfully obstructed recruiting." This law did not go far enough for Congress, so on October 6, 1917, it passed the Trading-with-the-Enemy Act, which provided for censorship of all foreign communications including those written in a foreign language. Still later, on May 16, 1918, the Sedition Act promised punishment to anyone publishing "any disloyal, profane, scurrilous or abusive language about the form of government of the United States or the Constitution, military or naval forces, flag, or the uniform of the army or navy.[62] The Postmaster General concluded that disloyal papers could not be mailed. The courts agreed. This decision meant that newspapers that printed critical comments about the government could not use the mails to deliver newspapers to subscribers. Some papers refused to buckle under the pressure and published information they deemed to be appropriate— including critical essays.

To control the flow of war information to newspapers and magazines, the Committee on Public Information (C.P.I.) was established and headed by journalist George Creel. The C.P.I. had two major divisions—the News Division and the Advertising Division. The News Division produced more than 6,000 press releases during the war, most with a strongly patriotic slant. Newspapers were free to select or reject the news releases, but most willingly reproduced the C.P.I.'s output, perhaps because they were generally factual.

Meanwhile, the Advertising Division, which did not purchase space, received many donations. The division created and coordinated patriotic advertising. With the exception of the Hearst chain, John R.

McLean's Washington *Post,* socialist, and German newspapers, most newspapers cooperated with the Advertising Division just as they did with the News Division.

In addition to its prolific news and advertising output, the C.P.I. wrote a voluntary censorship code—tightened when some newspapers appeared unwillingly to comply. On the whole, the C.P.I. tried to avoid outright media censorship, preferring to rely on persuasion. Also, the C.P.I. tried to remain as accurate as possible. Nevertheless, it was highly successful in promoting the government's point of view.

The war years brought about newspaper mergers. Increasing paper, equipment, and distribution costs forced newspapers to combine or close. Some morning papers added evening editions since they were cheaper to print with the equipment already there. One of the biggest consolidators was Frank A. Munsey, who merged the New York *Press* with the *Sun* (1916) and then purchased the *Herald* and *Evening Telegram,* both New York papers, and its Paris edition (1920). Although he sold some properties, he continued empire building with the *Globe and Commercial Advertiser,* a New York newspaper that could trace its beginnings to Noah Webster and the *American Minerva.*

Scripps continued to purchase and merge papers. The family holdings expanded by eighteen papers during the 1920s and three more were added in the 1930s. The chain acquired strong papers like the Pittsburgh *Press.* Some of the purchases were in cities where Scripps already had a paper. In these cases, the new paper was usually merged

---

THE WAR THAT DIDN'T END ON SCHEDULE

Just before noon Eastern Time on November 7, 1918, the United Press distributed the following cable:

UNI PRESS NEW YORK

PARIS URGENT ARMISTICE ALLIES GERMANY SIGNED

ELEVEN SMORNING

HOSTILITIES CEASED TWO SAFTERNOON SEDAN TAKEN SMORNING BY AMERICANS

HOWARD SIMMS

The cable was signed by the president of United Press, Roy W. How-ard, and the manager of the agency in France, William Philip Simms. Quickly UP flashed the bulletin across the nation and many newspapers followed with extras to proclaim peace in the world. But there were no follow-up reports explaining the peace. Soon it became apparent that a fake story had been sent, but no one could find the source. Some believed that the Germans had planted the story in an attempt to influence public opinion and bring an end to the war. Whatever the case, the war ended four days later.

Source: Webb Miller. *I Found No Peace.* (New York: The Literary Guild, 1936) p. 96.

---

with the existing one, such as in Akron, where the *Times* was merged with the *Press*. Within the Scripps empire there were three distinct family lines; the E. W. Scripps, Scripps-McRae (McRae was the business manager), and Scripps-Howard groups. By 1940, the three groups made up one of the strongest chains in the United States.[63]

The Scripps business formula consisted of purchasing 40 percent of a newspaper's stock while allowing local management to own the remainder as an incentive. The newspaper's local editor and business manager had almost total control over local news and business. All editors helped decide how to handle national issues. This formula gave much local control to the newspaper staff and an independence that allowed local management to use their creativity to build a strong newspaper. If the formula did not work, Scripps withdrew.

Hearst built his chain from his bases in New York and California. He added newspapers in Chicago, Boston, Atlanta, and California. Weak newspapers were combined with others to make stronger competitors in the marketplace. In Chicago, Hearst combined the *Herald* with the *Examiner* to make *Herald-Examiner* (1918) and in Boston the *Daily Advertiser* became part of the *Record*. In 1922 Hearst owned twenty dailies and eleven Sunday newspapers. He also owned two wire services—the INS and Universal Service—King Features, and six magazines. Hearst had interests in foreign newspapers, domestic motion pictures, and enterprises unrelated to the mass media. Chain ownership is discussed in detail in chapter 3.

BETWEEN WORLD WARS

Important structural changes in newspaper publishing took place between 1920 and 1940. One such change was the reorganization of the Kansas City *Star* after its founder, William Rockhill Nelson, died. The newspaper, offered at auction, was purchased by the employees. Many thought the experiment would fail, but within a few years the company had paid off its purchase loan and was showing a strong profit.

The tabloid newspaper was created when the *Illustrated Daily News,* shortened to the *Daily News,* was started in New York City by the Tribune Company (June 26, 1919).[64] Printed on pages much smaller than the standard newspaper, the tabloid was liberally illustrated with large pictures and headlines. The *Daily News* contained sixteen pages of four columns each. By 1922, the paper was selling over 400,000 copies. In 1926 it topped one million. In 1940 it had the second largest circulation of any newspaper in the United States.

Other tabloids quickly followed. Hearst first inserted a tabloid into his regular edition in 1921, but in 1924 he started a separate tabloid, the *Daily Mirror,* in New York City.

By 1929, optimism was as high as income. Then came the stock market crash. Advertising revenue dropped continuously year by year through 1933 when it finally bottomed out and began growing again. Newspaper circulation, however, dropped little. People still wanted their papers. The biggest drop in circulation, in 1930, was only 12 percent.

The National Industrial Recovery Act of 1933 required the formation of industry trade associations and codes of fair practices. To accommodate the new law, the American Newspaper Publishers Association formed a committee to create a fair practice code. The code was formed and retained even though the Recovery act was later declared illegal by the Supreme Court.

Several other laws affected newspapers. The Wagner Labor Relations Act permitted collective bargaining and prohibited employers from interfering with it. The Social Security Act added new taxes for employers and employees to pay and the National Wages and Hours Act initiated the minimum wage.

Changes in Format

Front page banner headlines came into general use during World War I. Publishers found them to be useful marketing tools because they were eyecatching. The size of the banner headline was keyed to the importance of the story—either the story's real importance or the story's ability to sell newspapers. Another layout change was the abandonment of the vertical line between columns.

Newswriting styles also changed. The standard who, what, where, when, and how became less important. In its place, who and what were fleshed out, followed by where, when, and how. Both styles still exist, of course.

The feature syndicate boomed after the war. Articles written in an interesting way and sold to many newspapers are the basis of feature syndicates. A syndication may be owned by a newspaper or magazine publisher, an independent business, or anyone interested in selling a writer's output to the media. Syndicated feature articles of this time were usually chatty, interesting stories with little news value. Walter Winchell wrote intensely personal stories about famous people in the theater and government. The columns reported who was in love, who was getting a divorce, and who was having children. To publicize such personal facts was unheard of in earlier times.

Political columns experienced a growing popularity as writers like David Lawrence and Walter Lippman provided both gossipy and serious political pieces.

Although comics had been around for some time, they boomed during the Depression. They included James E. Murphy's "Toots and Casper," Frank King's "Gasoline Alley," Al Capp's "Li'l Abner," and many others. The comics were syndicated to newspapers and came drawn with captions.

The news associations experienced considerable success between 1914 and 1940. AP increased its member newspapers from 100 to 1,400 and leased 285,000 miles of telegraph wires. United Press Association was doing just as well. International News Service had about 900 clients in 1940.

TABLE 2-3 Revenue of Daily/Sunday Newspapers

YEAR	RECEIPTS (IN MILLIONS)
1914	$ 283.6
1935	760.2
1950	2,435.1
1960	3,541.1
1970	5,870.9
1980	8,192.3

Note: Prior to 1960, figures reflect all revenues for daily/Sunday and weeklies; figures for 1960 and 1970 include advertising and subscriptions for daily/Sunday; 1980 includes advertising revenue only.

Source: *Editor and Publisher Yearbook* and *Annual Survey of Manufacturers* for years shown.

WORLD WAR II

On December 7, 1941, the Japanese bombed Pearl Harbor and rumors of war in Europe were no longer just rumors. Almost immediately, some 300 correspondents were sent to the war zones. Along with writers went photographers.

The armed services had their own journalists and papers, including the *Stars and Stripes* and the *Leatherneck.*

The best coverage of a military action in history was undoubtedly the D-Day story. Americans, English, and Canadians pooled their reporters to send back every detail of every event during the invasion. Seventy-eight reporters splashed ashore along with the landing forces. Some were injured and one was killed. Within 120 hours of the landing, some 200,000 words were sent home from the front.[65]

The war created its own censorship problems. The First War Powers Act created an office of censorship in 1941.[66] In time, the Code of Wartime Practices came into being. Sometimes news of important defeats was suppressed for weeks. Then in 1942, the Office of War Information (OWI), headed by Elmer Davis, was formed to distribute news. Like the Committee on Public Information in World War I, OWI worked with advertising agencies and journalists to see that appropriate messages were printed. After the war OWI was dissolved and was replaced by the United States Information Service in the Department of State to provide overseas information services.

On Sunday afternoon May 6, 1945, a small group of correspondents was called to cover an out-of-town operation. On the plane they were asked to swear that they would not divulge what they were about to see until given the authority. All the reporters thought they were going to another battle. Instead they arrived in Rheims, France, the next morning to witness the signing of a peace treaty between the Germans and the Allies. The reporters were told that the story would be released on Tuesday at 3 P.M.

The Germans released the information by radio earlier than the designated time, and reporters in England heard the report. Edward Kennedy, one of the few reporters at the signing, broke his pledge and released his own story to AP. As a result AP was excluded from further coverage for a time, but it had its scoop. Kennedy's action stimulated wide controversy among editorial writers. Many felt Kennedy had committed a serious breach of ethics.

ADDITIONAL READINGS

Conn, Frances. *Ida Tarbell Muckraker.* Nashville: Thomas Nelson, Inc., 1972.

Downie, Leonard, Jr. *The New Muckrakers.* Washington: The New Republic Book Company, Inc., 1976.

Eleyer, Willard G. *Main Currents in the History of American Journalism.* Boston: Houghton Mifflin Co., 1927.

Emory, Edwin. *The Press and America: An Interpretative History of the Mass Media.* Englewood Cliffs, N.J.: Prentice Hall, Inc., 1972.

Hudson, Frederic. *Journalism in the U.S. from 1690 to 1872.* New York: Harper and Brothers, Publishers, 1873.

Kobre, Sidney. *Development of American Journalism.* Dubuque, Iowa: William C. Brown, 1969.

Lee, Alfred McClung. *The Daily Newspaper in America: The Evolution of a Social Instrument.* New York: Octagon Books, 1973.

Lee, James Melvin. *History of American Journalism.* Boston: Houghton Mifflin Co., 1923.

Mott, Frank Luther. *American Journalism: A History of Newspapers in the United States through 260 Years: 1690 to 1950.* New York: The Macmillan Company, 1962.

Payne, George Henry. *History of Journalism in the United States.* Westport, Connecticut: Greenwood Press, 1970.

Penn, I. Garland. *The Afro-American Press and Its Editors.* New York: Arno Press, 1969.

Ross, Ishbel. *Leaves of the Press: The Story of Women in Journalism by an Insider.* New York: Harper and Brothers, Publishers, 1936.

Rutland, Robert A. *The News Mongers: Journalism in the Life of the Nation 1690–1972.* New York: The Dial Press, 1973.

Thomas, Isaiah. *The History of Printing in America.* New York: Weathervane Books, 1870.

Villard, Oswald Garrison. *Some Newspapers and Newspaper-Men.* New York: Books for Libraries Press, 1971.

Water, Victor Rose. *History of Cooperative News Gathering in the United States.* New York: D. Appleton & Co., 1930.

Wolsely, Roland E. *The Black Press, U.S.A.* Ames: The Iowa State University Press, 1971.

FOOTNOTES

1. Isaiah Thomas, *The History of Printing in America* (New York: Weathervane Books, MCMLXX), pp. 42–50.

2. Frank Luther Mott, *American Journalism: A History of Newspapers In The United States through 260 Years: 1690 to 1950* (New York: The Macmillan Company, 1950), p. 6.

3. Sidney Kobre, *Development of American Journalism* (Dubuque, Iowa: William C. Brown, Co., 1969), pp. 3–5.

4. Thomas, *History of Printing,* p. 89.

5. *New-England Courant,* February 11, 1723, p. 1.

6. George Henry Payne, *History of Journalism in the United States* (Westport, Connecticut: Greenwood Press, 1970), p. 38.

7. Ibid., p. 40.

8. John W. Moore, *Historical Notes on Printers and Printing: 1420–1886* (New York: Burt Franklin, 1968), p. 212.

9. Thomas, *History of Printing,* p. 433.

10. Moore, *Printers and Printing,* p. 62.

11. Thomas, *History of Printing,* p. 370.

12. William H. Taft, *American Journalism History: An Outline* (Columbia, Missouri: Lucas Brothers, 1975), p. 6.

13. Mott, *History of Newspapers,* pp. 32–33.

14. Williard Grosvenor Bleyer, *Main Currents in the History of American Journalism* (Boston: Houghton Mifflin, 1927), p. 65–67.

15. Arthur M. Schlesinger, *Prelude to Independence* (New York: Alfred A. Knopf, 1958), p. 65.

16. Mott, *History of Newspapers,* p. 44.

17. Bleyer, *History of Newspapers,* pp. 71–75.

18. Jonathan Daniels, *They Will Be Heard* (New York: McGraw-Hill, 1965), p. 3.

19. James Melvin Lee, *History of American Journalism* (Boston: Houghton Mifflin Co., 1923), p. 83.

20. Ibid.

21. Mott, *History of Newspapers,* p. 75.

22. Schlesinger, *Prelude to Independence,* pp. 85–109.

23. Thomas, *History of Printing,* p. 150.

24. "From a Correspondent," *Aurora,* March 6, 1797, p. 4. (*Aurora* was another name for *General Advertiser.*)

25. Bleyer, *History of Newspapers,* pp. 76–85.

26. Payne, *History of Journalism,* p. 178.

27. Ibid.

28. Pennsylvania *Evening Herald,* September 10, 1785.

29. Mott, *History of Newspapers,* p. 54.

30. Henry King, *American Journalism* (New York: Arno Press, 1970), p. 6.

31. Mott, *History of Newspapers,* pp. 169–170.

32. Edwin Emery, *The Press and America: An Interpretative History of the Mass Media* (Englewood Cliffs, New Jersey: Prentice-Hall, 1972), p. 134.

33. Ibid., pp. 160–62.

34. Ibid., pp. 138–40.

35. Payne, *History of Journalism,* p. 241.

36. Frank M. O'Brien, *The Story of the Sun* (New York: D. Appleton and Co., 1928), pp. 17–18.

37. *Sun,* September 3, 1833, p. 1.

38. Alfred McClung Lee, *The Daily Newspaper in America: The Evolution of a Social Instrument* (New York: Octagon Books, 1973), pp. 64–65.

39. O'Brien, *Story of the Sun,* pp. 112–113.

40. Meyer Berger, *The Story of The New York Times* (New York: Simon and Schuster, 1951), pp. 2–17.

41. Frederic Hudson, *Journalism in the United States from 1690 to 1872* (New York: Harper & Brothers, Publishers, 1873), p. 346.

42. Boston *Daily Times,* October 11, 1837, p. 1.

43. Sidney Kobre, *Foundation of American Journalism* (Westport, Conn.: Greenwood Press, 1958), p. 307.

44. Edwin H. Ford and Edwin Emery, eds., *Highlights in the History of the American Press* (Minneapolis: University of Minnesota Press, 1954), pp. 140–41.

45. Lee, *Daily Newspaper in America,* pp. 138–39.

46. Mott, *History of Newspapers,* p. 337.

47. "Will the Government Stand by the People?" *New York Tribune,* April 22, 1861, p. 4.

48. Emery, *Press and America,* p. 238.

49. Mott, *History of Newspapers,* p. 364.

50. Kobre, *Development of American Journalism,* pp. 530–31.

51. Ibid., p. 531.

52. Berger, *The New York Times,* p. 49.

53. Payne, *History of Journalism,* p. 362.

54. James Wyman Barrett, *Joseph Pulitzer and his World* (New York: The Vangard Press, 1941), p. 150.

55. Frank C. Waldrop, *McCormick of Chicago: An Unconventional Portrait of a Controversial Figure* (Englewood Cliffs, New Jersey: Prentice-Hall, 1966), pp. 86–87.

56. Barrett, *Pulitzer,* p. 139.

57. W. A. Swanberg, *Citizen Hearst: A Biography of William Randolph Hearst* (New York: Charles Scribner's Sons, 1961), p. 76.

58. *Atlantic Monthly* 98 (July 1906): 13.

59. Leonard Downie, Jr., *The New Muckrakers* (Washington: The New Republic Book Company, Inc., 1976), p. 7.

60. Frances E. Conn, *Ida Tarbell, Muckraker* (Nashville: Thomas Nelson, Inc., 1972), p. 92.

61. "The Press Agents War," *New York Times,* September 9, 1914, p. 8.

62. Sedition Act 40 Stat 553 (1918).

63. Oswald Garrison Villard, *Some Newspapers and Newspaper-Men* (New York: Books for Libraries Press, 1971), pp. 188–89.

64. Kobre, *Development of American Journalism,* pp. 605–7.

65. Mott, *History of Newspapers,* p. 755.

66. First War Powers Act 55 Stat 838 (December 18, 1941).

TODAY'S NEWSPAPER

During the years between the late 1940s and the 1980s, newspapers experienced many changes in production methods because of new technology. For a time, rising labor and materials costs threatened to drive many newspapers out of business or into consolidation with other newspapers. But offset printing, which uses photographic plates rather than stereotypes—the metal printing plates molded from raised printing surfaces—reduced the cost of producing printing plates. It undoubtedly saved some newspapers from bankruptcy.

The computer also became an important production tool during the 1960s and 1970s. Using video display terminals, reporters and editors can write and edit stories without ever using a piece of paper. Once the story receives approval from the editor, the computer produces a hard (paper) copy that is used in laying out the newspaper's pages. This process saves both paper and labor costs. By 1963, the Oklahoma City *Times* and the *Daily Oklahoman* were producing their entire news copy by computer.[1]

Another process that holds promise for newspapers is facsimile transmission of newspaper pages. The process, similar in some ways to television, transmits a page via telephone line to a receiving terminal. First attempted in the late 1940s by the *Philadelphia Inquirer* and the *Miami Herald* as a method for transmitting newspapers to homes and stores, it was given only limited trial. In 1979 and 1980 interest in electronic transmission was renewed. By that time cable television was offering vastly increased numbers of channels into the home and electronic newspaper transmission became more of a possibility. By 1980, for example the Knight-Ridder chain was sending newspapers via cable to a limited number of homes in the Miami area on an experimental basis.[2]

TYPES OF NEWSPAPERS

Although there are probably as many types of newspapers as there are newspapers, it is possible to characterize them somewhat by the audiences to which they appeal. Using this method one can identify major categories like quality, suburban, ethnic, college or university, special interest, and weekly. Certain newspapers—urban, middle-sized town, and small town—may not fit so neatly into the above categories.

The quality newspaper has been discussed by John C. Merrill of the University of Missouri and others. In his work Merrill has identified five characteristics of a quality newspaper.

1.   The newspaper is financially independent. Along with its independence, the newspaper must exhibit integrity, social concern, and good writing.

2.   The newspaper's content includes good interpretative and opinion pieces. Emphasis throughout is on content rather than on sensational layout.

3.   The newspaper places major emphasis on issues like politics, culture, economics, science, and education.

4.   The newspaper's staff is strong. Management seeks to maintain and improve its large, intelligent staff.

5.   The newspaper's readership is well educated, intelligent, and concerned about world issues. One of the newspaper's goals is to reach the opinion leaders.[3]

Merrill's study reviewed newspapers from throughout the world. In the United States Merrill found twenty-two newspapers that fit the quality mold. Among that group are the *New York Times,* the *Christian Science Monitor,* the St. Louis *Post-Dispatch,* and the Washington *Post.* The quality newspapers probably have more impact on public policy than any of the other newspapers. Moreover, their impact is wider than their readership, since many quality newspapers are read regularly by other media personnel as a guide to important news events.

Suburban Newspapers

A phenomenon of the 1960s and 1970s was the growth of suburban newspapers. One of the best known and successful suburban newspapers, Long Island's *Newsday,* was started in 1940 by Harry F. Guggenheim and Alicia Patterson. Many other cities like Los Angeles, San Francisco, Philadelphia, Cleveland, and Boston also have suburban newspapers.

Although suburban newspapers have often been criticized for being little more than community bulletin boards, many have made important journalistic contributions. *Newsday,* for example, has earned a Pu-

---

DEVELOPMENTS IN RECENT YEARS

1963	Oklahoma City *Times* and the *Daily Oklahoman* produce copy with a computer.		1980s	Afternoon newspapers begin to fail, led by the demise of papers such as the Philadelphia *Bulletin*. Circulation experiences a dip.
1960s	A new subjective journalism grows up with Tom Wolfe, Norman Mailer, and others.		1980s	Nearly 300 newspapers serve the needs of Black citizens.
1970	Newspaper Preservation Act allows competing newspapers to combine some facilities and staffs if needed to ensure survival.		1980s	Technology — videotext (newspapers on television), satellites (to transmit news), computer layout and editing, and improved film processing—change the way newspapers conduct themselves.
1970s	Newspaper circulation exceeds 60,000,000 copies daily.			

---

litzer Prize for public service, and the Sun newspapers of Omaha have earned the Sigma Delta Chi's public service award. Now, in the early 1980s, suburban newspapers are filling in the local news that the major metropolitan newspapers miss. However, a trend has started that may have long-range consequences for the suburban papers: the educated, affluent population is beginning to move back to the center cities. If this movement continues, it may well remove the support the suburban papers need to survive.

Minority Newspapers

Two ethnic groups—the Blacks and the Chicanos—have developed a number of newspapers. Black newspapers date from *Freedom's Journal* (1827). Little attention was given to Black newspapers until Gunnar Myrdal published his study, *An American Dilemma,* in the 1940s. At that time, about 150 newspapers were published by Blacks for Blacks, some with circulations as high as 257,000.

The Black press developed for some of the same reasons that other ethnic papers have: increased literacy, increased interest in political power, and greater self-awareness. Also, Black newspapers were virtually the only source of Black news until the civil rights movement of the 1950s and 1960s made white newspaper people more aware of Black readers. Then white newspapers began to devote space to Black issues and to hire Black reporters. But even with this new competition,

Black newspapers have continued to grow in number until there were more than 200 in the 1980s.

Other competition for Black newspapers comes from Black magazines like *Jet* and from radio stations that serve the Black population. Some television news shows feature Black reporters and stories. Nevertheless, newspapers such as the *Amsterdam News* in New York continue to provide the most thorough coverage of Black news and issues. The *Amsterdam News,* because of its appeal to the Black community, had a circulation of 53,178 in 1980.[4]

The growth of the Chicano movement in the 1960s gave rise to another group of ethnic newspapers. Some fifty newspapers designed to serve the Chicano population sprang up in California and the Southwest. The Chicano movement grew out of numerous factors such as low wages and lack of access to good jobs and housing. One of the leaders who brought Chicano concerns to national prominence was Cesar Chavez who led a group of farm workers out of the grapefields to start a strike.

Chicano newspapers concentrate on the human rights of Mexican-Americans, not always impartially. Most of the newspapers devote long pieces to politics and issues of importance to the Chicano community. Native American and Oriental papers also tend to be issue-oriented. Few of these newspapers accept advertising—perhaps because they are fearful of attempts to influence editorial policy—and most have lost money. Their survival depends on contributions from interested people.

Although no government agency has dictated the establishment of new minority printing and publishing enterprises, by 1972 about 3 percent of all printing and publishing enterprises were owned by minorities. However, the percentage of minority-owned print media is very small compared to number of minority group members in the U.S. population. Included in the 1972 minority ownership figures were newspapers, periodicals, books, commercial printing, blankbooks and bookbinding, printing trade services, and unclassified printing. Minority holdings in other media—broadcasting and motion pictures—were also found to be very modest.

College Newspapers

College newspapers are an often forgotten segment of the newspaper establishment. Although some eighteen hundred college newspapers are presently published, their style and quality varies greatly. Most are free and depend on advertising or the administration's contributions to keep them alive. College newspapers serve different functions depending upon the perceptions of students, faculty, and administrators. On some campuses there are problems over the degree of independence the newspaper can exercise from administrative control. One solution that's used is to set up a separate corporation to run the newspaper. Some of the larger college newspapers even hire full-time editors and key reporters, while others operate solely on volunteer labor.

Special Interest Newspapers

A variety of special interest newspapers serve the needs of ethnic, social, religious, business, and political groups. Many communities have "free shoppers," which are composed mainly of want ads and display advertising. To liven up the pages a bit, some of these shopper papers include short columns on matters of local interest. Shoppers are popular in rural areas as well as in some cities.

Business newspapers range from the national *Wall Street Journal* to regional publications like the *Long Island Commercial Review* and the *Los Angeles Daily Journal & Independent Review.* The regional newspapers have the advantage of being able to report local business news in greater detail than the national newspapers can.

Other special interest newspapers include military newspapers, free papers, prison newspapers, and alternative newspapers. This final category appeared in the 1960s to serve the needs of the new left in the United States and was characterized by papers like the *Village Voice,* which was started by Norman Mailer, Tom Wolfe, John Wilcock, and Ed Fancher. Begun in New York City's Greenwich Village, the *Village Voice* is liberal in its slant toward the news, advocating causes it considers important. Many other alternative newspapers have followed, including the Los Angeles *Free Press,* the *East Village Other,* and the San Francisco *Oracle.* Many have gone far beyond the *Voice* in their liberal views and disdain for traditional cultural mores.

Weekly Newspapers

Weekly newspapers seem to cluster at the very small and the very large end of the circulation lists. Some of the most famous weeklies, like the *National Observer* (1962), the *National Enquirer* (1974), and the *National Star* (1974), have huge circulations. Other weeklies, however, serve very small communities, many with 2,000 or fewer residents.

Although some weeklies seem doomed because their communities are dying, others are healthy and thriving in the early 1980s. Many have problems with editorial content because they lack the finances to support a strong news staff. Papers like the Newfield *News* in upstate New York use the services of unpaid reporters and concerned citizens who send information to the newspaper.

The quality of weeklies ranges as widely as their circulation. Some are poorly written and researched while others have a lively, crisp tone. The big growth of weeklies is in the suburbs where the population is large and rich enough to support a viable weekly. How the population movement back to the cities will affect the weeklies is yet to be seen.

NEW FORMS OF JOURNALISM

Many of the traditional journalistic values have come under attack in the middle to late twentieth century. A new kind of journalism with its own standards seeks to displace the old. Everette Dennis, University of

Oregon, defined five categories of emerging journalism: underground, alternative, advocacy, precision, and nonfiction.

> *Underground journalism*—The underground movement has been characterized by its resistance to the establishment and its devotion to certain causes and interests including music, drugs, and sex. Reporting usually does not attempt to be objective. The style is often a cross between nonfiction and advocacy.
>
> *Alternative journalism*—This form of journalism is a return to the muckraking journalism of the early twentieth century, in which the reporter tries to give strong evidence on the ills of society.
>
> *Advocacy journalism*—Advocates live up to their name by becoming subjectively involved in the stories they report, writing their final stories from an obvious point of view. These reporters make no attempt to be objective. Although most editors frown upon advocacy in news stories, they approve and actively support advocacy journalism on the editorial pages of the newspaper. Advocacy becomes unacceptable when it so permeates the newspaper that it destroys its credibility with readers.
>
> *Precision journalism*—With this technique, the reporter tries to apply social science methods to journalism, collecting as much of the data as possible in a systematic way. The tools of the precision journalist include computers and questionnaires.
>
> *Nonfiction reporting or New Journalism*—The term "new journalism" began emerging in the literature about the middle of the 1960s to describe a group of reporters who were writing in a style similar to short stories. The work of writers like Tom Wolfe, Hunter S. Thompson, Truman Capote, Gay Talese, Rex Reed and others reflects this style.

Wolfe has argued that these journalists saw newspapers as a stopping point en route to writing "The Novel."[5] That sense of ultimate destiny, of course, has plagued more than reporters, but starting in the early 1960s reporters began to allow their passion for fiction to influence their reporting and writing. Columns read more like short stories than like the formal newspaper prose of the 1950s. Dialogue, intimate sketches of famous persons' lives, and the emotions surrounding events characterized the New Journalism.

To achieve the sense of being there that is so important to the New Journalism, reporters have to visit the scene of the event and soak up the environment. Jimmy Breslin started writing a column for the *Herald Tribune* in 1963 that characterized the new style. When covering an event, Breslin would arrive early to watch, listen, and question the participants. He stayed for the entire affair and anything that happened afterward. The published story reflected the perspiration and tension of the event along with the facts. The New Journalism genre has a realism that didn't exist in earlier periods.

The New Journalism may be described this way—reporting from the scene with writing that embodies realism and emotion. Realism is created by using four devices—scene by scene construction, dialogue, third person point of view, and detail. This final device involves recording everything from a character's gestures, habits, and manners to the details of furniture, clothing, and decoration.

New Journalism has continued in some form into the 1980s in books like Gay Talese's *Thy Neighbor's Wife,* without displacing other forms of reporting and writing.

Some of the new techniques of journalism really are not new—muckraking (now alternative journalism) was being practiced at the beginning of the twentieth century. However, at least two of the new categories—nonfiction and precision journalism—require so much time and effort they are undoubtedly found more often today in magazines than in newspapers.

OWNERSHIP AND OPERATING PATTERNS

Increasing costs and, in some cases, decreasing circulation conspired to make the newspaper business more financially difficult in the 1960s and 1970s. Money was needed to invest in modern equipment, and labor costs increased rapidly. The new equipment required fewer workers in certain areas, but unions were reluctant to make changes. One solution to financial problems was the Newspaper Preservation Act of 1970, which allowed competing newspapers in some communities to combine advertising staffs and printing facilities (though not editorial staffs) to reduce costs.[6] Other trends that helped some newspapers were the demise of competing dailies in many cities and the growing size of newspaper chains.

The joint operating agreements sanctioned by the Newspaper Preservation Act created some controversy. For example, the law led to an arrangement between the San Francisco *Examiner* and the *Chronicle* that divided morning and afternoon markets between the two papers and formed a jointly owned subsidiary to print the two newspapers. Profits were shared fifty-fifty. This arrangement led to the demise of a semi-monthly printed by the San Francisco Bay Guardian Company.

The Bay Guardian Company filed suit against the *Examiner* and the *Chronicle,* holding that the Newspaper Preservation Act had allowed an agreement that created a local monopoly. The Federal District court that heard the case held that the law was constitutional and did not violate any local laws. However, the judge did question the nature of the agreement between the *Chronicle* and the *Examiner,* suggesting that the question of an illegal local monopoly would have to be resolved in another case.[7]

Whatever the problems with the Newspaper Preservation Act, by 1982 twenty-four joint operating agreements existed and *Editor and Publisher* was defending the practice as essential to the survival of many newspapers.

sidebar

BUILDING A CONGLOMERATE—FOR WHOM?

The desire to build ever bigger media corporations with more newspapers, magazines, and television stations does have its lighter side. When his wife's birthday arrived in 1959, Newhouse bought her *Vogue, House & Garden, Bride's Magazine, Glamour,* and *Vogue Pattern Book*—not just a single copy of each but the entire publishing enterprise of each—for some $5 million. As it turned out, Newhouse did not stop with those five—within months he had added seven more magazines.

Source: Ben Bagdikian, "Newspaper Mergers—The Final Phase," *Columbia Journalism Review,* March-April 1977, p. 20.

TABLE 3–1 Growth of Chains—1900–1980

YEAR	NUMBER OF CHAINS	NUMBER OF CHAIN-OWNED DAILIES	NUMBER OF DAILIES
1900	8	27	—
1930	55	311	1942
1945	75	368	1749
1960	109	552	1763
1971	157	879	1749
1980	162	—	1745

Source: Data from Christopher H. Sterling and Timothy R. Haight. *The Mass Media: Aspen Institute Guide to Communication Industry Trends* (New York: Praeger Publishers, 1978) p. 63, except 1980 data, which is from *1981 Editor and Publisher Yearbook*, pp. 357–363.

CHAINS

Although the development of newspaper chains began much earlier, the rapid growth of chains is very much a twentieth century phenomenon. As recently as 1945, there were fewer than 400 newspapers owned by chains. That number had risen to more than 1,000 by 1976. Undoubtedly, one of the reasons for the recent growth of chains is the amount of capital needed to operate a viable modern newspaper. Not only has the number of chains increased, but so has the number of newspapers held by each chain. For example, in 1972 E. W. Scripps owned forty-nine newspapers, Gannett owned fifty and Newhouse owned twenty-three. Table 3–1 shows how the number of newspaper chains has grown since 1900. Total circulation for the top ten newspaper groups amounted to 22,145,000 in 1976, an increase of 1,207,000 in four years (Table 3–2). Moreover, by 1976 71 percent of all daily newspapers were printed by chain owners.

Knight-Ridder owns newspapers in Akron, Miami, Detroit, Charlotte, and Philadelphia. Meanwhile, the Hearst organization, which was so large at the beginning of the century, has had to sell some of its newspapers to cover mounting expenses.

CROSS-MEDIA OWNERS

Another modern trend, this one appearing as early as the 1930s, is owners with holdings in several media. For instance, Cox Broadcasting Company, the Atlanta-based company, owns newspapers, book publishers, magazine publishers, film distributors, radio and television stations, and television production houses. The New York Times Company has holdings in book publishing, newspapers, magazines, educational film production, radio and television stations, educational recordings, a news service, and a data bank. Many other companies have similar holdings reflecting a wide range of media interests. Some other cross-media owners include American Broadcasting Companies, Inc., RCA, Inc., CBS, Inc., Time Inc., Washington Post Co., and Newhouse Newspapers.

The pros and cons of cross-media ownership, chains, and joint operating agreements have been debated by many people over the years, including former Vice-Presidents Spiro Agnew and Hubert Humphrey. To clarify the terms, cross-media ownership refers to a company which owns properties in two or more media such as newspapers and television or newspapers and book publishing. A chain owner holds two or more properties in the same medium, such as several newspapers in various communities. Joint operating agreements exist when two newspaper publishers sign an agreement to use the same printing or distribution facilities and to divide profits by an agreed formula. Those who defend the existence of large newspaper holdings argue that the improved economic leverage makes possible more thorough news coverage. The rich companies can hire large and diversified news staffs who have the time to cover the news in detail. The same people also assert that financial strength gives newspapers independence from the political pressures that might influence a weaker paper.

Those who oppose the concentration of media power contend that local news monopolies can exercise a form of censorship by refusing to cover certain types of news or events. A local news monopoly exists when one company owns all or most of the news media in a community. For example, a monopoly would exist if one person owned a community's only daily newspaper, only television station, and one or two radio stations. The organization, if it refused to carry advertising for a sponsor, would effectively prevent the advertiser from reaching the public. And if the owner refused to cover a political candidate, that candidate would not be able to reach the public. Table 3–3 lists some of the bigger cross-media owners and the nature of their holdings.

Studies conducted on the effects of newspaper ownership of broadcast stations include work done by the Ohio University Research Center under contract to the National Association of Broadcasters. This study revealed no reduction in the free flow of news in a cross-ownership situation.[8] Similar findings were reported by Resource Management Corporation based on a study of 546 television and 357 newspapers. The study found that cross-ownership had no effect on newspaper advertising rates.[9]

TABLE 3–2 Circulation of Ten Largest Chains	
Chain	**Circulation**
Knight-Ridder	3,725,000
Newhouse	3,530,000
Chicago Tribune	2,995,000
Gannett	2,940,000
Scripps-Howard	1,750,000
Times-Mirror	1,750,000
Dow Jones	1,700,000
Hearst	1,550,000
Cox	1,200,000
New York Times	1,005,000

Source: Sterling and Haight, 1978, p. 83.

NEWSPAPERS AS A PROFITABLE INSTITUTION

Although increasing costs and, for some decreasing circulation have conspired to make the newspaper business more difficult in the 1960s and 1970s, the newspapers that have survived generally show increased profits. Total receipts for newspapers increased from $1,917 million in 1947 to $3,628 million in 1958. That figure reached $10,468

TABLE 3-3   Companies Owning Media Properties in At Least Three Media Industries—1981

NAME OF COMPANY	PUBLISHING HOLDINGS	BROADCASTING STATIONS HOLDINGS	OTHER MEDIA HOLDINGS
Capital Cities	8 Newspapers	13 Radio 6 TV	Cable
Cox	24 Newspapers	12 Radio 5 TV	Cable
Donrey Media Group	38 Newspapers 37 Weeklies	5 Radio 3 TV	Cable
Fuqua Industries		2 Radio 3 TV	198 Movie Theaters Film production/ processing
Gannett	82 Newspapers 22 Nondailies	13 Radio 7 TV	Outdoor advertising Satellite
General Cinema Corp.		2 Radio 1 TV	663 Movie Theaters Film Production
Harte-Hanks Newspapers	26 Newspapers 68 Nondailies	4 TV	Cable, market research firms
Jefferson-Pilot Corp	6 Newspapers 10 Nondailies Shoppers	11 Radio 2 TV	Cable
Knight-Ridder Newspapers	35 Newspapers plus stock in others	4 TV	
Metromedia		13 Radio 7 TV	Spanish network Production house Cole Publications Outdoor advertising
Multimedia	14 Newspapers 22 Nondailies	12 Radio 6 TV	Cable
Newhouse	16 Newspapers	5 Radio	Cable
Park Newspapers	20 Newspapers 24 Weeklies	14 Radio 7 TV	Outdoor advertising
Post Corporation	4 Newspapers Suburban papers	3 Radio 5 TV	Printing firms TV production house
RKO General		12 Radio 4 Television	Cable
Seaton Stations	8 Newspapers	5 Radio 1 TV	
State Telecasting	5 Newspapers	3 TV	
Storer Broadcasting		1 Radio 7 TV	Cable in 19 states

TABLE 3-3 continued

TABLE 3-3 Companies Owning Media Properties in At Least Three Media Industries—1981 (continued)

NAME OF COMPANY	PUBLISHING HOLDINGS	BROADCASTING STATIONS HOLDINGS	OTHER MEDIA HOLDINGS
Times Mirror Co	8 Newspapers	7 TV	Cable
Westinghouse Broadcasting		12 Radio 6 TV	Cable
WGN Broadcasting (Tribune Co)	8 Newspapers	4 Radio 2 TV	Cable
Wometco		1 Radio 6 TV	Cable

Sources: *Broadcasting Cable Yearbook 1981* and *Editor and Publisher Yearbook 1981.*

million in 1975.[10] Although total receipts for 1981 were not available at this writing, revenue for advertising reached $9,631 billion—and this is in addition to circulation fees. Of course the effects of inflation made this increase less than the figures suggest, but on the whole, the newspaper industry has fared well.

One way to examine newspaper finances is to look at a typical newspaper with a 250,000 circulation. If one does this, one finds that advertising revenue has risen from $5,174,000 in 1950 to $23,340,000 in 1976. Advertising in those two years accounted for 70.8 percent and 76.6 percent of total newspaper revenue. Other revenue, including circulation revenue, resulted in $2,120,000 and $7,257,000. Meanwhile, net income before taxes (profit) remained a relatively constant fraction

TABLE 3-4 Economics for Typical Newspaper of 35,000 Circulation—1979

REVENUE			OPERATING EXPENSES
Advertising—Local	$2,526,124	Newsprint	938,357
National	262,387	Press	197,791
Classified	1,141,447	Composing	299,126
Legal	70,444	Advertising	608,911
Preprints	416,258	Circulation	443,222
Total	$4,416,660	Editorial	803,961
Circulation	1,883,491	General & Administration	540,771
Other Operating Revenue	172,684	Building	113,422
Total Operating Revenue	$6,472,835	Employee Benefits	377,746
Other Income	92,855	Depreciation	189,897
Total Revenue	$6,565,690	Bad Debts	35,013
		Total Operating Expenses	$4,548,217

Source: *Editor and Publisher*, April 5, 1980, p. 16.

TABLE 3-5 Daily
Newspaper Circulation
— 1900–1980

Year	Circulation of Dailies
1920	27,791,000
1930	39,589,000
1940	41,132,000
1950	53,829,000
1960	58,882,000
1970	62,108,000
1976	60,977,000
1980	62,201,840

Note: Although circulation was lower in 1976 than 1970, 1976 reflects an increase in circulation over the low in 1975.

Source: *Editor and Publisher Yearbook* for appropriate years.

of total income, but increased in dollar amount from $1,349,000 to $5,530,000.[11] Of course, some of that increase was lost to inflation and higher taxes, but the 250,000 circulation newspaper did experience a real increase in income and revenue.

A similar economic analysis also has been done for a typical newspaper of 34,000 circulation. For such a newspaper, net income before taxes rose from $314,000 in 1972 to $623,000 in 1976.[12] Table 3–4 shows total revenue and operating expenses for a similar newspaper in 1979.

Circulation is critically important to newspapers. Back in the days of yellow journalism, sensational news was used to improve circulation. Without circulation, newspapers could not interest advertisers in using their publication for advertising. Rates are directly related to circulation figures. The Audit Bureau of Circulation, an independent research organization, performs periodic examinations of circulation to verify the reach of newspapers. That information is used to persuade advertisers to purchase space. Tables 3–5 and 3–6 show circulation statistics for daily newspapers, past and present.

Circulation is achieved by delivering newspapers, one at a time, to subscribers; most are delivered directly to homes and offices by carriers. Sometimes the carriers are employed directly by the newspaper; more frequently, the little merchant system is used, in which private contractors purchase newspapers at a reduced price to be delivered at the regular price. The difference between the two prices is the profit for the merchants, usually young people on their first job, who sell their newspapers at daily, weekly, and sometimes monthly rates.

Other methods for selling newspapers include single copy sales at newsstands, newspaper boxes, and through the mail. This last method is limited mostly to rural, sparsely populated areas.

Recently the use of young carriers has been questioned by newspaper publishers because the turnover is so high—exceeding 100 percent a year in some cases. Training programs have been hard to maintain in such a high turnover situation. Moreover, the National Labor Relations Board has questioned whether the young merchants are really independent businesspeople or only employees of the newspaper.

Circulation has always been a tenuous situation, but since the late 1970s it has become even more difficult. The number of special circulation magazines, the instantaneous news coverage of radio and television, the increased leisure time people spend away from home—all raise new problems for circulation managers. In the 1980s, the increased options on cable television channels have raised more problems. As the number of specialized channels devoted to sports, culture, movies, or old syndicated programs increases, viewers will have more and more alternatives to reading newspapers in their leisure time.

Even paper shortages threatened circulation in the 1970s by limiting the quantity of paper available to newspapers. Although a number of solutions to the paper shortage were proposed, none had been found by the early 1980s that would adequately solve the problem.

ADVERTISING

Advertising tries to persuade people to do something—buy a product, consider a candidate, change their opinion of a business or industry. Whatever its purpose, advertising cannot force anyone to do anything. Some of the most promoted products of the past have failed in the marketplace because citizens were unmoved by the best advertising campaigns. One frequently mentioned example is the Edsel automobile built by Ford Motor Company at a high cost. After a few years of production losses, the car was removed from the market. In 1981 newspapers devoted 62.3 percent of their space to advertising.

Newspaper Advertising comes from several sources—national, local, classified, and legal. National advertising is done by large companies that do business throughout the nation, such as automobile manufacturers, soft drink producers, and household product companies. Local advertising, sometimes called retail advertising, is usually purchased by supermarkets, department stores, or local car dealers. These advertisements are usually displays prepared by the advertiser or the newspaper staff. Sometimes local advertising agenices help advertisers plan and place the advertisement. National advertising, on the other hand, is almost always handled by agencies specializing in the packaging of advertising messages. Classified ads are usually single column short ads purchased by very small businesses or individuals. Legals are those notices required by law. Usually published in fine print, the notices are produced by government agencies and others to meet specific legal requirements.

Although advertising can be cited for some excesses—misrepresenting a product, encouraging the public to buy items it does not need, and creating markets where none existed—it also has many benefits. Without strong national advertising, it is doubtful that the modern system of mass production would ever have developed to the extent it has. Mass production requires very large markets for its products and advertising has been instrumental in creating those markets. The result, defenders of advertising say, has been products produced at lower costs than would have been possible on a smaller scale, thus the consumer benefits by being able to buy more for less.[18]

Advertising, its proponents argue, creates competition, which leads to the development of better and safer products. At its best, advertising also informs consumers of the strengths and weaknesses of products so that they can make educated choices.

Whatever its advantages, advertising has often been accused of being offensive to audiences who would rather not be inundated with certain of its forms. For example advertising for personal products is often crude to many and is considered "bad taste." Some advertisers sell half-truths.

To deal with questionable advertising, newspapers have joined with other media in self-regulation. One result was the formation of the

TABLE 3–6 Ten Top Daily Circulation Newspapers (Sept. 30, 1980)

1. Wall Street Journal	1,838,891
2. New York News	1,524,641
3. Los Angeles Times	1,000,942
4. New York Times	873,255
5. Chicago Tribune	784,388
6. Chicago Sun-Times	655,332
7. New York Post	639,604
8. Detroit News	629,598
9. Detroit Free Press	604,062
10. Boston Globe	501,520

Source: *1981 Editor and Publisher International Yearbook* (New York: Editor and Publisher, 1981), p. 299.

TABLE 3-7 Cost of Reaching 1,000 People Through Various Media

Daily newspapers	$12.90
Sunday supplements	6.95
Consumer magazines (color)	8.70
Radio (network)	1.84
Radio (spot)	2.28
Television (prime time network)	4.43
Television (day network)	1.82

Note: Data from 1979.

Source: *Marketing & Media Decisions*, August 1980, p. 70, 71.

National Advertising Review Board in 1971.[14] The board reviews complaints about advertising to determine if there is reason to demand a change. When the board has found an advertiser guilty, it attempts to persuade the advertiser to correct its ways. If the advertiser refuses, the board may release its findings to the Federal Trade Commission (FTC), to citizen groups, and to the public. The FTC is an agency of the federal government set up to regulate many aspects of business such as illegal advertising.

Apart from legal or trade association restraints on advertising, newspapers have considerable latitude in regulating advertising. The United States Supreme Court in 1971 held that newspapers were not common carriers and as such had the right to refuse advertising with or without an explanation.[15] Many have refused to carry advertising for X-rated motion pictures, for example.

Advertising has experienced many changes in the past few years—some from outside and some from inside the newspaper business. Many states have started imposing some form of tax on advertising revenue in the form of a gross receipts tax or sales tax just like the tax paid for products bought at a department store. The American Newspaper Publishers Association expressed its opposition to the tax through a booklet entitled "7 Reasons Why You Can't Afford a Sales Tax on Advertising." You can't afford it because it would probably be added to the cost of the product.

Another advertising problem is piracy. Because newspapers had switched to offset printing, ads could easily be taken from a regular newspaper page and used in a shopper. In this way the advertiser did not have to pay to have the advertisement laid out a second time. Some newspapers moved to prevent piracy by obtaining copyrights on their layout and including assignment clauses in their rate cards and advertising contracts.

Advertising and a Newspaper's Income

A newspaper's income comes from two sources—advertising and circulation payments. However, advertising accounts for about 65 percent of the total income of most newspapers. A figure of considerable importance is the "cost per thousand." CPM, as it is sometimes called, is a measure of how much an advertiser has to pay to reach 1,000 readers. Table 3-7 shows approximately how much advertisers have paid for typical advertisements in various media over the past thirty years. In reading the table remember that it is based on some assumptions about the size of the advertisements and the length of commercials. The table, therefore, only provides typical examples.

Because of the importance of advertising to a newspaper's survival, the newspaper industry has an interest in both the amount of money spent on advertising in the United States and the percentage of that devoted to newspaper advertising. Since 1956, newspapers have had between 29 percent and 33 percent of every advertising dollar, with local advertising being more important than national in most cases. No other medium comes close to newspapers' share of the advertising business—television is a distant second with about 20 percent.[16] In the years prior to 1956 newspapers' share of advertising was also fairly constant—ranging between 32 percent and 45 percent.

As new media have entered the market they have generally carved out a share of the existing expenditures for advertising, which has lead to a decline (Table 3–8) in the fraction devoted to any one existing medium. Since the sum of money devoted to all advertising has been increasing—as has the gross national product—in most years of the twentieth century, newspapers have never experienced any real decline in total advertising revenue.[17]

ORGANIZATION OF NEWSPAPERS

Like most businesses, newspapers are divided into departments with administrative heads directing their units. At the top of the chart is the owner. Reporting to the owner is the publisher, who is often also the owner on medium and small papers. The publisher is responsible for the day to day operation of the newspaper. Reporting to the publisher are the managers of five broad areas: production, personnel, business, news, and editing.

Production

A good newspaper is the product of many skills and many people working together to produce the final product. The obvious personnel are the reporters and editors; but others, such as compositors, photo-engravers, and presspersons also make important contributions. In recent years new technologies have reduced the need for certain production people at the newspaper, such as linotype operators. However, newspapers' increasing circulation has led to more jobs, so the industry as a whole is far from phasing out personnel.

Personnel

In 1950 some 280,100 people worked in the newspaper industry. By 1960 that figure had risen to 325,200 and in 1970 the number was 372,200. Through the 1970s, the number of people working in the newspaper business continued to grow—in 1980 414,000 people were employed by newspapers. (Like circulation, employment in newspapers saw a slight decline in 1975.)[18]

Another indicator of job status and security is the average salary of a newspaper employee. The average salary of all employees experienced a continual, but slow growth, In 1947, the weekly salary averaged $61.96. By 1950 the average salary was $75.36; in 1960 it was $105.70; in 1970 it had reached $150.59; and in 1981 it was $275.04. Although much of this increase was the result of inflation, the average salary for

TABLE 3–8 Fraction of Advertising Revenues Received by Various Media—1976

Newspapers	30
Magazines	5
Farm Publications	Less than 1
Television	20
Radio	7
Direct Mail	14
Outdoor	1
Other	23

Source: Sterling and Haight, 1978 p. 131.

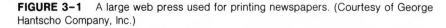

FIGURE 3-1 A large web press used for printing newspapers. (Courtesy of George Hantscho Company, Inc.)

newspaper employees has stayed between ten dollars and 20 dollars per week ahead of the average for all manufacturing industries.[19]

Averages can be deceiving, however, because lumped into one group are the production workers, reporters, editors, and everyone else involved in a newspaper. Strong unions have worked to bring production workers' salaries into line with other industrial workers. However, reporters have not been as successful financially. Although large city newspapers usually pay their reporters much more than small community newspapers, the salaries of reporters and editors working for most newspapers are in need of improvement.

Employment opportunities for women and minorities in the newspaper business changed during the 1960s and 1970s (Tables 3–9 and 3–10). In 1973 when the Equal Employment Opportunity Commission conducted a study of the newspaper industry, men dominated, holding some 74.4 percent of all jobs. White employees dominated all other groups by a wide margin—92.4 percent were white. Both of these figures were slightly better than they had been in 1970, but the change was still less than 5 percent in both cases.[20] At best, one can say that opportunities for women and minorities are slowly improving. Black employees are the largest minority group employed by the industry, with other groups making very small showings.

How are employees to improve their salaries and other benefits? At many newspapers all or part of the staff is unionized, but a strike, even when it is justified because of inadequate working conditions or salaries, can have a devastating effect on the community. With no newspaper available, an important avenue of news and opinion is cut off. Supermarkets, theaters, and other advertisers cannot reach the public. Bargain hunters lose an important source of information. Apartment and house hunters lose access to listings. The effects of a newspaper strike are so widespread, one could make a case for prohibiting newspaper employees from striking. Yet, no other arrangement exists for employees to get management's attention.

Business Department

The business department, which is responsible for circulation, advertising, promotion, and accounting, has changed dramatically in the years since the computer was invented. Many of the operations of the business department, such as billing, accounting, and payroll, are now handled by computers.

A major responsibility of the business department is to sell advertising. To fulfill this role, the department employs salespeople, usually on commission or commission plus a small salary, to contact clients. Armed with information about the newspaper's reach, cost per thousand and content, salespeople can show clients what they will receive for their investment.

Another area of concern is promotion—the job of increasing the circulation, visibility, and image of the newspaper. Ads in the newspaper and commercials on radio and television have been used successfully. Posters on buses, on subways, and at subway stations and roadside billboards have worked also. Advertising people themselves are reached through their trade magazines.

News and Opinion Department

The news and editorial department typically is independent of the business side of the newspaper to insure that advertisers have little opportunity to influence the news and editorial content. Although cases of excessive influence can probably be found, many newspapers work hard to insure the news and editorial departments their needed independence. Perhaps one of the weakest points of many newspapers is the business page, where some of the stories are little more than free advertising for local businesses. But, generally, editorial freedom is alive and healthy.

Its independence has helped make the newspaper an important source of news for most Americans. Table 3–11 shows how frequently that public has turned to newspapers compared to other sources for news over the past few years. Most people used television for their primary news source, but newspapers maintained a fairly constant portion of the news seeking public. The total percentages usually exceeded 100 percent indicating that many people used two or more media to get news. For example, people may have used radio and television for headline coverage and newspapers to fill in the details. News magazines may have provided detailed follow up on the week's news.[21]

TABLE 3-9   Women Employed in the Mass Media

	BOOK INDUSTRY		NEWSPAPER INDUSTRY		PERIODICALS INDUSTRY	
	NUMBER OF WOMEN EMPLOYEES	PERCENT OF TOTAL EMPLOYEES IN INDUSTRY	NUMBER OF WOMEN EMPLOYEES	PERCENT OF TOTAL EMPLOYEES IN INDUSTRY	NUMBER OF WOMEN EMPLOYEES	PERCENT OF TOTAL EMPLOYEES IN INDUSTRY
1960	30.7	43.9%	65.2	20.0%	31.3	44.5%
1961	30.8	43.4	66.1	20.3	31.4	44.4
1962	30.8	42.9	67.8	20.7	31.6	45.3
1963	31.0	42.6	69.9	21.3	31.9	46.8
1964	32.7	42.5	72.6	21.6	32.5	47.4
1965	34.7	42.7	75.9	22.0	33.1	47.5
1966	39.2	44.3	80.3	22.9	34.3	47.8
1967	42.8	45.9	84.0	23.7	35.5	47.3
1968	44.7	46.9	88.0	24.6	35.7	47.0
1969	46.5	47.2	93.9	25.5	35.8	47.5
1970	48.6	48.4	97.7	26.2	36.6	49.0
1971	48.4	49.8	99.7	26.7	35.0	52.6
1972	49.7	52.0	106.1	27.8	33.9	53.4
1973	49.8	52.1	112.5	29.1	33.9	51.9
1974	50.7	51.8	116.9	30.5	36.2	54.1
1975	50.2	51.3	119.5	31.7	37.4	54.9
1976	49.9	51.9	125.7	32.7	39.4	55.7
1977	52.2	52.6	132.5	33.5	42.7	57.2
1978	54.6	53.2	142.3	35.0	47.0	59.8
1979	54.1	53.1	151.1	36.0	50.3	61.3
1980	53.8	53.5	157.6	37.5	54.1	60.4
1981	53.9	53.8	161.0	38.1	57.1	59.3

Note: All employee figures are in thousands.

Source: U.S. Bureau of Labor Statistics, *Employment and Earnings. United States, 1909–1978*, pp. 808, 809, 727, 726, 624, 622 and *Supplement to Employment*

The results found in Table 3–11 were contested by the American Newspaper Publishers Association, which commissioned a study by the Gallup organization to find "the news source used yesterday." ANPA believed that finding out just exactly what people did use, not what they thought they would use, would provide a more accurate indication of actual newspaper consumption. This study has been conducted several times since 1957 with consistent results. In 1973, the survey found that 70 percent used newspapers yesterday, 62 percent used television and 50 percent used radio.[22]

Newspapers traditionally have been an important part of the news diet for most Americans. With this in mind, reporters have long worked to achieve objective news coverage. Interpretation has generally been reserved for the editorial page and labeled as opinion. But complete objectivity is probably not possible. A reporter who covers a story sees the story only from a certain perspective based on experience, training, and personal interests.

Moreover, because the world has become increasingly complicated, the mere reporting of facts in the newspaper is of little benefit to most readers. It is becoming more important to place the facts in the per-

TABLE 3-9 Women Employed in the Mass Media (continued)

	MOTION PICTURE INDUSTRY		BROADCASTING INDUSTRY		TOTAL NON-AGRICULTURAL LABOR FORCE	
	NUMBER OF WOMEN EMPLOYEES	PERCENT OF TOTAL EMPLOYEES IN INDUSTRY	NUMBER OF WOMEN EMPLOYEES	PERCENT OF TOTAL EMPLOYEES IN INDUSTRY	NUMBER OF WOMEN EMPLOYEES	PERCENT OF TOTAL NON-AGRICULTURAL LABOR FORCE
1960	66.3	35.0%	20.9	22.6%	N/A	N/A
1961	64.1	34.4	21.4	22.8	N/A	N/A
1962	60.7	34.0	21.4	22.5	N/A	N/A
1963	59.8	33.9	22.2	22.4	N/A	N/A
1964	58.8	33.1	23.0	22.4	19,672	33.7%
1965	59.1	33.3	23.6	22.1	20,660	34.0
1966	60.8	32.4	24.8	21.8	22,168	34.7
1967	64.4	33.1	26.9	22.5	23,272	35.4
1968	66.4	33.9	28.3	22.8	24,395	35.9
1969	69.5	33.6	31.2	23.8	25,595	36.9
1970	70.7	34.6	32.2	23.4	26,132	36.7
1971	71.4	35.5	33.8	23.6	26,466	37.2
1972	73.0	35.6	34.1	23.9	27,541	37.4
1973	76.7	37.0	35.7	24.7	28,998	37.8
1974	76.5	36.9	38.1	25.5	30,124	38.5
1975	76.5	37.1	40.7	26.8	30,178	39.2
1976	76.6	36.6	42.9	26.8	31,570	39.8
1977	79.0	36.3	47.0	28.0	33,252	40.3
1978	81.5	37.0	51.9	29.3	35,349	40.7
1979	84.5	37.1	58.5	31.0	37,096	41.3
1980	81.8	37.7	63.8	32.0	38,186	42.2
1981	85.4	39.4	67.5	32.5	39,019	42.8

and Earnings Revised Establishment Data June 1982, pp. 148, 149, 179, 217.

spective of their larger circumstances. In many cases, the story needs to be related to events that have occurred in the past to give it perspective and meaning.

Reporters need standards to judge whether their work is satisfactory. Herbert Brucker of the *Hartford Courant* posed this question as a guide: "Is [the reporter] digging up the truth in the dispassionate spirit of the scientist, collecting all the relevant facts he can get—on both sides—or is he openly and subtly arguing a case, plugging a point of view?"[23] Recalling the four theories of the press in chapter 1, the United States ideally looks to news as the means by which the public can make rational choices, which they then turn into votes for or against issues and candidates. The reporter makes the greatest contribution by presenting the facts clearly, delineating both sides of the argument, and providing enough background to make the story understandable to the average reader. When a reporter does this, the reader will not know on which side the reporter stands. As A. M. Rosenthal, managing editor of *The New York Times* once said, "The duty of every reporter and editor is to strive for as much objectivity as humanly possible."[24]

TABLE 3-10   Minority and Male and Female Employees in Selected Industries

	PRINTING/ PUBLISHING INDUSTRY		NEWSPAPER INDUSTRY		MOTION PICTURE INDUSTRY	
	1966	1973	1971[a]	1979	1966	1979
All Employees	100.0%	100.0%	100.0%	100.0%	100.0%	100.0%
Male	69.1	59.8	77.6	67.3	70.2	61.4
Female	30.9	40.3	22.4	32.7	29.8	38.6
White Employees	N/A	87.1	93.2	88.5	N/A	81.9
Male	N/A	52.6	72.2	59.8	N/A	50.4
Female	N/A	34.5	21.0	28.7	N/A	31.5
All Minority						
Employees	N/A	12.9	6.8	11.5	N/A	18.1
Male	N/A	7.2	5.4	7.5	N/A	11.0
Female	N/A	5.7	1.4	4.0	N/A	7.1
Black Employees	4.8	8.1	4.7	7.6	5.1	8.1
Male	3.1	4.3	3.8	4.9	3.7	4.7
Female	1.7	3.7	.9	2.7	1.4	3.4

Source: *Equal Employment Opportunity Report* No. 1 (Washington, D.C., 1966), c11, c55, EEOC, *1979 Report* (Washington, D.C., 1981) I-35, I-36, I-152.

NEWS SOURCES

Newspapers maintain sizable staffs of reporters to gather, write, and edit local and regional news. Most reporters have beats—areas that they cover—so that they become thoroughly familiar with news sources in those areas. Typical beats include the police station and city hall. Sometimes newspapers use part-time reporters or stringers to cover certain areas that do not usually provide enough news to justify hir-

TABLE 3-11   Sources of News

	RADIO	TELEVISION	MAGAZINES	NEWSPAPERS	OTHER PEOPLE	ALL SOURCES MENTIONED	DON'T KNOW/ NO ANSWER
1959	34%	51%	8%	57%	4%	154%	1%
1961	34	52	9	57	5	157	3
1963	29	55	6	53	4	147	3
1964	26	58	8	56	5	153	3
1967	28	64	7	55	4	158	2
1968	25	59	7	49	5	145	3
1971	23	60	5	48	4	140	1
1972	21	64	6	50	4	145	1
1974	21	65	4	47	4	141	—
1976	19	64	7	49	5	144	—

Source: Television Information Office (1977), p. 3, using data developed by The Roper Organization.

THE REPORTER'S LIFE

The popular view of a reporter's life which emerged after the famous work of Bob Woodward and Carl Bernstein, who exposed the Watergate events, had reporters clandestinely meeting informants who told of evil deeds in government. For the reporter who followed every lead there waited fame and honor for heroic efforts. While that titillating view undoubtedly led many people to choose journalism as a career, most reporters live quite a different life—one that is more ordered and perhaps more routine. Typical of the work of many reporters is that of Melissa Mills Herring of *The Columbia Record*.

Herring's responsibilities involve covering the State Board of Education, the Commission on Higher Education, the University of South Carolina Board of Trustees, a technical college, and local school districts. Primarily these responsibilities involve reporting regularly scheduled and some special meetings. By law the meetings must be announced to the press in advance, so that reporters can plan to attend the meetings. At these sessions some of the organizations provide press tables where reporters can compile stories.

Only infrequently does the schedule of the meeting deviate from the usual course. In the case of a local technical college, which experienced a major investigation leading to the indictment of its former president,

Herring experienced unusual difficulties. In that case, officials did not return calls, people were "unavailable" for comment and others hung up on her. By placing enough calls to enough persons, however, Herring was able to trace the story for her readers.

The education beat, then, follows a predictable set of events most of the time. While other reporters, such as those assigned to police beats, may also follow a schedule, the events often are less predictable. Accidents, robberies and arrests do not occur on an advertised schedule. Moreover, police or rescue personnel may be less willing to cooperate with a reporter trying to complete an assignment.

The beat reporters must constantly seek to discover all sides of an issue so that readers are not misled—and that demands time and perseverance. The two goals—timeliness and accuracy—sometimes conflict with each other. Being first with a story leads readers to look to that medium for the latest information on events. Accuracy builds reader confidence so that readers will return to the newspaper regularly for the best news. However, information rushed into print to be first is subject to greater chance of error, while waiting until every detail is correct may leave the publication last in its market. The conflict, of course, can never be resolved.

ing a full-time person. These stringers are paid on a per-story basis for the news they deliver. Some of the larger newspapers have their own reporters in distant cities like Washington D.C. to cover national news.

Most news from outside a newspaper's region comes from the wire services, UPI and Associated Press. Some of the larger newspapers like *The New York Times,* however, operate their own wire services.

A second major source of news is the feature syndicate. Syndicates provide editorials, and articles on food, fashion, and the arts, as well as how-to-do-it and advice columns. Comics are also a product of news syndicates. Over 350 news syndicates are operating today in the United States.

Sometimes news must be interpreted or additional information must be gathered. In these cases, the newspaper's library serves a valuable function. Reporters find not only books and magazines there, but also old newspapers that can give information about how the matter stood in the past. Most larger newspapers maintain some form of library—at the very least one containing past copies of the newspaper and usually containing much more.

Finally, newspapers use news releases from local organizations that are trying to promote themselves. The responsible editor or reporter uses the news release only as a starting point, checking facts and information for accuracy before anything is printed. News releases come from many sources: governmental agencies, religious groups, sports organizations, business groups, civic associations, and politicians, among others.

SECTIONS OF A NEWSPAPER

Because of the growing diversity of news, most newspapers divide their newspapers, and the assignment of their reporters, into departments or sections. Besides the news section, newspaper departments include the arts, business, sports, fashions, the home, and special sections such as religion, real estate, travel, and book reviews. Not every section appears in the newspaper everyday. Some are limited to the weekend and others to selected week days. In the past, most newspapers had a women's page, but that section is disappearing from many newspapers as women become more a part of the work force. The matters once treated on women's pages now often appear under departments like home, food, or fashion and are read by men as well as women.

The sports pages of many newspapers appear as a section that can be separated from the rest of the newspaper for easy reading. Although sports pages give the usual final scores, much of the sports writing today has a distinctly feature quality. Articles include interviews with coaches or players, analysis of upcoming or past games, and other material that is not part of a television play-by-play broadcast. Most sports sections cover not only the major sports of football, basketball, and baseball, but also sports like golf, tennis, ice hockey, swimming, and track.

Like sports, other sections of the paper also specialize in serving the particular needs of readers. Arts sections announce forthcoming events

THE POLICE REPORTER

His day starts at 5:45 a.m. but not in quite the manner of most Americans. John Goyer, police reporter at the Columbia *Record,* rolls out of bed at that early hour to call the ambulance service for information about injured or dead persons. Although the information Goyer finds will not have the official stamp of a police investigation, he may secure important leads to be followed later in the day. With luck, a little more sleeping may be possible before Goyer tries to reach a community police department at 6:30 a.m. Both of these calls need to be made before the night shift goes home.

Dressing and breakfast out of the way, Goyer makes his way to the newsroom at the *Record* by 7:15 a.m. where the day starts with a re-write of police stories appearing in the morning paper coowned with the *Record.* Facts need to be updated. Style must match the afternoon paper's format. New information must be added. The task is completed at one of the newspaper's VDTs positioned on an oak-colored desk top in front of Goyer.

But rewriting earlier stories is only the beginning. By 8:30 or 9:00 a.m., after the first budget meeting, Goyer heads to the police and sheriff departments in Columbia and Richland County. Here, seasoned judgments help inform Goyer when to believe he has the whole story and when facts are being withheld. Of course, it is not possible to fill in every detail because sources resist imparting information, but the reporter's instinct often leads Goyer to ask more questions or seek information from other persons.

Accuracy and completeness must guide the police reporter just as they do other reporters. To keep on top of developing stories Goyer has compiled a list of persons to contact throughout the area served by the *Record.* They include the ambulance service, local police department dispatchers, fire department assistant chiefs, highway patrol officers, and informal conversations with people inside and outside police departments. Some of these sources, such as local police dispatchers, may be reached with a telephone call, but the larger departments like the county sheriff and Columbia Police Department require frequent visits. The visits serve to let police department officials know Goyer and develop trust in him, but the trips also make possible review of reports and other printed matter.

This particular morning Goyer arrives at the Columbia Police Department about 9:00 a.m. The police sergeant engages in a friendly debate over the finer points of the freedom of information laws, then lets Goyer review police reports for the day. The conversation starts the day with a more pleasant tone than one might expect in this headquarters building. Some of the reports Goyer quickly rejects as too insignificant, but he selects several stories and compiles notes on a pocket pad. To fill in details Goyer quizzes several officers around the station. The lieutenant has disappeared into his office with several other officers. Goyer senses a story and waits 30 minutes to talk to the lieutenant. Deadline is pushing hard and Goyer tries to find the details elsewhere— the matter turns out to be a personnel issue, so Goyer heads to the sheriff's office.

There, the first stop is the adjoining magistrate court to check the criminal docket for leads. The victims of four arrests were held on large bonds—a sure sign something big might have happened. Goyer writes the names down and seeks out the captain, who has just returned from vacation and has little information. After some conversation Goyer returns to his office hoping to get updates later.

Now less than an hour remains before deadline and Goyer must write his stories for the afternoon newspaper. One of the most serious problems the police reporter has to face is a police department reluctant to release information, fearing publicity may jeopardize their case. The telephone calls, the trips from department to department, the conversations with those who might know more information are an essential part of reporting the story accurately.

The result of all this reporting is four stories in the day's *Record* covering two major robberies, a continuing story on a woman who threw her lover over a railing to his death, and a story on a person apprehended in another state for a crime that was committed in Columbia.

---

and review current ones. Arts coverage has probably been at its best in *The New York Times,* which has an extensive Sunday section as well as more limited coverage during the week. Most newspapers, however, reprint news releases and syndicated columns for their arts coverage. Coverage of the arts has been uneven at best. Some reasons may be advanced: readers are not sufficiently interested in books, plays, and other arts to justify the cost or space; reviews of a play, some reporters fear, are little more than free advertising; and, typically, few news people were trained in the arts.

Many newspapers also publish a weekend magazine, often in color, that reviews entertainment, restaurants, and activities in the area. Written in feature style, the weekend magazine provides a good place for leisure advertising.

The news media have often fallen short in providing thorough coverage of business. What is needed as the 1980s begin is thoughtful assessment of business decisions and their effects on consumers, employees, and the public. Why don't newspapers bring the same care to covering business that they do to other areas? Some believe that newspapers fear retaliation from advertisers—a refusal to purchase advertising—should the newspaper print unflattering articles. But in a day when advertising is so important to their survival, businesses can hardly afford to reject a medium as large and important as newspapers.

The religion department has received varying amounts of attention over the years, but most newspapers devote at least some space to it. Religion coverage provides information on weekend services and some analysis of religious issues. Nevertheless, coverage does not seem to match the public's current interest in religion. The American public is spending more money on religion than on sports, and more people attend religious services each week than attend sporting events. Yet, more space is still devoted to sports than to religion in newspapers.

One of the most popular parts of most newspapers is the comics section. Surveys indicate that everyone reads the comics—adults, teens, and children. Although some comics undoubtedly serve to promulgate the political or social ideas of their creators, comics entertain different and specialized audiences.

EDITING

No matter how good the copy or the photographs may be, there is no newspaper until everything is put together in a style pleasing to the reader. Each story, headline, and picture reaches its final place in a newspaper because of conscious decisions made by editors. A large newspaper may have managing editors, copy editors, picture editors, and others who assist in preparing the final product.

Copy editors read copy for accuracy, style, spelling, and grammar. They also check for libelous comments. The copy editor may also write headlines or rewrite a story that needs to be printed soon but is not written well. Picture editors select pictures and arrange their layout on the final page.

Not all stories make it to print. The quantity of advertising, the available supply of newsprint, and the cost of production dictate the space available for news. Editors must select just enough news to fill the space. Many stories must be shortened, some must be eliminated, and others must start on one page and continue on inside pages. Decisions about the size of pictures and headlines must also be made, and, finally, the placement of each story must be decided. Which stories will occupy the front page? All of these placement decisions are made by editors, also known as gatekeepers. The term gatekeeper symbolizes the job of the editors and reporters—they decide when to open the gate to allow information to reach the reader through the printed page.

With the advent of television and other competing media, the final newspaper page must be continually improved for newspapers to remain a viable medium in the marketplace. Some newspapers are beginning to use more open layouts, larger pictures, and livelier graphics to meet the challenge of visual media in the 1980s. The *New York News* and other tabloid size newspapers use these graphic techniques to achieve their goals, but the trend has spread to many other newspapers.

Although there have been critics who have predicted the demise of the newspaper, as the 1980s began newspapers seemed as healthy as ever—indeed newspapers supplied a service that no other medium could—a daily detailed coverage of the events.

GOODBY P.M., HELLO, ALL DAY!

Since around 1970, the number of evening newspapers has been slowly declining while morning newspapers have been growing in both circulation and number. Among the evening newspapers to recently go under are *The Washington Star* (August 7, 1981), the evening edition of the New York *Daily News* (a short-lived attempt that failed in 1981) and thirty-nine evening newspapers that switched to morning publications. Other evening newspapers such as the Detroit *News* and the Philadelphia *Bulletin* have been experiencing declines in advertising and circulation. The *Bulletin* finally folded in the spring of 1982.

Factors cited for the loss in popularity of evening newspapers are the movement of middle-class citizens to the suburbs and the rising popularity of television news. But perhaps more important to the demise of the evening paper has been the changing climate of retail advertising. Retail advertising decisions have been shifting from local stores to central headquarters as retail chains have grown. To reduce advertising expenses, the central offices have decided to buy advertising only in the largest circulation newspaper in a community—often the morning newspaper—leaving the smaller circulation papers without strong local advertising sales. Since newspapers receive as much as 70 to 80 percent of their revenue from advertising, any significant decline may create a crisis.

Many newspapers, morning and afternoon, have gone to a twenty-four hour news cycle. Advertising and features remain the same, but important news stories are updated throughout the day. This reduces production and editorial costs. Some all-day newspapers are the Detroit *News*, New Orleans *Times Picayune*, and *The Daily News* (Washington, Pa.)

Source: Jonathan Friendly, "What Future for the P.M. Papers?" *The New York Times*, August 16, 1981, p. 4F.

TABLE 3-12   The Most Believable News Sources

	RADIO	TELEVISION	MAGAZINES	NEWSPAPERS	DON'T KNOW/ NO ANSWER
1959	12%	29%	10%	32%	17%
1961	12	39	10	24	17
1963	12	36	10	24	18
1964	8	41	10	23	18
1967	7	41	8	24	20
1968	8	44	11	21	16
1971	10	49	9	20	12
1972	8	48	10	21	13
1974	8	51	8	20	13
1976	7	51	9	22	11

Source: Television Information Office (1975), using data developed by The Roper Organization.

The definition of news appears to be changing. Television news, often more like headlines, is one kind of news, but the in-depth analysis of a good newspaper is another. Audiences are being segmented as the information in Table 3–12 might indicate. For some people, the television news is the "hard" news and they look no further. For others, the hard news alone is meaningless.

Newspapers Today

New technologies have changed and will continue to change newspaper production. Here are some of the new developments:

■ Video display terminals (VDT) hooked up to a central computer provide a framework for compiling news stories. Using a keyboard like a typewriter, the reporter writes the story and views the results on a television screen. Editorial changes, additions, and deletions can later be inserted into the story. In the composing room, layout people find that the VDT takes an increasing role in laying out newspaper pages before a hard or paper copy is made. Most reporters, therefore, use pencils and paper only to collect notes—not to write up stories.

■ Satellites now transmit wire stories for both Associated Press and United Press International. Although the conversion is still underway, both wire services have found the new means of transmission reduces costs.

■ Electronic newspapers, once a novel idea, now is a reality. Newspapers on paper will continue, but the electronic counterpart sent by cable to subscribers' homes has been tested in markets in the South, Midwest, and far West. As the electronic services expand, newspaper publishers will supply some information almost exclusively to electronic channels while reserving other information for print. The electronic information might include sports statistics, stock quotations, and movie and restaurant listings.

■ Computer-operated sorting equipment will continue to make it easy to send specialized inserts to specific geographic areas.

■ Satellites will continue to transmit national editions of several newspapers, such as *The New York Times,* to regional printing plants. This will make possible nearly simultaneous delivery of newspapers all over the nation.

■ New photographic processes are shortening the time from taking a picture to producing a finished print—compressing the time required to produce photographs for a printed newspaper story.

■ Telerams, small boxes that weigh about twenty-four pounds and look like a briefcase, provide reporters with a lightweight alternative to a typewriter when they are on assignment. The units contain small computers and a keyboard. To use them, a reporter keys a story into the Teleram, making editorial changes on a small screen. When the story is completed, the reporter calls the newspaper's home computer, connects the telephone handset to the Teleram, and relays the story into the main computer's memory. Telerams are especially popular with sports reporters who build a story while a game is in progress and send the story back minutes after the game is finished.

■ Computer-produced pages ready for preparing printing plates are not far in the future. When fully developed the new technology will remove the need to cut up and typeset copy and paste up pages. Limited computer layout is already being done in advertising departments of newspapers, but as existing limitations disappear, the editorial composing departments, too, will give up their wax, knives, and other layout tools in favor of a "tube." When that time comes, the newsroom will have much more direct access to the composing process.

■ The national daily newspaper concept received a boost with the appearance of Gannett's *USA Today* (from Washington, D.C.) on September 15, 1982. Initially, the paper was published in a few markets, but others are being added in many parts of the nation.

■ Daily newspaper circulation declined some in 1982 because of a reduction in the number of papers in publication from 1745 to 1730 (September 30, 1982), but if the national daily concept works, the trend may be reversed.

■ What has been called the most modern newspaper plant in the world became fully operational September 19, 1982 when the Chicago *Tribune* switched its printing to its new building. The facility uses computerized equipment to load paper on presses, insert advertising supplements, sort newspapers by routes, control printing processes, and mix inks. For years to come the *Tribune* will be a model for the industry.

In sum, many newspapers that survive into the 1990s will do so because they have adopted the best of the changing technologies to reduce costs, improve flexibility, and offer subscribers a variety of services that take advantage of more than print. The newspapers that have already adopted new communications technologies into their operations have become more viable in the market.

ADDITIONAL READINGS

Friendly, Jonathan. "What Future for the P.M. Papers?" *New York Times,* Sunday, August 16, 1981, p. 4F.

Hohenberg, John. *The New Front Page* New York: Columbia University Press, 1966.

Hohenberg, John. *The News Media: A Journalist Looks at his Profession.* New York: Holt, Rhinehart & Winston, 1968.

Hynds, Ernest C. *American Newspapers in the 1970s.* New York: Hastings House, Publishers, 1977.

Merrill, John C. *The Elite Press: Great Newspapers of the World.* New York: Pittman Publishing Corp., 1968.

Rucker, Frank W. and Williams, Herbert Lee. *Newspaper Organizations and Management, Second Edition.* Ames, Iowa: Iowa State University Press, 1965.

FOOTNOTES

1. Ernest C. Hynds, *American Newspapers in the 1970s* (New York: Hastings House, Publishers, 1977), p. 83.

2. "Knight-Ridder to Test an Electronic Newspaper," *Wall Street Journal,* April 18, 1979, p. 26.

3. John C. Merrill, *The Elite Press: Great Newspapers of the World* (New York: Pitman Publishing Corp., 1968), pp. 30–31.

4. *Ayer Directory of Publications* (Philadelphia: Ayer Press, 1980), p. 600.

5. Tom Wolfe and E. W. Johnson, *The New Journalism* (New York: Harper & Row Publishers, 1973).

6. Newspaper Preservation Act 15 U.S.C.A. 1801 (1970).

7. "Newspaper Preservation Act Upheld in First Court Test," *Editor & Publisher,* July 8, 1972, pp. 13, 30.

8. Armando M. Lago, "The Price Effects of Joint Mass Communication Media Ownership," *The Antitrust Bulletin* (Winter 1971): 789–813.

9. "Paper-Owned Stations Hailed," *Atlanta Constitution,* July 6, 1971, p. 10A.

10. *Editor and Publisher,* June 1, 1974, pp. 9, 25; April 26, 1975, p. 15; May 1, 1976, p. 24; March 13, 1982, p. 19.

11. *Editor and Publisher,* June 1, 1974, pp. 9, 25; April 26, 1975, p. 15; May 1, 1976, p. 24; March 26, 1977.

12. *Ibid.*

13. Hynds, *American Newspapers,* pp. 140–41.

14. *Ibid.*

15. Richard L. Tobin, "The Right to Turn Down Advertising," *Saturday Review,* June 12, 1971, p. 55.

16. Christopher H. Sterling and Timothy R. Haight, *The Mass Media: Aspen Institute Guide to Communication Industry Trends,* (New York: Praeger Publishers, 1978), pp. 130, 131.

17. *Ibid.*

18. (For 1950 to 1970) Bureau of Labor Statistics, *Employment and Earnings 1939–1978.* (WashIngton, D.C.: U.S. Government Printing Office, 1979) (1980, 1982) Bureau of Labor Statics, *Supplement to Employment and Earnings Revised Establishment Data* (Washington, D.C.: U.S. Government Printing Office, 1982) p. 149.

19. Ibid., Employment, p. 621, Supplement, p. 149.

20. Equal Employment Opportunity Commission (1976).

21. The Roper Organization data prepared for Television Information Office (1978).

22. Gallup Poll submitted to American Newspaper Publishers Association (1974), p. 41.

23. Robert A. Juran, "The decline and fall? of objectivity," *The Quill* (August 1968), p. 24.

24. Stanford Sesser, "Journalists: Objectivity and Activism," *The Quill* (December 1969), p. 7.

BOOKS

In 1976, Samuel Vaughan, president of the Doubleday Publishing Division, delivered the Bowker Memorial Lecture at the McGraw-Hill auditorium in New York. He had this to say:

> Whatever we think of ourselves, we can take comfort from the fact that few others think of us at all (to paraphrase Ayn Rand). "Publishing is usually ignored by the intellectual community," say the editors of the Annals, a scholarly magazine which last year devoted a special issue to the subject.
>
> We are ignored economically, as well. Few forecasters find the price of books or title output or unit sales a telling indicator—certainly not to set beside freight car loading or new housing starts. Book statistics are a fleck of ink on the vast Xerox of the Gross National Product. Still, don't feel left out. If ours are not as gross as some national products, that seems a small loss.
>
> Everyone knows, or should by now, that the value of books transcends their economics. And publishers should not head for our accustomed place at the wailing wall. It is too crowded there anyhow, with agents, re-sellers, and the Authors League.[1]

Book publishing in America followed the trends of Europe in terms of both quality and quantity. Most early books were paperback. Sermons, for example, were a popular kind of reading and were published in paper because it was the cheapest method. Some of these pamphlets or books even anticipated modern paperbacks in their use of the "skyline," a selling phrase or sentence on the cover that summarizes the contents.[2] Government documents, always one of the main forms of published materials, had paper covers as well. Early law books, since they were meant to be bound together eventually, were published without title pages or covers.

Literary historians invariably note the lack of creative literature published in colonial times. The reasons were obvious enough. The authorities who controlled the press and used it as a civil and ecclesiastical tool were uninterested in employing it in the cause of "belles lettres."[3] Webster defines "belles lettres" as literature that is an end in itself (as most poetry, fiction, and drama) and not practical or purely informative, often of a facile or sophisticated nature. Government control was the handicap. The Massachusetts General Court was so afraid of "the general diffusion of printing" that by its order the Cambridge Press enjoyed a half-century of monopoly. Toward the end of the seventeenth century, the authorities quickly ended the first attempt to establish a press in Pennsylvania, and no printing was permitted in Virginia until 1730.[4]

The ultimate importance of the Cambridge Press has been well established. "Almost every printer and publisher in New England and many of the great houses of New York can trace their ancestry to the little college printery operated by the Days and Greens . . . "[5] In addition to the usual almanacs, primers, law and psalm books, the press began to turn out other fare. In 1662 the press published the country's first best seller, the Reverend Michael Wigglesworth's *Day of Doom,* a chilling exposition of Calvinist theology done in doggerel verse; in 1669 it printed Nathaniel Morton's *New England's Memorial,* the first history of an English colony to be printed in America.[6] Along with these native products, Cambridge Press published reprints of current English literature, including Thomas Vincent's story of the great London plague and fire.

As the output of the press broadened, government became nervous. In 1662 the General Court made an attempt to establish censorship by appointing a board of licensers. The law was repealed at the next session of the legislature, apparently because of complaints that the licensers had been arbitrary in their judgments, but the bill was reenacted in 1665 with an additional provision forbidding printing in any Massachusetts town except Cambridge. This frustrated the Cambridge Press's planned move to Boston. Very limited in freedom already, it was not until the approved move to Boston in 1674 that the press moved away from religious control and became relatively independent.

One of the first bookbinders was John Sanders, who probably bound copies of the *Bay Psalm Book* and other issues of the Cambridge Press. He brought his craft from England and did his work in the style of the day, that is, using plain leather without any ornamentation. Another early binder was John Ratcliff, who was sent by the missionary society in England to work on an Indian Bible. Bookbinding flourished and developed in the eighteenth century, but it was not until 1827 that binding in cloth was introduced, establishing a method now universally used in book publishing.[7]

THE 1800s

Like the newspaper industry, the book publishing industry can point
to the mid-1800s as the beginning of real growth. It wasn't so much
that books had suddenly become popular; it was that the nation had
changed—more people were educated and interested in reading.
There was also a wider choice of book topics. In 1834, largely through
George Palmer Putnam's efforts, the first systematic table of book production in the United States was compiled and printed in the *Booksellers' Advertiser and Register of New Publications, American and Foreign.* Before then, the earliest figure available was an estimate made in
1820 that the gross dollar value of books manufactured and sold in
America was $2.5 million, with schoolbooks leading at $750,000, followed by classical books, theology, law, medical books, and all others.
Ten years later the gross value of books manufactured and sold in the
United States was estimated at $3.5 million.[8]

The production tables of 1834 showed that the average retail price
of a book was about $1.20 for books by American authors and about
seventy-five cents for English and other foreign reprints. In 1840 gross
sales were at $5.5 million, and by 1850, sales had advanced 125 per-
cent to a total of $12.5 million. In 1853, it was estimated that there
were 733 new works published in this country, of which 278 were reprints of English books, and 35 were translations of foreign authors. It
should be noted that before the Civil War, most of the books read in
the United States still came from Europe. This is not surprising because until 1891, American publishers could pirate material from England rather than pay for material from American authors. The copyright
revision of 1891 protected authors in Europe; they would have to be
paid. Although there were some fifty thousand American titles available, about 70 percent of the books read in this country at the time
came from Europe.

In the 1800s there was a fiction boom. By 1850, there were slightly
more than 1,700 works of fiction, about 800 of which had been published in the preceding decade.[9] The public appetite for fiction appeared to be insatiable. English-produced imports declined as American production grew; fiction surged forward until by its summer list of
books for 1874, Harper could offer thirteen novels, although only one
was written by an American. Whatever their origin and although most
of these early novels ranged from average to mediocre, the demand for
them grew steadily.[10]

Women were particularly prominent in the manic surge toward fiction. Before 1800 only four American women had been able to get
their work published, but in 1872, nearly three-fourths of the American
novels were written by women. A year earlier, Peterson & Brothers in
Philadelphia had announced a uniform edition of forty-three volumes
of Ann Stephen's works. If one had to establish a turning point when
the fiction mania really began, however, it would probably have to be

when Edward Payson Roe's *Barriers Burned Away* was printed in 1872.

By 1880, the flood of fiction was so strong that a backlash set in, sponsored by those who were convinced for moral or religious reasons that novels were the opiate of the masses and the producers of social degeneracy. A magazine called *The Hour* warned: "Millions of young girls and hundreds of thousands of young men are 'novelized' into absolute idiocy. Novel-readers are like opium smokers; the more they have of it the more they want of it, and the publishers, delighted at this state of affairs, go on corrupting public taste and understanding and making fortunes out of this corruption."[11]

When the Civil War ended, a great cultural stirring emerged in the nation. Much of this came about because free public libraries emerged and their popularity led to increased readership; many people found themselves wanting to buy books for their own libraries.

Just as important in this cultural regenerance was the unique system for marketing novels that developed. Most novels were first printed in magazines and later transformed to books. The popularity books earned through the magazine led many people to purchase them. This was the way authors like Henry James got started. Later, films were added to the process. Fiction in a magazine became a book which, if popular enough, became a movie.

It was logical to try out novels in magazines because many of the large book publishers of the late nineteenth century also owned magazines. Without really considering marketing, publishers thought because books and magazines both used printing presses, they could easily be combined in one operation. This was actually a myth. Books required then, and still require, equipment quite different from that used to print magazines; distribution and sales were and are different, as well. In time, book and magazine publishing separated.

Another reason that publishers printed American novels first in magazines was that their authors were often unknown. Before the Civil War there were few established American authors, and realistic publishers were leery of the unestablished. Even though they tried to be astute, they made mistakes—as they do today. For example, five publishers turned down a book by Upton Sinclair called *The Jungle*. When the book was finally published in 1906, it became a best seller. Five houses declined to publish Mary Roberts Rinehart's *The Circular Staircase* which went on to sell very well.

There is a sense of continuity in publishing that is quite different from that in any other American business. This continuity is both a strength and a weakness. The strength lies in publishing's extraordinary line of succession from father to son, beginning before the Civil War and continuing today, although the transition to corporate anonymity now nears completion. From the pre-Civil War establishment of the great houses--Harper's, Scribner's, Appleton, Wiley--an unbroken line of sons, grandsons, and other family members has guided these firms. They are the publishing establishment.

These old-line firms were unfortunately set in their ways and resisted change. They were joined on occasion by newcomers like Henry
Holt, but he outdid the early founders' conservatism. Holt became one
of the leaders in a losing struggle against the increasing role of agents,
the rise of advertising, and the mass market production of fiction that
stressed entertainment rather than morals values.[12]

F.N. Doubleday could be considered a transitional figure between
the old and new eras. Energetic, aggressive, and not particularly bound
by the customs of the past, he was at first regarded with great suspicion by the old guard. Yet, in the onrush of events and the tremendous
acceleration of history that began with World War I and continued into
the 1920's, Doubleday emerged as conservative, too.[13]

It would be a mistake to dismiss the old guard for its conservatism
too quickly. After all, it was men like Charles Scribner and William
Appleton who were among the publishing leaders in the long battle
for international copyright, protection of the author's rights in the
western world. Nor were they totally incapable of change. Scribner's
published the best of the new writers of the 1920s, and Harper's survived the spectacular bankruptcy of its house in 1899 to emerge as one
of today's publishing leaders. If they resisted a changing world in
which books were regarded more as merchandise than as intellectual
art objects, they were at least in tune with Teddy Roosevelt, who was
applying the brakes on the unrestrained greed of corporations who
have not stopped screaming since.[14] But publishers exploited, too, by
treating authors as an unnecessary evil rather than as the main force of
their business.

The other weakness caused by this sense of continuity in publishing
lies in the difficulty publishers have in breaking out of old patterns.
Publishers Weekly is still full of complaints from booksellers and publishers about the overwhelming crush of books that appear in the fall
season, particularly during the holiday weeks. But still the publishers
make no move to do anything about the traditional spring and fall
seasons in the trade, although those periods were originally determined by the movement of ice in and out of rivers that carried books
from the eastern publishers to the country's interior early in the nineteenth century. Publishers are still selling books with the movement of
river ice.[15] Another way to put this is that to the "old liners," the old
ways are the best ways. They do not yet think of book selling as mass
marketing.

THE TWENTIETH CENTURY

Until the close of the Civil War, publishing was not a business dominated by the bottom line even though publishers, like other businessmen, tried to show a profit. To this day, there is in book publishing
still that conflict between business and art. Publishing a book still involves the publisher's excitement, or at least confidence, in the au-

thor's manuscript, and the booksellers' confidence or faith in it. But, finding the customers has become more and more important in recent decades.

There were more book customers as the twentieth century began. Urbanization continued, which was good for book sales because people in cities have always been better prospects for books, probably because of the larger number of bookstores and libraries, and the easier access to newspapers and publications that review and advertise books. Also illiteracy decreased from 7.7 percent among persons ten years old and older in 1910 to 2.9 percent in 1940.[16]

School enrollments and the number of educational institutions rose steadily from 1915 to 1940. Textbooks and educational books have always sold well. With the baby boom following World War II, almost a billion dollars worth of books were sold each year out of a total book market of a little more than three billion dollars. With the birth rate declining today, the relative importance of the textbook market may change.

It is amazing that books sell so well today, considering current literacy figures:

> When we use the criterion of high school completion to help delineate the population that has not achieved functional literacy, we arrive at essentially the same figure as that arrived at by those who used competency levels: somewhere between 54 and 64 million (in 1978). The total population of the United States in 1978 was estimated to be about 218 million.[17]

Paperbacks

Although early books were really all paperbacks, and garish "dime" novels have been around for a long time, the term paperback has come to mean an economical substitute for hardback books based on large volume production. Early in 1920, the Reynolds Publishing Company of New York City, which is the main center of book publishing, began printing a series of standard fiction books that retailed for ten cents each. These volumes were snapped up at once by the Woolworth Company stores, but Reynolds offered them to anyone who would buy in lots of 100,000 or more of a single title. These books were all the same size, 4-⅜ by 6-½ inches, printed with large type, and each was exactly 96 pages long.[18]

This venture did not prepare publishing for the standardized *Little Blue Books* of E. Haldeman-Julius, however. Julius was remembered by a friend as a young man who had a sparkling way about him. The *New York World* said of him in a 1928 review of his career, "He starved, he sparkled, and always he wrote—sketches, poems, stories . . . He lived in an unheated room somewhere . . . in Greenwich Village . . . and his leisure hours were spent with other young radicals discussing books and the revolution at the Dutch Oven or some such bygone eating place of Bohemia."[19]

TABLE 4-1 Estimated Total and Per Capita Expenditures on Books by U.S. General Consumers—1970, 1975, 1980

	POPULATION (000,000)	DOLLARS (000,000)	1967 DOLLARS (000,000)	UNITS (000,000)	PER CAPITA DOLLARS	PER CAPITA 1967 DOLLARS	PER CAPITA UNITS
1970							
Adult trade hardbound	142.90	165.62	142.77	29.85	1.15	.99	.20
Adult trade paperbound	142.90	34.54	29.77	22.14	.24	.20	.15
Juvenile trade hardbound	43.20	59.70	51.46	16.01	1.38	1.19	.37
Juvenile trade paperbound	43.20	1.29	1.11	1.64	.02	.02	.03
Religious	186.10	112.92	97.34	29.45	.60	.52	.15
Book clubs	186.10	186.90	161.12	164.44	1.00	.86	.88
Mail order publications	186.10	168.62	145.36	18.39	.90	.78	.09
Mass market paperbacks	186.10	193.97	167.21	228.97	1.04	.89	1.23
Subscription reference books	186.10	302.50	260.77	1.82	1.62	1.40	*
1970 TOTAL EXPENDITURES	**186.10**	**1226.06**	**1056.94**	**512.71**	**6.58**	**5.67**	**2.75**
Sales through retailers	186.10	566.01	487.93	317.80	3.04	2.62	1.70
Direct-to-consumer sales	186.10	660.05	569.00	194.91	3.54	3.05	1.04
Total hardbound sales	186.10	926.73	798.90	128.71	4.97	4.29	.69
Total paperbound sales	186.10	299.33	258.04	384.00	1.60	1.38	2.06
1975							
Adult trade hardbound	155.70	392.07	243.52	56.87	2.51	1.56	.36
Adult trade paperbound	155.70	114.54	71.14	37.20	.73	.45	.23
Juvenile trade hardbound	42.00	61.74	38.34	18.03	1.47	.91	.42
Juvenile trade paperbound	42.00	24.64	15.30	21.61	.58	.36	.51
Religious	197.70	237.75	147.67	63.61	1.20	.74	.32
Book clubs	197.70	312.07	193.83	188.37	1.57	.98	.95
Mail order publications	197.70	284.27	176.56	30.50	1.43	.89	.15
Mass market paperbacks	197.70	431.83	268.21	326.45	2.18	1.35	1.65
Subscription reference books	197.70	207.68	128.99	.90	1.05	.65	*
1975 TOTAL EXPENDITURES	**197.70**	**2066.59**	**1283.59**	**743.54**	**10.45**	**6.49**	**3.76**
Sales through retailers	197.70	1250.16	776.49	505.13	6.32	3.92	2.55
Direct-to-consumer sales	197.70	816.43	507.09	238.41	4.12	2.56	1.20
Total hardbound sales	197.70	1358.16	843.57	189.91	6.86	4.26	.96
Total paperbound sales	197.70	708.43	440.01	553.63	3.58	2.22	2.80
1980							
Adult trade hardbound	168.30	870.10	352.26	96.54	5.16	2.09	.57
Adult trade paperbound	168.30	321.27	130.06	75.37	1.90	.77	.44
Juvenile trade hardbound	37.80	105.65	42.77	25.41	2.79	1.13	.67
Juvenile trade paperbound	37.80	82.95	33.58	46.15	2.19	.88	1.22
Religious	206.10	428.09	173.31	78.90	2.07	.84	.38
Book clubs	206.10	524.05	212.16	211.08	2.54	1.02	1.02
Mail order publications	206.10	556.89	225.46	48.26	2.70	1.09	.23
Mass market paperbacks	206.10	974.07	394.36	425.40	4.72	1.91	2.06
Subscription reference books	206.10	286.48	115.98	.90	1.39	.56	*
1980 TOTAL EXPENDITURES	**206.10**	**4149.55**	**1679.97**	**1008.01**	**20.13**	**8.15**	**4.89**
Sales through retailers	206.10	2715.96	1099.57	713.39	13.17	5.33	3.46
Direct-to-consumer sales	206.10	1433.59	580.40	294.62	6.95	2.81	1.42
Total hardbound sales	206.10	2508.48	1015.57	265.17	12.17	4.92	1.28
Total paperbound sales	206.10	1641.07	664.40	742.84	7.96	3.22	3.60

Source: Population data from U.S. Census—actual for 1970, 1975; projected (series II) for 1980. Sales data from "Book Industry Trends" (*Book Industry Study Group*), based on surveys by U.S. Census, AAP, ECPA, ABA, NACS, et al.

*Less than one hundredth annually.

FIGURE 4–1 Early
paperback novel. (Culver
Pictures)

If there was anything really radical about Julius, it was his move to Girard, Kansas, in 1915 to help publish the national socialist paper, *Appeal to Reason.* The money for Julius's share came from his wife, Marcet-Haldeman, thus, Haldeman-Julius. In the year he bought the *Appeal,* Haldeman-Julius published its first *Little Blue Book.*

They had been preceded by a series of Socialist Classics that the paper had issued at twenty-five cents each. Through advertising in the *Appeal,* these books about the socialist cause filtered through the country. The first *Little Blue Book,* however, was un-political, and even immoral by socialist standards, since it was the laissez-faire verse of *The Rubaiyat of Omar Khayyam,* with a somewhat incongruous introduction by Clarence Darrow. But the second volume, Wilde's *Ballad of Reading Goal,* was more in the revolutionary tradition, and subsequent titles, mostly in the public domain . . . free to reprint . . . were of the same kind—Paine's *Age of Reason* and books by or about Ingersoll, Spencer, Huxley, Rousseau, Balzac, Hugo, Shelley, Shakespeare, Moliere, and Ibsen. A few Greek classics were mixed in with socialist propaganda; Shaw and George Moore rubbed elbows, and they were soon joined by volumes on sex and psychology, biographies of great men, and familiar family items like *The Face on the Bar-Room Floor,* in the spirit of Prohibition, and *Casey at the Bat.*[20]

The books had semi-stiff blue cover stock, indifferent typography, and careless production. They averaged about sixty-four pages in the beginning, at a retail cost of twenty-five cents. A single advertisement for *The Little Blue Books* in the first volume of the *Appeal* produced 5,000 replies. Haldeman-Julius then gambled $150 on a second advertisement in the St. Louis *Post-Dispatch,* which returned another $1,000 in orders. A little later he produced the masterpiece of mail-order advertising that began, "Would you spend $2.98 for a college education?" and the stampede began.[21]

By the time he died in 1951, Haldeman-Julius had sold more than 300 million copies of his *Little Blue Books* at a nickel a copy, and his full pages of advertising that had appeared in newspapers across the country, listing thousands of titles in fine print with numbers to be circled in an accompanying coupon, were an American institution.[22]

Haldeman-Julius had no hesitation about renaming his merchandise so that it would sell. De Maupassant's *Tallow Ball* was moving at only 15,000 copies a year until he retitled it *A Prostitute's Sacrifice,* after which sales reached about 55,000 annually. *Room No. 11,* another de Maupassant classic, was similarly unpopular until Haldeman-Julius renamed it *What Happened in Room No.11?* [23]

Julius's main sin was obviously using misleading advertising. Another example of his effective advertising technique was when he claimed that the five-cent price of his books would rise soon, so it was wise to stock up. That "soon" never came, but people did stock up.

Today's Haldeman-Julius's books would be called mass paperbacks because of the large numbers printed, as distinguished from the trade paperbacks, which are printed in lots of 10,000 or 20,000 and are usually about the same size as hardback books. Trade paperbacks are usually sold through the nation's approximately 1,000 bookstores, and the 1,000 variety and stationery stores with large book departments. The average price for a trade paperback now is around $10. Mass market paperbacks are two dollars or three dollars and can be purchased at drugstores and supermarkets—more than 100,000 outlets altogether. Robert F. DeGraff started the movement away from exclusively bookstore sales when he sold his Pocket Book series to chain stores and newsstands in 1939. That year he published thirty-four titles and sold 1.5 million books.

Paperback publishers today talk of their growth in terms of increasing sales volumes, but a large part of that increase in sales volume has come from inflation. A few years ago trade paperbacks sold for about the price of today's mass paperback; now the price is five times higher. Nevertheless, paperbacks are doing so well that they may someday push hardback books completely out of the market—especially if the cost of a hardback book continues to increase. The question is, will the public pay twenty dollars for a permanent cover, better printing, and graphics, when they can have the same information in a somewhat poorer form?

In 1981, mass market paperbacks accounted for $847.6 million in book sales. This represented a rise of more than 12 percent over the 1980 figure. Trade paperbacks show a 10 percent increase over 1980.[24] When inflation is considered, the growth was nil.

The profit margin on hardback books is low. The physical production of a hardback book can cost ten dollars out of a book's total retail cost of fifteen dollars. Then advertising, promotion, and administration costs must be added in. Finally, there is the author. Amazingly, even though authors are the main architects of books, they may receive only one dollar out of the fifteen dollar sale price.

Large market paperbacks do not earn much money per copy either. By the time a publisher has purchased reprint rights or author fees for original work, and has paid wholesalers and distributors, the profit margin is about the same as that for hardback books.

Contrary to popular belief, paperbacks do not yet dominate the book business, at least from the publisher's point of view. The reader's point of view is another matter; apart from textbooks, more than two-fifths of all the books sold in this country are paperbacks.

Trade Books

Samuel Vaughan asks:

Is the popular book more or less popular than 20 years ago? The Doubleday research department answered my question by taking a number one novel of the mid-50s and setting it out beside one of the mid-70s. In 1955, Doubleday published Herman Wouk's *Marjorie Morningstar*. It was the leading novel in sales. In 1974, we published a first novel, Peter Benchley's *Jaws*. Each had book club and paperbound reprint editions and each was made into a movie. Hardcover trade sales for *Marjorie Morningstar* were 212,000 copies. For *Jaws* around 200,000. Book club sales for *Marjorie* were 234,000; for *Jaws* 192,000 copies. Paperback sales for *Marjorie* were about one-and-a-half million copies; for *Jaws,* nine million copies.

Taken together then, the total sale for *Marjorie Morningstar* was just under two million copies in its first three U.S. versions. For *Jaws,* a little over nine million copies—and still swimming . . .

Seen that way, one popular book of the 70s has reached nearly four times as many Americans as did one of 20 years ago.[25]

When most people hear the word "book," they immediately think of trade hardback books. A trade book is defined by purpose, for general circulation through bookstores or libraries. It is not a textbook and is not sold by subscription. Most of the nearly 40,000 new titles published in the United States every year are trade hardbacks. Aside from some 3,000 to 4,000 novels, most trade hardbacks are devoted to specific subjects like agriculture, art, and biography, and are printed in limited quantities.

Trade hardbacks offer a wealth of culture, information, and entertainment, but less than 5 percent sell more than 5,000 copies before going out of print. Americans buy fewer than 50 million hardback trade books a year. That's less than one book for every four people in the country.

Despite the limited appetite of most readers for hardback trade books, book publishing, which includes paperbacks and hardbacks of all kinds, is a profitable industry. Dollars received by book publishers in 1981, according to the Book Industry Study Group, showed an increase of 9.7 percent over the 1980 figures of $6.716 billion. (Inflation was not considered.) Sales of units were estimated at $1.860 billion for 1981, an increase of about 3.5 percent.[26] Many of the big name publishing houses—Macmillan, Random House, Doubleday—acquired new subsidiaries or were themselves acquired by profit-seeking conglomerates. Motion picture companies, often as parts of bigger conglomerates, have bought publishers, as have television networks. CBS now owns Holt, Rinehart & Winston, and Warner Brothers owns Warner Publishing. The price of publishing stocks and the size of publishing organizations have soared because of the attention. Television and films companies bought into publishing because they want books with some kind of track record, and the television and film versions of a story can help sell the book to a mass audience. The result of all this has been high-priced bidding for paperback rights to best-selling hardback books. This success created a publishing boom in the late 1960s and 1970s that came as a surprise to the industry, which has traditionally been very conservative.

Best sellers are the flashy part of the business—volume can be very high, but there is also tremendous financial risk. *Jaws* took off because of the movie. The James Herriot series, including *All Creatures Great and Small,* was helped by the television show. Herriot's *All Things Wise and Wonderful* sold over 500,000 copies, and was excerpted in *McCall's, Family Circle,* and *Reader's Digest.* It was also a Literary Guild selection. *All The President's Men* was a best seller because of the well-known events surrounding Watergate. But for every best seller that makes it, there is also a potential best seller that flops despite heavy promotion. One balances the other and in the end, best sellers wind up responsible for only a small part of publishing profits.

As already mentioned, most of the money in publishing is made on textbooks, juvenile books, reference books, and how-to-do-it trade hardback and paperback books. The income of a publishing company is determined largely by its backlist—the number of books it has that achieve small but steady sales year after year.

The book most commonly published, remember, is a trade hardback. An editor reads the manuscript and guesses that it might sell about 5,000 copies at fifteen dollars a copy. Adding up the expenses of printing, distribution, and overhead, the editor calculates that 5,000 sales will yield a net profit of about $11,000. On the basis of these figures, the publisher offers the author a contract, a 10 percent royalty with a guaranteed advance of $3,000. A year or two later (publishers work slowly), the book comes out. If it sells the expected 5,000 copies, the author earns back the $3,000 advance plus an additional $1,000 in royalties. The publishing company keeps the remaining $7,000 as its profit. If the book sells only 2,000 copies to most of the bigger libraries and all of the author's friends, the author gets to keep the advance and the publisher loses a few thousand dollars. And if by some miracle the book sells a few hundred thousand copies, the author gets rich and the publisher gets richer. Most books either earn a few thousand dollars or lose a few thousand dollars. It's a slow way to get rich.

This example really refers to the good years of the 1960s and early 1970s. Today, inflation has hit publishing hard. Profit margins are getting smaller and smaller. The cost of manufacturing a book has at times risen almost 100 percent a year. Paper costs are the biggest villain. The price of paper shot up, depending on its quality, anywhere from 35 to 80 percent each year in the mid-1970s.

In response to rising costs, publishers have had to raise their prices. In 1961, Joseph Heller's first novel, *Catch 22,* was priced at $5.95. His second novel, *Something Happened,* published in 1974, sold for $10.00 a copy. It is no longer unusual for a standard biography to carry a $12.95 price tag, and $17.50 is now an acceptable price for a major work of nonfiction.

With prices that high, publishers are assuming that people will buy and read more selectively. So, they have begun to trim their lists of new titles. In 1976, Macmillan was among the first to announce a sharp cutback in the number of titles it planned to publish. Experts predict

FIGURE 4–2 Early Book-Of-The-Month Club ad. (Photo by Joe DiMaggio)

that new authors, and authors with mediocre sales records, will now have a harder time finding publishers. Advances to authors and promotional budgets are also expected to decline. Fiction will be the hardest hit, with the exception of those few books that are already sold to movies.

What is the trade hardback book's future? With the decline of mass circulation general interest magazines, the trade hardback book provides one of the few remaining opportunities for serious, lengthy journalism like *The Pentagon Papers.* There is no question that the death of the *Saturday Evening Post, Collier's, Life,* and other general interest magazines has given birth to more journalistic books.[27]

Book Clubs

In 1926 Harry Scherman launched the modern book club idea with his Book-of-the-Month Club. Scherman's first job was reporting on books, theater, politics, and New York social life for Louis Lipsky's weekly paper, *The American Hebrew* which was owned by Cyrus Sulzberger, whose son became the proprietor of the *New York Times.* In 1913, Scherman got a job with the advertising agency Ruthrauff & Ryan writing booklets, direct mail pieces, letters, and circulars. He liked the work. "I turned out to be particularly good at selling books by mail because that was my interest. I had always noticed how people could be influenced to read books by what was said about them." A year later he was hired by the mail-order department of J. Walter Thompson.[28]

In 1916, Charles and Albert Boni showed Scherman their dummy of the first production of their Little Leather Library book, *Romeo and Juliet.* Scherman told the Bonis that one of the major tobacco companies had enclosed a tiny volume of Shakespeare in each of its packs, and he suggested proposing to the Whitman Candy Company that they include a book inside every box of their candy. Whitman seized on the idea. Scherman and the Bonis were asked for 1,000 copies each of fifteen Shakespearean plays at ten cents a copy for the Library Package.[29] The partners had no actual books and no capital, but with the order in hand they were able to borrow $5,000 to produce them. Scherman resigned from J. Walter Thompson.

Scherman, the Bonis, and Maxwell Sackheim, one of J. Walter Thompson's top copywriters who had joined them, were assured of success when the Woolworth chain began to distribute the Little Leather Library. The books, also distributed in bookstores, drugstores, and by mail, sold millions of copies. When the sales totals passed 25 million, the Bonis sold out to Scherman and Sackheim and went off to launch the Modern Library with Horace Liveright. The surviving partners assumed they were reaching the saturation point and so diversified their company by forming the advertising agency Sackheim and Scherman in 1920.[30]

Sackheim suggested that the library enterprise could be prolonged if they concentrated on mail order and stopped dealing with the stores. But, as Sackheim later wrote, "We had decided that the mail-order business was no good unless some sort of repeat-sales feature could be worked out."[31] The feature they devised was the Book-of-the-Month Club, which promised a classic book each week so that buyers could acquire culture on the installment plan. This was a technique borrowed from the magazine subscription business. But even at the bargain price of five dollars a year, the idea failed.[32]

The problem turned out to be the "classic" books. Sackheim said, "We knew the pull of popular selections. We knew the importance of repeat sales. We had already experienced the feel of the book club potential. It was only a step to the use of popular books and to the Book-of-the-Month Club idea."[33] A panel of judges was set up to pick the best selections from those offered by book publishers. The judges limited their choices to current books at no more than three dollars list price. Some publishers complained that this was tough on four-dollar and five-dollar books, but were reconciled by the fact that an assured 40,000 first printing would make three dollars viable.[34]

The club was well advertised in full pages in the *New York Times, Herald Tribune, Literary Digest, Atlantic,* and similar periodicals.[35] In the late 1920s and 1930s, the Book-of-the-Month Club concept became an institution and featured books like *Elmer Gantry* by Sinclair Lewis, *Grant Hotel* by Vicki Baum, *The Good Earth* by Pearl Buck, and *Gone With The Wind* by Margaret Mitchell.

Competition from companies like the Literary Guild sprang up immediately. Today, readers can join a host of specialty book clubs such as travel book clubs, mystery book clubs, and psychology book clubs. The 1981 gross income of all book clubs was $571.5 million. In about fifty years of operation, the book club system has not changed much. Members are notified of the next selection a few weeks in advance. If they do not reject it, the book is sent automatically. Many a book has been bought just because the member forgot to reject it, a clever marketing scheme on the part of the club. Publishers initially feared that book clubs would hurt bookstore sales. They had the same fear about paperbacks. Neither has happened. Mail-order operations have created hundreds of thousands of new book buyers in areas where booksellers are scarce or nonexistent.

A complete mailing list of retail book outlets would not have numbered more than 2,000 in 1921. Ben Huebsch made an analysis and offered some predictions in a lead article in *Publisher's Weekly* in 1924:

1.   Although America is beginning to be a book-reading nation, the industry is not prepared to meet "the new impulse" because there are too few retail shops in some places, none in others, and too many (at the moment) in a few areas.

2.   A sudden interest in book selling has attracted too many people with insufficient experience and capital.

3.   Erratic fluctuation is characteristic of the new interest in book buy-

ing, and, consequently, there is difficulty in adjusting the new shops, especially to rapidly changing demands.

4.   It is difficult to start a well-stocked shop without abundant capital, and any distribution reform movement would have to be directed toward making more shops possible in places where they are needed, and with smaller amounts of capital.

5.   Sales are being lost every day because most shops are far from the source of supply, and because their limited capital restricts the amount of stock they can carry.

6.   Selling methods employed by publishers are "cumbersome, archaic and inadequate." While Huebsch was willing to grant a "high order of intelligence" among publishers, he asserted that there was too much emphasis placed on sales to dealers instead of sales to the public through them.[36]

To some extent the problems faced by the book publishing industry are the same today. But, extensive advertising, promotion, and publicity have helped. The testimonial ad, invented in 1928 by Alfred Knopf, uses socialites and celebrities to endorse books. Publicity departments treat new books as news and work to get space and time for them in newspapers, magazines, radio, and television. None of this works, however, without solid "word of mouth" advertising—one reader telling another of a good book.

CENSORSHIP

Over the years various organizations and states have attempted to censor certain works of fiction because of what they considered to be questionable content. These books often dealt with sexual themes, as was the case with *Elmer Gantry, An American Tragedy, Lady Chatterly's Lover,* and *Ulysses.* However, with time and the growing sophistication of the public, these books were found by most courts and the general public to have "redeeming value."

The concept of redeeming value has been developed over the last twenty years by the courts, film boards, and other organizations involved in media censorship. The concept of redeeming value is used as a measuring stick to determine whether a creative work has crossed over the line from validity in dealing with real human relationships and social issues, to out-and-out pornography with its subsequent exploitation of the consumer. Many books, with their plots full of sex and violence to the exclusion of all other themes and their super-hype accompanying promotional campaigns, fall into this category.

Another type of book that attracts censorship are textbooks that explain scientific theory and historical fact. An example of the former is Charles Darwin's *Evolution of the Species,* which raised a public outcry in its time because of its total exclusion of the Bible's interpretation of the evolution of man. Many special interest groups, such as Blacks, Jews, and feminists, do not feel that some history books reflect historical fact in dealing with their minority group. Also, books that deal with current events, such as the Watergate book *All The President's Men*, are often criticized because of the haste in which they were prepared, which often does not leave time for an accurate assessment of what took place.

BOOK PUBLISHING TRENDS

A new form of journalistic book is the "instant" book. These are quickie books, books by journalists writing white-hot accounts of the latest Presidential campaign, of the first 100 days or of the final hours.[37] Publishers are able to publish books for selected markets because unlike magazines, they do not have advertiser influence to consider. Audiences can be small. All kinds of topics can be covered from the responsible to the reprehensible.[38]

The public does not expect Socratic dialogue in the *Daily News* or instant wisdom on Channel 4. They do have reason to expect that a book will continue to mean something special, something fuller, longer, and better than anything that can be produced quicker and cheaper and faster elsewhere.[39]

Biographies were another mainstay of the old general interest magazines that books have now inherited. Their sales have remained steady as have how-to books and histories—books on how to ski, the history of sea shell collecting, or the sinking of the Titanic are pretty much assured at least a few thousand sales to libraries and devoted fans of the topic. A novel by an unknown author, on the other hand, has no guaranteed audience at all.

As sales of hardback fiction decline, the paperback grows in influence. Instead of simply buying the paperback reprint rights to a hardback best seller or what they hope will become a best seller, some paperback publishers are now signing contracts for the original publication to be in paperback. William Peter Blatty's *The Exorcist* was originally signed by Bantam Books, a paperback publisher. Avon Books, another paperback house, has built up a stable of authors whose books do not appear in hardcover at all.

Book publishing, in general, is simultaneously a tight-knit monopoly and a wide open field. Ninety percent of all book titles are published by the 350 biggest publishing companies and a mere two dozen publishers account for two-thirds of the nation's books. But there are 6,500 publishing houses in the country. Most of them have just one or two editors, hire job lot printers to produce their books, and publish only a few titles a year. The big companies inevitably earn most of the money because they publish most of the books. But anyone can compete with them.

In the 1960s, small-scale publishers often competed by using flashy promotional campaigns, taking advantage of the conservatism of main-stream publishers in a time of rapidly expanding markets. Some paper-back people say the most important part of a book is its cover design and title.

In the 1980s, competition will probably force publishers to publish books on the smallest possible budgets. Both big and small publishing companies will be cutting corners, but editors who can deliver will continue to make higher salaries.

A book with a small potential audience has little chance of being published and even less of a chance of getting the promotional sup-port that will let readers know it exists. But, for the favored few con-tenders for big money, the competition among publishers is fierce. With eleven major paperback houses doing 90 percent of the paper-back business, the demand for best-selling books greatly exceeds the supply. And today, paperback houses have access to far more money, in part because the top eleven paperback houses are owned by affluent corporate parents. Moreover, rising volume has generated larger cash flows.

Paperback houses pay huge advances for reprint rights because they need best sellers as "leaders" to head their monthly lists of titles, which may include anywhere from fifteen to thirty books for each of the major houses. In the past, the leaders served to direct traffic to the Bantam rack or the NAL/SIGNET rack, where the customer's eye might be caught by one or two less well known books. Without an adequate number of leaders, distributors would often reduce a company's rack space in the stores they service, with a consequent drop in the pub-lisher's sales volume. And of course, publishers hoped that the leaders themselves would be highly profitable. This marketing strategy does not work as well as it did ten years ago because of the increased num-ber of new titles, but the demand for leaders persists because they have the largest potential for making money. The publisher makes money on the leaders not only by selling a lot of copies, but also by making movie deals and making special arrangements with hardback publishers.

For the hardback publisher, dealing with paperback publishers is often a question of survival. A decade ago a successful hardback pub-lisher could show an annual profit with several books losing money, others earning modestly, and occasional best sellers generating enough revenue to offset the losers. Subsidiary income was just that, an extra. Today, most large publishers say that they lose money on their hardback books. The Association of American Publishers says that the pretax profit margin on such books runs about 1.7 percent above cost with a 15.1 percent profit on income from subsidiaries. It is clear that hardback book publishers would be in the red without paperback sales and movie deals.

It is difficult to make money on trade hardback fiction, largely be-cause it involves a multiplicity of unrelated titles produced in low vol-ume, only a few of which can be promoted adequately, and most of

EDITORS

Editor Jonathan Segal Stalks Big Best Sellers and Great Works, Too

Jonathan Segal had visions of editing works by great authors, championing new literary talent and spending long, leisurely hours with manuscripts. But that was before he landed a job as a book editor eight years ago.

"I thought I was going to do good books and not worry about the money part," he says.

The bespectacled 35-year-old Mr. Segal, now a senior editor of the Summit Books imprint of Simon & Schuster Inc., still relishes book editing. But he admits he has put out commercially successful books, such as one on bird watching, that "I just wasn't passionate about." He doesn't have time for much leisurely reading, except at night and on weekends. And, as for great authors, Mr. Segal says, "Graham Greene isn't offered to me every day."

Mr. Segal also didn't expect to be spending his days writing book-jacket promotions, preparing sales memos, meeting book-club officials and lunching with agents. But he does do all that, and so do many of the 500-odd editors of hardcover, general-interest fiction and nonfiction books in New York City. The changing life of the trade-book editor has its defenders, particularly among publishing conglomerates that see benefits in the broadening of responsibilities. Others, however, say that literary quality is often sacrificed to commerce.

"The pace for book editors used to be slower," says A. Scott Berg, the biographer of Maxwell Perkins, the archetypal literary editor of Ernest Hemingway, F. Scott Fitzgerald and Thomas Wolfe. "But modern editors constantly have a financial gun to their heads," says Mr. Berg. "I don't know if Max Perkins could survive in this publishing world."

One source of financial pressure is the ownership of major publishers by large corporations such as Gulf & Western Industries, which acquired Simon & Schuster in 1975. "Book publishers are expected to make a return on investment comparable to other big companies," says Jonathan W. Galassi, a senior editor of Random House Inc., which now is owned by a Newhouse family trust. "There's more pressure on editors to find products that will float."

Another source of anxiety is the heightened competition for authors, the most salable of whom commonly auction themselves off to the highest bidder. "It's a fact of life that sometimes an author abandons a good editor to make more money," says Henry Morrison, an authors' agent. "The closeness between editor and author is disappearing."

To survive, editors must become better businessmen, says Walter Powell, an assistant professor at the Yale University School of Management. "They no longer can spend mornings reading manuscripts and afternoons meeting authors." Instead, editors are orchestrating every aspect of a book's publication, from cover design to marketing.

Some reviewers claim to see evidence in the books they read that editors nowadays are left little time in which to edit. "Readers depend on editors to know when a manuscript has gone on too long or the dialogue is unnecessary or silly or an idea is a cliche," says *New York Times* critic John Leonard. Because he detects more such flaws in the books he writes about, Mr. Leonard suspects that "there must be less glamour for editors in the pencil work and more in lunches with agents at the Grill Room of the Four Seasons."

To find publishable works, Mr. Segal screens some 50 manuscripts, proposals and letters each week, most of which are sent to him by agents. Of these possible projects, he usually gives only one or two further consideration. One reject: a diet book that recommended chewing wood chips to curb appetite. Five days a week Mr. Segal lunches with agents and other contacts, sometimes learning of authors who want to switch editors. Mr. Segal says he spends about $60 a day on business entertainment. He recalls that Simon & Schuster's president, Richard E. Snyder, once told him, "You're not going out to lunch enough." Nowadays, Mr. Segal sometimes also schedules business breakfasts.

Much of Mr. Segal's day is spent trying to stir interest in the books he does buy. For instance, he recently sent galley proofs of a new humor book called *For Better, For Worse* to Erma Bombeck and other humorists, hoping to get back comments for the book jacket. It is important

"to get the hype going," he says. Mrs. Bombeck didn't reply.

There are obstacles to sales. Simon & Schuster, seeking to avoid warehousing too many copies, has reduced the size of first printings of many new titles by 15% to 20%. This policy annoys Jeffrey Goodman, author of *American Genesis,* whose first printing of 12,500 copies fell below Mr. Goodman's hopes and, in his opinion, "jeopardized the making of a big book."

Mr. Segal says that the "problem with small first printings is that if a book starts to run, there won't be enough copies. It takes two or three weeks to get reprints into the stores, and by that time who remembers that the author was on the Phil Donahue show?"

Making big books is no less a priority for Mr. Segal than for his writers, though, to date, "I've done very few best sellers," he says. But he is well aware that a best-seller success would boost his own stature among agents representing big-name writers. "They want to go with a winner," he says.

A best seller is important to an editor's career," says James H. Silberman, the president and editor in chief of Summit and Mr. Segal's boss. "Jon's instincts seem to be good, but it's a little early to tell if his writers will go the distance."

Source: Daniel Machalara. "Bookworm's Turn, Editor Jonathan Segal Stalks Big Best Sellers and Great Works, Too," *The Wall Street Journal,* June 22, 1981. Reprinted by permission of *The Wall Street Journal,* © Dow Jones & Company, Inc., 1981. All rights reserved.

which are saleable for only a short time. In contrast, hardback staples like professional books, how-to books, and textbooks are saleable for a long time and have a pretax profit margin of 14 to 18 percent. Most prominent firms in hardback book publishing show a respectable profit only because of nonfiction departments like these. Partly to help compensate for the vicissitudes of fiction, Random House recently invested $4.5 million to publish a huge, handsome one-volume encyclopedia to be sold in bookstores. It's a big gamble, but if it catches on, the encyclopedia will provide a steady flow of income year after year.

Authors

Some authors do make it. At a time when star athletes often are paid more than top corporate executives, it surely fits the contemporary pattern that best-selling books have turned into huge sums of money for a few authors. In the past few years, the biggest bonanzas have been the enormous advances —often over a million dollars—paid for paperback reprint rights. These huge advances reflect the new financial dominance of mass-market paperback books over general audience hardback books.

Although Harlequin or Silhouette paperback romances do not usually offer memorable literature, their top writers can earn $30,000 for a single 150-page volume. Janet Dailey, who has 80 million copies of fifty-seven novels in print, produces eight books a year for a six-figure income. Who's Janet Dailey? "It's not Joyce Carol Oates under a pseudonym," says Gallen Book editor Judith Sullivan. Bantam Vice President Rollene Saal says, "I have a fantasy that as the sun sets across the land, the typewriters come out and the ladies go to work.[40]

Harlequin Enterprises

What is Harlequin Enterprises? It is a Canadian publishing house that since 1971 has prospered not by pursuing celebrity authors and stalking spots on the best-seller lists, but by churning out a line of modestly priced contemporary romantic fantasies written to a formula and promoted as brand name products more in the manner of soap than of books.

Founded in 1949 as a book reprinter and distributor, Harlequin bought a London publisher of romantic fiction in 1971. In ten years, the company's unit volume has ballooned from the 25 million books it published in 1971 to the 190 million it published in 1980. Sales growth has averaged 41 percent in each of the past five years. In 1980, Harlequin earned $21.7 million on revenues of $223 million, a performance that was the envy of the U.S. book industry.[41] (In 1982, however, the company had problems. It has been so successful that many newcomers have been attracted to the field and are taking a share of the market.)

TABLE 4-2 American Book Title Production—1979, 1980, 1981

DOMESTIC AND IMPORTED HARDBOUND & PAPERBOUND BOOKS; FROM *WEEKLY RECORD* LISTINGS; 1981 FIGURES ALSO INCLUDE MASS MARKET DATA FROM *PAPERBOUND BOOKS IN PRINT*

Categories with Dewey Decimal Numbers	1979 TITLES (FINAL) ALL HARDBOUND AND PAPERBOUND			1980 TITLES (FINAL) ALL HARDBOUND AND PAPERBOUND			1981 TITLES (PRELIMINARY) HARDBOUND & TRADE PAPERBOUND ONLY			ALL HARD- & PAPER-BOUND
	New Books	New Editions	Totals	New Books	New Editions	Totals	New Books	New Editions	Totals	Totals
Agriculture (630–639; 712–719)	432	106	538	382	79	461	327	59	386	391
Art (700–711; 720–779)	1,718	303	2,021	1,437	254	1,691	1,126	201	1,327	1,334
*Biography	1,557	485	2,042	1,399	492	1,891	1,153	364	1,517	1,589
Business (650–659)	1,057	305	1,362	935	250	1,185	874	270	1,144	1,156
Education (370–379)	952	169	1,121	876	135	1,011	801	130	931	946
Fiction	2,313	951	3,264	1,918	917	2,835	1,697	628	2,325	5,107
General Works (000–099)	1,248	223	1,471	1,428	215	1,643	1,211	205	1,416	1,493
History (900–909; 930–999)	1,546	614	2,160	1,569	651	2,220	1,422	424	1,846	1,891
Home Economics (640–649)	767	130	897	767	112	879	674	133	807	816
Juveniles	2,704	348	3,052	2,585	274	2,859	2,376	191	2,567	2,780
Language (400–499)	435	125	560	433	96	529	361	98	459	477
Law (340–349)	873	345	1,218	816	286	1,102	851	258	1,109	1,113
Literature (800–810; 813–820; 823–899)	1,298	451	1,749	1,317	369	1,686	1,171	212	1,383	1,426
Medicine (610–619)	2,609	648	3,257	2,667	625	3,292	2,568	541	3,109	3,142
Music (780–789)	219	170	389	236	121	357	244	94	338	338
Philosophy, Psychology (100–199)	1,082	295	1,377	1,097	332	1,429	949	224	1,173	1,250

DOMESTIC AND IMPORTED HARDBOUND & PAPERBOUND BOOKS; FROM *WEEKLY RECORD* LISTINGS; 1981 FIGURES ALSO INCLUDE MASS MARKET DATA FROM *PAPERBOUND BOOKS IN PRINT*

Categories with Dewey Decimal Numbers	1979 TITLES (FINAL) ALL HARDBOUND AND PAPERBOUND			1980 TITLES (FINAL) ALL HARDBOUND AND PAPERBOUND			1981 TITLES (PRELIMINARY) HARDBOUND & TRADE PAPERBOUND ONLY			ALL HARD- & PAPER-BOUND
	New Books	New Editions	Totals	New Books	New Editions	Totals	New Books	New Editions	Totals	Totals
Poetry, Drama (811; 812; 821; 822)	1,084	277	1,361	962	217	1,179	853	117	970	996
Religion (200–299)	1,861	464	2,325	1,635	420	2,055	1,570	326	1,896	1,913
Science (500–599)	2,563	593	3,156	2,551	556	3,109	2,291	522	2,813	2,863
Sociology, Economics (300–339; 350–369; 380–399)	6,422	1,293	7,715	5,876	1,276	7,152	5,452	1,013	6,465	6,610
Sports, Recreation (790–799)	931	191	1,122	808	163	971	771	148	919	1,064
Technology (600–609; 620–629; 660–699)	1,922	469	2,391	1,923	414	2,337	1,759	376	2,135	2,246
Travel (910–919)	519	115	634	413	91	504	307	83	390	401
Total	**36,112**	**9,070**	**45,182**	**34,030**	**8,347**	**42,377**	**30,808**	**6,617**	**37,425**	**41,538**

* Includes biographies placed in other classes by the Library of Congress.

Source: "1981: The Year in Review," *Publishers Weekly*, March 12, 1982, pp. 29–43.

Note: Titles listed in Bowker's *Weekly Record* are the source of all 1979 and 1980 figures above; these figures, however, reflected a considerable undercount of mass market paperbacks. *Weekly Record* is also the source of the *preliminary hardbound and trade paperbound* totals for 1981. Those figures are combined with the *new* mass market count (from *Paperbound Books in Print* to form the preliminary 1981 total of *all* hardbound and *all* paperbound (mass market and trade) titles thus far recorded and given in the righthand column above.

Book Packaging

A more recent development in book publishing is the appearance of the book packager, a person who signs a contract with a publisher and may deliver an entire project ready for printing. "What used to be a hallowed publisher-author relationship is being forfeited to packagers, and I think to the detriment of publishing," according to Dan Okrent, a packager who has been an editor at Knopf, Viking Press, and Harcourt Brace Jovanovich. Some packagers are just matchmakers who come up with an idea, hire writers, and sign a contract to deliver a finished manuscript to an interested publisher. Other packagers also edit the books. Packagers of photo or art books provide illustration and design. Some packagers deliver a finished book ready for printing.

Packaging is the one way that would-be publishers can get started without a lot of capital. For the small publishing house with just a few editorial people it may be a great idea; hiring a packager is like adding to the staff without incurring the personnel costs. To the older, established publishing houses, the packagers' injection into the editor-author-publisher relationship is questionable. Is the packager interested in quality? How will the packager change the role of the house editor?

Packaged books tend to be nonfiction heavily illustrated trade paperbacks. A packager is particularly attractive to publishers when the packager's book is specialized and that particular expertise is not available in-house. Many book people think packaging will never work with fiction, which cannot be manufactured like soap and where the authors work for years and need the traditional nurturing relationship with their publishers.[42]

The most important factor influencing the change in book publishing has been the paperback revolution. Because it can be published more cheaply and, therefore, sold at a lower cost to the consumer, the paperback has presented a serious challenge to the hardback trade book, particularly in the novel category. Will the hard back price itself out of the market? People may become unwilling to pay twenty-five dollars for a book they may read only once, but they may continue to invest in durable hardback books that they will refer to many times, like a reference book.

Paperback novels may run into trouble because of the huge advances that are given to authors. In the early 1980s, the tie-ins with films and television that involved so much advance money have not always been commercially successful. Novels that make it have to support the losers; the number of losers must be minimized. If such a balance can be achieved, it is likely that the trend toward paperbacks will grow stronger and eventually all trade books will be published only in paperback.

1981—A Tough Time for Publishers

The changes in publishing that first began to show in 1980 continued to create upheaval in 1981. Old ways of doing business were altered; new marketing philosophies began to play a more important role; and seemingly well-established relationships between hardback and paperback publishing, between publishers and booksellers, even between publishers and authors showed signs of permanent strain. And the weak economy did not help.

■ There were frequent job changes among top-ranking people who had become identified with their companies. A number of them seemed to involve deep-rooted differences of approach between experienced editorial executives and strongly marketing or sales-oriented officials.

■ There was antitrust action in which the Justice Department and CBS, Inc., signed a consent decree whereby the communications giant was allowed to retain Fawcett, subject of a three-year antitrust suit, but was ordered to sell Popular Library.

■ There was increased activity by District 65, a union affiliated with the United Auto Workers, which has been trying to organize publishing employees.

■ There were some attempts made by publishers to stop discrimination in favor of big retail chains regarding discount policies.

■ There was the continued unraveling of the old relationship between hardback and paperback books as more and more paperback "originals" were published.

■ There was the beginning of the Reagan administration, which seemed to encourage would-be censors—books were removed from libraries or school reading lists for a variety of reasons.

■ There was the industry going electronic to cut costs, particularly labor costs. Included among the electronic equipment of 1981 were microprocessor controls on presses, remote word processors linked via telecommunications interface to publisher-owned typesetters, scanning machines that read directly into a typesetter, a vision of laser plate-making systems for making book plates, text-processing systems, and even plans for an entire electronic manufacturing plant.

■ There was growing evidence that writers, who in some cases had seen their royalties and advances cut as publishers struggled with their own cash flow problems, were becoming increasingly restive. A study prepared for the Authors Guild Foundation by a group of social scientists at Columbia University showed that the median income from the writing of 2,239 authors of (mostly trade) books in 1979 was only $4,775.

ADDITIONAL READINGS

Anderson, Charles B., (ed). *Bookselling in America and the World: Some Observations and Reflections: in Celebration of the American Booksellers Association.* New York: Quadrangle, The New York Times Book Co., 1975.

Burke, William Jeremiah and Howe, Will D. *American Authors and Books 1640-1940.* New York, Gramercy Publishing Co., 1943.

Littlefield, George Emery. *Early Boston Booksellers, 1642-1711.* New York: B. Franklin, 1969.

Jenison, Madge. *Sunwise Turn: A Human Comedy of Bookselling.* New York: E. P. Dutton and Co., 1923.

Wroth, Lawrence C., Lehmann-Haupt, Hellmut, and Silver, Rollo G. *The Book in America: History of the Making and Selling of Books in the United States.* New York: Bowker, 1952.

FOOTNOTES

1. Samuel Vaughan, "Medium Rare: Samuel S. Vaughan Takes a New Look at the Book," *Publishers Weekly,* November 22, 1976, p. 28.

2. John Tebbel, *A History of Book Publishing in the United States: Volume I* (New York: R.R. Bowker, 1972), p. 14.

3. Frank Luther Mott, *Golden Multitudes: The Story of Best Sellers in the United States* (New York: The Macmillan Company, 1947), pp. 11–23.

4. Ibid., p. 23.

5. Lawrence G. Starkey, "Benefactors of the Cambridge Press: A Reconstruction," *Studies in Bibliography: Papers of the Bibliographical Society of the University of Virginia* (Charlottesville: 1950).

6. Tebbel, *History of Book Publishing,* p. 19.

7. Hellmutt Lehmann-Haupt, Lawrence C. Wroth, and Rollo G. Silver, *The Book in America: A History of the Making and Selling of Books in the United States* (New York: R.R. Bowker, 1952), p. 148.

8. Ibid., p. 123.

9. Tebbel, *History of Book Publishing,* p. 23.

10. Lyle H. Wright, "A Few Observations on American Fiction" (Worcester: American Antiquarian Society, reprinted from the proceedings, April 1955), p. 81.

11. *Publishers Weekly,* August 14, 1880, p. 186.

12. Tebbel, *A History of Book Publishing in the United States: Volume II* (New York: The Macmillan Company, 1972), p. IX

13. Ibid.

14. Ibid., p. X.

15. Ibid.

16. U.S. Bureau of the Census, "Education of the American Population, a 1960 Census Monograph" (Washington, D.C.: U.S. Government Printing Office, 1967), p. 114.

17. *Adult Illiteracy in the United States: A Report to the Ford Foundation* (New York: McGraw-Hill, 1979), p. 28.

18. Tebbel, *A History of Book Publishing in the United States: Volume III* (New York: The Macmillan Company, 1978), p. 202.

19. Ibid.

20. Ibid., p. 205.

21. Ibid.

22. Ibid.

23. *Time,* August 8, 1949, p. 47.

24. *Publishers Weekly,* April 30, 1982, p. 15; February 19, 1982, p. 17.

25. Charles Lee, *The Hidden Public: The Story of the Book-of-the-Month Club* (New York: Doubleday & Co., 1958), p. 23.

26. Tebbel, *History of Book Publishing, Volume III,* pp. 287–88.

27. Ibid., p. 288.

28. Lee, *Book-of-the-Month Club,* p. 24.

29. Tebbel, *History of Book Publishing, Volume III,* p. 288.

30. Lee, *Book-of-the-Month Club,* p. 25.

31. *Publishers Weekly,* November 27, 1926, p. 208.

32. Tebbel, *History of Book Publishing, Volume III,* p. 290.

33. Ben Huebsch, "Some Notes on Future Book Activities," *Publishers Weekly,* August 16, 1924, p. 531.

34. Vaughan, "A New Look at the Book," p. 28.

35. *Publishers Weekly,* April 30, 1982, p. 15.

36. Vaughan, "A New Look at the Book," p. 30.

37. Ibid.

38. Ibid.

39. Ibid., pp. 30–31.

40. "From Bedroom to Boardroom," *Time Magazine,* April 13, 1981, p. 101.

41. "Harlequin: A Romance Publisher Adds Men's Novels and a Touch of Mystery," *Business Week,* July 6, 1981, p. 93.

42. "Book Packagers Come of Age," *New York Times,* July 20, 1981, p. 13.

5

MAGAZINES

A magazine as defined by Webster's Dictionary is a publication that appears at regular intervals and contains stories, articles, etc. and, usually, advertisements. A newspaper is more current; a book is less so; and a pamphlet has a more specific content area.

After the American Revolution, magazines were a better source of information and entertainment than newspapers, even though they imitated English periodicals. As a collection of features and fiction, they were an important element in raising the country's cultural level. The first periodical (1741) arrived a century after the first book, *The Bay Psalm Book*, emerged from the press at Cambridge. Most of the early magazines were short-lived because none of them ever had more than 1,600 subscribers. Therefore, magazine work was not profitable for printers and they avoided it.[1]

As to who established the first periodical in America, it was nearly a draw between Benjamin Franklin and Philadelphia printer Andrew Bradford. Franklin's *The General Magazine, and Historical Chronicle, for all the British Plantations in America* came out the same week that Bradford issued *The American Magazine, or a Monthly View of the Political State of the British Colonies.* Franklin and Bradford were rivals in newspaper publishing, nearly every other field of publishing, and for the postmastership of Philadelphia. Franklin was usually the winner. *The General Magazine* was not a success, however, and ran for only six issues or a total of 426 pages.[2]

One of Andrew Bradford's complaints about his rival was that as postmaster of Philadelphia, Franklin sent out his magazine without paying the nearly prohibitive postal rates demanded of others.

A major difficulty of magazines was their distribution. The mail service was erratic, often over roads that were really no more than rough trails. Postmasters often considered magazines a nuisance because of their bulk and gave them the lowest possible priority. In the Postal Act of 1794, the government grudgingly recognized the new medium, stating that magazines "may be transported in the mails when the mode of conveyance and the size of the mails will permit it."[3]

The cost of distributing the typical early magazine ran anywhere from forty-eight cents to ninety cents, depending on the distance. The rates did not decline even as the roads were improved and the routes were extended. In fact, when the aftermath of the War of 1812 precipitated a general rise in prices of all kinds, postage went up 50 percent in every category.[4]

Easily the most important magazine between 1794 and 1825 was Joseph Dennie's *Port Folio*. Dennie was the first magazine editor in the modern style, a man of charm and wit who began his career as a newspaper writer and editor of the *Farmer's Museum* in Walpole, New Hampshire. Besides Dennie's own polished writing, the *Port Folio* boasted a distinguished list of contributors. Although articles were not signed, many of the authors, like John Quincy Adams, were known to the readers. The heart of *Port Folio* was Dennie's "La Preacher" essays. His topics were varied—literature, politics, morals, and manners—and his columns were all graceful, witty, informed, and entertaining. Even though it was the most successful literary periodical up to that time, the *Port Folio* was nevertheless no more financially viable than its predecessors. Dennie died on January 7, 1812, and the magazine passed on to others and declined.

Although the monthly general magazines were the most important part of the growing magazine industry, the weeklies were the most prolific. Weekly magazines sprang up in every part of America. There was scarcely any community of any consequence that did not have one, although few lasted for long.[5] Most weeklies made no pretense at enlightenment. They were entertaining, but not always original; they borrowed freely from other publications.

One of the few weekly magazines with any staying power was *The Saturday Evening Post*, published in the same printshop where Franklin's *Pennsylvania Gazette* expired six years earlier. The *Post* began its spectacular career on August 4, 1821, the enterprise of twenty-four year old printer Charles Alexander and fellow printer Samuel Coate Atkinson.[6]

In the early 1800s, magazines diversified and began to reflect the multiplying interests of the new nation. Religion remained a staple, but other specialty audiences such as the vast women's audience were also beginning to be tapped. Farmers, teachers, scientists, lawyers, doctors, musicians, theatrical people, college students, mechanics, and historians were other specialty magazine audiences. Increasingly popular with nearly everyone was the comic magazine which stemmed from the comic almanacs and jest books printed by book publishers.[7] Specialized magazines mirrored the state of whatever field they served. What appeared in the general magazines was less authentic and often less interesting.[8]

Biographies were a staple in magazines, as they have been in one form or another ever since. They were usually about the lives of military or political heroes, and borrowed heavily from English magazines for similar portraits of those abroad. The biographical material was contemporary history to many readers, and in a time of national self-doubt before the Civil War, readers found reassurance that the American past had been glorious. No American magazine of the time would have dared to tell them anything different.[9] Readers from the Union might have considered it "treason", and secessionists did not want to change history either--they wanted the status quo.

Besides essays and biographies, magazine readers were particularly fond of travel stories. The *Port Folio* carried John Quincy Adam's account of his journey through Silesia, and other magazines were soon publishing letters from Americans traveling in Europe. Much of the travel writing, however, consisted of excerpts from books, which were almost as abundant as travelers.

THE GENERAL MONTHLY MAGAZINE

The year 1825 was a turning point in both Europe and America. It marked the rapid spread of education, the technological revolution, and the rise of the cities. Expansion was everywhere and magazines were no exception. Notable additions in this period were the *Knickerbocker Magazine* (1833), *Graham's Magazine* (1840), the *New York Mirror* (1823),[10] and *Ladies' Magazine* (1828), which soon merged with *Godey's Lady's Book*.

During the Andrew Jackson era, the menacing cloud of slavery appeared. There was also controversy surrounding the National Bank, the economic issues raised by the panic of 1837, and the Mexican War, which was as bitterly opposed as it was supported. Although women's magazines and religious publications were not politically oriented, most general interest magazines were. There was little attempt to be neutral. Politics remained in an uncomfortable juxtaposition with "belles-lettres."[11]

The quarterly magazine was ailing after the Civil War, but not so the monthlies. The weeklies might have been livelier, but monthlies like *Harper's*, *The Atlantic*, *Scribner's*, and *The Galaxy* were the intellectually exciting, prestigious, and successful magazines. They were able to overcome financial problems caused by the loss of southern subscribers. As for the weeklies, the popularity they developed among the men in the Federal army helped. For magazines in the South, the war meant disaster.

A major marketing development for magazines was the first use of premiums to sell subscriptions.[12] The *Youth's Companion* was an outgrowth of a Boston congregational paper, the *Recorder*, one of the earliest religious weeklies. In the late 1860s, the paper started issuing every October a "premium list number" containing pictures and descriptions of the treasures that might be had for obtaining two, three, or more subscriptions. The list, which covered thirty six pages of the *Companion* by the 1880s, included everything form magic lanterns to dolls. For more than fifty years, readers waited for that annual issue as eagerly as they waited for Santa Claus, and its circulation grew until the *Companion* led all other magazines for a time, with a subscription rate of 400,000 in 1887 and half a million in 1898. The subscription price was not high; it remained $1.75 a year. The success of the premium idea spread through the magazine world, often reaching the point of absurdity, and it caused the premature death of some magazines.[13]

At the end of the century, several trends were apparent. Book and magazine publishing had headquarters in New York City. Periodicals had become more national in character. The editor of *The Writer* stated the case clearly in 1899: "No one section of this country can or will support a magazine of general literature, and the country as a whole will not support such a magazine if it is published as the representative of any single section."[14] But there was a difference between regionalism and the new configuration, urban vs nonurban areas. Although regionalism was waning, this was the time of the rise of the urban weekly, in a sense the forerunner of today's *New Yorker*, a national magazine with a blend of news, amusement, literary work, and politics, but these early weeklies also carried a quantity of local society gossip.[15]

One of the national magazines established during this period was *Collier's* (1888-1957).

PETER COLLIER

Peter Collier came to America from Ireland at seventeen and by twenty-four was already in the book publishing business, directing his first lists towards Catholics but gradually expanding into the cheap reprint business, and then into the selling of "library sets" of standard authors, on the installment plan and by mail. Branching out into the periodical business in 1888 with *Once a Week*, a popular magazine that attained a 250,000 circulation by 1892, Collier changed the name of the periodical in 1895 to *Collier's Weekly*, subtitled "An Illustrated Journal," and under that name it went on to great success. *Collier's* coverage of the Spanish-American War, both in pictures and text, was outstanding. Later, in the early 1900s, it was Norman Hapgood, the editor, and his crusading editorials, tied to the magazine's articles that made *Collier's* one of the leading magazines. By 1942 *Collier's* circulation was over three million.

Source: John Tebbel, *The American Magazine: A Compact History* (New York: Hawthorn Books, 1960) pp. 157-59.

FIGURE 5-1 Peter Collier. (Culver Pictures)

Around 1890 the ten cent magazine, not a new idea, had remarkable success. Although not strictly a member of this genre, *The Ladies' Home Journal* showed the way. Its first half million in circulation was achieved at a five cent price; at a price of ten cents it was up to a circulation of 700,000 by 1893. *The Journal* and others were aided by cheap paper, and by the invention of the halftone, a new and cheaper method of reproducing pictures.[16]

The high point for the ten cent magazine began with the founding of *McClure's* in June, 1893, which forced its already established rivals, *Munsey's* and *Cosmopolitan*, to lower their prices to ten cents. *Peterson's* and *Godey's* also went down to ten cents. The basis of the ten cent magazine's popular appeal was its liveliness and variety, its many well-printed illustrations, its coverage of world events and developments at home, and most of all, its head-on confrontation with contemporary social problems.[17] The "muckraking" pioneered by *McClure's* was widely imitated in other magazines and the result was a social dimension that periodicals did not have before. The magazines were no longer just mirrors of national life, but critics of it. Naturally, there were abuses, and not all muckraking was backed by careful research. In the end, the movement wore itself out by shouting. Nevertheless, magazines would never be quite as bland again.[18]

CYRUS CURTIS

Unlike most of his publishing contemporaries, Curtis made no pretense of being an editor. His particular genius lay in knowing how to establish magazines' properties, and in finding the editors to edit them. He had the consummate good sense to leave these editors alone, and they rewarded him by giving him, in the *Ladies' Home Journal* and the *Saturday Evening Post*, two of the most successful magazines ever produced in America, and, in the *Post*, one of the most beloved.

Born in Portland, Maine, in 1850, his first job was carrying newspapers on a route, but at thirteen he was publishing his own newspaper, *Young America*, on a $2.50 press. In 1872 he started the paper, *The People's Ledger*, and carried it on for six years. In 1879 he founded another paper, the *Tribune and Farmer*. His wife, Louisa Knapp, was editor of the woman's supplement and the supplement was so successful it became clear to Curtis that he would do well to sell the parent publication and keep the supplement. The supplement came under his direction and sole ownership in December, 1883, as the *Ladies' Home Journal*.

Source: John Tebbel. *The American Magazine: A Compact History* (New York: Hawthorn Books, 1960), pp. 181, 182.

FIGURE 5–2 Cyrus Curtis. (Culver Pictures)

For the most part, newspapers successfully resisted the natural inclination of advertisers to influence or control editorial content. The influence that existed in so much of the small town press was the result of the economic facts of the situation, the newspaper's total dependence on advertisers for its existence. In urban centers, advertising was of primary importance, but circulation was still essential, too; and there was at least a degree of mutual dependence between advertisers and newspapers.

Because magazine advertising was national and not local, and the cost of production far exceeded subscription revenue, advertisers were in a far stronger position. Magazine circulation was not so much a primary source of income; it was a bargaining force in the competitive struggle for the advertising dollar, which had to be spread out among all media. With the arrival of radio and television, this situation, became much more intense.[19] The result was a relationship between advertising content and editorial content that virtually ended editorial independence in all but a few magazines.

THE TWENTIETH CENTURY

After World War I, the radio threat was real. Motion pictures were a problem, too, but radio was more of a problem because it directly competed for the reader's time at home. Adding to the gloom was the fact that many of the old, established magazines that had dominated the business for so long were dying. Such was the fate of the *Century*, *St. Nicholas*, *Judge*, and *The Delineator*.[20]

Several factors were responsible for the deaths of magazines. The inability of publishers to alter old formulas in an era of dramatic changes was very significant. Several periodicals that tried to adapt to the new age failed because they did not do so quickly enough. Another reason magazines failed was because of competition from innovators. One older operation that remained unscathed was the Hearst Corporation, which survived because its magazines were in the specialized, rather than the general magazine field. By 1955, Hearst was publishing *Motor*, *Motor Boating*, *American Druggist*, *Harper's Bazaar*, *House Beautiful*, *Town and Country*, *Good Housekeeping*, *Cosmopolitan*, and *Sports Afield*. The real secret of the Hearst Corporation's success, however, was its diversity. Besides its newspapers and magazines, Hearst owned newspaper supplements, a newsreel company, a book publishing house, radio and television stations, subscription agencies, paper mills, and real estate. Its annual gross revenue was approximately $350 million in 1955 and the Hearst magazines accounted for only a seventh of that total.[21]

Among the magazine innovators there are three that serve as excellent examples: De Witt Wallace of the *Reader's Digest*, Harold Ross of *The New Yorker*, and Henry Luce of *Time*.

De Witt Wallace startled the magazine world with the *Reader's Digest* (1922), not by introducing a new idea, but by taking an old one and improving it. He reprinted pieces from other publications, but he made sure they had "lasting value" in his own estimation. The *Reader's Digest* mirrored the personality of Wallace, who once remarked, "I simply hunt for things that interest me, and if they do, I print them."[22] Wallace's magazine emphasized constructiveness and perennial optimism.

The imitators of the *Reader's Digest* began to spring up in the late

1920s, despite Wallace's attempt to hide his publication's success by keeping its circulation figures a secret. As the number of imitators grew, some of the newcomers limited their content to special areas instead of carrying the wide variety of articles that the *Digest* did. For instance, there was a *Science Digest*, a *Catholic Digest*, a *Negro Digest*, and a *Children's Digest*.[23]

Harold Ross became a major innovator by following the concept of the urban magazine and making an extremely sophisticated version— *The New Yorker* (1925). Ross said, "The New Yorker will be a reflection in word and pictures of metropolitan life. It will be human. Its general tenor will be one of gaiety, wit and satire, but it will be more than a jester. It will assume a reasonable degree of enlightenment on the part of its readers. It will hate bunk.[24]

Like the founder of the *Reader's Digest*, the young men who established Time Inc. in 1922 were without professional magazine experience, as were the editors they hired to staff *Time*. Even after Time Inc. had grown into one of the largest magazine publishing houses in the world and had many experienced professionals on its staff, there were still traces of amateurishness in its open-minded approach to publishing problems and procedures. Like Wallace, Briton Hadden and Henry Luce had a strong streak of the missionary in them. As the *Reader's Digest* generated a whole new class of magazines, two publications of Time, Inc. were responsible for new classes–the news magazine and the picture magazine—*Time* and *Life*.[25]

HENRY LUCE OF *TIME*

The idea for what became *Time* was conceived by Briton Hadden and Henry R. Luce at Yale, where they collaborated on managing the undergraduate newspaper. They nurtured the idea during service together at an officers' training camp in World War I, and they developed it further while working on Frank Munsey's Baltimore *News*. Early in 1922 they quit their jobs on the *News* (with the understanding that they could return if their project failed) and set about raising money for a "paper" of their own which they referred to as *Facts*. That "paper" became *Time* and they founded it on $86,000 raised with the help of friends and acquaintances.

Source: Theodore Peterson. *Magazines in the Twentieth Century* (Urbana: University of Illinois Press, 1964), p. 235.

FIGURE 5–3 Henry Luce. (Time, Inc.)

Time's method was to assign writers to one or more stories as their week's work. These assignments were made by a departmental editor, who was in turn responsible to a senior editorial executive who was responsible only to Luce. A style of writing developed that was very informal and inventive. New words like "tycoon" were freely invented by writers.

The magazine was a popular success, but critics did find fault. They said the news was packaged as entertainment, there was an overall conservative point of view, and facts were mingled with judgments.[26] Despite the early criticism, news magazines are very influential today. *Time, Newsweek,* and *U.S. News and World Report* do sway political opinion, even though they are brief, subjective, and their stories are developed by groups—dozens of researchers, writers, and editors who collaborate on each major article. The success of American news magazines has spawned a raft of imitators around the world: *Tiempo* in Mexico, *Akis* in Turkey, *L'Express* in France, *Der Speigel* in Germany. Maybe news magazines are more subjective because, unlike television with its headline format, they can deal with stories in depth.

Luce also created *Life.* In November, 1936, after months of experimentation and promotion, *Life* finally appeared on the newsstands, and the modern picture magazine was born. For a dime, purchasers of that initial issue got ninety-six large pages full of photographs—including the first photograph of an obstetrician slapping a baby to consciousness, captioned, "Life Begins." That issue of *Life* was sold out almost at once. Customers put their names on news dealer's waiting lists or bought secondhand copies for as much as a dollar. *Life* was the most successful picture magazine and its success bred dozens of imitators.[27]

Time Inc. then added *Sports Illustrated* and *Fortune.* Today, Time, Inc. is the country's largest magazine publisher, a cable system operator, with interests in forest products and book publishing, and is developing a magazine to serve the growing number of cable subscribers.[28]

KEYS TO SUCCESS

Economists have noted that over the years magazine revenue from national advertising has matched consumer spending. Richard G. Gettell, chief economist for Time Inc., once suggested that consumer spending is an important forecasting tool, for if one can obtain reasonable predictions about the economy as a whole, one can guess pretty closely how many dollars magazines will get from national advertising.[29]

From 1935 to 1950, Gettell noted that changes in the amount of money that consumers spent for goods were matched by almost exactly proportional changes in the amounts spent on national advertising in all print media. The media did not share the same percentage of national advertising throughout the whole period, but the share that magazines received was the most stable of any medium in relation to both consumer spending and total advertising expenditures. As consumer spending rose or fell, so did magazines' advertising income. Interestingly, economists of the Federal Communications Commission concluded in 1947: "Broadcast appears to be the least sensitive to changes in disposable personal income, magazines most sensitive."[30]

In the 1920s, as Americans spent increasing sums to raise their material standard of living, magazines benefited from the expanding market for advertisers' goods and services. But the publisher, besides selling a service to the advertisers, had his own product to market in competition with other claims on readers' time. Helping him sell his magazines in spite of the competition were a number of changes in American life—increased leisure time, advances in education and literacy, population growth from 67 million in 1893 to 178 million in 1950, and most importantly, people with money to spend.[31]

Because advertising volume fluctuates with the general movements of the economy, the fortunes of magazines rise and fall with the economy, too. Therefore, there are periodic predictions that the magazine industry is in dire trouble. The loss of advertising pages over a year's time in an established periodical may by a signal of serious trouble, but it also may only reflect the general state of the economy and hence, of advertising.[32] One thing learned from the history of magazines in America is that people who have new ideas that are acceptable to large numbers of readers will be successful in establishing new magazines whether times are good or bad, and regardless of the industry's current condition.

Successful publishing ventures generally have these things in common:[33]

1.   They are designed for markets that have been previously overlooked or inadequately served.

2.   They reflect the personalities of their publishers.

3.   They (with the possible exception of the *Reader's Digest*) change constantly as conditions and reading tastes change.

4.   They are usually characterized by good business management.

5.   They usually have solid promotional efforts.

Harlan Logan, a former publishers' consultant and former editor of *Scribner's*, noted that the following weaknesses were always present in magazine failures.[34]

1.   Lack of editorial reason for existence.

2.   Lack of clearly defined editorial pattern.

3.   Lack of advertising reason for existence.

4.   Lack of realistic budget projections.

5.   Lack of realistic schedule of time required to gain either reader or advertising acceptance.

6.   Lack of knowledge of the magazine field in general and of the specific competition.

7.   Lack of accurate information about the personnel hired to produce the new magazine.

8. Lack of an objective and independent (nonstaff) audit of the potentialities of the new magazine and of the publishing program that has been set up.

ADVERTISING AND CIRCULATION

Until about 1880, advertising agencies were generally space brokers that bargained with publishers for large blocks of space and sold it, in smaller units, to their clients. These agencies' prices were not standardized and they offered their clients no services like copywriting or layout. By 1890, however, advertising agencies were numerous, and they had begun to base their charges for space on magazine circulation.

To get their money's worth, some advertisers tried to improve the effectiveness of their advertisements. They heard talks on the use of psychology in advertising and they began to test the drawing power of their advertisements by key numbers and checking systems. This led to placing ads in the proper editorial climate aimed at the right audience, and, by the 1920s, placing ads in magazines with the largest circulations possible.[35]

Throughout the 1920s, the weekly magazine in which the reader could have best seen the expanding volume of advertising was the *Saturday Evening Post.* A monument of sorts was the issue of December 7, 1929. Weighing nearly two pounds, the 272-page magazine carried 214 national advertisers. Curtis Publishing took in revenues estimated at $1,512,000 for that one issue.[36]

Magazine advertising continued to climb, even when radio was in its prime. In the early 1920s, a successful publisher might gross $2 million a year in advertising. After World War II, some magazines carried that much advertising in one issue.[37]

Mammoth circulations began in 1937 when the *Saturday Evening Post* first topped 3 million. But the greatest circulation gains of most magazines came after World War II. Part of the growth of magazines in the 1950s and early 1960s arose from the determination of some publishers to compete with television on its own ground. If television could reach millions, so could they, and their single-minded drive for mass audiences made the term "number's game" a part of the publishing vocabulary. *Reader's Digest, Saturday Evening Post,* and *Look* boasted in 1960 that a single advertisement placed in them would reach every other person in the United States 2.3 times. Two years later, *McCall's* bought space in the trade press to compare its audience reach with that of television. In the dozen years after 1950, *Look* and *McCall's* more than doubled their circulations. This pace probably speeded up the death knoll for magazines.

As single copy sales accounted for a declining share of their circulations, magazines conducted massive direct mail campaigns to lure readers with reduced prices. Bargain rates accounted for a substantial proportion of subscriptions and renewals for some publications.[38] More and more, general audience magazines were selling magazines for less than they cost and depending on advertising—to keep the circulation large in order to compete with television's large audience.

Cut-rate subscriptions generate circulation and advertising when the economy is right; when the economy is not right, cut-rate subscriptions lose a lot of money for publishers. Recently, publishers have tried to return to the ideal point where subscribers pay for most of the cost of production.

In the early 1900s, one economy magazine publishers developed was the non-mailed copy. Retail outlets were expanding and publishers used them to sell their magazines. By 1915, an estimated 50,000 retail outlets sold magazines as a part of their stock; after 1930, many drugstores, department stores, and grocery stores began to carry magazines for the first time and the number of outlets grew to about 80,000 by the mid-1930s. In the 1950s and 1960s, the number of outlets seemed to be stationary at about 100,000, but this is slightly misleading. Large supermarkets were replacing small, local markets and were more efficient, better organized outlets for book and magazine sales[39]

The supermarket was the most important new outlet circulation people discovered in the 1930s. From 1930 onward, several publishers produced magazines for exclusive distribution by variety and grocery chains. For example, in 1930 the Dell Publishing Company agreed to publish *Modern Romances* and *Modern Screen* for sole distribution by the S. S. Kresge and S. H. Kress variety chains in towns where they had stores and for newsstand sale elsewhere.[40] Not only was this an exciting new marketplace, it saved on the cost of distribution. The cost of mailing never has stopped rising at a quick pace. Today, the post office is still in financial trouble. In 1974, Congress agreed to the concept of raising postal rates for publications more slowly, spreading them out over years. That reduced some of the burden then, but was no solution for the long-term problem. So far, no major magazine has been put out of business by the Postal Service alone, but many small magazines are in financial trouble and many publications may never even start because of the high cost of mailing.

As postal rates continue to climb, magazine circulation will inevitably move from the mails to the chain store racks. Highly specialized magazines will still have to rely on mail subscriptions, but more general magazines may well abandon the postal system just as they retreated from cut-rate subscriptions. This change is striking. In 1972, only 4 percent of *Life's* readers paid the cover price at the newsstand; in 1973, 80 percent of *Playboy's* readers did.

The move away from cut-rate subscriptions has meant a move away from subscriptions altogether. As the gap between the subscription price and the newsstand price has narrowed, more and more readers have chosen to buy their favorite magazines, when they feel like it, at the store. For magazines like *TV Guide, Reader's Digest, Family Circle,* and *Woman's Day*, supermarket and drugstore sales have proved even more successful than newsstand sales. The stores like this trend because their commissions are high—25%, for example, on a *TV Guide*. And the publishers like the arrangement because they save on overhead costs and have a simplified, cheaper distribution method.

If the public sometimes gets the impression by the disappearance of national institutions like the *Saturday Evening Post* that the magazine business is dying, they could not be more wrong. At the beginning of 1969, circulation and advertising revenues in the magazine industry had reached any all-time high. In the decade of the 1960s, 676 new magazines appeared, and only 176 periodicals disappeared through sale, merger, or suspension. In 1968 alone, 94 new magazines were started, while only 9 were merged and sold, and 12 were suspended.[41] The death of a *Post* or a *Look* is not caused by the public not reading. To sell successfully, magazines must be strong in circulation and advertising, as well as in editorial content. These factors are interdependent. Loss of advertising is usually the direct cause of a magazine's death, but it is usually brought on by weakness in the other areas. The *Post's* problem was its attempt to compete for a mass audience with television. There was no way it could reach the same numbers as cheaply. It increased circulation of home delivery by cutting the price almost to cost, counting on advertising to make up the difference; but, television could still do it cheaper and advertising was lost. *Look* and *Life* had the same problem. The mass magazine, commonly called a consumer publication, has declined, and they were the flashiest of the consumer publications. Their demise accounts for why many people think the magazine industry has died. The flashy magazines dominated the newsstands and made the headlines, but they were really only the most visible part of periodical publishing. There are more than 16,000 publications today, and more than half of them are business magazines with a total circulation of more than 60 million. (Company magazines or house organs account for a good share of this.) McGraw-Hill specializes in special interest business publications, although it also publishes *Business Week.*[42]

SPECIALIZATION

The magazine world is extremely fluid. Of the twenty most profitable magazines published in 1927, half were gone by 1951. Of the top twenty magazines in 1962, fifteen had not yet been founded in 1920. It is possible, in other words, to start a magazine today and be an instant success tomorrow. Even more important, the specialization of magazines allows plenty of latitude for editors and writers with unique ideas. One newspaper is pretty much like another; it has to appeal to all the readers in town. A magazine, on the other hand, can aim at attracting a small, devoted readership. Publishers who are quick to sense new interests of the public and act quickly can do very well.

When moviegoers grew curious about the private lives of film stars, *Photoplay* was started to satisfy their curiosity.

The first issue of *Bride's Magazine* went to press in September, 1934, with only New York, New Jersey, and Connecticut as its market. It reached out for a national distribution five years later. In the early 1960s, advertisers were spending more than $2 million to reach its 220,000 subscribers. The major problem it had was distribution. Could the publishers of *Bride's Magazine* get copies into the hands of women immediately after they had become engaged? At first, the plan was to scout out newly engaged women through announcements on the society pages of newspapers and mail them free copies. After the magazine became known, free distribution was eliminated and it was sold on newsstands and by subscription. This was a good market for advertisers because newly marrieds spent money to set up households.[43]

Playboy was a magazine phenomenon of the 1950s. It summarized its editorial pitch in its first anniversary issue: "*Playboy* is an entertainment magazine for the indoor man—a choice collection of stories, articles, pictures, cartoons, and humor selected from many sources, past and present, to form a pleasure-primer for the sophisticated, city-bred

HUGH HEFNER OF *PLAYBOY*

Hugh Hefner worked for *Esquire* magazine but he wanted to work for himself. He wanted to start with a girlie type magazine to capture an audience and then gradually increase the quality to a state of taste and sophistication. He borrowed $600 from a bank and from a finance company and sold stock to his friends to raise another $7,000. He ordered 70,000 copies of his first issue which came out in December, 1953, although it bore no date because Hefner was not sure there would be a second issue. A girlie feature that helped sell 70 percent of the copies of that first issue was a much discussed nude calendar photograph of actress Marilyn Monroe. Hefner did not solicit advertising until 1956 because he knew he could not attract the kind that would be most profitable and in keeping with his ideas for the magazine. That date is just about the time that the major shift to quality was made. By the end of the first year, *Playboy* was selling 175,000 copies, and early in its second year the circulation began to shoot up rapidly.[48]

At present, expansion into bunny clubs, movies, etc., has caused great financial concern. Hefner has had to take in new partners and cut back on expansion into new areas, but *Playboy*, by itself, is still a financial success because its cost per thousand readers (CPM) to advertisers is very good, as are its demographics—a select audience, particularly suited to particular products.

Source: Theodore Peterson. *Magazines in the Twentieth Century* (Urbana: University of Illinois Press, 1964), p. 317.

FIGURE 5-4 Hugh Hefner. (*Playboy*)

male. We never intended *Playboy* to be a big circulation magazine; we've never edited it to please the general public. We hoped it would be welcomed by that select group of urban fellows who were less concerned with hunting, fishing and climbing mountains than good food, drink, proper dress, and the pleasure of female company."[44]

Specialized magazines appeal to advertisers because they offer particular readers: what better place to sell boating products than through a boating magazine? Specialized magazines also attract more attentive readers who are often willing to pay high subscription prices for just the right magazine.

There are two ways for a specialized magazine to earn a profit. By offering advertisers just the right market for their products and services, it can justify high advertising rates. And, by offering readers editorial content tailored to match their interests, it can justify high subscription rates. Many of the most successful specialized magazines are able to make money from both ends, the advertiser and the reader.

With small magazines like *Wild World of Skateboarding* or *Kosher Home* doing well, a number of new or refurbished magazines are even attempting to reach wider audiences again while maintaining selectivity. Here are three examples.

> *Outside* (projected circulation 100,000; single copy $1.00 is about the outdoors in the same way that *Rolling Stone* is about music. William Randolph Hearst left his family's publishing empire to edit the new monthly. Launched by *Rolling Stone* editor Jann Wenner, *Outside* is a kind of glossy *Whole Earth Catalogue* filled with rich nature photography and lively prose on subjects like white water canoeing, wind power, and unusually beautiful places to camp.

> *US* (estimated circulation 750,000; single copy 50 cents) is the largest imitator of Time Inc.'s *People.* Familiar faces are the cover staple: Paul Newman, Henry 'the Fonz' Winkler, Princess Grace of Monaco. It's published by the New York Times Co. and aided by the supermarket distribution network of the firm's *Family Circle.*

> *Horizon* (circulation 98,000; single copy $2.50) has been around since 1958, but in 1977 it underwent such a face lift that any resemblance to the old, hardback quarterly is coincidental. Inside the soft cover magazine are heavily illustrated essays on such trendy topics as women in film, a new gymnastic fever, and photograph collecting.

The prime objective of the publishers is to find as much of the select audience as possible while breaking demographics down as finitely as possible.

Another way of offering a select audience is to publish regional or special editions of national magazines—a section of the magazine is printed separately and is different depending on location and audience. For example, *Better Homes and Gardens* publishes special zip-coded editions for high-income areas. *Time* has a college student edition, a doctor's edition, and an educator's edition for advertisers interested in reaching these particular audiences. For an audience of readers who earn more than $15,000 a year, *Reader's Digest* charged advertisers $11.25 per thousand copies for an ad versus $3.33 per thousand for the *Digest's* regular edition. In this example, editorial content was identical, only the ads were different. This tactic can earn a national magazine solid extra income, but in the long run it does nothing to rid the magazine of its poor readers, the people advertisers can reach easily on television. Probably the only real financial solution is to force readers to pay the full cost of the magazine and let the circulation drop, hoping that the attractive readers will continue to buy it.

MAGAZINE STAFFS

The typical magazine staff is much smaller than most people would imagine. *Wastes Engineering*, for example, a successful monthly for the sanitation industry, has one editor, one associate editor, one managing editor, one editorial assistant, and one part-time editorial consultant. It does have an editorial advisory board of eighteen, but they work only a few hours a month.

Besides staff writers, new magazines often hire free lance writers. Free-lancers are paid by the article, at rates ranging form $20 to $3,000 an article. Although there are perhaps 25,000 writers in this country who consider themselves free-lancers, most work only part time. Fewer than 300 of them earn $10,000 or more a year from their writing. A few dozen free-lancers do 90 percent of the writing in the top-paying magazines.

As with newspapers, each magazine article begins with an assignment. Free-lancers usually think up their own topics, then query editors at various magazines to see who's interested. Staff writers, of course, are often told what to write. Either way, one editor is always responsible for approving the topics, research approach, and finished manuscript. On most magazines, the top editor does this for every article. Some of the larger, more decentralized magazines have department editors who do this job. *Better Homes and Gardens,* for example, has twelve of them.

Once a manuscript is approved, it goes to a copy editor for the finishing touches. At the same time, a copy of the article is sent to the art department, which begins to work on drawings, photographs, and other illustrations for it. The art director and the managing editor rough out the approximate layout, then tell the production editor to prepare the article for the printer. The printer sends back galley proofs. A proofreader checks these for errors, while the production editor cuts and pastes them into a dummy of the magazine. The printer uses the dummies to prepare a set of page proofs, a one-color version of the magazine. After final adjustments are made on the page proofs, color proofs are prepared and checked. Finally, the magazine is okayed for printing.

CENSORSHIP

Ralph Ginzberg set out in early 1962 to pull the sex magazine out from under the counter and to put it on the living room coffee table with *Eros,* a quarterly "on the joy of love," which he sold for fifteen dollars a year. Just as *Time, Reader's Digest,* and *The New Yorker* were all products of circumstance, Ginzberg said in his prospectus, so *Eros* was the product of a climate of sexual candor, an offspring of court decisions that "had realistically interpreted American obscenity laws." Designed by a leading graphic artist, printed in black and white and lavish color on presses at home and abroad, and bound between hard covers, *Eros* gave textual and pictorial treatment to such topics as Japanese love-making manuals, the contraceptive industry, and the proper interpretation of the sexual passages in *Lady Chatterley's Lover.*

A government attorney called *Eros* "pornography for snobs" and in December, 1963, Ginzberg was sentenced to five years in prison and fined for sending *Eros* and other publications through the mails. This was the first of many brushes with the law for Ginzberg, with the courts calling his work pornography without social redeeming value, and Ginzberg claiming his First Amendment rights.[45]

See the next chapter for a detailed discussion of the law and the press.

FREEDOM OF THE PRESS—ANOTHER POINT OF VIEW

Ralph K. Winter, professor of law, Yale Law School: "As the law presently stands, I think that the press is fully protected in publication. That has been demonstrated in case after case, no matter how often the justices on the Supreme Court are replaced by new Justices.

To the extent that the law presently allows unnecessary intrusion into the workings of the press—unnecessary in the sense that the intrusion serves no particularly important governmental interest—then the press is deserving of more freedom. But it seems to me that the recent claims to an 'absolute' privilege for the press, even when another important interest calls for a minor intrusion, are very hard to justify. It is certainly as hard to justify an absolute privilege for the press as it is to justify an absolute privilege for the president of the United States."

Source: John Charles Daly et al., *The Press and the Courts: Competing Principles* (Washington: American Enterprise Institute for Public Policy Research, 1978), p.3.

EFFECTS OF MAGAZINES

The most important effects of magazines are probably imperceptible and cumulative. Reading a magazine does not change a reader, but exposure to magazines throughout a lifetime may have profound effects.[46]

There are two specific areas to consider—editorial and marketing. Timeliness and continuity separate magazines from books. Magazines do lack the immediacy of broadcasting and newspapers, but they are timely enough to deal with the flow of events; magazines provide a forum of discussion by carrying responses from their audiences, and they can sustain stories over a period of time so that the effect is cumulative. The available space and the reading habits of magazine audiences allow for greater length, and, therefore, greater depth than broadcasting. Like the other print media, the appeal of magazines is more to the intellect than to the senses and emotions. Magazines are not as transient as broadcasting, nor do they require attention at a given time. Periodicals are not soon discarded like newspapers; they remain in readers' homes for weeks or months, a fact that publishers are quick to point out to advertisers.[47]

Like the other media, magazines bestow prestige upon people, organizations, institutions, movements, and issues. They give a certain importance to whatever they mention in their articles and advertising.[48]

As major carriers of advertising, magazines certainly have played a significant role in raising the material standard of living in the twentieth century. The system may be disliked by some, but magazines have undoubtedly served mass production and mass distribution by bringing together the buyers and sellers of goods and services.[49]

Magazines of an earlier time were a collection of features and fiction designed to please everyone. Before television, the mass circulation magazine was America's visual medium—magazines like *Life* and *Look* were filled with full-color artwork and pictures. Then television came along and the large mass circulation magazines responded to the new medium by trying to increase their circulations even more. During the 1950s, *McCall's* and *Look* doubled their circulations. So big had the circulation of the large magazines become that the *Saturday Evening Post, Life, Look,* and *Reader's Digest* could claim that their combined circulation reached half of the population 2.3 times every week.

Increases in circulation were not accidental—the magazines had carefully designed strategies for increasing circulation. They reduced the cost of home delivery to the point where it was almost unthinkable not to subscribe, and although newsstand sales declined, subscriptions increased dramatically. Only about 10 percent of the magazine industry's sales were at the newsstands by the early 1960s.

But, as magazines lowered their subscription prices, they had to face the problem of rising production and distribution costs. Publishers expected advertisers to make up the difference, but the time came when advertisers could reach large audiences through television cheaper. The large consumer magazine was doomed. The 1960s and early 1970s saw the death of *Life, Look, The Saturday Evening Post,* and a number of other magazines, but magazines had something that the best of television could not compete with—the specialized magazine.

Specialized magazines displaced most of the mass circulation magazines by providing stories, articles, and information to people with special interests. Anything, everything was possible material for forming a new magazine. The specialized magazine won two ways: it usually appealed to an audience willing to pay a higher price to receive it, and advertisers were willing to pay more for its select audiences.

TRENDS IN THE '80s   Magazines Today

New technologies will alter distribution systems, fracture markets into smaller and smaller pieces, weakening the position of national magazines.

■ Postal rate increases have been a constant problem for home circulation magazines since the 1700s. Even higher rates in the 1980s may make home delivery too expensive to continue.

■ Alternative forms of distribution will continue to develop. Just as publishers discovered the supermarket chains in the 1970s, other store outlets will be investigated.

■ Cable television offers a home delivery system that may rival any retail outlet for efficiency and cost effectiveness. Videotex (putting the magazine on the television screen) may be the form of the new magazine. If current magazine publishers do not explore this distribution concept, upstarts who do use the new system may become strong competition. Major publishers will probably explore videotex.

■ Because of cable and videotex, the national magazine that went to regional editions in the 1960s may have to go to several hundred separate editions, catering to an extremely small area, to survive.

■ Because of new distribution systems and segmented reader interest, specialized magazines will continue to do well. Time, Inc., for instance, came out with a cable programming magazine.

■ The growth of national magazines, if there is any, will be sluggish because of the population demand for specialized material and the developing ability to deliver it economically.

ADDITIONAL READINGS

Ferguson, Rowena. *Editing the Small Magazine.* New York, Columbia University Press, 1958.

Flannes, Robert et al., *Plain Talk About the Word Business.* Washington, Public Affairs Press, 1970.

Mogel, Leonard. *The Magazine: Everything You Need to Know to Make It in the Magazine Business.* Englewood Cliffs, N.J., Prentice-Hall, 1979.

Page, Walter Hines. *A Publisher's Confession.* New York, Doubleday, 1905.

Unwin, Stanley. *Truth About Publishing.* London, Allen & Unwin, 1947.

FOOTNOTES

1. John Tebbel, *The American Magazine: A Compact History* (New York: Hawthorn Books, 1960), p. 5.

2. Ibid., p. 7.

3. Frank Luther Mott, *A History of American Magazines 1741–1850* (Cambridge: Harvard University Press, 1957), p. 119.

4. Tebbel, *The American Magazine,* p. 17.

5. Mott, *History of American Magazines,* p. 126.

6. Joseph C. Goulden, *The Curtis Caper* (New York: G.P. Putnam's Sons, 1965), p. 23.

7. Tebbel, *The American Magazine,* p. 21.

8. Ibid., p. 35.

9. Ibid., p. 41.

10. Mott, *History of American Magazines,* pp. 342–52.

11. Tebbel, *The American Magazine,* p. 57.

12. Mott, *History of American Magazines,* p. 7.

13. Tebbel, *The American Magazine,* p. 105.

14. Ibid., p. 142.

15. Ibid.

16. Mott, *History of American Magazines,* pp. 536–55.

17. Ibid., pp. 589–607.

18. Ibid.

19. Tebbel, *The American Magazine,* pp. 195–96.

20. Ibid., p. 206.

21. Ibid., p. 212.

22. *Time,* December 10, 1951, p. 64.

23. Theodore Peterson, *Magazines in the Twentieth Century* (Urbana: University of Illinois Press, 1964), p. 336.

24. Tebbel, *The American Magazine,* p. 234.

25. Peterson, *Magazines,* p. 234.

26. Robert T. Elson, *Time, Inc.: The Intimate History of a Publishing Enterprise 1923–1941* (New York: Atheneum, 1968), pp. 81–93.

27. Peterson, *Magazines,* p. 345.

28. *New York Times,* June 25, 1981, p. 17.

29. Richard Glenn Gettell, "What Will Advertising Be Like in a Mobilized Economy," (Talk delivered at Thirty-second Annual Meeting of the American Association of Advertising Agencies, White Sulphur Springs, W. Va., April 20, 1951).

30. Federal Communications Commission, *An Economic Study of Standard Broadcasting* (Washington, D.C.: 1947), p. 60.

31. Peterson, *Magazines,* p. 47.

32. Tebbel, *The American Magazine,* p. 221.

33. Peterson, *Magazines,* pp. 260–61.

34. Harlan Logan, "Tomorrow's New Magazines," *Magazine Industry* (Summer 1949): 19.

35. Peterson, *Magazines,* p. 22.

36. Ibid., p. 23.

37. Goulden, *Curtis Caper,* p. 84.

38. Ibid., p. 93.

39. Peterson, *Magazines,* p. 104.

40. Ibid., p. 105.

41. Tebbel, *The American Magazine,* p. 249.

42. Ibid., p. 243.

43. Peterson, *Magazines,* p. 263.

44. Ibid., p. 316.

45. Ibid., p. 379.

46. Ibid., p. 441.

47. Goulden, *Curtis Caper,* p. 87.

48. Peterson, *Magazines,* p. 442.

49. Goulden, *Curtis Caper,* pp. 26–27.

THE PRESS AND THE GOVERNMENT

Congress shall make no law respecting an establishment of religion, or prohibiting the free exercise thereof; or abridging the freedom of speech, or of the press; or the right of people peaceably to assemble, and to petition the government for a redress of grievances.

First Amendment to the U.S. Constitution

The Bill of Rights was added to the United States Constitution in 1791 so that citizens would have the liberty to speak, worship, and publish. But, the wording of the First Amendment was left vague, undoubtedly because of the vigorous debate in progress at that time over just how much freedom citizens should have from governmental intervention. What were the limits of freedom of speech or the press to be? Finding the answer to that question was a chore left to the courts that were to review future cases.

Writing a few years before the American Revolution, the prominent English scholar Sir William Blackstone expressed his views on the meanings of liberty of the press—attitudes that were to influence American legal tradition:

The liberty of the press is indeed essential to the nature of a free state: but this consists in laying no previous restraints upon publications, and not in freedom from censure for criminal matter when published. Every free man has an undoubted right to lay what sentiments he pleases before the public: but if he publishes what is improper, mischievous, or illegal, he must take the consequences . . .[1]

The liberty of the press that Blackstone saw as essential was embodied in the First Amendment to the U.S. Constitution. However, federal courts originally applied that amendment only to the federal jurisdiction and left each state free to define the amendment within its own jurisdiction. Then in 1868, the Fourteenth Amendment was added to the Constitution, declaring that states could not "deprive any person of life, liberty, or property without due process of law. . . ." But not until *Gitlow* v. *New York*[2] was the Fourteenth Amendment's liberty expanded to include freedom of the press. In *Gitlow,* the court observed that the freedom of speech and press were "among the fundamental personal rights and 'liberties'" protected by the Fourteenth Amendment. This was the first time that federal and state laws regarding freedom of speech and press came under the same standards. Moreover, this meant that the Supreme Court then assumed the right to examine state as well as federal abuses.

The fundamental question regarding Constitutional guarantees of freedom is whether those freedoms are absolute. Blackstone did not believe that they should be. He opposed prior restraint, but proposed a penalty for those who abused the freedom to criticize. The meaning of the First Amendment freedoms has been hotly debated in and out of courts for most of the history of the United States. Courts have not always interpreted these freedoms identically.

A few scholars, such as the late Supreme Court Justice Hugo Black, have argued that press and speech freedoms are absolute and that there should be no penalties imposed through defamation or other laws, nor should there be criminal or civil restrictions. Few, however, have shared Black's absolutist views.

The remainder of this chapter is devoted to finding the boundaries imposed on the freedom to speak and print. These boundaries have been the subject of countless court cases and a number of statutes in this country. As the composition of the Supreme Court and other courts has changed, the limits of freedom have changed, too.

During the 1950s when the nation was afraid of the Communists, some members of Congress tried to draw a very strict interpretation of the First Amendment, believing that it was better to repress the free expression of some people in order to safeguard the nation for the majority. At times of national crisis, such as impending war, the government has prosecuted people accused of sedition—a written or spoken criticism of government perceived as dangerous to its existence. Sometimes sedition has been written into statutes; other times it was the result of judicial decisions.

SEDITION

Although American printers had more freedom from governmental restraints than their counterparts in England and elsewhere in Europe, many methods were nevertheless used to restrict what was printed.

When a printer published a news sheet that did not have official sanction, such as Benjamin Harris's *Public Occurrences, Both Foreign and Domestic,* the government prevented the publication of a second edition.

The First Amendment to the Bill of Rights reflected the culmination of centuries of the best legal, journalistic, and political thinking in Europe and America. The pamphleteers, the courageous printers of banned newspapers, the juries and lawyers in trials like Zenger, the writings of Milton, and much more influenced the Bill of Rights. But was the new proclamation absolute? Did it give writers and editors the absolute right to publish anything they wished without regard for the consequences?

A major test of press freedom came with the Alien and Sedition Acts, which were in effect from 1798 to 1800. The two acts were passed at a time when the United States was experiencing increasing pressure from warring France and England. In the United States, the Republicans favored France and the Federalists stood with England. The Sedition Act made criticism of the Congress, the President, or the federal government a crime. Because Congress was heavily Federalist and President John Adams was a member of the same party, and because support for England and France was divided along party lines, the Sedition Act penalized the out-of-power Republicans.

The first conviction sent Representative Matthew Lyon to jail, fined for $1,000. Anthony Haswell, editor of the *Vermont Gazette,* defended Lyon and was himself fined and imprisoned. So angry did the Alien and Sedition Acts make the electorate, that the Federalists were defeated at the polls in 1800. The new Republican President, Thomas Jefferson, allowed the laws to lapse, and Congress did not enact another peace time sedition law for 140 years.[3]

At the state and local levels, however, sedition appeared under the guise of criminal libel during much of the nineteenth century. Several newspaper attacks on judges led to contempt citations. The right of judges to deal with the misbehavior of reporters in or out of their courtrooms was upheld by the United States Supreme Court in *Patterson* v. *State of Colorado* (1907) and *Toledo Newspaper Co.* v. *U.S.* in 1918.[4] These early twentieth century decisions were later substantially modified, as will be discussed later.

Sedition appeared again in the early twentieth century when various groups began demanding changes in government. When President William McKinley was assassinated, three states passed laws restricting the speech and printing freedoms of those who wished to overthrow the government. Congress followed with its own Immigration Act (1903) designed to keep people who advocated the overthrow of the United States out of the country. The 1917 Revolution in Russia did not help matters—Congress passed the Espionage Act of 1917, which was later amended to outlaw sedition.[5]

About 2,000 people were prosecuted under the new law. Some newspapers and magazines lost their bulk mailing privileges because they were accused of illegal conduct. Included in this group were the New York *Call* and *Masses* and the Milwaukee *Leader*.

The Supreme Court rendered an opinion on the repressive legislation in the 1919 case *Schenck* v. *U.S.*:

> We admit that in many places and in ordinary times the defendants in saying all that was said in the circular would have been within their constitutional rights. But the character of every act depends upon the circumstances in which it was done.[6]

In the Schenck case Chief Justice Oliver Wendell Holmes established the famous "clear and present danger" test in which a publication's seditious qualities were to be evaluated with the question, does the communication "bring about the substantive evils that Congress has a right to prevent?" Schenck, the defendant in the case, was found guilty of publishing his opinion that citizens should resist the draft even in war time. Although the ruling in this case was not used by the Supreme Court to expand speech and press freedoms, the case did reject as too narrow the old standards for sedition. This was the first of several cases that materially improved press freedoms.

The Congress passed a sedition act in 1940, in the form of the Alien Registration Act, also known as the Smith Act. The Smith Act was employed against Communists in the United States. The first case, in 1943,[7] involved a splinter group and was much less important than the later Dennis case, which involved eleven Communist leaders and was heard by the Supreme Court in 1951. The Communists had been engaged in producing newspapers, pamphlets, and books. The extended trial in the lower courts produced a large amount of evidence regarding their "illegal" activities.

The Supreme Court used the clear and present danger test and found that the eleven were actively trying to persuade a nation to overthrow its government. Although the group was so small and unpopular that they could not possibly have succeeded, the majority of the Court believed that the probability of success should not be the standard for judging if a clear and present danger existed. The simple attempt to overthrow the government was sufficient cause to decide against the defendants. The conviction and jail sentence were allowed to stand.[8]

Justices Douglas and Black vigorously disagreed with the opinion of the majority, noting that the eleven had no chance of success in overthrowing the government. Without the possibility for success, Douglas and Black thought there was no danger to national security and that therefore, the case should be dismissed.

Cases against Communists continued until 1957 and *Yates* v. *U.S.* The majority opinion in Yates held that the Smith Act distinguished "between the advocacy or teaching of abstract doctrine and the advocacy or teaching of action. . . . The statute was aimed at the advocacy and teaching of concrete action for the forcible overthrow of the Government."[9] The case foreshadowed the demise of a number of cases against Communists and the Smith Act fell into disuse.

DEFAMATION

Each state defines defamation, but generally it is defined as any communication that tends to damage another person in any of five ways: injury to a person's esteem or social standing; ridicule of a person; damage to a person by suggesting that that person has an undesirable disease or mental illness; injury to a person's ability to engage in business, trade, or occupation; or, injury to a corporation's integrity, credit, or ability to conduct business.[10]

SEDITION, DEFAMATION, AND THE GROWTH OF PRESS PROTECTION

Sedition

1798–1800	Alien and Sedition Acts in force and some editors sent to jail or fined.
1917	Congress passes the Espionage Act.
1918	U.S. Supreme Court upholds right of judges to deal with reporters in and out of courtrooms.
1919	U.S. Supreme Court supports Espionage Act.
1940	Alien Registration Act passed and enforced against Communists.
1950s	Powers of Alien Registration Act begin to fall with *Dennis* v. *U.S.* (1951) and *Yates* v. *U.S.* (1957).

Defamation

1897	R. A. Reid unable to recover damages against the Providence Journal Company.
1969	Gertz awarded damages for being labeled a communist fronter.

Press Protection

1964	In a case involving the *New York Times* the U.S. Supreme Court grants some protection to newspapers which cover public figures. Some error is permitted.
1971	In a case involving George Rosenbloom, a person engaged in wholesale selling of magazines, the U.S. Supreme Court extends the protections of *New York Times* (1964) case to any situation where a person was engaged in a public interest activity.
1974	The liberal Rosenbloom interpretation begins to fall in *Gertz* v. *Robert Welch*.
1980s	Large damages awarded to some public figures who brought libel charges, including Carol Burnett and president of Mobil Oil Company.

Defamation can be committed in two forms—libel and slander. Libel usually refers to printed defamation; slander to spoken defamation. With the arrival of radio and television, the distinction between libel and slander has become less clear-cut as will become apparent in chapter 12.

Libel

The libel that is being discussed here is civil defamation or communication that injures a person, corporation, or other private entity. Libel cannot be committed against general groups without precise boundaries. Therefore, one does not defame political parties, business-persons in general, or other vague groups. It is possible, however, to defame small, well-defined groups. The following paragraphs examine the nature of libel in each of its five categories.

The first area of libel, damaging a person's social standing or esteem, can be done by someone improperly writing, for example, that that person has murdered, perjured, or committed arson. To accuse someone of committing a crime in the absence of a judicial conviction injures that person's esteem. Courts have awarded damages under such circumstances.[11]

In a Pennsylvania case (1971) Lillian Reis Corabi won a defamation case against the *Saturday Evening Post* because the magazine had tied her to murder and robbery before she was tried.[12]

Although improperly accusing someone of a crime is libelous, every hint of criminal activity has not automatically led to an adverse judgment. In 1897, R. A. Reid was unable to recover damages from the Providence Journal Company over a published story that said that several fires had started in his office.[13]

In *Gertz* v. *Robert Welch, Incorporated* (1969) the court awarded damages to Gertz because a John Birch Society publication had called him a "communist-fronter" and had used other terms associating him with the Communist party.

Some of the terms that have led to judgments against a writer or publisher have included these: liar, skunk, drunkard, hypocrite, and hog. The point is that in any printed story that includes these or similar words, the writer must be able to support the claims—a very difficult task in the case of some words.

The second libel area, committing defamation through ridicule, does not include innocent jesting such as sometimes occurs at parties. However, any excessive ridicule of another can lead to a libel action. The boundary between good-natured humor and vicious ridicule, of course, is for the courts to determine, but some guidelines can be noted from past cases.

One case involved Mary and Letitia Megarry, who did not like an unknown individual parking in a no-parking zone in front of the Megarrys' business. To protest, the Megarrys left a note in the car saying that they would solicit police help if the illegal parking continued.

The car's owner left a sign conspicuously posted outside the Megarrys' business, which said, "Nuts to you—you old witch." The Megarrys won $5,000 in damages because they had been held up to ridicule and contempt.[14]

The third area of libel is when someone claims that a person has a "loathsome, infectious or contagious disease" when in fact that person does not have the disease. Some of the diseases that have been considered loathsome include venereal disease, leprosy, and smallpox. Accusing someone of a disease that carries moral connotations, such as alcoholism, is particularly dangerous.[15]

Fact magazine once described Barry Goldwater, then the Republican candidate for president, as a "paranoid" person whom "everybody hates." The comments resulted in $75,000 in punitive damages and $1 in compensatory damages.[16]

The fourth area of libel, injuring a person's ability to practice his or her chosen trade, occupation, or profession through false statements, has led to a number of judgments. Calling a person an embezzler, incompetent, or untrained can be libelous. The distinction between libelous and acceptable statements is often fuzzy and frequently requires judicial interpretation. For example, David Brown sued for libel on the basis of a headline that said, "Have the 'Skids Been Greased' at City Council?" Brown thought that the publication implied that he had bribed the City Council. The court disagreed, but noted that if the statement had said, "palms are greased at City Council," then a libelous statement would have been printed. The distinction was that the actual printed statement only implied political pressure, while the second statement implied actual bribery.[17]

Courts sometimes have held that accusing a person of a single error or mistake is not grounds for libel, although this rule has been applied unevenly. More general negative statements are never protected; therefore, questioning a person's ethics is simply not protected.

The last category of libel deals not with individuals but with corporations or other business organizations. One defames a corporation by making statements that adversely affect its ability to conduct business in the community. Accusing a company of fraudulent activities, shaky credit, or unethical business practices can lead to a finding of libel.

Libelous publications can be printed words, but they can also be pictures, headlines, cartoons, and associations (such as pictures tampered with to show a person in an undesirable place they had never been). Moreover, libel is not restricted to the news copy of a newspaper. Injurious comments can appear in both advertising and editorial content. Libel can even be committed in materials not written by the newspaper staff, such as syndicated columns. Sometimes libel has been committed through mistaken identity. A story about a fictional Sam Jones might be libelous if there is a real Sam Jones. Reporting a crime as having been committed by *Sam Jones,* when actually *Samuel Jones* committed the crime, may lead to a libel suit.

Words themselves can be libelous, as was pointed out earlier. Words like thief or whore are *libel per se*—defamatory on the face. In recent years, libel per se has been less and less successful. But there is another kind of libel, *libel per quod,* in which the circumstances outside the words make the story libelous. For example, saying that a married woman had twins is not ordinarily libelous, but if that woman had been married only a month and had not yet had children, then the circumstances make the words libelous.

For an individual or a corporation to bring a libel suit, that person or corporation must allege that three conditions existed: publication, identification, and defamation or false and injurious statement. The courts are charged with determining if these three conditions are met—when a jury or judge decides that they have been, damages can be awarded to the offended party.

Defenses against libel fall into two broad categories—constitutional and traditional. Using the constitutional defense, the media claim their First Amendment rights and their obligation to inform the public. This defense is called the *public principle.* The traditional defenses against libel are that the publication was true, that the media had a right to make fair comments, or that they used privileged—legal and legislative records—materials. The protection granted to publish privileged records arose from the view that the public has both a right and need to be informed on matters that come before the attention of government.

Constitutional Defenses Against Libel

In a democracy such as the United States, the news media serve the important function of informing the electorate so that they may make intelligent decisions on how they wish to be governed. The news media, therefore, must be free, unbridled by artificial restrictions, to publish anything that will help the electorate make those intelligent decisions. To fulfill their responsibility, the news media must be free from excessive libel restrictions when covering public persons and public issues.

Thus arose the *public principle* standard articulated by the Supreme Court in 1964. Arising from a political advertisement printed in *The New York Times,* the *New York Times Co.* v. *Sullivan* decision held that criticism of public officials did not assure libel damages unless the defendant could prove *actual malice.* Otherwise, a wide, robust national debate would be inhibited by the media's fear of libel. The advertisement expressed the views of a group of Black leaders on the handling of several incidents in Montgomery. L. B. Sullivan had been police commissioner in Montgomery, Alabama, during the time described in the advertisement and he felt that the advertisement libeled him.

In *New York Times Co.* v. *Sullivan,*[18] the Supreme Court established several important standards for determining how to handle libel cases.

1. Although the alleged libel was committed in a paid advertisement,

the Supreme Court said that that fact alone was not grounds for a finding of libel. If advertising automatically opened the door to libel, newspapers would be unable to sell editorial advertising and a large segment of the population would be denied access to a medium in which they could express potentially unpopular political views.

2. Although the Supreme Court found some factual errors in the advertisement, those errors did not automatically make the advertisement

---

FIGURE 6–1 An example of an editorial advertisement. (American Friends for the State of Israel)

The Real Issue

The very criticism of Israel demonstrates international faith in Israel's high moral standing.

Tens of thousands of Lebanese civilians were murdered in the course of seven years of incessant bloodshed in Lebanon.

They were murdered by the PLO.
They were murdered by the Syrians.
They were murdered by Lebanese Moslems.
They were murdered by Lebanese Christians.
They were murdered in the darkness of the night and in broad daylight, women and children, young men and old.

For seven consecutive years.

The free press reported it, but did not cry out.
The world expressed regret, but did not intervene.

No Western leader did anything to stop the bloodshed. The governments of the free world saw it as an internal Lebanese affair, as a problem that was not worth sacrificing the lives of their own men.

Last month, several hundred innocent men, women and children were massacred in Beirut. Arabs were murdered by Arabs. Again.

No one demanded that the murderers pay for the blood they spilled. Instead, guilt was placed on Israel, the single nation in the world to display genuine concern for civilians caught in war—even at the cost of its own soldiers.

Israel is held guilty because it believed that those who wore uniforms would conduct themselves as soldiers. Israel is held guilty because it trusted military officers who gave their word they would not hurt the innocent.

Is the press entitled to preach morality to Israel? **No—but this is not the issue.**

Is the free world, which did nothing to prevent bloodshed in Lebanon, entitled now to make that very charge against Israel? **No—but this too is not the issue.**

The issue is much more profound.

The fact that the world was shocked by the possibility that Israel might not have done its utmost to prevent the massacre in the refugee camps demonstrates the high moral standard that the world attributes to Israel.

The more sincere the shock, the more clearly was demonstrated the level of expectation from Israel—because Israel is expected not to permit, under any circumstances, what other nations of the world freely allow: the bloodshed of innocents.

The criticism levelled against Israel was, paradoxically, a demonstration of faith in Israel's moral standing, a public acknowledgement that the moral standards of Israel are higher—far higher—than those of other nations.

This fact Israel has been proving since its inception. In all its wars. In its most recent war.

This is the real issue: the world expects more from Israel.

In launching an investigation into its own conduct, Israel has taken upon itself the challenge that its own high level of morality demands.

AMERICAN FRIENDS FOR ISRAEL
3 West 16th Street, New York, NY 10011

Here is my contribution of $_____
to help spread this message.

NAME_____

STREET_____

CITY & STATE_____ ZIP_____

libelous. The Court conceded that factual errors frequently creep into any vigorous debate, but occasional errors of human judgment must be tolerated for the greater benefit of the frank discussion of all sides of an issue.

3. For a public official to recover damages from a claim of libel, that official must be able to prove that the medium printed the message with actual malice. Actual malice was defined as printing the message with the "knowledge that it was false or with reckless disregard of whether it was false or not."[19]

Although the *New York Times* case involved an official in Alabama, other states that had libel statutes similar to Alabama's were also affected. A series of cases involving officials in Connecticut, Pennsylvania, and elsewhere failed to award libel damages to a former mayor, a deputy sheriff, and a police sergeant after the *New York Times* ruling was made.

In several opinions following the *New York Times* case, the courts extended the notion that public officials must prove actual malice to include public figures, as well. The principles enumerated in the *New York Times* case were to be invoked anytime the media covered a public figure—someone engaged in an activity of interest to the public. Included was anyone on the public payroll—janitor, governor, and contractors, as well as any other people whose activities made them of interest to the public. An example was George Rosenbloom of Philadelphia, who distributed magazines that some described as "smut literature." He became a public figure when he was arrested for his business activity. The Supreme Court held that Rosenbloom could not recover damages from an alleged defamation over radio station WIP, because his business made him a matter of public interest.

Although the Rosenbloom case virtually destroyed the concept of a private person, this liberal interpretation of the libel law began to crumble when the Supreme Court issued its opinion in *Gertz* v. *Robert Welch, Inc.,* in 1974.[20] Justice Powell, writing for the majority, said that there were both public and private figures and that they should be treated differently. In this case, Gertz was found to be a private individual. Public figures could still recover damages only when actual malice was shown—the rule established in *New York Times* v. *Sullivan* remained.

Justice Powell noted that public figures had greater access to the media and therefore had a greater opportunity to defend themselves than private individuals did. Moreover, public figures usually attained their status by choice—by running for office or selecting a position that placed them in the public view. Because private individuals had less access to the mass media and, correspondingly, less opportunity to respond, Powell thought that the state had a legitimate interest in protecting them from the results of false statements. No longer would private individuals have to prove actual malice. The majority opinion held that states could establish their own standards for imposing liability, "so long as they do not impose liability without fault."[21] That phrase rejected libel per se—courts no longer could impose liability solely on the basis of words that were agreed to be libelous. Fault was defined by Powell as negligence.

Powell and the majority restricted recoverable financial damages for public figures to those paid for "actual injury," except in cases where the media knowingly or recklessly falsified a communication. In 1981, Carol Burnett sued the *National Enquirer* and won on this basis.

Powell also laid down two standards upon which to judge if a person was a public figure. First, some people are public figures in all circumstances because of the fame or notoriety they have achieved. Politicians or famous criminals are examples of people who fit this category. Other people, like certain businessmen, are so powerful or influential that they always are public figures. Second, many people become public figures in only certain circumstances, because they chose to become involved in a public debate in order to influence the outcome of that debate. A person who serves on a temporary government commission, designed to suggest solutions to an energy crisis would be a public figure during his or her tenure on the commission. Powell noted that some people might be brought involuntarily into the public figure category under this test.

Gertz v. *Welch,* in the view of many members of the mass media, represented a retreat from the liberal interpretations of the *New York Times* and *Rosenbloom* decisions. The earlier two opinions had effectively eliminated the private figure concept, leaving the mass media free to write about most people as long as they avoided actual malice.

In the years since *Gertz* v. *Welch,* the courts have been struggling to distinguish between public and private figures, but as one judge observed, "Defining public figures is much like trying to nail a jellyfish to the wall."[22] The implied warning to the mass media is that they must carefully consider each publication, and hope that their decision on whether a person is a public figure is correct. If a reporter must commit an error in judgment in covering an individual, assume that the person is private.

Courts have had some difficulty in determining what constitutes reckless disregard of the truth. One court found that for a publisher to testify that a statement was published without actual knowledge of its falsity was not enough to reach a verdict in favor of the publisher. If there is evidence in the story or elsewhere that the reporter may have had questions about the accuracy of data, the courts will probably decide against the publication.[23]

However, the courts have not always required a newspaper to verify every fact because to do so would be very costly. For example, *The Washington Post* was not required to verify a story written by Drew Pearson, despite Pearson's reputation for inaccuracy.[24] But in another case, a radio station lost a libel suit because it did not use a delaying device during a live call-in show. A listener who called the station defamed a local person and the station was found to have violated the reckless disregard of the truth standard.

Only occasionally has the second part of the *New York Times* standard—knowledge of falsity—been the cause for awarding damages. Most reporters will not consciously print something that they know to be false.

Traditional Defenses Against Libel

Truth.   Generally, evidence that a news story or headline is true provides complete protection from defamation claims—although some state laws are unclear on this point. The old notion of truth as defense is worth remembering. In many cases a measure of untruth has been tolerated before the truth defense was destroyed. The degree of error that the courts will accept is always an unknown quantity, so reporters who push the limits of truth are treading on dangerous ground.

Fair Comment.   Fair comment holds that newspeople have the right to fairly criticize "matters of public concern." The basis for fair comment rests on the concept that the news media have a right and an obligation to evaluate events for the readers so that they can more easily make informed choices. Critics who write about plays, concerts, ballets, or books use fair comment as their protection for the unflattering comments they make in their reviews. As it can with other defenses, a showing of malice can destroy the fair comment defense. Therefore, the writer should be careful. Writers who produce negative reviews of their competitors' work must be particularly cautious, as they may be accused of writing with malice.

In recent years, the constitutional defense has overshadowed the fair comment defense because of the strong similarity between the two and because the constitutional defense is always stronger than a statutory defense. Also, writers lose fair comment protections when they write as fact something that is not fact. Careful reporting and evaluation therefore become more important with newswriting.

Qualified Privilege.   The news media have a responsibility to keep the public informed about government, consequently when the media publish something from a public record, such as the official transcript of a legislative or court hearing, they are granted immunity from libel damages just as the source of their information is protected or privileged. People who speak at the original hearings are granted immunity so that they can speak freely. Although the record may contain defamations, the mass media have the same protection as the original speaker as long as they repeat exactly what was said without distortion.

A careless reporter can jeopardize the protections of qualified privilege by omitting or adding facts that change or distort the meaning. Because of the ease with which a reporter can destroy this defense, any would-be reporter or editor should take a course in journalism law to learn exactly how to go about publishing hearings.

Two examples of how qualified privilege can be lost may be instructive. At the outset of a case, three defendants were being sued for illegal actions; later, the case against one was dropped, but the newspaper printed a story saying that all three had been found guilty. The third defendant won libel damages. In another example, misspelling the name of a defendant suggested that an innocent party had committed a crime; again, the innocent person recovered damages. The point is obvious: professional reporters check their facts before sending a story to print.

Libel Damages

Three kinds of damages can be recovered in a libel suit: compensation for real damage to one's reputation, compensation for actual pecuniary losses, and public policy payments. Real or compensatory awards repay defamed people for the real injury to their reputations as a result of the defamation. Pecuniary loss payments repay the injured for an actual financial loss like a lost job. Public policy payments are actually fines for improper actions. The court can also add on *punitive* or punishment damages if it wishes.

A prompt retraction of a defamatory published statement can often save a publication from paying punitive damages and may reduce the amounts of other damages, because the retraction shows that no malice was present.

PRIVACY

Another legal area where the public's right to know and individual rights conflict is privacy. The question is: How much can I protect my privacy against your right to know about me? Technology has advanced so far by the early 1980s that almost anything a person does can be observed by another person using the right instruments. Night vision scopes, tapping of telephone lines, unauthorized access to confidential computer files, and many other methods open up private lives to outside scrutiny in ways that were just not possible in earlier times. Consequently, privacy is a popular and controversial topic.

PRIVACY LAW DEVELOPMENTS

1890   Samuel Warren and Louis D. Brandeis write an article detailing their concept of privacy—a new legal concept.

1903   New York passes first privacy statute.

1971   Entering a person's home and taking pictures invades privacy.

1975   Information copied from court records held to be open for printing in Cox Broadcasting case.

sidebar

GOING TO COURT

Filing a case against the media (or the other way around) costs a considerable sum. Of course, the costs of every situation are different, but one case illustrates the point. During July, 1982, the Reporters Committee for Freedom of the Press went to court asking that a restraining order approved for Mobil Oil Company be overturned. The restraining order permitted Mobil to keep all documents involved in a court case secret for 24 hours and some documents that Mobil felt contained sensitive trade information secret permanently.

When the two sides went to trial on July 7, each had spent more than $1 million and a year and a half of preparation. During the weeks, months or years required to complete the case, costs will continue to mount.

Although immigrants who settled in America were trying to escape the tyranny of the state, the new American settlers sometimes lapsed into their own form of repression—one that forced dissidents to leave one colony and seek out another. Nevertheless, the founders of the United States apparently wanted some form of personal protection. As Nelson and Teeter wrote:

Although privacy was not mentioned in the Constitution by name, its first eight amendments, plus the Fourteenth Amendment, include the right to be secure against unreasonable search and seizure and the principle of due process of law. Taken together with the Declaration of Independence's demands for the right to "life, liberty and the pursuit of happiness," it can be seen that the men who founded the nation had a lively concern for something like "the right to be let alone."[25]

Many legal scholars have traced the beginnings of privacy law to an article written by Samuel D. Warren and Louis D. Brandeis (later a Supreme Court justice) that appeared in the *Harvard Law Review* in 1890. The two lawyers believed that "the press [was] overstepping in every direction the obvious bounds of propriety and of decency."[26]

Although similar thoughts had been expressed in earlier writings, Warren and Brandeis were the first to clearly describe the concept of privacy in their writings. Like many other legal concepts, privacy has had to follow a meandering course in its development.

The first state to establish a privacy statute was New York. The center of the publishing business, New York enacted its statute in 1903. Today, most states have statutes or case law that deals with privacy. A few states have chosen to blend the concepts of privacy and defamation, while others have kept them distinct. Some states ignore privacy or hold that such a concept does not exist.

One legal scholar concluded there were four ways one's privacy could be invaded: intruding on physical solitude; publishing private matters; attributing views to a person that that individual did not hold; or using a person's likeness or name for advertising.[27]

Very few cases have been filed against the mass media accusing them of intruding into a person's home or physical solitude. Cases in this category that have been successful arose because a reporter or photographer used surreptitious means to gain entry into a person's home.[28] In such cases, courts have held that the legitimate news gathering responsibilities of the mass media do not protect them from prosecution. Lying to gain entry to a person's home or using concealed electronic devices have led to adverse decisions. However, courts have not prevented reporters from receiving and printing news that was secured illegally. The reporters themselves, however, must not have engaged in the illegal acts.

The mass media have found themselves involved in a variety of cases when they have published private matters. However publishing private matters from the public record is provided the defense of qualified privilege. In 1975, the Supreme Court clarified its views on privacy and the public record. A Georgia newspaper had found the name of a rape victim in a court record and published the name. Although the newspaper was fined in a lower court, the Supreme Court held that people who are involved in court cases relinquish that aspect of their privacy associated with the judicial proceedings.[29] At one time in California there appeared to be a variation in privacy law. After long time lapses, private citizens regained some or all of the privacy they had lost during a judicial proceeding. However, the lapsed time test has not been used often in recent years and may not provide much protection for private citizens.

Even photographs can give editors and newspapers privacy problems. Photographs taken in public places have been protected, but photographs taken in private places and printed have led to judgments against more than one publisher. Moreover, when captions are written for photographs, their wording can create a false impression that may lead to an adverse decision. In one case, a couple was able to recover damages from one publication because of a photograph's caption, but they were unable to recover damages when the same photograph was published in another magazine with a different caption.

Fictionalizing, or changing the facts, has also been grounds for privacy judgments when there was evidence that the publisher had "published knowingly reckless falsehoods."[30]

Perhaps one of the most amusing cases, although certainly not for the plaintiff, involved a film studio which sent as a promotional gimmick, the following letter from a fictional character in one of its films to 100 men in the Los Angeles area.

> Dearest:
>
> Don't breathe it to a soul, but I'm back in Los Angeles and more curious than ever to see you. Remember how I cut up about a year ago? Well, I'm raring to go again, and believe me I'm in the mood for fun.
>
> Let's renew our acquaintanceship and I promise you an evening you won't forget. Meet me in front of Warner's Downtown Theatre at 7th and Hill on Thursday. Just look for a girl with a gleam in her eye, a smile on her lips, and mischief on her mind!
>
> Fondly
> Your ectoplasmic playmate,
>
> Marion Kerby

Unfortunately, there was a real Marion Kerby and she had a telephone number listed in the Los Angeles telephone book. Kerby received several unpleasant telephone calls as a result of the letter, and in due course she sued the studio and won damages.[31] A simple check of the telephone directory would have revealed her existence and the incident could have been avoided.

In some cases, courts have allowed the publication of a person's likeness or name when the publication was incidental to the larger purpose of the printed matter. However, remember that it is for the courts to decide just what is incidental. In still other situations, libel and privacy have both been issues in the same case and the courts had to decide on the merits of one or both matters.

Finally, when a person dies, that person's privacy protections usually vanish. Heirs who believe that they can protect their deceased relative's privacy have not been successful in most cases.

Although it is not uniformly applied, the malice test of *New York Times* v. *Sullivan* has been used by the Supreme Court to deal with invasion of privacy cases. In *Time* v. *Hill* [32] Justice Brennan quoted from *New York Times* v. *Sullivan,* concluding that the plaintiff had not shown malice on the part of *Life* magazine. *Life* had carried an article claiming to tell the true story of the James Hill family. The Hill family alleged that the facts reported in the story were inaccurate, but Brennan and the majority of the court decided that the family could gain damages only if they could show malice.

Two other defenses from privacy suits need to be mentioned—newsworthiness and consent. Newsworthiness is difficult to determine. Neither the courts nor the editors have been able to devise a universally accepted definition of newsworthiness. Although the courts have tended to accept the definitions of journalists, one must still exercise care in determining newsworthiness. Recency is one measure of newsworthiness; the more recent an event the more likely the courts are to decide that the event is newsworthy.

Consent forms, signed by the subjects, should always be obtained before any story or picture is published. Although a consent form is no guarantee that the signer will not take legal action, a properly completed consent form weakens the plaintiff's case.

COPYRIGHT

The press must also be careful when expressing the ideas of others. Almost all authors and publishers protect their works from unauthorized use through copyright. Inside the front cover of a book is the word copyright or a "C" in a circle, a date, and the organization or person who has copyrighted the work. Often there is also a statement on the uses that can be made of the copyrighted work. The phrase, "All rights reserved," sometimes appears in books, indicating the publisher's desire to protect the book from any unauthorized republication.

Copyright is the means by which writers can preserve their property rights to their literary efforts. The copyright holder reserves the right to profit from the work and to tell others how they may use the work.

Without copyright protections, few people would be inclined to pro-duce, because they would not be able to gain financial rewards.

Individuals may copyright their work in their native country and in other countries. In the United States, Article I, Section 8 of the Consti-tution forms the basis for copyrighting works. This article grants Con-gress the power to promote science and the useful arts by protecting writings and inventions for their creators over a limited time.

The concept of copyright dates from 1469, when John of Speyer re-ceived the exclusive right to print the letters of Pliny and Cicero. In the United States both the Constitution and the Fourth Amendment anticipated copyright. The most recent copyright law went into effect on January 1, 1978. This law, which had been in the making since 1961, was passed by Congress and signed by President Gerald R. Ford in 1976.

The new law clarified what could be copyrighted. Any original work in a medium that existed at the time the law was written or that came later can be copyrighted. Included in the 1978 law were literature, music, drama, pantomines, choreography, graphic art, other art, in-cluding sculpture, motion pictures, audio recordings, and audiovisual productions.

The work itself—the words on the page, the sounds on the record, or the images on the film—is copyrighted. Copyright protection does not include "any idea, procedure, process, system, method of opera-tion, concept, principle, or discovery, regardless of the form in which it is described."[33] These are covered under patent law.

To secure a copyright through the Register of Copyrights in the Li-brary of Congress in Washington, the creator of a work must complete the necessary form secured from the register and return it with two copies of the work. The copyright remains in effect fifty years beyond the death of the creator. Not only the original producer of a work en-joys copyright protection; the heirs also have a protected interest in the work for the term of the copyright.

If a person fails to secure a copyright by completing the appropriate forms, the statute allows up to five years after the work is completed to register it—even if the work has been published during this five-year period. For the copyright to be valid, every copy of the protected work must include a notice of copyright, the © or with sound recordings, a ℗.

Only original works may be copyrighted. Originality says nothing about the quality of the work, its marketability, or its aesthetic worth. All that is required is that the work not be a duplicate of something that already exists. Originality does not mean that the work needs to be unique. After all, authors base their ideas on the work of those who have written before them. A person's work is original when it reflects modification, exaltation, or improvement on other's work.[34]

The Supreme Court spelled out its standard for originality: "The right secured by copyright is not the right to forbid the use of certain words or facts or ideas by others; it is a right to that arrangement of words which the author has selected to express his ideas which the law protects."[35]

Copyright Infringement

What if someone plagiarizes or copies a copyrighted work? Such a person is called an "infringer." If someone infringes on a copyrighted work, the holder of the copyright has the right to recover losses through the courts. Although, the government will not take the necessary legal actions to protect the copyright (that is the copyright holder's job), the law is on the side of the copyright holder.

From a successful lawsuit, a plaintiff may regain a reasonable lawyer's fee and statutory damages ranging from as little as $250 to as much as $50,000. In addition, actual damages and profits may be recovered. The recovery of profits may only be the sum that remains after all expenses are deducted from the gross selling price. So, if a pop music album sells for $8.95 and it costs $7.50 to produce, distribute, and pay other fees, the copyright holder would receive just $1.45 for each record whose sale was lost. Finally, a restraining order will keep the infringer from further use of the record.

Although much of what has been said about copyright applies to creative works like music and plays, under some circumstances the courts have provided protection for news, as well. Some newspapers copyright their copy and most syndicated services copyright their work. In one case, a court in Pennsylvania stopped a radio station from using uncopyrighted news from a local newspaper on the grounds that the two were in direct competition.

The foregoing does not forbid all use of copyrighted materials. The courts have allowed the development of the doctrine of fair use, which means that limited use may be made of copyrighted works without fear of infringement. The length of the passage allowed by fair use is most closely related to the total length of the work. For long works like books, many publishers have adopted the standard of 200 words. The same standard does not apply when quoting from a poem or a two-page essay. The 200-word limit has not been made part of statutory or common law, but it seems to be reasonable for most longer works. When quoting from a poem or short work, the limit may be closer to one or two lines.

The length of the quote is not the only consideration when determining fair use. Courts also have looked at the purpose for which a work was quoted, the financial loss that the copyright owner might sustain from the uncompensated use of the quote, and even the nature of the use of the quote. When a work has been quoted for scholarly or critical purposes, the courts have tended to be more lenient than if the purpose was strictly commercial.

In any event, any quoting or paraphrasing of another's work should be accompanied by a footnote, so that readers will know the true source. Also, the footnote provides a means by which statements may be verified.

The problem of copyright has been compounded in recent years because of the ease with which books, journals, and newspapers can be mechanically copied. When it revised the copyright law in 1975 and 1976, Congress adopted several provisions permitting the limited photocopying of works for educational use. (17 U.S.C.A. 107). The new law permits teachers to photocopy single copies of a chapter, article, short story, chart, graph, etc., for teaching and research purposes. In addition, teachers may make one copy of a work for each student in a class if the copied work meets certain tests. No more than 250 words of a poem may be copied, but if the poem is shorter than 250 words the whole poem may be copied. The limit on prose is 2,500 words or 10 percent of the work (the smaller amount applies, although 500 words may be copied regardless of length). Some restrictions on photocopying deal with spontaneity—the teacher must have just thought of the idea—and its cumulative effect—and the teacher cannot copy excessively throughout the semester.

THE PRESIDENT AND THE PRESS

Although the news media have a proper concern for government infringement of their First Amendment rights, sometimes public officials feel abused by the media. Presidents, particularly, have had differing feelings about newspapers. Here are some:

Rutherford B. Hayes thought newspapers a waste of time—they spent too much time on the trivial.

James Garfield liked reporters and invited them to the White House. In fact, some of his friends were among the press corps.

Grover Cleveland found reporters infuriating, but he had cause. Cleveland was married while president and reporters dogged him and his new bride throughout their honeymoon. Presumably, stories about the honeymoon made newspapers across the nation.

In more modern times Richard Nixon had a fighting relationship with the media throughout most of his public career. As Vice-President he had to defend a story about a campaign contribution and as President, stories and rumors drove him from office.

FREE PRESS—FAIR TRIAL

Like other legal matters discussed in this chapter, the fight of free press-fair trial is over two apparently conflicting rights—the right of an individual to a fair and speedy trial and the right of the public to know. On the one hand, extensive pretrial publicity in the mass media may prejudice potential jurors, ruining the accused's chance for a fair trial. On the other hand, the mass media serve as watchdogs of the judiciary, just as they do for the other branches of government, by exposing the judicial process to public view. Presumably, public exposure of problems will lead to the public pressuring for corrective action.

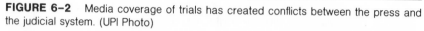

FIGURE 6–2 Media coverage of trials has created conflicts between the press and the judicial system. (UPI Photo)

Some of the events of the 1960s served to focus particular attention on the free press-fair trial issue. The assassination of President John F. Kennedy in 1963 was one such event. The Warren Commission report on the assassination criticized the mass media and others for their extensive and questionable coverage of the assassination that probably prejudiced the case against Lee Harvey Oswald. According to the Warren Commission, Oswald could probably not have received a fair trial if he had lived.

The assassination of Senator Robert Kennedy in 1968 and the public statements made by local officials regarding Sirhan Bishara Sirhan, the person arrested in connection with the murder, had the effect of pre-biasing the jury. Several trials of lesser known persons also were accompanied by media coverage that had deleterious effects.

Many years ago, the American Bar Association decided there was a conflict between the public's right to know and the defendant's right to an impartial trial. As a result, the ABA produced Canon 20 as part of their Canons of Professional Ethics:

Newspaper publications by a lawyer as to pending or anticipated litigation may interfere with a fair trial in the courts and otherwise prejudice the due administration of justice. Generally they are to be condemned. If the extreme circumstances of a particular case justify a statement to the public, it is unprofessional to make it anonymously. An *ex parte* reference to the facts should not go beyond quotation from the records and papers on file in the court.

Although the old Canons of Professional and Judicial Ethics have been superseded with a more recent Code of Professional Responsibility, the standards that guide lawyers in their dealings with the media remain.

All of this concern with media coverage of a trial may seem overdrawn, but pretrial publicity concerns every lawyer who has defended someone, and has had trouble finding a jury without an opinion on the guilt or innocence of the person to be tried.

Such was the case of Leslie Irvin, who allegedly murdered six persons near Evansville, Indiana. The six murders were committed in a four-month period during 1954 and 1955. Shortly after the murders, Leslie Irvin was arrested in connection with burglary and bad check charges. Soon, local newspapers were carrying stories about "Mad Dog Irvin" who had supposedly confessed to the slayings. After Irvin was indicted for one of the murders, his court-appointed attorney requested a *change of venue*—or place of the trial to a county where extensive publicity had not reached prospective jurors. The court granted a change to a nearby county, but residents of that county also had heard of Irvin's alleged involvement with the murders. The court denied a second change of venue request because Indiana law permitted only one change.

Irvin's attorney appealed the conviction to the state's Supreme Court, which denied his motion for a new trial. An appeal to the United States Supreme Court led to a decision that Irvin had been denied a fair trial because of the pretrial publicity and its influence on jurors. A new trial in a new location was ordered.

In his concurring opinion, Justice Frankfurter expressed strong views regarding the conflict between the press and a defendant's right to a fair trial. After noting that every year the Supreme Court was asked to review cases involving the news media's trial coverage, Frankfurter observed:

> Claims are made that a jury trial has been distorted because of inflammatory newspaper accounts . . . exerting pressures upon potential jurors before trial and even during the course of trial.

Such extraneous influences on prospective jurors, in violation of the decencies guaranteed by our Constitution, are sometimes so powerful that an accused is forced to forego a trial by jury.[36]

In Louisiana, Wilbert Rideau had the same problems over a television interview regarding a bank robbery, and related kidnapping and murder Rideau was alleged to have committed. The local sheriff interviewed Rideau after his arrest, and unknown to Rideau, recorded the interview on motion picture film. Later the film was broadcast on KLPC-TV in Lake Charles, Louisiana, and was seen by about two-thirds of the residents of the parish.

Rideau's attorneys tried unsuccessfully to secure a change of venue; Rideau was convicted and sentenced to death. After a fruitless appeal to the state supreme court, a successful appeal was lodged with the United States Supreme Court.

Justice Stewart, who wrote the majority opinion, observed that every accused person has certain rights under American laws: "right to counsel, right to plead not guilty, and the right to be tried in a courtroom presided over by a judge."[37] Stewart went on to write that Rideau had been tried by a sheriff on television without appropriate legal counsel. He ordered a new trial in a new area.

Pretrial publicity has not been the only concern of the Supreme Court or of attorneys who defend the accused. The Lindberg Case in the 1930s was so riddled with irresponsible news covererage during the trial that the ABA convened a committee of lawyers, editors, and publishers, which ultimately issued a scathing report on the trial and its media coverage. Because of this report, the ABA produced Canon 35, which prohibited taking photographs of or broadcasting trials.

Years later, a hearing of Billy Sol Estes, the famous Texas financier, was covered by television (1962). During the hearing, television cameras, cables, and other implements of the television journalist's trade were conspicuous. After the two-day hearing, the judge established media standards for the trial. He limited the number of cameras and their placement, and established other rules to insure an orderly trial.

Later, the Supreme Court reviewed the trial, but not the hearing. Although the judge had taken elaborate precautions to protect the defendant's rights, the Supreme Court ruled that television cameras should not be allowed into the courtroom, because they might impair the quality of testimony given by witnesses. Justice Clark summed up the majority's opinion by saying, "Trial by television is . . . foreign to our system."[38] The majority believed that television cameras might influence the testimony of witnesses and that television deprived the accused of due process of law. Moreover, prohibiting cameras, both still and television, in a courtroom did not discriminate against the electronic media because television and radio stations could send reporters to trials just as other medium could. The unique characteristic of television did not require courts to treat television reporters differently.

In the 1980s this has changed. Cameras are now allowed again in some courts. Sometimes witnesses even appear on videotape rather than live. But, the courts are moving cautiously because it is difficult to determine the effects these changes may have.

What the Judge Can Do to Insure a Fair Trial

The trial has five ways to protect the defendant's rights in the event of heavy media trial coverage. They are these: change of venue—moving the trial to a new location where an unbiased jury might be found; continuance or postponement—giving up the right to a speedy trial in order to allow the publicity to subside; voir dire—examining potential jurors to decide if they are prejudiced; sequestration—isolating the jury from outside information arising from personal or mass media sources; and contempt of court—the judge uses contempt to punish reporters who violate standards of the court. Penalties may be imposed such as a fine or exclusion from the courtroom.

In the case of Dr. Sam Sheppard of Ohio, who was on trial for the murder of his wife, the jury was not sequestered during much of the trial, nor was their sequestration complete while they decided the case. Jurors were able to call relatives and friends without the bailiff's knowing what these people were saying on the other end of the line. Coverage of the trial was so extensive and sensational that jurors probably could not help but be aware of what was being said. The Supreme Court said that the news media, the police, the coroner, and the trial court had been irresponsible, and called for a new trial.

Besides the strictly legal controls, bar associations have attempted to exercise self-regulatory measures to protect the rights of defendants. Various bar associations have issued guidelines for handling criminal proceedings. The U.S. Attorney General has prepared a "Statement of Policy Concerning the Release of Information by Personnel of the Department of Justice Relating to Criminal and Civil Proceedings" designed to protect the rights of defendants.

Most of the guidelines have amounted to restrictions on what the news media may publish. These restrictions are also called gag orders. Or, the guidelines may be outlines for what law enforcement people can release to the press or public. The Supreme Court had an opportunity to express its view on gag orders that amount to prior restraint on the press in the 1976 case *Nebraska Press Association* v. *Stuart.* Lincoln County, Nebraska, district court judge Hugh Stuart, had issued an order prohibiting the press to publish in five areas related to the case. The Nebraska Press Association and others filed petitions that ultimately led to the Supreme Court review.

Although Chief Justice Burger, writing for the majority, believed that there might be some circumstances when a restrictive order was tolera-

sidebar

PRETRIAL HEARINGS

Many states have laws permitting the public access to a courtroom during pretrial hearings but excluding reporters. While the contradiction may appear laughable, it has been real enough for many reporters. In a 1982 decision the Supreme Court of Georgia struck down the law for that state except in "the very rarest" cases.

In Georgia, a lower court judge had ruled that reporters were not members of the public and then evicted the reporters. Not all states have such unusual laws, but the issue remains far from adequately resolved.

FREE PRESS—FAIR TRIAL DEVELOPMENTS

1954   Excessive media coverage may so bias a jury that the right to a fair trial may be compromised, according to a case involving Leslie Irvin. U.S. Supreme Court reaches its decision in 1961.

1963   When Wilbert Rideau had the same problems when a local sheriff allowed a videotaped interrogation to be shown on television, the U.S. Supreme Court concludes that Rideau's right to a fair trial in the community had been lost.

1965   Television in the courtroom compromises Billy Sol Estes' rights.

1976   U.S. Supreme Court in a Nebraska case decides that the news media must retain freedoms notwithstanding the fair trial issue.

1980s   Some states allow electronic media into courtrooms.

ble, he said that it should be the final course of action, and applied only when there was a compelling indication that the defendant's rights would be jeopardized. Such was not the situation in the Nebraska case, he said. Although *Nebraska Press Association* v. *Stuart* appeared to be a victory for the news media, the statement that limitations might be tolerable in certain situations left open the door for restraining orders. The prior restraint debate still rages in the 1980s. One way judges have avoided First Amendment questions is to gag the participants in the case—lawyers, witnesses, jurors—rather than the press.

ACCESS TO GOVERNMENT INFORMATION

In England and Europe in the fifteenth century, authoritarian rulers used licensing and governmental contracts to restrain printers from publishing certain information. In modern America, security classifications, printing contracts, and many other means have been used to restrict the flow of information to the mass media.

Every president since George Washington has, undoubtedly, wanted to keep some things from the public view. Washington was the first to indicate the need for secrecy on some matters. The courts have not used the Constitution to force government to release any and all information to the news media. Rather, the courts have encouraged the lively tug-of-war between the government and the mass media in which the media have striven for access to information while the government has struggled to keep some information private.

Two statutes that substantially changed the government's procedures for maintaining secrecy were the Federal Public Records Law (1966), known as the Freedom of Information Act, and the Government in the Sunshine Act (1977). The first law made many of the government's records public and the second made many governmental meetings public.

The FOI Act which took effect in 1967, as amended in 1975, required federal agencies to publish information explaining their administrative structure and how citizens can secure information from them. Although the statute authorized nine categories in which records could be kept secret, Congress intended for most information to be available to the public. Included in the nine exemptions were personnel rules and practices, memoranda indicating how personnel felt about matters, personnel files—the release of which would be an invasion of privacy, and data on geological and geophysical exploration. Some of the exemptions were designed to protect individuals and companies, but a few protected governmental secrecy.

Perhaps the biggest problem with the FOI Act was that it allowed agencies to circumvent the law without ever violating the requirements. Although not actually refusing information, the delays, high charges for finding the material, high duplication costs, and bureaucratic resistance these agencies used frustrated the public and the media. A series of amendments designed to tighten the law were produced, but in the 1980s, problems still exist.

Meanwhile, another law, entitled the Privacy Act of 1974, was passed, which required the government to protect the privacy of citizens on whom it had collected files, and to make the files available upon demand to the persons involved. Thus, if someone knew that the government had a file on them, that person could request a copy and take action to have the file corrected. Under the law, the government had to publish categories of people upon whom it held files.

The Sunshine Act of 1977 did for federal meetings what the FOI Act did for records. It required that meetings held by some fifty agencies be conducted in public. Ten categories of meetings, however, could be held in secret. Among them were meetings dealing with national defense, foreign policy, personnel matters, and legal issues that were required to be kept secret.

Many states have passed their own records and meetings laws that require that all or part of state-level meetings be conducted in public.

ARE THE MEDIA BIASED?

Although the mass media promise to cover the major issues of the day, some have argued that a systematic bias among reporters and editors excludes some points of view from a hearing in the media. The charge surfaced again in an article appearing in *The Atlantic Monthly* written by R. J. Herrnstein, who is an Edgar Pierce Professor of Psychology at Harvard University.

Herrnstein stated that his views have been systematically kept out of the *New York Times,* while contrary views were treated at least fifteen times in the book review section, and five articles appeared elsewhere in the newspaper about Sir Cyril Burt, a controversial research psychologist who may have fabricated data in his studies.

Herrnstein, who is a psychometrician, has argued that IQ scores are largely related to genetics and only slightly related to a person's environment. Quotations are offered that suggest that heritability constitutes about 80 percent of the determinate factors in IQ. The controversial point arises when Herrnstein suggests that average IQ varies somewhat among ethnic groups—although Herrnstein quickly points out that every group has the same wide range of intelligence.

The issue here is not the validity of Herrnstein's argument, but the decision of the media not to cover points of view at variance with their own. According to Herrnstein, the *New York Times* was not the only newspaper excluding or attacking his views—the *Boston Globe,* after covering a Herrnstein speech, published a highly critical review. Other media coming under Herrnstein's attack include *Science, Time,* and the *Washington Post.* In each case, he said the media treated one side extensively, but failed to provide adequate treatment of the opposition.

Source: R. J. Herrnstein. "IQ Testing and the Media," *The Atlantic Monthly* (August 1982), pps. 68–74.

Since there is considerable variation, reporters should take care to learn what their state law requires.

Finally, although the mass media may often cover the public parts of trials and hearings, they are usually excluded from the parts of meetings where secrecy appears to be important. For example, some pretrial hearings have been closed. When trade secrets were to be revealed in court, judges have taken that information *in camera*—in secret. Some classes of civil cases such as divorce, family relations, and juvenile cases have been closed to the public and the mass media.

CONTEMPT

Myron Farber, a reporter for the *New York Times,* was convicted by a New Jersey court in 1978 for refusing to turn over some confidential files to a judge who believed that the files were important to solving the case. Farber was sentenced to serve six months in jail—he actually served only forty days—and Farber's employer was fined $285,000. New Jersey had a *shield law* based on an earlier Supreme Court decision that was designed to protect the confidentiality of a reporter's sources from investigation by a court. In the Farber case neither the *Times* nor Farber received a hearing, despite several requests for one, and an appeal to the Supreme Court was refused.[39] Although Farber's sentence was later suspended, the effect of the New Jersey decision stood.

Farber's experience illustrates the type of contempt known as *direct contempt.* Direct contempt may result from disobeying a court's order, creating a disturbance in a courtroom, attempting to influence a decision, or refusing to testify. A second form of contempt, called *indirect contempt,* occurs when a person tries to influence a case by putting pressure on witnesses outside the courtroom. The contempt power is held by legislative and administrative bodies as well as by the courts.

The federal power of judicial contempt has its basis in an 1831 law created by Congress. States have similar statutory or common law provisions granting judges the right to use contempt.

In recent years, contempt powers have been increasingly used against various news organizations, particularly when one of their reporters refuses to testify about confidential sources. During a two-and-a-half year period in the early 1970s, over 120 subpoenas were reportedly served on CBS and NBC asking for information related to their news—subpoenas that were mostly refused.

In a 1972 case *Branzburg* v. *Hayes,* the United States Supreme Court ruled that there was no protection under the Constitution or existing statutes to protect newspeople from subpoenas. However, the Court observed that states were free to create their own shield laws if they wished. As a result, some twenty-five states have adopted statutes providing for qualified or absolute protection. One of the earliest states to enact an absolute privilege statute was Alabama, whose law, passed in 1935, predated the Supreme Court's opinion by many years. California's recent Proposition 5 placed a shield law into its constitution.

Reporters generally support absolute privilege and are often willing to go to jail because of their beliefs. They believe that absolute privilege is essential if news sources are to be preserved. Should sources know that their anonymity may be compromised, they may refuse to provide information. On the other hand, a reporter may be obstructing justice. All the facts may not come out in a trial and the reporter's source of information cannot be called as a witness.

Not every device for restraining press freedoms involves direct censorship. For example, the government sometimes simply refuses to issue passports to reporters who engage in activities they disapprove of. When China proposed to trade an equal number of United States reporters for Chinese reporters during the 1950s, the United States refused, and chose instead to provide the news media with its own reports on events in China. On other occasions, the government has tried to prevent American citizens from going to Vietnam, Cuba, or elsewhere. If reporters from the United States media are not in a foreign capital, the government can more readily provide its own version of the news to the media.

William Worthy, a reporter for the *Afro-American* (Baltimore), prepared some controversial reports that were later broadcast by CBS. First, the State Department got CBS to kill some of the reports, and later when he had returned to the United States, it revoked Worthy's passport.

ADVERTISING

The standard of old England, *caveat emptor* or let the buyer be aware, hardly applies to modern society. The twentieth century has seen a changing climate towards advertising that can injure citizens who lack the information to make informed judgments.

Newspapers and magazine reporters and other writers of the early twentieth century exposed many fraudulent and misleading advertising schemes—from worthless medical cures to valueless cosmetics. Although considerable self-regulation existed, many newspapers still accepted misleading advertising, so legal restraints grew rapidly. The passage of laws creating the Food and Drug Administration, the Securities and Exchange Commission, the Federal Trade Commission, and the Federal Radio Commission (later replaced by the Federal Communications Commission) led to trade and advertising regulation.

The agency most directly responsible for advertising regulation is the Federal Trade Commission (FTC). Despite its work in regulating business and advertising, the FTC has been criticized by many people and organizations, including consumer advocate Ralph Nader, and the American Bar Association. So harsh was the criticism in the early 1970s, that the FTC was reorganized and expanded; a Bureau of Consumer Protection with seven divisions was added.

The original statute that created the FTC declared: "Unfair methods

SELF-REGULATORS

The threat of government intervention has been enough to induce some industries to create mechanisms for self regulation. Advertising agencies and the advertising they create have long raised questions of public interest. In 1971 the American Advertising Federation, the American Association of Advertising Agencies, the Association of National Advertisers, and the Council of Better Business Bureaus formed the National Advertising Division and the National Advertising Review Board.

The two joint organizations review complaints about advertising and monitor advertising to make independent judgments. Complaints arise from consumers, local business groups, and competitors. When the NAD/NARB concludes that a violation has occurred, the advertiser is under no requirement to make changes. Adverse publicity may lead to corrections, however.

One of the benefits of the NAD/NARB is reduced litigation costs. During early 1982 five of eleven actions concluded when the advertising was withdrawn or modified.

of competition in commerce, and unfair or deceptive practices in commerce, are declared unlawful." But early attempts by the FTC to regulate advertising got pitifully little encouragement from the courts. As late as 1931, the Supreme Court was still deciding that the buyer must beware when purchasing. Although the FTC in *FTC* v. *Raladam Company* (1931) had found strong reason to believe that the Raladam Company's reducing medication, Marmola, was unsafe and improperly advertised, the Supreme Court ruled that the FTC had overstepped its bounds and held that section 5 of the FTC Act did not rule out advertising that deceived the public.

Congress amended the FTC Act in 1938 with the Wheeler-Lea Amendment, which gave the FTC additional powers. The amendment read in part: "It shall be unlawful for any person, partnership, or corporation to disseminate, or cause to be disseminated, any false advertisement. . . ." The new law went on to define false advertising.

Although the Wheeler-Lea Amendment and subsequent court cases have supported the FTC's regulation of misleading and fraudulent advertising, the FTC has always had too little money to regulate the giant $30 billion advertising industry. At best, the FTC has regulated by example—selecting some industries and getting the changes it desires. The FTC hopes that then other businesses and industries will conform to the intent of its successful cases.

The FTC's powers include the following: letters of compliance—an informal promise to comply with the FTC's wishes; stipulations—an agreement by the advertiser to cease and desist from practices the FTC has found to be misleading; and consent orders—formal complaints produced by the FTC with a formal agreement from the offender to cease. None of these first three powers have the force of law. However, the fourth power—the cease and desist order—is issued after the FTC has made a finding of guilt. If the offending party does not appeal to the courts, the order becomes final in sixty days. Apart from these administrative remedies, the FTC may publicize its actions in an attempt to gain support for its views.

In order to help companies understand its thinking, the FTC conducts trade conferences, publishes industry guides, issues advisory opinions, and promulgates trade regulations. All of these actions are designed to guide industry and business into initiating their own compliance with FTC standards. Needless to say, such voluntary compliance has not always been forthcoming.

One of the FTC's biggest problems has been following through on lawsuits. Many of their cases have required years and large sums of money to prosecute, and while the case was pending, the offending company was free to continue its offensive practice.

Former FTC Chairman Earl Kintner once spelled out his view on how and what could be regulated. According to Kintner, the government should not have to prove that the offending company either knew of the falsity of its advertising or had an intent to deceive. Rather, the FTC could demand a change if the advertising had a tendency to deceive. Kintner said that the most literal truth was required, and sometimes that was insufficient if the literal truth was stated in such a way that it tended to mislead the customer. The FTC has not always been upheld in its attempt to enforce the literal truth standard, but there have been enough examples when it was to recommend that advertisers should exercise caution.

One of the more famous deceptive advertising cases was *FTC* v. *Colgate Palmolive Company* (1965), in which the FTC found that a Rapid Shave commercial showing sand being shaved off sandpaper immediately after the application of Rapid Shave did not represent the truth. It turned out that some eighty minutes of soaking were required before the pictured results were obtained. In addition, the FTC found that Rapid Shave had used plexiglas with sand spread on it rather than sandpaper. As a result, the FTC issued an order forbidding the use of mockups that tended to misrepresent reality. The United States Supreme Court ultimately affirmed the FTC's final regulation.

An important power in the hands of the FTC during the late 1960s and 1970s has been corrective advertising. Corrective advertising requires that an offending advertiser purchase advertising that corrects the error that appeared in its earlier advertisements. Some of the offending companies that have had to purchase corrective advertising include Profile Bread (an ITT company) and Listerine. The FTC has viewed corrective advertising as one of the best means for providing the public with new information to correct earlier misinformation. When the FTC issues a corrective advertising order, it specifies how much advertising the advertiser must buy and for how long a period the advertiser must carry the correction. The FTC also usually specifies the wording of the correction.

Other agencies interested in regulating aspects of commerce include the Food and Drug Administration, which regulates misbranding and false labeling, the Federal Communications Commission, which is discussed in detail later; the Post Office, which regulates the use of the mails; the Securities and Exchange Commission, which regulates the stock markets; and the Bureau of Alcohol, Tobacco and Firearms of the Internal Revenue Service which oversees advertising claims regarding alcohol and tobacco.

ANTITRUST

The Sherman Act was created in 1890 to prevent or dissolve businesses that were engaged in "restraint of trade or commerce." The law permitted government to dissolve monopolies and other agreements, contracts, or arrangements that jeopardize the free flow of commerce. Congress was so concerned that it provided criminal prosecution for offenders. When a company's monopolizing or trade restraint practices caused another company to sustain losses, the law provided that the injured party could recover treble damages—three dollars for every dollar lost. Laws that followed, like the Clayton Act of 1914, further expanded the government's powers.

Can newspaper, radio, and television organizations be prosecuted under antitrust laws despite their First Amendment protection? Court cases have arisen over this question because the number of dailies declined from about 2,580 in 1914 to 1,745 in 1981, with a large number of those remaining being absorbed by chains. Moreover, the number of newspapers that either hold or are held by other media has been increasing. Ben Bagdikian, professor of journalism at the University of California in Berkeley, observed that the groups and people that

DEVELOPMENT OF ANTITRUST REGULATION

1890 Sherman Act appears to stop activities that restrain trade.

1945 In *Associated Press* v. *U.S.* the U.S. Supreme Court sees no conflict between the First Amendment liberties and the application of antitrust laws to newspapers or wire services.

1951 The conclusion of AP (1945) is applied directly to the Lorain *Journal,* a newspaper.

1957 Kansas City *Star* finds itself coming under the restrictions of AP and Lorain.

1970 Newspaper Preservation Act allows some activities in order to keep newspapers from folding.

1980s A number of newspapers have joint operating agreements allowed under the 1970 law.

control journalism are becoming dominated by firms with holdings in nonmass media areas where conflicts of interest might exist.[40]

Newspaper antitrust cases have arisen because of the abiding importance of a diversity of journalistic voices from which the electorate may sift the truth. As the number of independent voices declines in both print and broadcasting, the mass media's ability to provide the competing editorial voices people need has been questioned.

An early antitrust case involved the Associated Press (1945). The Associated Press (AP) bylaws at that time included a provision about determining the admission of new newspapers to AP membership. The rule said that when one newspaper opposed the membership of a new newspaper, the entire membership would have to be polled and a majority vote obtained for membership. In effect, one newspaper could almost certainly deny membership to a new applicant.[41]

When Marshall Field wanted the Chicago *Sun* to join AP, the Chicago *Tribune* objected and the government went to court. The majority Supreme Court opinion, written by Justice Hugo L. Black, decided against the AP provisions. AP and its member newspapers argued that applying the antitrust laws to newspapers would be a violation of the freedom of press protected under the First Amendment to the Constitution. Black held that newspapers were engaged in business as well as in news handling. Although news and information were protected by the First Amendment, the business aspects of newspapers did not enjoy the same protections and were thus regulated just like any other business.

Black's opinion continued by noting that if anything, the First Amendment supported the need for governmental regulation of practices that restrained business or ruined competitors. "The First Amendment rests on the assumption that the widest possible dissemination of information from diverse and antagonistic sources is essential to the welfare of the public."[42] Because the AP bylaws represented a clear restriction on commerce, the Supreme Court made AP drop its bylaws restricting membership. The Supreme Court delivered a similar opinion in 1951 in *Lorain Journal Company* v. *United States.*[43] The Lorain *Journal* controlled most of the media in Lorain, Ohio. When another company attempted to set up radio station WEOL there, the Lorain *Journal* told its advertisers that if they used WEOL, they would not be allowed to advertise in the *Journal.* Since the *Journal* controlled 99 percent of the media market, local advertisers could not survive without access to it.

Justice Harold H. Burton's opinion treated each of the newspaper's contentions in turn. First, Burton agreed that a newspaper had the right to sell or refuse to sell advertising to whomever it chose as long as it made no attempt to restrain trade. Second, Burton saw no conflict between the freedom of the press guarantees and an injunction applied to a publisher who was attempting to monopolize. Again, the Supreme Court drew a line between the business and freedom to publish aspects of a newspaper.

The Supreme Court's opinion that harmless business practices should be allowed to continue was decided in *Times-Picayune* v. *United States* (1953).[44] This case revolved around an arrangement in which businesses who chose to buy advertising in either the *Times-Picayune* or the *States* newspaper (both owned by the same company) would be required to buy advertising in both. The Supreme Court held that there was nothing illegal about tying the two media together.

However, as in the case of the *Kansas City Star* (1957),[45] courts have generally opposed any business arrangement made by a newspaper or other mass media holder that made business more difficult for other mass media holders.

Another example of the Court's refusal to accept anticompetitive business practices was its refusal to allow a merger between the largest newspaper in Los Angeles—the Los Angeles *Times*—and the San Bernardino *Sun,* which is located forty miles from Los Angeles. The Supreme Court refused to permit the purchase to take place on the grounds that an anticompetitive environment would be created.[46] (The Supreme Court affirmed the lower court's decision without adding its own opinion.)

Another area of antitrust regulation involves joint operating agreements, a topic that is discussed in chapter 3.

In conclusion, freedom of the press is a fact in the United States, but there are restraints that go with it, because there are other interests that also must be served. For example, freedom of the press should not overshadow individual freedoms; but there are certain government secrets that should remain so. Freedom will be a relative state dependent upon checks and balances as long as there are individuals and institutions that want more than their share.

TRENDS IN THE '80s

The Print Media and the Law

The growing trend of courts to grant large awards to persons libeled by the media has reduced many reporters' feelings of freedom to cover events. A $9.2 million judgment was exacted in 1981 of the *Alton* (Ill.) *Telegraph* which nearly bankrupted the paper and a $14.5 million judgment was made in the same year against *Penthouse* magazine (and the $14.5 million figure represented a reduction from the jury's original verdict of nearly twice that sum). In addition Carol Burnett won a $1.6 million judgment against the *National Enquirer* in 1981.

■ Shield laws—laws designed to protect reporters who refuse to reveal their sources—need to be strengthened, most reporters feel. *Editor and Publisher* has produced cartoons showing courts in pursuit of reporters.

■ The Freedom of Information Act, which protects the right of the public and reporters to see government information, has been subjected to continuing attacks from Congress and the executive branch. Some twenty bills on the subject appeared in the House and Senate during 1981 and early 1982. None were passed and signed into law by the President, but the President did approve an executive order restricting access.

■ Reporters long have enjoyed the right to cover pretrail and trial events in criminal cases, but those rights have never been extended to include civil cases. In a civil case in 1982 involving Mobil Oil Company, its president, the Reporters Committee for Freedom of the Press, and the *Washington Post,* the issue of reporter access to pretrial civil case documents has been reviewed. The trial court in Washington decided for Mobil but the case probably will end at the United States Supreme Court where the issues under consideration might include the constitutionality of secrecy orders (an order issued by a judge that keeps a company's records secret from reporters or the public), and the court's right to impose prior restraints on reporters gathering pretrial information for publication.

■ Another part of the case involved a libel claim by Mobil's president. The jury agreed that libel had been committed and awarded damages of just over $2 million in July 1982.

■ *Editor and Publisher* reported that 1981 was a year of deteriorating press freedom in the world, from the United States and Canada to Afghanistan, Angola and elsewhere. For example President Reagan's proposed reform of the Freedom of Information Act amounts to curbs on what the press can cover.

■ Although a newspaper may own as many newspapers, magazines, or book publishing companies as it wishes, the FCC has limited the number of broadcast outlets a newspaper can own. However, the current deregulatory movement in Washington may lead to a loosening of restrictions on broadcast outlet ownership; many government officials have proposed changes. At present, a local newspaper can own one television station or one AM and one FM station in the same community, but may not own both radio and television outlets.

■ Taxes offensive to newspaper publishers did not disappear with the Revolution. The U. S. Supreme Court is slated in 1982–83 to hear a case in which the Minneapolis Star and Tribune Company complained about a $100,000 use tax on paper and ink imposed by the state of Minnesota. The newspaper holds that the tax restrains First Amendment rights and amounts to a tax on knowledge.

ADDITIONAL READINGS

Bagdikian, Ben. "Newspaper Mergers—The Final Phase." *Columbia Journalism Review,* March-April 1977, p.20.

Franklin, Marc A., and Franklin, Ruth Korzenik. *The First Amendment and the Fourth Estate: Communications Law for Undergraduates.* Mineola, New York: The Foundation Press, Inc., 1977.

Nelson, Harold L., and Teeter, Dwight L. Jr. *Law of Mass Communications: Freedom and Control of Print and Broadcast Media.* Mineola, New York: The Foundation Press, Inc., 1978.

Prosser, William L. "Privacy." *California Law Review* 48(1960):383–423.

Zion, Sidney. "High Court vs. the Press (Part II)." *The New York Times Magazine,* November 18, 1979, p.144.

FOOTNOTES

1. Blackstone Commentaries 151, 152.

2. Gitlow v. New York, 268 U.S. 652, 666 (1925).

3. U.S. v. Hudson and Goddwin, 11 U.S. (7 Cranch.) 32 (1812).

4. Patterson v. Colorado, 205 U.S. 454 (1907) and Toledo Newspaper Co. v. U.S., 247 U.S. 402 (1918).

5. Espionage Act 40 Stat 217 (1917).

6. 249 U.S. 47 (1919).

7. Dunne v. U.S., 138 F.2d 137 (8th Cir. 1943).

8. Dennis v. U.S., 341 U.S. 491 (1951).

9. Ibid.

10. Harold L. Nelson and Dwight L. Teeter, Jr., *Law of Mass Communications: Freedom and Control of Print and Broadcast Media* (Mineola, New York: Foundation Press, 1978), p. 56.

11. Frechette v. Special Magazines, 136 N.Y.S.2d 448 (1954).

12. Corabi v. Curtis Pub. Co., 441 Pa. 432 (1971).

13. Reid v. Providence Journal Co., 20 R.I. 120 (1897).

14. Megarry v. Norton, 137 Cal App.2d 581 (1955).

15. Lewis v. Hayes, 165 Cal. 527 (1913).

16. Goldwater v. Ginzburg, 414 F.2d 324 (2d Cir. 1969).

17. Brown v. Newman, 224 Tenn. 297 (1970).

18. New York Times v. Sullivan, 376 U.S. 254, 84 S.Ct. 710 (1964).

19. *Sullivan,* 279, 280.

20. Gertz v. Robert Welch, Inc. 418 U.S. 323, 94 S.Ct. 2997 (1974).

21. Ibid.

22. Rosanova v. Playboy Enterprises, Inc., 411 F.Supp 440, 443 (SD Ga. 1976).

23. St. Amant v. Thompson, 309 U.S. 727 (1968).

24. Washington Post Co. v. Keogh, 125 U.S. App. DC 32, 365 F.2d 965 (1966).

25. Nelson and Teeter, *Law of Mass Communications,* p. 162.

26. Samuel Warren and Louis D. Brandeis, "The Right to Privacy," *Harvard Law Review* 4 (1890): 196.

27. William L. Prosser, "Privacy" *California Law Review* 48 (1960): 383–423.

28. Dietemann v. Time, Inc., 449 F.2d 242 (9th Cir. 1971).

29. Cox Broadcasting Corp. v. Cohn, 420 U.S. 469 (1975).

30. Cantrell v. Forest City Publishing Co., 419 U.S. 245 (1974).

31. Kerby v. Hal Roach Studios, Inc., 53 Cal.App.2d 207 (1942).

32. Time v. Hill, 385 U.S. 374 (1967).

33. Copyright Act of 1976, 17 U.S.C.A. 102.

34. 8 Fed.Cas. 615, No. 4, 436 (CC Mass. 1845).

35. Holmes v. Hurst, 174 U.S. 82 (1899).

36. Irvin v. Bowd, 366 U.S. 717 730 (1961).

37. Rideau v. Louisiana, 373 U.S. 723, 727 (1963).

38. Estes v. Texas, 381 U.S. 532, 549 (1965).

39. Sidney Zion, "High Court vs. the Press (Part II)" *The New York Times Magazine,* November 18, 1979, p. 144.

40. Ben Bagdikian, "Newspaper Mergers—The Final Phase," *Columbia Journalism Review* (March-April 1977): 20.

41. Associated Press v. United States, 326 U.S. 1 (1945).

42. Ibid., 326 U.S. 1, 20 (1945).

43. Lorain Journal Company v. United States, 342 U.S. 143 (1951).

44. Times-Picayune v. U.S., 345 U.S. 594 (1953).

45. United States v. Kansas City Star, 240 F.2d 643 (1957).

46. United States v. Times-Mirror Corp., 274 F.Supp. 606; 390 U.S. 712 (1968).

PART II

Visual / Sound

7

MOTION PICTURES: DEVELOPMENT

It may soon appear that an inordinate amount of time is spent on film theory and popular genres. The reason, as Marshall McLuhan, the media philosopher, suggested, is that new technology absorbs the old. Thus, television is what it is to a great extent because film became what it did.

Behind the finished product of television lies a very expensive process. Following is one day on the set that completed two minutes of film for the released picture.

A Day on the Set of a Motion Picture: *Blown Away*
Location: Ithaca, New York   Date: March 1, 1982

6:00 A.M.   Susan wakes up from a deep sleep. The friendly voice on the other end of the line says, "Make-up in one hour." The phone rings in the adjoining room and the same message is repeated to Debbie.

6:15 A.M.   Director Sam Ruttle is having a cup of coffee with his cinematographer, David Lance. "Do you think we'll be able to do twelve set-ups today?"

"You keep asking me that!"

Sam smiles. "The producer keeps asking me that."

"If the weather holds."

Judy enters and sits down. "Here are all the permissions from the city. Buffalo Street is being blocked off right now. The police will be there at 7 A.M. The Porsche and Triumph have been repainted and tuned. The stunt drivers will be on location at 7:30. David, your people have a question about one of the camera locations."

"I'd better get out there."

Sam looks down at his shot list for the day. "I'll be out there as soon as I go over the script with Susan and Debbie again."

7 A.M.   Make-up in a motel room that has been turned into combination make-up and dressing room. Susan and Debbie are being made up when Sam points to a spot near Susan's nose. "Be sure to get that grease smudge right there, or we won't have a match. Six close-ups to do today." He turns to a woman who is ironing. "Make sure the dresses look a little more tired. Supposedly, twelve hours have passed."

"Everything under control."

Sam discusses the dialogue with the two leads as they finish their make-up.

7:45 A.M.   Sam arrives at the bottom of Buffalo Street. Brute lights are being put in their final positions. There are six cameras being readied to cover the downhill chase between the Porsche and Triumph. David calls Sam on the radio, "Join me at location 3."

Sam trudges half way up the hill to a camera position set in a huge hole built so that the lens will be right at street level. "This what you had in mind, Sam?"

"You sure we'll get the sense of speed?"

"As long as those three houses are in the background to establish the spacial relationship."

"Good."

8:15 A.M.   Sam calls for a rehearsal. The stunt drivers barrel down the hill at 90 miles per hour. Dave consults with Sam afterwards.

"Everything looked all right to me. I just want to put some dulling spray on the Porsche. Too much glare. I want to add one more brute near location four. I should be ready in fifteen minutes."

8:25 A.M.   It suddenly starts to snow. Judy approaches Sam, who is talking to the stunt drivers. "What do you want to do, boss?"

"What does the weather report say now?"

"Same thing it said last night. Clear and sunny."

Sam frowns. "Call a coffee break. Fifteen minutes."

"Okay."

9 A.M.   It is snowing harder. Sam is talking to Judy. "I think we're in trouble."

"Do you want to move to the dining room interior? I think we could be set in two hours."

"That would be right at the lunch break. It'll probably take four hours to do that scene. Maybe we can do it in four hours. We'd have to. I don't want to go on overtime again today." He laughs. "Remind me to make my next picture a studio one, no matter what. Or, at the very least, a place that has consistent weather."

Judy laughs. "I'll remind you."

"Okay. We'll switch to the dining room."

1 P.M.   The dining room scene is set for action. The two actresses have different outfits and make-up. They are ready to confront each other in a booth.

Sam speaks up. "Put an inky on the left side of Susan's face."

There's a call for quiet on the set. Sam finally gets the first shot of the day off at 1:15 P.M.

The rest of the afternoon goes very well. Six different camera set-ups. He gets all of the master shots, and will pick up the close-ups on the next day with weather problems.

7:30 P.M.   Sam has dinner with Judy and Dave. They go through the set-up for the next morning. The weather is supposed to be clear tomorrow. They'll try to get the chase down Buffalo Street. Judy and Dave leave to reorganize the Buffalo Street shoot.

8:30 P.M.   Sam has a meeting with Susan and Debbie about some slight changes he wants out of them in the close-ups of the Buffalo Street location.

10:00 P.M.   The entire cast and crew assemble to look at the rushes from the previous day. They look pretty good. Sam holds a short conversation with Susan and Debbie.

11:30 P.M.   Sam is in his room, making arrangements for the next day with Judy and Dave. The city was reluctant at first to give permissions to block Buffalo again.

12:15 A.M.   Sam looks over the script to see if there is some way he can alter the script so that it won't matter what the weather is at Buffalo street tomorrow.

There isn't. It has to be sunny and clear.

1:10 A.M.   Sam falls asleep, script in hand.

THE DEVELOPMENT OF MOTION PICTURES

Movies are expensive to make and audiences have to pay the entire cost. For the most part, films have no ads or commercials to support them. Luckily, they are fun, interesting, or important to watch or they would not sell.

The outside income for films comes from popcorn, candy, and other concessions products. A generation ago, Saturday afternoon at the movies constituted a ritual for children, and popcorn was a major part of that ritual. Profits from concession stand sales almost equalled the profit from admissions at that time.

Today, going to the films is not a regular habit in the United States; television has replaced film as the most common form of entertainment. Each motion picture has to be sold as a special item; each has to stand on its own.

The need to be entertained always has been part of the human experience. The arts have taken many forms—music, drama, mime, and projected images. At least as early as Athanasius Kircher's magic lantern, invented in 1646, people have been projecting drawings on screens for pleasure. In the eighteenth century, entertainers traveled around Europe amusing paying audiences with lantern projectors, much as the modern slide show amuses today.

The first photographs were made by Joseph Nicéphore Nièpce in 1826 using a *camera obscura.* This device, invented during the Renaissance, consisted of a sealed chamber or box with a tiny hole in one wall. The hole acted as a lens to focus light from the outside, and thereby the image of the object, onto the opposite wall. This simple optical principle makes possible all photography. Nièpce added the final step by fixing the image thus projected onto a pewter plate covered with chemical emulsions. The exposure time, however, was eight hours and Nièpce died in 1833 without making further innovations. His partner, Louis-Jacques Mande Daguerre, contributed the introduction of a silvered copper plate, which reduced the exposure time to fifteen minutes making photography a practical reality. The technology became a part of books, magazines, and newspapers, and was vital to the conception of motion pictures, because a series of drawings could be replaced by individually posed "phase photographs." This was accomplished by Eadweard Muybridge in 1877.[1]

By using multiple magic lanterns, inventors attempted without success to make images move, but in the mid-nineteenth century, Alexander Black combined slides, photography, and narrative to tell a story. He soon added live actors. Audiences were entertained, but they still wanted motion. The principal front runners in the technical international competition to make motion pictures were Thomas Edison and Thomas Armat of the United States; Louis Le Prince, and Louis and Auguste Lumière of France; Max and Emil Skladanowsky of Germany; and William Friese-Green of England.

Before projecting films to audiences, one viewer at a time saw moving images through individual peephole machines called mutoscopes, large photographs mounted sequentially on individual cards on a rotating wheel. The pictures were better in detail and clarity than the kinetoscope, an Edison/Dickson invention of 1890, but they did not use a continuous strip of film. The first kinetoscope parlor opened on Broadway in New York City (April 14, 1894) when Andrew Holland had ten kinetoscopes available with no waiting.

Projecting movies to more than one person began in the United States on April 20, 1896, at Koster and Bial's music hall in New York. Involved were Thomas Alva Edison, William Kennedy Dickson, Thomas Armat, and a machine called the vitascope. Handcranked, noisy, and using 35-mm film, the projector did not break the film thanks to the invention of the *American loop* by Greg and Otway Latham. The films were simple and short and emphasized motion.

The Edison Company produced some of the early films under the direction of Dickson. Other films were pirated from the Lumière brothers, who had their first showing in Paris on December 28, 1895,[2] some four months earlier than Edison. This international film piracy characterized the early years in the new industry. (Technically Edison put the elements of motion pictures together, but the Lumière Brothers probably deserve the credit for putting film together as an art.)

Dickson constructed the first motion picture studio for the Edison Company at West Orange, New Jersey, in 1894. Nicknamed the Black Maria, it was painted black inside and out. Although the studio was wired for an electric camera, it had no connection for lights. Instead, the roof slid open to admit sunlight and the entire studio rotated to keep up with the sun.

Adjusting to the New Medium

From the beginning, the new communications medium captured people's imagination. It thrilled people and made them happy. But it remained a novel apparatus, a curiosity of penny arcade peep shows, an unwilling exile of vaudeville theaters, and an inhabitant of noisy, storefront nickelodeons until theater people took the calculated risk of infiltrating the new medium as actors, writers, and directors.

They did so reluctantly and anonymously at first, lured by the prospect of an easy five dollars a day, or between five and fifteen dollars for a picture idea. Edison's sexy sensation of 1896, *The Kiss,* was from a contemporary drama starring stage actors John Rice and May Irwin. His *The Milk White Flag* (1896) was from a popular Charles Hoyt play. In 1897, Wallace "Old Man" McCutcheon, husband of Pearl White, directed stage actor Joseph Jefferson in *Rip Van Winkle* for the American Mutoscope and Biograph Company. George Méliès, film pioneer extraordinaire, used amateur actors in his early productions because French actors shared the snobbery toward film. Méliès, a magician-turned-cinema manufacturer, eventually lured professionals before his camera after he had proven that even nonactors could make successful films. Méliès ingeniously directed and wrote films, designed and painted sets, and acted as his own choreographer, costumer, prop man, producer, and distributor. He not only acted in his own films, he also employed his magic tricks to make himself double on the screen. It was of this man that America's pioneer film director D. W. Griffith said, "I owe him everything." Méliès' films are credited with creating the initial split between fiction and nonfiction film.

Another attempt at drama prior to 1900 was the 1897 production, *The Burglar on the Roof.* J. Stuart Blackton and Albert Smith produced the film for their company, Vitagraph. Blackton, a newspaper reporter and illustrator, starred. In 1898, the same entrepreneurs faked what was purported to be an actual event in the Spanish-American War. With Smith at the camera, Blackton tore down a miniature Spanish flag and hoisted an equally miniature American flag.

As early as 1895, William Kennedy Laurie Dickson produced a brief (less then a minute) drama for the Edison Company called *The Execution of Mary, Queen of Scots.*

These first faltering steps did little for cinematic technique or the motion picture's reputation with the theater crowd. But, they did indicate an initial lack of understanding of film's potential as a new, creative medium independent of theater. The early American companies, Edison (1889), American Mutoscope and Biograph (1897), Lubin (1897), and Vitagraph (1896), all treated the camera as an immobile audience member viewing a stage play, with the action taking place within the prescribed perimeter of stage left, stage right, upstage, center stage, and downstage.

The camera ground away, recording the theatrical performance on celluloid, but with the disadvantage of having it pantomimed on a flat, two-dimensional screen instead of spoken and acted by live players in front of a supportive audience. Film had to do better than act as an insensitive recording instrument of another medium's performance if it was to become an art rather than a public curiosity. Susanne Langer said, "The medium in which we naturally conceive our ideas may restrict them, not only to certain forms but to certain fields."[3] Cinema had to break the ties with theater to survive. And it did, becoming the unstaged, fortuitous, endless flow of life that film theorist Siegfried Kracauer[4] advocated. He thought that anything less than a totally spontaneous affect was uncinematic.

THE THEORY OF FILM

As obvious as it sounds, the key difference between the still photograph and the motion picture is movement. One is inherently static, an immobile record of a person, place, or thing; it exists to be studied at leisure. If a person who owns a photograph places a great value on the subject, that person will place the picture in a strategic position, where it can be seen and thus possessed frequently.

The same difference exists between the motion picture and paintings. One is inherently mobile and transient, to be possessed only in memory; the other an object whose physical reality is permanent and aesthetic.

Home video systems, like snapshots, place personal cinematography within the reach of the masses. Sixteen millimeter films, smaller image size than films projected in theaters are usually produced by professionals. They are commissioned by corporate sponsors who impose the subjects they value on us—in schools and nontheatrical documentary, or public service television. Because of their great cost—from $250,000 to $6 million or more—35-mm films seen in theaters are made by artists, at the sufferance of bankers, to be sold back to the movie-going public on a rental basis. The subjects must be general enough to sell tickets, and universal enough to satiate the drives that pull viewers away from other activities.

Inevitably, discussion returns to comparisons between motion pictures and staged plays. Both range widely in cost and subject matter; neither has an aesthetic objective reality—an empty theater or an unproduced play has no more physical attraction than an idle motion picture projector or an esoterically coded film script; both are designed to present moving images and thus are mobile and transient; in both cases the audience enters a darkened room to be possessed by sounds and visuals in motion—changes in the perceptual field.

Film and television use sound stages and sets, but not in the theatrical sense of a fully developed stage setting. While the film or TV director has the same control over what the viewer sees, he or she points the camera at only selected fragments of incomplete sets. Why bother to dress the entire stage if the camera's eye, the surrogate for the viewer's eye, is not permitted to sweep the scene at will?

Beyond the footlights of the theater, actors perform for live audiences who are ready for the bewitching spell of drama. But there is no such direct performer-viewer relationship when technology intervenes. The film actors' immediate audience is a mixture of hardware and production staff: lights, cameras, tripods, dollies, booms, sound equipment, director, camera crew, electricians, sound crew, and so forth. The film actors' stage is controlled chaos. They wait; they repeat; they work under the pressure of time. No one applauds, unless the project is being shot live for television. But if it is a theater film rather than a television film, it is unlikely that the actors are actually working on a stage. Modern portable equipment, the pressure for economy, and the desire for realism combine to make the world a stage. Real streets, apartments, and towns provide the authenticity that modern viewers demand.

Films and videotapes are staged reality; it is the audience that has become unstaged, absent at the moment of creation and disassociated by its lack of physical proximity to the performers. Hundreds of scenes are staged and shot out of time-place sequence, assembled by an objective expert who probably never had any prior contact with the production. Then, after sound mixing and special effects printing, the camera's eye view of this artificial reality is reflected from a screen into the viewer's eye. No matter where the viewers sit in that black box of the theater, they are psychologically shifted into the black box of the camera and transported into the scene—foreground or middleground or background—to peer objectively or subjectively through the unblinking, single eye of the camera at the intimacies of the action.

THE ART OF FILM

In 1915, the American poet Vachel Lindsay wrote that the motion picture can encompass "The sea of humanity, not metaphorically but literally; the whirling of dancers in ballrooms, handkerchief-waving masses of people in balconies, hat-waving political ratification meetings, ragged glowering strikers, and gossiping, dickering people in the marketplace. By the law of compensation, while the motion picture is shallow in showing private passion, it is powerful in conveying the passions of masses of men."[5] Lindsay was talking about movement, conflict, and change. Films about internal conflict that fail to show its external manifestation invariably fail. Physical change within a person is hard to capture on film, and yet without change that can appear on the screen, film cannot move. Yet, it must move if it is to be perceptually stimulating and satisfying.

The Russian filmmakers recognized this basic cinematic characteristic, although they overemphasized editing, forgetting that the camera can move also. Vsevolod Pudovkin (1893-1953)[6] said, "The foundation of film art is editing." Carefully adjusting the tempo of cutting to emotional content, alternating one tempo with another to articulate the film's overall rhythm, is a valid concern of editing and is really a question of orchestrated change. Pudovkin points out that to alter the order of shots in a scene, without any internal alteration of the shots themselves, may suffice to change the meaning of the scene. It also offers more possibilities for producing the unexpected and reinforces Kracauer's principles. Pudovkin quotes what he describes as a crude example, composed of three close-ups: 1) a person is smiling; 2) a revolver is pointed; 3) the same person is looking frightened. Sequenced this way, the person is frightened. But reverse the first and third shots and the person is brave. Pudovkin was so preoccupied with this relationship, called "linkage" of individual shots, that he claimed the shots in and of themselves had little value. But he would concur with Kracauer that the processes of film construction and viewing are inductive. In a parts-to-whole evolution, both filmmaker and viewer assemble and reassemble the symbology according to perceptual principles of diffusion (a fuzzy, vague notion of the film context), differentiation (clear, recognizable figures that begin to emerge from the diffused "ground"), and integration (persons, places, objects, and events that mesh into an understandable context).

Sergei Mikhailovich Eisenstein (1898-1948),[7] the other great Russian theorist of editing, or montage as it was called in Russia, saw everything in terms of change, too. Although his ideas seemed to clash with those of Pudovkin, their differences seemed stronger on paper than they did on film. He said his theory was the dialectic or collision of opposites within the frame, and from frame to frame, rather than linkage. Eisenstein's collision of shots can be one of attraction of similarity, or it can be one of opposites. These conflicts can be of ideas related to story line, or ideas as symbols. They can also be conflicts of composition or style—for instance, the conflict of lines, size, shape, or angle.

Editing

The cut is the filmmaker's quickest and easiest way to produce change in a person, place, object, or event. The filmmaker can cut for continuous action and leave out those incidents of life that weaken drama.

Action can be accelerated, as in a race to a finish line. Or, the filmmaker can cut back and forth to two simultaneous actions, as when Indians chase cowboys. Cutting or film editing separates film and television from the other arts, as does a camera that can move between and within shots. Lewis Jacobs[8] put it this way: Griffith, the director of *Birth of a Nation* (1915), "suddenly understood how the art of the movie director differs from that of the stage director; in movie making, guiding the camera, even more than directing the actor, is the trick." Jacobs continued, "Editing gave the film director unprecedented control over movement in what is essentially an art of movement; by playing on shot duration, and on the relationship of actions in successive shots, he [Griffith] was able to move his audience by skillfully constructed movement within the frame and frame to frame."

The Need for Change in Characters

The need for change carries over to characterization. No longer do audiences accept the complete hero; predictability or stereotypes were satisfying only to less sophisticated audiences. In the early 1900s, a physical fight or a rush of action was all that was required to capture and hold an audience's attention. Characterization changes were not necessary. Today, even the stereotypes often do unpredictable things.

SOCIETAL INFLUENCES ON FILMS

From a story point-of-view, Depression-era audiences chose rapidly paced, visual-aural situation comedies like *It Happened One Night* and colorful, action and conflict-filled adventures like *Mutiny on the Bounty* to momentarily remove them from their stultifying, static world. In contrast, visually slow moving thematic pictures like *Gentleman's Agreement* were preferred right after World War II because audiences were satiated with rapid change in the environment. They wanted themes that would give them time to think about where they had been and where they were going, and to evaluate the human condition after living through the most violent global-scale social disruptions in modern times.

Audience choices of particular films during certain periods are partly based on sociological and psychological conditions in society. People go to the movies to massage their senses, to move into another environment in time and space, to seek rest or rapid change, to compare and contrast, and to receive fresh insights and information.

The Need for Change in Events

If the art of moving pictures is based on a theory of change, it finds ultimate expression in one of its most durable forms—the chase, a suspenseful sequence of events building in momentum, the outcome of which is uncertain. "The chase," said Alfred Hitchcock,[9] "seems to me the final expression of the motion picture medium." All of the elements associated with the theory of change are major attributes of a good chase sequence on film, and are probably responsible for the chase scene's longevity as well as its development in so many genres—western, gangster, private eye, adventure, horror, and comedy.

The Chase

Ferdinand Zecca (1864–1947) directed some of cinema's first chase films for the French Pathé Company in the early 1900s. Edwin Sidney Porter established the chase film tradition, along with the western, in this country. D. W. Griffith made a major contribution to the chase with his crosscutting technique known as the Griffith last minute rescue or "meanwhile, back at the ranch." Mack Sennett clasped the

FIGURE 7-1 The western became part of the chase and a stereotype. (Movie Star News)

JOHN WAYNE in "THE BIG STAMPEDE"~ A Warner Bros · First National Picture

TECHNICAL DEVELOPMENTS

1844
–55
Michael Faraday publishes the results of his work with electromagnetic induction, leading to the generator in "Experimental Researches on Electricity."

1869 Celluloid, the first of the plastics, is discovered.

1879 Edison perfects his first practical incandescent lamp.

1883 Edison observes thermionic emission in a lamp bulb.

1886 Charles Martin Hall and Paul Heroult develop the process of electrolysis of alumina.

1887 Edison and Kennedy begin their research and experimentation with motion pictures.

1889 Kodak introduces the flexible film stock celluloid, one type of which still forms the base of film stock today, and film projection as it is now known becomes possible.

There is not actual movement within a film frame. A piece of motion picture is a long strip of still pictures, each photograph slightly different from the one before or after it. It would seem, then, that one might expect to see a long series of still pictures on the screen. This is not the case because long before the invention of pictures, philosophers and scientists discovered that when a picture, or image, is held up before the eye and then removed, the eye retains the image of the picture for a moment before it fades. Later experiments concluded that by projecting a series of still pictures, each slightly different from adjacent ones, the eye would fill in the blank spots, creating the illusion of motion. They were right.

1890 Edison develops this country's first motion picture studio, the so-called Black Maria. It is curious that the incandescent light he invented in 1879 was not used. The Black Maria's exterior surface was painted flat black. A pulley was operated to open and close shutters that allowed sunlight through the steep pitched roof. To keep up with the earth's rotation, the entire studio swung on pivots, thus insuring a longer shooting day. It was within these confining black walls that Dickson filmed the shirt dance of Annabelle Whitford Moor, the leaping muscles of Sandow the Strong Man, the sensational kiss of John Rice and Mary Irwin, and other pantomimed variety acts. Dickson also felt the frustrations and limitations of working with an immobile camera in a small room.

"I consider that the greatest mission of the motion picture is first to make people happy . . . to bring more joy and cheer and wholesome good will into this world of ours. And God knows we need it."

This was Edison speaking of his new invention, that "interesting and novel apparatus . . . that curiosity . . . with no very large practical possibilities."

Interestingly, to Edison it was so much a toy he did not have the foresight to register international patents on the motion picture technology he invented.

1906 Joseph Thomson discovers the electron.

Source: Gerald Mast. *A Short History of the Movies.* New York: Pegasus, 1971.

chase to his zany bosom in about 1912 and made it explosively funny as a major element of his Keystone Cops series.

The chase galloped along through the westerns of the 1920s; rode the running boards of the gangsters in the 1930s; donned khaki as the good guys of the Allies fought the bad guys of the Axis in World War II; flew in a balloon *Around the World in 80 Days* in the mid 1950s; crawled back into the saddle in the 1960s with *Butch Cassidy and the Sundance Kid*; and in the 1970s rode a tank with *Patton*, romped with the cavalry in *Little Big Man,* and transformed a peaceful civilian's car into junk in *The French Connection.*

The chase scene satisfies the audience's desire for rapid perceptual changes despite Alvin Toffler's[10] suggestion that people are satiated with change and want to arrest its almost uncontrollable growth. The chase genre actually offers relief from the Toffler syndrome. The audience can take pleasure in the sensual massage bouncing from the screen without having their personal lifestyles radically altered. This may give them the feeling that they are controlling change, although they are not; and it may give them a respite from the external world—the more violent the change the more stimulating the massage. Film audiences have always liked a chase. Technological progress has allowed cinema to perfect it with a moving camera and location shooting.

Westerns—Stereotypes

Western films deal with guns—physical objects designed to kill which have postures associated with their use that form visual and emotional reactions about law and order, freedom and restriction, etc. Underlying and in conflict with the simplified morality of the western tale is the essential immorality implicit in the law of the gun. But Americans have always liked to feel that they are freewheeling individuals who can break out of the mold to do their own thing. Westerns appeal to this illusion of individualism and unrestricted freedom. America has always had a violent nature; in the western, violence is universalized in a love-hate relationship that binds anti-hero, anti-villain, and villain, a situation in which murder is socially acceptable and desirable. In fact, murder becomes the only satisfactory way of serving justice. This western philosophy of life is a satisfying emotional experience for an audience that often feels cornered by legal restrictions.

ARTISTIC DEVELOPMENTS

Nonfiction

1888   In Leeds, France, Louis Aime Augustin Le Prince films actuality or documentary scenes of traffic on Leeds Bridge.

1895   In France, Louis and Auguste Lumière shoot actuality scenes like *Train Arriving at the Station.*

1896   Englishman Bert Acres takes his camera which was constructed by Robert W. Paul, who got started in the business by copying without permission the Edison-Dickson Kinetoscope design when it was exhibited at the Chicago World's Fair in 1893, makes a film of the Derby races and then *The Sea Waves at Dover* (1896).

1901   The Edison Studio re-
-02   sponds to these early nonfiction films with the *New York Fire Brigade, Niagara Falls,* and *New York in a Blizzard.*

Narrative

1897–   Georges Méliès, a profes-
1913   sional magician who owned and operated the Theatre Robert-Houdin in Paris (which became the first public movie theater in the world by 1896) begins putting tricks into films: He makes *The Cabinet of Mephistopheles* (1897), *Cinderella* (1899), *The Man with the India-Rubber Head* (1901), *A Trip to the Moon* (1902), *The Palace of the Arabian Nights* (1905), *Twenty Thousand Leagues Under the Sea* (1907), and *Conquest of the Pole* (1912).

1902   Edwin Porter creates one of this country's first storytelling films, *The Life of an American Fireman.*

1903   Porter directs *The Great Train Robbery* for the Edison Company, which is considered to be one of America's first truly dramatic films. It is the first American film that is not merely a photographed play. The story builds from shot to shot, cuts back and forth between two simultaneous actions, and manipulates time and space.

1908   Griffith and his wife, Linda Arvidson, go to work for Biograph, an early competitor of the Edison Company, at the going price of five dollars a day. Within a few months, Griffith has directed his first film. During his five years at Biograph, Griffith either directs or manufactures (the early word for producing) some 150 films. His last film for Biograph is *Judith of Bethulia* in 1913, because the company decides he is too extravagant and eases him out of production.

Source: David Bordwell and Kristin Thompson. *Film Art: An Introduction.* Menlo Park, Calif.: Addison-Wesley, 1979.

Actually, the typical western is set during the late nineteenth century, when rapid economic expansion and land development created chaotic conditions in which bandits and outlaws operated casually, often with the cooperation of sheriffs and police. Yet, even through this period, acts of violence were a comparatively minor aspect of social history; headlines puffed them up to legendary dimensions, out of proportion to the realities of western development. Legends are virtually indestructible, however. And the legends of the West have persisted in the debunking glare of fact to relieve American tensions.

The westerns' romantic settings offer release from the thwarted dreams and moral uncertainties of the present.[11] Today's problems are transferred to a false past. The alienated man becomes a rugged individualist, a Tom Mix astride his faithful Tony. The myth feeds the audiences' fantasies and relieves their reality, showing men with ruthless courage and quick guns who have satisfactory answers to problems over which in real life people actually have little control. This myth of rugged individualism on a new frontier has been comforting to a society feeling more and more restricted by rapid growth and change.

ETHNIC GROUPS IN FILM

Ethnic groups rarely receive sympathetic or realistic treatment in Holywood's celluloid versions of American life. How different things might have been if, from the beginning, filmmakers had presented in-depth, honest studies of minority groups, instead of falling back on simplistic clichés as an easy way to sell stories. Nonetheless, many critics consider stereotypes to be a recognized and valuable literary device.

Cowboys—Wasps

America's first cowboy film, *The Great Train Robbery* (1903), mercifully omitted Indians. This was probably because the filmmakers' westward movement had not yet begun, so they hadn't discovered the vast American prairies and the dramatic potential of cowboys and Indians.

Max Aronson of Little Rock, Arkansas, became America's first cowboy star. He appeared in *The Great Train Robbery* in several roles, although Aronson and film historians disagree over just which roles. However, they all agree that he tried to mount his horse from the wrong side and was thrown off.

In 1907, Aronson and George Spoor of Chicago formed the Essanay Film Manufacturing Company; Spoor was the 'S', Aronson the 'A'. Charlie Chaplin was their biggest star. Between 1909 and 1915, Aronson was responsible for nearly 400 films. He acted in many of them as "Bronco Billy" Anderson. He recalled that he'd write them in the morning and film them in the afternoon. Sometimes the scenario would be written as they filmed.

Although some companies, like Vitagraph, were active in the East, by 1908 the westward movement had begun. Thomas Ince was one of the first American directors to exploit the vast space of the West. He shot his westerns on an 18,000-acre California ranch known as Inceville. Thomas Ince was to producers what D. W. Griffith was to directors: he literally defined the producer's function and separated it from the creative role of the director.

Ince's most popular cowboy star was William Hart, a middle-aged actor from Broadway. His stiff theatrics made real cowboys laugh, but his popularity with audiences spanned the decade from 1915 to 1925.

The action in cowboy movies made them very popular with audiences. Cowboy stars included Tom Mix, Hoot Gibson, Ken Maynard, and William Boyd, who made sixty-six films as Hopalong Cassidy. Although most of the cowboy actors were on straight salary and did not share in profits, Boyd was different—he got all his savings together in 1948, negotiated 1,500 separate contracts, and for $350,000 bought the television rights to his films. The good guy who always wore black made a fortune.

Hopalong Cassidy was as far from the rough riding Mixs and Maynards of the twenties and thirties as Gene Autry was. Autry claims that he was encouraged to enter films one rainy night in Chelsea, Oklahoma, where he was working as a relief telegraph operator around 1930. During a quiet hour, he was strumming his guitar and singing to himself when a man came by to send a wire and stayed to hear Autry sing. The man was Will Rogers and he advised the young Autry to work his way to Hollywood via radio. By 1970, Gene Autry owned radio stations, oil wells, and a baseball team, holdings worth more than $100 million.

Sidekicks and character actors gave badly needed color and comic relief to the tired western plots. George "Gabby" Hayes of Wellesville, New York, was Hopalong Cassidy's partner. Gabby never rode a horse until he was fifty and he hated westerns. Slim Pickens started riding at age two and became the highest paid rodeo clown in history before he started making pictures. John Carradine was a trained Shakespearean actor who was made a super villain after his entry in *Tol'able David* (1930). He was featured in many John Ford films, including *Stagecoach* (1939), which is considered the movie that raised the western from a Saturday afternoon and popcorn diversion to a respectable art.

Another player in *Stagecoach* was former prop man John Wayne. Wayne's first starring role was in *The Big Trail* (1929). He tried to make it as a singing cowboy, did a lot of cheapie westerns, and finally became a star in *Stagecoach*. John Ford saw him moving furniture on the back lot and asked him if he wanted to act. That was the beginning of an historic film career for the former University of Southern California football player.

Gangster Pictures—The Italian Atmosphere

In Hollywood, the mood of the Depression was reflected in gangster films.[12] Real gangsters were shooting real bullets during the 1930s: Al

FIGURE 7–2   Edward G. Robinson personified the 1930s gangster. (Movie Star News)

Capone, "Ma" Barker, "Pretty Boy" Floyd, John Dillinger, the Barrow Gang. Hollywood modeled its tough gals and guys after them, emulating such underworld tactics as the 1929 St. Valentine's Day Massacre in Chicago.

Edward G. Robinson.   In 1931, Caesar Enrico Bandello, mobster kingpin, was gunned down by police. The film dramatization, *Little Caesar* (1931), was directed by Mervyn LeRoy and was Edward G. Robinson's second film at Warner Brothers. *Little Caesar* established Robinson as the crime czar. His dying line was "Mother of Mercy, is this the end of Rico?" That was just the beginning—Robinson went on to make over a hundred films. His one hundred and first, before dying at the age of 79, was *Soylent Green* with Charlton Heston. Robinson was a fine actor, on both stage and screen. He preferred to be remembered for his role as Dr. Paul Erlich (1940), who searched for the microbe that causes syphilis or as the tormented sea captain in Jack London's *The Sea Wolf* (1941), whose credo was "Better to reign in hell than to serve in heaven." But it was as a snarling, cigar-smoking racketeer that he would be remembered—as Johnny Rocco in *Key Largo* (1948).

James Cagney.   In April, 1931, Warner Brothers released *The Public Enemy,* which was directed by William Wellman, and starred James Cagney, Jean Harlow, Joan Blondell, and Mae Clarke. *New York Times* critic Andre Sennwald described *The Public Enemy* as "just another gangster film, weaker than most in its story, stronger than most in its acting,'' but it went on to become a classic of its genre.

James Cagney was one of the cockiest, most self-assured, aggressive gangsters in filmland. His role as George M. Cohan in *Yankee Doodle Dandy* (1942) won him an Academy Award, but most film fans remember him pushing a grapefruit into Mae Clarke's face in *Public Enemy.* Cagney is credited with sixty-three feature films; his last was *Ragtime,* filmed in 1981.

In 1933, Cagney played a Broadway producer in Lloyd Bacon's *Footlight Parade.* In 1938, Cagney, Bogart, Pat O'Brien, Ann Sheridan, and the Dead End Kids did *Angels with Dirty Faces.* Cagney played a cynical and sentimental thug who blamed society for his predicament. In *City for Conquest* (1940) Cagney played a boxer who sacrificed himself to further the musical career of his gifted brother, played by Arthur Kennedy in his film debut. Cagney's flair for comedy appeared in Raoul Walsh's *The Strawberry Blonde* (1941) with Olivia de Havilland.

In 1949, director Raoul Walsh and Cagney revived the gangster film in *White Heat* with Edmond O'Brien and Virginia Mayo. *New York Times* critic Bosley Crowther described it as, "One of the most explosive pictures Cagney or anyone has ever played—the acme of the gangster-prison film." Cagney played a psychopathic hood with a mother obsession. Edmond O'Brien played an undercover treasury agent who delivered Cagney's epitath: "Cody Jarret, he finally made it to the top of the world. And it blew up in his face."

ESCAPISM

The films of the 1930s were really all like westerns with only the locale and costumes changed. In westerns, it was man against man and nature. In gangster films, it was man against man, the city, and big business. In comedies, it was man against man and big business. All three suggested the dream of the American psyche—to eliminate problems through escape or violence. These films are still popular for the same reason. They offer relief for minds that know there are few frontiers left. This yearning after an uncharted refuge may explain the popularity of recent films offering new frontiers, such as *2001: A Space Odyssey* or *Star Wars.* Of course, the Buster Keatons, William S. Harts, and Jimmy Cagneys have always been surrogate Don Quixotes for those of us more inclined to sit at home and dream. Even when America's physical and economic frontiers were plentiful, only a few actually dared to prove their dreams.

America watched, enthralled, as real astronauts rode buggies on the moon, but few would have traded secure seats on golf carts or lawn tractors for that billion dollar lunar ride. Most people prefer to let surrogates chase after distant planets, whether they be Neil Armstrong, astronaut, or William Shatner, *Star Trek's* Captain Kirk.

Source: Peter Klinge and Lee McConkey. *Introduction to Film Structure.* Washington, D.C.: University Press of America, 1982.

Humphrey Bogart. Sometimes art is a direct reflection of reality. In 1930, inmates at Auburn prison disarmed guards, murdered one official, held the warden hostage, and laid siege. Six hours and eight deaths later, the riot was subdued. An aide to New York Governor Franklin Roosevelt said it was one hell of a way to begin a depression. The Auburn riot influenced a hit Broadway play, *The Last Mile,* starring Spencer Tracy, and in Hollywood, Fox Films quickly assembled *Up the River* directed by John Ford. Although Fox had previously tested Tracy and rejected him as not much good and too ugly, Ford convinced Fox that Tracy was right for the part. He also had to sell Fox on Broadway actor Humphrey Bogart, who had just debuted with Fox that same year in *A Devil with Women.* Directors around the studio referred to Bogart as Beauregarde Humphries; but Ford got his way, and Spencer Tracy nicknamed Bogart "Bogie." *Up the River* was Tracy's first feature film and Bogie's second.

After a few forgettable films, some all-knowing Hollywood producer decided that Beauregard Humphries had no future in movies. His contract with Warner Brothers was dropped because film executives said that women would never go for a man with a scarred lip and a slight lisp. Bogart went back to a depressed Broadway and had some very dry seasons there before he created the role of "Duke" Mantee in Robert Sherwood's *The Petrified Forest* (1935). Leslie Howard played the lead.

Warner Brothers bought *Petrified Forest,* signed Leslie Howard and picked Edward G. Robinson to play "Duke" Mantee, but Leslie Howard told Warner Brothers that he would not do the film unless Bogart played Mantee. The studio subjected Bogart to fifteen screen tests before signing him to a $400-a-week, 40-week contract. After the film was released in 1936, no one called him Humphrey anymore. He was known as "Bogie."

In the late 1930s, Warner Brothers used Bogie as a cold, implacable, rotten-to-the-core villain against their "good" heavies like Cagney, Raft, and Robinson.

World War II was rough on Hollywood's American gangsters, who were gradually replaced by international hoods. But, before they faded, there was time for Raoul Walsh to direct Bogart as the tough and bitter Roy Earle in *High Sierra* (1941). The National Board of Review gave Best Acting awards to Bogart and Ida Lupino and gave the film its Best Picture award.

THE RISE OF THE ANTI-HERO

The transition to international films began with pictures like John Huston's *The Maltese Falcon* (1941). The decade of the gangster film was about to yield to a new genre, the detective film. *The Maltese Falcon* was not the first detective picture, but it served as a model for films tough, worldly, amoral private eyes who are still around four dec-

FIGURE 7–3 Humphrey Bogart as anti-hero. (Movie Star News)

ades later. *The Maltese Falcon* was Sydney Greenstreet's film debut at age 61 and was the first meeting of Peter Lorre and Greenstreet. Bogie continued the American gangster-to-detective-to-international intrigue transition in Michael Curtiz's *Casablanca* (1942). *Casablanca* won the 1943 Academy Award for best picture, and nominations for Bogie and Claude Rains. Its cast included Ingrid Bergman, Paul Henreid, Conrad Veidt, Sydney Greenstreet, Peter Lorre, and Dooley Wilson, the piano-playing Sam of "Play it again, Sam" fame.

In 1944, forty-five-year-old Bogie played opposite 19-year-old Lauren Bacall, who was making her screen debut. The film was Howard Hawk's production of Ernest Hemingway's *To Have and Have Not.* This time the piano player was Hoagy Carmichael as Crickett. The immortal line went from Bacall to Bogart: "If you want me, just whistle." The setting, again international, was Martinique rather than Casablanca.

John Huston directed Bogie, Tim Holt, and his father, Walter Huston, in *The Treasure of Sierra Madre* (1948). Considered to be one of the strongest films of the decade, it was not popular with filmgoers. Huston borrowed a lot from Erich Von Stroheim's 1923 film, *Greed.* Neither was a popular film but both survived to become classics. Academy Awards went to John Huston for screenplay and direction, and to his father, Walter, for his role as the toothless, philosophical prospector. The National Board of Review, *Film Daily, Time,* and the New

York film critics all named *The Treasure of the Sierra Madre* as one of the best pictures of 1948.

In July, 1948, John Huston again teamed with Bogie to do an unsuccessful reprise of the American gangster genre. Robinson's Johnny Rocco was a faded version of his 1931 Caesar Enrico Bandello. But in 1951, that elusive Academy Award finally caught up with Bogie. It was John Huston's *African Queen* that drew a sympathetic combination of toughness and tenderness out of Bogart. Katharine Hepburn, the female lead, was nominated, too, but lost to Vivien Leigh for her performance in *A Streetcar Named Desire*.

Bogie was nominated again in 1954, this time for his psychotic Captain Queeg in *The Caine Mutiny,* but he lost to Marlon Brando for *On the Waterfront*. In 1956, Bogie made his last film, *The Harder They Fall.* Bogart, who died of cancer on January 14, 1957, has become a film legend.

Robinson, Cagney, and Bogart were the three big crime actors. But, there were others active in the crime genre: Sylvia Sidney and Gary Cooper in Rouben Mamoulian's 1931 *City Streets;* Paul Muni in Mervyn LeRoy's *I am a Fugitive from a Chain Gang* (1932); William Powell and Myrna Loy in Woody Van Dyke's series, *The Thin Man;* Warner Oland, Sidney Toler, and Roland Winters in the Charlie Chan films; and Basil Rathbone as Sherlock Holmes.

Sherlock Holmes came to symbolize crime and the detective genre. His line, "Elementary, my dear Watson" is still remembered when few can recall Robinson's "Mother of Mercy, is this the end of Rico?" or Cagney's "Made it Ma! Top of the World!" Crime films had run their course by the end of the thirties, but they sputtered on through the forties with the help of novelty, comedy, and the bizarre.

Horror Pictures—The Monster Era

Since Freud and Jung, interest in psychology has not waned. The human spirit is fascinated by its darker side, disordered psyches. And no nation was more interested in this topic than the Germans after World War I.

Although such films as *The Execution of Mary, Queen of Scots, Dr. Jekyll and Mr. Hyde,* and *Frankenstein* appeared in America before 1910, it was not until after World War I that a full-fledged film horror school developed. Horror movies developed from the German school of expressionism, of which Robert Weine's 1919 *Cabinet of Dr. Caligari* is the most famous title. The calculated distortions of expressionism were designed to reveal a meaning beyond reality.[13]

Karl Freund, director of photography on such expressionistic films as *The Last Laugh* and Fritz Lang's *Metropolis,*[14] was one of the talents who left Germany before the rise of Hitler and helped develop the horror tradition in America. He was director of photography on Tod Browning's *Dracula* (1930) and director of *The Mummy* (1932) with Boris Karloff. Then Freund won an Oscar for his cinematography on

FIGURE 7-4 Frankenstein is tame by today's standard of horror. (Movie Star News)

The Good Earth (1937), and he continued to move away from horror films for the rest of his career, which he ended doing the photography for "I Love Lucy."

One of the first and probably the best of the vampire movies was Fred Murnau's silent film *Nosferatu* (1922). The Dracula character was originated by novelist Bram Stoker. The Dracula tradition reached the United States with famous movies starring Bela Lugosi, but no one ever topped Fred Murnau's *Nosferatu*.

Lon Chaney filmed a classic, *Phantom of the Opera,* in 1925. Without monster make-up, Chaney did Tod Browning's *The Unknown* (1927). Chaney was later to have played Dracula under Browning, but he died before the film was produced. Lon Chaney, Jr., continued in his father's footsteps, acting in *Son of Dracula, The Mummy's Curse,* and *The Wolf Man.* But his most memorable role was as the feeble-minded Lenny in Lewis Milestone's *Of Mice and Men* (1940).

In a word association test, it is likely that horror would be linked to the monster that British novelist Mary Shelley created in her novel *Frankenstein.* And that monster would be linked just as likely with British actor William Pratt, who became Boris Karloff in 1911. Karloff acted in several monster films, including *Frankenstein.* Incidentally, the scene where the monster tossed the little girl into the lake to see if she would float was censored from the film for being too shocking in 1931.

Karloff made three films as the monster. In 1935, James Whale, an English director working in the United States, put Karloff in *The Bride of Frankenstein* with English actress Elsa Lanchester, the wife of Charles Laughton.

The Bride of Frankenstein has been criticized for "humanization" of the monster. Boris Karloff objected to this humanizing because he felt that speech weakened the character. This schizophrenia of a human monster was partly caused by the fact that the original screenplay was written as a satire, but was later altered by producer Carl Laemmle into a horror film.

Universal revived the monster film in 1939, *The Son of Frankenstein,* which marked Karloff's third and last appearance as this collection of spare parts. In this finale film, British actor Basil Rathbone played Baron Wold Von Frankenstein, who had been played in the previous films by British actor Colin Clive. For *The Son of Frankenstein,* Karloff was joined by fellow horror star Bela Lugosi as Ygor, a half-crazy, evil shepherd who commands the monster to murder. In the film, Ygor is shot and the monster plunges to a horrible death in a lake of boiling sulphur. Some of Karloff's other films include Karl Freund's *The Mummy* (1932); James Whale's *The Old Dark House* (1932); *Isle of the Dead* (1945); and *Abbott and Costello Meet the Killer* (1949).

There were other film monsters. Claude Rains made his acting debut in James Whale's *The Invisible Man* (1933). Willis O'Brien, the special effects man, created the animated, lovable, prehistoric beast *King Kong* (1933). Henry Hull played the first werewolf in a sound film in the 1935 film *Werewolf of London.* And Miriam Hopkins played Campagne Ivy to Fredric March in *Dr. Jekyll and Mr. Hyde* (1932). Director Rouben Mamoulian and cinematographer Karl Struss solved Jekyll's transformation into Hyde by using color transparencies. The transformation was accomplished in one continuous shot that revealed more and more of the actor's make-up through different color filters. The make-up consisted of various shades of red, green, and blue. A red filter absorbed the red make-up, a green filter absorbed the green make-up and so on. Mamoulian kept his technique a secret for thirty-seven years. The sound effects that accompanied the transformation marked the first use of synthetic sound in film. Struss and Mamoulin photographed light frequencies from a candle, recorded a gong and played it backwards, and recorded Mamoulian's speeded up heartbeats as he ran up and down a staircase.

The true horror genre ended in the forties with films like *I Walked with a Zombie* and Peter Lorre in the macabre *The Beast with Five Fingers.* During the fifties, directors mixed horror with science fiction, sex, violence, and murder.

Films are rarely categorized by genre today. When hundreds of pictures were released every year, it was a helpful way of organizing movies. Now, when less than a hundred features are produced a year, titles can be remembered without using categories.

BLACKS—EVEN MORE OBVIOUS STEREOTYPES

Since the days of Griffith, Blacks have been stereotyped on film as "fetch and carry" characters; but, it must be remembered that Griffith said he had no intention of slighting Blacks. He made *Intolerance* to prove it. Like Griffith, most early filmmakers found it easier to deal with a story in which Blacks were stereotyped than one in which they had multi-dimensional characteristics.

Shirley Temple's Black manservant with a heart of gold, not much of a brain, and a talent for singing and dancing, was typical of how Blacks were portrayed in films, as is the mammy in *Gone With the Wind.* It was not until the sixties and pictures like *Guess Who's Coming to Dinner* (1967) that Hollywood finally recognized Blacks as real people. In that film, a Black man wants to marry a white girl and the problems of an interracial marriage are considered by the girl's family. But here, the part of the Black is played by Sidney Poitier, a man who seems and acts more like a man from the white, middle class background.

WOMEN IN FILM

Until very recently, film women have usually been warm, supportive, not too bright, and attractive—all characteristics designed to catch or keep a man. Recently, many film females have lost their purity and have become extremely sexy, rather than just the girl any man could bring home to mother. This is more a reflection of the changing mores in American society than an attempt to avoid stereotypes. A woman can be sexy, might have had a fling, and can still go home to meet mother.

When Bette Davis, Barbara Stanwyck, or Rosalind Russell played hard-driving intelligent women in films, they also were either eccentric, comedic, or slightly shady. When a woman played a businesswoman, she was to be sympathized with by the audience. She often acted more like a man than men did; audiences were made to feel that something was amiss in her early childhood. Such rationalizations for women who hold professional jobs are no longer necessary in today's society, in which it is considered more "normal" for a woman to hold a job.

Bette Davis played roles typical of the early stereotypes which undermined strength in women by teaming it with shallowness. One of

MOSTLY STEREOTYPES

Hollywood has stereotyped most minority groups. Gansters were Italians; Indians were drunken heathens; cowboy stars wore white hats; women were usually the adjunct to men; and Blacks were faithful servants. Multi-dimensional characterization has never been Hollywood's strong suit. John Wayne and Gary Cooper played the same types picture after picture. A movie that deals with the complexities of human nature, like *The Great Santini* (1979), is the exception to the rule.

As deplorable as film stereotypes may be, the real problem has always been the small number of Blacks and women employed in the film industry. Although women may be breaking through the barrier in the early 1980s, no one is sure yet; Blacks have still made little progress. Only pictures designed specifically for Black audiences, like *Shaft,* have offered long-term employment for Blacks, and very few pictures are made today specifically for this group.

Source: Peter Klinge and Lee McConkey. *Introduction To Film Structure.* Washington, D.C.: University Press of America, 1982.

her early specialities was the erotic and vicious rich girl, sexually tantalizing to males. Being a woman, she was expected to be forgiven almost anything, but there was rarely much character development. In *Cabin in the Cotton* (1932) she is rich, sexy, and mean. In *Jezebel* (1938) she is the perverse Southern belle who goes to the antebellum ball in a red gown instead of the conventional demure white dress. She is headstrong, selfish and spoiled. In *The Letter* (1940) Davis is the bored and errant plantation wife. In *The Little Foxes* (1941) she plays the Southern belle again, ruthlessly driven by greed. In one scene, she stands unemotionally in closeup in the foreground as her husband in the midst of a heart attack futilely tries to climb the stairs in the background. Davis argued with the director, William Wyler, that the character was not being rounded out emotionally, but Wyler got his way. Until recent times, if women were strong-willed or ambitious, there had to be a large and obvious flaw in the character.

VIOLENCE SELLS FILMS WITH SOCIAL THEMES

Americans love the spectacular visual and audio changes inherent in violence. Three of the all-time top movie moneymakers in this country have dealt with violent themes: *The Birth of a Nation* (1915), which was about the Civil War and the trauma of Reconstruction; *Gone with the Wind* (1930), also about the Civil War and Reconstruction; and *The Godfather* (1972), about family war and war against society. Each of these films also featured some kind of a race, which builds momentum and suspense very much like a chase does. In *Birth of a Nation*, it was the last-minute race of the Ku Klux Klan to save the supposedly put-upon Southerners from the unprincipled Reconstructionists. In *Gone with the Wind*, the race was Scarlet O'Hara's and Rhett Butler's attempt to get out of a burning Atlanta in time. In *The Godfather*, Sonny lost his race to save his sister from a brutal husband. It ended in his dance of death, caught in a hail of bullets, as he rushed to her side.

KEEP THE PLOT SIMPLE

In 1920, Metro was casting *The Four Horsemen of the Apocalypse*, based on a novel by Vincente Blasco-Ibanex. The plot of the picture is complex. It involves an aristocratic expatriate German family living in South America. The Four Horsemen symbolized War, Conquest, Famine, and Death; the pros and cons of these elements are interwoven with class struggle, personal conscience, and the inevitable love triangle. This was director Rex Ingram's third film for the young company headed by Marcus Lowe. *The Four Horsemen of the Apocalypse* cost $750,000 to produce and it grossed $4.5 million. Its success launched Rudolph Valentino to stardom, and made Ingram's reputation as a director. It salvaged the tottering economy of Metro, which was soon to merge with Sam Goldwyn and Louis B. Mayer's studio into the powerful MGM. Adhering to the Hollywood maxim that "nothing succeeds like success," MGM did a remake of the picture in 1962 against a WWII background and starring Glenn Ford.

The first silent version about loyalty to the Kaiser was a success because the plot was fast-paced and easy to follow. The second failed because along with having too much dialogue, it tried to deal with too many issues—division over the Nazis, the demise of the aristocracy, and the rise of the working class. After thirty-five years, motion was being sacrificed to lengthy philosophical discussions. The 1921 version, with no sound, by necessity avoided philosophical depth, no doubt adding to the movie's appeal, and kept the action moving quickly.

When American films attempt to deal with the realities of war, they usually follow a structure established by Griffith and the western—the sweep of history reduced to human terms and a few standardized emotions—love, jealousy, and courage. *The Big Parade* (1925), directed by King Vidor, was just such a war picture.

War and western films often have a lot in common; they are both mass movement against an epic background. This is probably one reason for the success of *The Big Parade*, but the more obvious reason was that the film's action was combined with a mixture of sentimentality and realism well suited to the Jazz Age. Americans no longer looked at war idealistically and sentimentally, but they did look at themselves that way. Empathy was created with a plot that showed humans caught in machinery, in this case war, over which they had no control.

FILMS TODAY

Far fewer films are made for theatrical release in the 1980s. Movies today cost more, run longer, and their exhibitors charge the public more. They are not necessarily high quality, but they are sensational. Films like *The Exorcist* or *Dressed to Kill* do particularly well at the box office. Promotion is often the key to a movie's success, and often just as much money is spent on advertising, promotion, and publicity, as is spent on the picture itself. The primary objective of all this effort is to create "word of mouth" advertising, in which one viewer tells another to see a film. When Fred Goldberg was vice-president of advertising at United Artists, he used to say that you can promote the hell out of a picture, but it will be word of mouth that makes or breaks it in the end. Peter Guber, the producer of *The Deep,* would agree. He took a run-of-the-mill picture, created word of mouth advertising by spending as much on advertising as on the picture, and made a great deal of money. Hype blinded viewers to the true value of the picture. Critics complain that moviegoers do not listen to their own instincts anymore.

Profits can be fantastic if a movie hits on the right combination. Universal made *Jaws* for $8 million, and spent more than $2 million on promotion, but the film got all this money back in just three weeks. Twentieth Century Fox spent $7 million on *Star Wars* and made that back in a couple of weeks. *The Godfather* has grossed over $80 million. Experts predict that *Jaws* will gross more than $300 million before it is all over, and the same is predicted for *Star Wars.* A movie like *Rocky* is an exception to this trend of big-budget pictures with big action because its price tag was closer to $1 million, and though it does not have lots of big action, it grossed $54 million. Nonetheless, the movie industry in this country is not healthy because there are many more failures than hits. Most movie profits now come from network and cable television sales. A great number of potential filmgoers like their movies noncontroversial, fantasy-filled, sexually understated, fast-moving, straightforward, and square like *On Golden Pond* (1981), but most pictures still seem to be targeted for the teen-age to twenty-five-year-old market. Other viewers either go along with teen-age entertainment, stay home and watch television, or go to the movies only occasionally. *E.T.* is the exception. It might be argued that Hollywood is making its non-targeted product for television, not movie theaters.

People are going to some movies, however, and in larger numbers. Although about half the people in the country do not go to even one film a year, a surprisingly large number of people who were nonfilmgoers are lining up at the box office. Maybe it is the times that have brought the change. There is a premise that movies prosper in times of depression or recession because people want to forget their troubles through escape and excitement. This may be true, but movies were not very successful during the recessions of the 1950s; however, the reason in this case might have been that television was still so new that films could not pull audiences away.

A more likely overall explanation for the success of some recent movies is the movies themselves. Hollywood has returned to making movies with an emphasis on action and adventure, and has become adept at making, marketing, and advertising them. Book tie-ins are a case in point. A lot of money was put into pushing the paperback of *The Deep*. In return, a lot of people went to the film.

The big or moneymaking picture is an entertaining one. Take a look at the list of movies that made the most money in one week in 1982. There are very few thematic films listed here.

There are few films like the *Graduate, Easy Rider,* or *M*A*S*H* on this list. Most of the current winners are intellectually light, filled with fantasy, fun, sexual romps, comedy, and adventure. This is not to say that these films are any worse or better than message pictures, but some critics say that such films are evidence that anti-intellectualism is on the rampage in America. This is a convenient answer. It seems that anti-intellectualism is always said to be on the rampage when there is discussion of a product used by most of the populace; anyway, intellectualism has never been favored by this country or by the film industry. It is just that for a time, because of television, the film industry thought it could counter the fluff with the serious. Now the young filmmaker who approaches the studio with a daring and controversial idea will rarely get financing, or if some financing is available, it will not be enough. Film is not a social cause medium unless the market demands it. The people in Hollywood, creative people as well as business executives, study the potential audience for a film as closely as a Proctor and Gamble media buyer studies the potential audience for a magazine ad.

Dennis Friedland, the producer of *Joe,* an immensely powerful movie with a strong message, says that before he makes any type of movie, he wants to know the most money that type of movie has made, the least, and the average. Then, he figures out a budget that will pretty much guarantee a profit.

What do these new trends do to the "art" of moviemaking? Or was moviemaking ever really an art? There certainly have been artistic films, even American artistic films. For example, there is the early work of Griffith, Chaplin, and Hitchcock. Some critics go as far as to say that the movie is America's major artistic contribution to the world, but most American films are not art, and never were. Ninety percent of American movies have always been products to be marketed to an audience, just like any other product.

Cinema in the 1980s has an almost unlimited ability to go anywhere and do anything because of technological advances like better cameras, sound recorders, and film. And the aesthetics of cinema cannot be separated from electro-mechanical discoveries and developments. The desires of the filmmaker and the tools available to him are inseparable. *Citizen Kane* (1940) is considered to be a film that represented a substantive advance in the art of cinematography because of its depth, with action in the background, middleground, and foreground

TABLE 7–1 Top 15 Movies (Week Ending April 14, 1982)	
Film	**Gross**
1. *Some Kind of Hero*	$2,208,741
2. *Porky's*	$1,897,842
3. *Victor Victoria*	$1,353,181
4. *Chariots of Fire*	$1,288,169
5. *Deathtrap*	$1,133,266
6. *On Golden Pond**	$1,073,358
7. *Richard Prior Live on the Sunset Strip*	$875,865
8. *Cat People*	$800,616
9. *Robin Hood*	$732,793
10. *Quest for Fire*	$728,359
11. *Silent Rage*	$723,795
12. *A Little Sex*	$432,200
13. *Penitentiary II*	$371,694
14. *Raiders of the Lost Ark**	$363,572
15. *I Ought to be in Pictures*	$354,909

Variety, April 21, 1982, p. 9

*Raiders has the highest grand total to date, followed by *On Golden Pond.*

I GOT A LOOK AT THE TECHNOLOGY

The list of adventurous businessmen attracted to Hollywood along with starstruck youngsters is not long but it is interesting. In the 1930s Joseph Kennedy and John Hay Whitney backed films. In the 1960s Charles Bluhdom bought Paramount. The big news today is that Denver oilman Marvin Davis is paying over $700 million for 20th Century-Fox. Less noticed, but potentially more revolutionary for the movie business, is that Jack Singer is putting up $8 million to back Francis Ford Coppola.

Who is Jack Singer? He's one of Canada's biggest real estate developers, as well as a big shareholder in that country's Dome Petroleum, an oil driller in Oklahoma and Texas, Phoenix and Tucson and the holder of 330 acres in Los Angeles' exclusive Bel Air section.

Has Singer been sniffing too much greasepaint? He shrugs when asked such a question. "No," he replies quietly. "I got a look at the technology Francis is using and I think he already is where the rest of the film industry will be going. He's a modern-day Thomas Edison."

The technology—what Coppola likes to call his electronic cinema—is the simultaneous use of both 35mm film and videotape in the making of *One From the Heart.* Coppola uses videotape as if it were an electronic drawing board on which to plan and realize his film. Ultimately the videotape version serves as a kind of stencil, allowing for a fast, computerized editing of the film version.

It is the speed of editing—amid the chaos of a grossly overbudget film on which Coppola has spent $6 million alone to recreate Las Vegas on a Hollywood set—that caught Singer's entrepreneurial eye. "After only six weeks Francis had a rough version of the film shown to an audience in Seattle," says Singer. "This kind of speed is unheard of."

The potential for cost-saving is impressive. While most directors would take a year or more to edit a film—running up postproduction costs that can account for up to 25% of budget for a complicated musical—Coppola has scheduled a four-month edit for *Heart.*

The ultimate prospect, of course, is for a complete replacement of film by videotape.

Source: Michael Kolbenschlog. "I Got a Look at the Technology." *Forbes,* July 6, 1981, Reprinted by permission. © 1981, Forbes, Inc.

at the same time. But its depth, like so many cinematic techniques, evolved with the development of faster film stocks, better lighting, and better lenses.

Today, more sophisticated video technology resulting in better cameras, lenses, tape, and computer editing, is making great strides and is being employed by filmmakers. Editing is often done with video. In the near future, film and video technology may become completely integrated. If production is now becoming integrated, viewing already is; more film is seen on television than in the theaters.

NONFICTION FILM: NOT SO POPULAR

Hollywood theatrical films do not represent the sum total of film. There are newsreels, instructional films, industrial films, promotional films, and documentaries. There is a film on how to read a book (educational), a film on a manufacturing plant (industrial), a recruitment film for the army (promotional), and a film on ecological subjects (documentary). Government productions alone are worth over a billion dollars a year, making the government one of the major film producers in this country.

The word documentary has often been used to define all of the above categories, but a stricter definition came out of the World Union of Documentary in 1948:

> ...all methods of recording on celluloid any aspect of reality interpreted either by factual shooting or by sincere and justifiable reconstruction, so as to appeal either to reason or emotion, for the purpose of stimulating the desire for, and the widening of human knowledge and understanding, an of truthfully posing problems and their solutions in the spheres of economics, culture, and human relations.[15]

Obviously, some of the news-oriented programs on television are documentaries by this definition, and films that sell a product or idea are not.

More recently, the term nonfiction has replaced the word documentary as a result of its use in describing Truman Capote's novel *In Cold Blood*. This represented a radical shift in thinking because the implication is that any story based on fact may be included. Currently, the term docu-drama is in vogue, particularly on television. In a docu-drama, the story is based on fact but the producers admit that the plot has been structured for dramatic purposes. Many features made outside the Hollywood system—called independents—fall loosely into this category because they have strong messages based on facts.

Finally, this unnameable area of film can be categorized along the lines of narrative and nonnarrative. This approach offers room for the experimental film, like Andy Warhol's film about the Empire State Building, which is more like a picture that is altered a bit over a long period of time than an actual moving picture, or Walter Ruttmann's *Berlin: Symphony of a Great City,* which is an expression of feeling about a city without a strong narrative line.

When they began, United States narrative documentaries were defined by one man—Robert Flaherty. He was the first important filmmaker to document real life using real people and real locations, although it would be misleading to think of Flaherty as the originator of the sociopolitical, didactic film. He was a romantic and a poet, not terribly concerned about social messages or box office. Although his first film, *Nanook of the North* (1922), eventually did received a money-making theater release, most of his work did not. His last film, *Louisiana Story,* was made for the Exxon Corporation (1948). It's the story of how an oil well is installed near a bayou swamp family without disrupting the environment. From a public relations standpoint, the film was a great success for Exxon—the picture was shown to special interest groups and film clubs all over the country, and eventually on television.

After Flaherty's initial success with *Nanook,* the next documentary excitement came with the Depression and the election of Franklin Roosevelt, who arranged for several films to help implement his policies. *The Plow that Broke the Plain* (1936) was made to explain why the Oklahoma farmers in their dust bowl situation were not the cause of the problem, and they should be helped in their plans to resettle elsewhere. *The River* (1937) was made as part of a campaign for the Tennessee Valley Authority to explain why the flooding had to be stopped, and how the water could be harnessed to produce energy and productive towns.

During World War II, most of the documentary films gave way to promotional films made to serve the country. Films were produced to tell the citizens why the United States was in the war, how the war was going, and what the future would be. One example is the *Why We Fight* series. After the war, the documentary finally found a permanent and financially viable distribution system—television.

TRENDS IN THE '80s Motion Pictures

Occasionally, a documentary has such strong entertainment appeal that it receives theater release, such as *Woodstock* (1970), but this is usually rare.[16] The promotional, industrial, and public relations film will still be made for distribution to film clubs, special groups, etc. These films are usually financed by sponsors for the same reason that companies advertise; they have a point of view to communicate that will bring dollars back into the company if they are able to reach the right audience. However, as video players become more common, most of these projects will be shot on videotape because video production can be much more economical than film production.

■ It would not be overstating the case to repeat that theatrical films in this country are a popular form of entertainment. Thematic pictures or documentaries do not have mass appeal. Top grossing pictures will continue to be light entertainment, fantasy, or adventure, like *E.T., Raiders of the Lost Ark,* and *Star Wars.* Pictures appealing to specialized audiences will begin to be shot in a 16mm format or Super 16, in hopes that a distributor will be found who will blow the picture up to the theatrical release 35mm print. If the picture is not picked up for theatrical release, it will remain in a 16mm format, appropriate for a network television sale, a pickup by pay television, or cable.

■ High risk ventures of every type and genre will involve videotape versus film. As a new generation of television receivers with higher picture and sound standards becomes available with matching production equipment, making moving pictures with film will probably become as old fashioned as the stagecoach as a means of transportation. Already, video editing is becoming popular, a process by which the raw film stock is transferred to video, the video is coded by computer and the editing process is performed at a video console.

■ In the *Journal of the University Film and Video Association,* Summer 1982 issue, Eric Smoodin reminds us that large television screens had their first public showings in motion picture theaters in 1935. At the time the image was not satisfactory when compared to the film image. But in the near future, technological advances should produce an image that will satisfy a viewing audience. Combine this with the possibility of delivering the programs via satellite, and the movie theater may not be a dying animal. In fact, such a situation might revitalize the production of theatrical product by reducing costs. First, a program beamed from satellites would not need a print for each theater, resulting in a large financial savings. Second, one copy could be released to the world in one evening. (The cost of distributing pictures to theaters is very high and takes a long time.) Besides, if the release is immediate all over the world, the producers can get their money back much faster; in turn, the producers can pay their backers quickly and save interest money on their debt.

ADDITIONAL READINGS

Baxter, John. *The Gangster Film.* Cranbury, N.J.: A. S. Barnes, 1970.

Folsom, James K., ed. *The Western.* Englewood Cliffs, N.J.: Prentice-Hall, 1979.

Jacobs, Lewis, ed. *The Emergence of Film Art.* New York: W. W. Norton, 1979.

Mast, Gerald. *A Short History of the Movies.* Indianapolis: Bobbs-Merrill, 1981.

Sklar, Robert. *Movie-Made America: A Cultural History of American Movies.* New York: Random House, 1975.

FOOTNOTES

1. David A. Cook, *A History of Narrative Film* (New York: Norton & Co., 1981) pp. 2–3.

2. David Bordwell and Kristin Thompson, *Film Art: An Introduction* (Menlo Park: Addison-Wesley, 1979), p. 291.

3. Susanne Langer, *Philosophy in a New Key* (New York: New American Library, 1951), p. 210.

4. Siegfried Kracauer, *Theory of Film: The Redemption of Physical Reality* (New York: Oxford University Press, 1960).

5. Vachel Lindsay, *The Art of the Motion Picture* (New York: Macmillan Company, 1915).

6. Vsevolod I. Pudovkin, *Film Technique and Film Acting* (New York: Lear, 1949).

7. Sergi Mikhailovich Eisenstein, *Film Form, The Film Sense* (New York: World Publishing, 1964).

8. Lewis Jacobs, *The Rise of the American Film* (New York: Teachers College Press, 1968), p. 110.

9. *New York Times Magazine,* October 29, 1950, pp. 22–23.

10. Alvin Toffler, *Future Shock* (New York: Random House, 1970).

11. John Lawson, *Film, The Creative Process* (New York: Hill & Wang, 1967), p. 64.

12. Thorold Dickinson, *A Discovery of Cinema* (New York: Oxford University Press, 1971), p. 67.

13. Lotte H. Eisner, *The Haunted Screen* (Berkeley: University of California Press, 1969).

14. Frederick W. Ott, *The Films of Fritz Lang* (Secaucus, N.J.: Citadel Press, 1979).

15. Jay Leyda, *Kino: A History of the Russian and Soviet Cinema* (London: Allen and Unwin, 1960), p. 200.

16. Richard Meran Barsam, *Nonfiction Film: A Critical History* (New York: E.P. Dutton, 1973).

SOUND PICTURES AND RECORDS

Thomas Alva Edison, the wizard of Menlo Park, constructed the miracle of the 19th century in 1877 and called it the phonograph, which means sound writer. The phonograph quickly made the record business, as well as becoming an important element in radio broadcasting and film production.

Edison and his associate, William Dickson, invented the kinetograph or motion writer in 1889. Dickson was immediately assigned to invent a Kineto-Phonograph that would combine pictures with sound on Edison's cylinders. He actually did it, but the pictures were too small and difficult to focus on the curved cylinder.[1] So, it was not until 1895 that the Edison Company tried to market a Kinetophone that synchronized pictures and sound. The public was not buying, however, and the kinetophone was discontinued after selling fewer than fifty machines. Finally in 1922, sound and picture were successfully mated. However, it should be noted, that from the very beginning, live musicians played music to accompany films and also played while the films were being shot to give the actors a feeling of pace and mood.

Dr. Lee De Forest, who in 1906 invented the audion tube, which is the key to sound reproduction, started developing sound-on-film talking pictures in 1913. By 1922, his phonofilms were producing synchronized sound-on-film talking pictures with performers like the team of Weaver and Fields. The next year he did musicals, and in 1926, two of De Forest's former associates sold his system without his permission to William Fox, who used it in the Fox Movietone News service. De Forest sued and won.

That same year, the debut of Warner Brothers Vitaphone Sound Movies went practically unnoticed. While *Son of the Sheik* was playing at the Mark Strand Theater in New York, with Rudolph Valentino making personal appearances, Warner Brothers held a gala premiere at the Warner Theater on August 5, 1926, featuring *Don Juan* with John Barrymore and Mary Astor. *Don Juan* did not have talk, but it had a synchronized music score played on a sixteen-inch phonograph record. The Bell Telephone Lab had improved on the Edison-Dickson Kinetophone.

Will Hays, president of the Motion Picture Producers and Distributors Association of America, an organization of producers that formed when demands of actors, writers, production crews, and others got too strident, introduced the evening's program in lip synchronization from the screen. In addition to *Don Juan*, the studio presented talking and singing shorts, including one featuring opera star Giovanni Martinelli.

Part of the success of any major film company in the 1920s and 1930s was its ability to control production and distribution, studios, and theaters. Warner Brothers took a desperate gamble on the Vitaphone Sound System in order to avoid imminent bankruptcy, which was brought on by its inability to control a chain of first-run theaters in which to show its films. Warners gambled on the Vitaphone system even though other studios had turned down offers to buy the patents. Even after the *Don Juan* program received good reviews, most exhibitors were reluctant to install the very expensive sound equipment. There was no big splash in the industry, but people kept coming to the show. Warners decided to try again, and approached George Jessel to re-create his stage role in *The Jazz Singer* for the movies. Unable to get Jessel, they turned to Al Jolson. Warners offered Jolson stock, but he insisted on cash.

END OF THE JAZZ AGE

Perhaps the last significant film event of the Jazz Age occurred on October 6, 1927, at the Warner Theater in New York where *The Jazz Singer* dropped a bomb on the motion picture industry. It was not the best film of 1927. *The Jazz Singer* is not remembered for its theme (maudlin), relevance to the Jazz Age, or its acting (burlesqued pantomime). It was popular because of seven lip synchronization sequences: the jazz singer as a little boy; as a dinner club singer; at a performance of religious songs; at an informal chat and song session with his mama; at a rehearsal for a Broadway show; as a fill-in cantor for his father; and in the "Mammy" finale.

As *The Jazz Singer* marked the crossfade from visual to sound motion pictures, from pantomime to talk, so did the late twenties mark the transition from a brash young America, full of itself for having saved the world, to a country in a Great Depression.

Source: David A. Cook. *A History of Narrative Film.* New York: W.W. Norton & Company, 1981, p.240.

There were less than 300 spoken words in *The Jazz Singer,* and many of them were ad-libbed.[2] The plot was poor and the sound was harsh, but enthusiastic audience reaction to the film lifted Warner Brothers from being a company on the brink of economic disaster to a company that was worth almost $300 million in a few years.

In the first year of its existence (1927-28), the Academy of Motion Picture Arts and Sciences, ignoring *The Jazz Singer,* presented its awards to silent films. Best picture award went to Paramount's *Wings,* directed by William Wellman. The first best actor award went to Emil Jannings for two films, *The Way of All Flesh* and *The Last Command.* Jannings also had the distinction of being the first actor to be absent on presentation night. He collected his Oscar early, and left for Germany after the studio told him that his German accent would be unacceptable for talkies. He tried his voice in an English version of *The Blue Angel* starring Marlene Dietrich, but American audiences were not buying.

The last silent film in the United States was produced in 1931. Robert Flaherty, who had traveled to Hudson Bay for *Nanook,* was sent by Paramount to Tahiti to film *Tabu.* The father of the documentary refused to do a Hollywood story so the job was turned over to Fred Murnau who refused to take sound seriously. *Tabu* was released with title inserts and music track. Thus, Murnau, whose first American film, *Sunrise* (1927), won an Academy Award for Janet Gaynor, had the distinction of directing America's last silent film. It was also his final picture; he died in an automobile accident shortly after *Tabu* was released.

THE MUSICAL

During the Great Depression, Americans needed and sought out escapist entertainment. There is no question that Hollywood, in the interest of its own survival, avoided heavy themes, and although many theaters were forced to shut down, business was good for those that survived. The trouble-forgetting musical was a major reason for their survival. Hollywood swung into the Depression with MGM's *The Broadway Melody* (1928) and musicals have never stopped being produced since. *The Sound of Music* (1965), one of the most successful of all musicals, grossed one hundred million in its first release and did almost as well in its second release. The form continues to do well on television as the musical variety show.

This is the story of the block busting musical: a long, successful Broadway run; a successful road company; a big-selling album featuring the Broadway cast; hits from the show sung on television and in night clubs; recordings from the show made by popular singers. Once sound track recordings were technically perfected, they became billion dollar sellers on their own.

FIGURE 8-1 Fred Astaire. (Movie Star News)

FIGURE 8–2   A Busby Berkeley number. (Movie Star News)

RECORDS

The technologically improved sound of post-World War II records spawned a giant new industry, helped by radio, which pushed songs by stars like Bing Crosby and Frank Sinatra. Performers were cross-promoted in radio, films, and records, and made money from each.

Records really hit their stride with the arrival of rock 'n' roll, in the 1950s. First there was Elvis Presley, then the Beatles; records, a business that rivaled movies, had arrived. In 1974, Americans paid $1.7 billion at the movies, but they spent $500 million more than that on records and tapes. The $2.2 billion that Americans spent on rock records was more than three times what they spent on football, hockey, basketball, and baseball put together.[3]

BUSBY BERKELEY AND FRED ASTAIRE

A dance director from the New York Stage, Berkeley came to Hollywood to work for Samuel Goldwyn in 1930 but did not reveal his genius until he moved to Warner Brothers in 1933. There, as dance director for musicals like *42nd Street* (Lloyd Bacon, 1933), *Gold Digger of 1933*, (Mervyn LeRoy, 1933), *Footlight Parade* (Lloyd Bacon, 1933), *Dames* (Roy Enright, 1934), *Gold Diggers of 1935* (Busby Berkeley, 1935), *In Caliente* (Busby Berkeley, 1935), and *Gold Diggers of 1937* (Lloyd Bacon, 1937), he developed a flamboyant visual style which turned the production numbers of pedestrian backstage romances into surreal fantasies for the eye. Based upon the use of swooping aerial photography (or crane choreography), kaleidoscopic lenses, highly expressive camera movement, and sophisticated montage techniques, Berkeley's production numbers come closer to an experimental cinema of abstract impressionism than to anything in the traditional narrative film.

Fred Astaire, by contrast, achieved a much greater integration of music and dance with narrative in the series of RKO musicals in which he played opposite Ginger Rogers between 1933 (*Flying Down to Rio*, Thornton Freeland) and 1939 (*The Story of Vernon and Irene Castle*, H.C. Potter). Beginning as a performer, Astaire went on to direct and choreograph his dance sequences in *The Gay Divorcee* (Mark Sandrich, 1934), *Roberta* (William Seiter, 1935), *Top Hat* (Mark Sandrich, 1935), *Swing Time* (George Stevens, 1936), *Shall We Dance?* (Mark Sandrich, 1937), and *Carefree* (Mark Sandrich, 1938), and he developed a sophisticated but highly functional camera style in which the camera itself became a partner in the dance through both cutting and movement. Furthermore, Astaire's RKO musicals contributed significantly to the development of creative recording techniques through their rhythmic pairing of sound and image.

Source: David A. Cook. *A History of Narrative Film.* New York: W.W. Norton & Company, 1981, pp.259-260.

The record business of the fifties was dominated by a small number of major record companies who had the distribution systems to get the records to the retail market. But, these companies were initially hostile to rock 'n' roll, preferring the old dependables like Perry Como. Thus, rock spawned scores of new record companies that were willing to deal with the jungle beat. Many of these independents had already learned something about distributing records in the black "rhythm and blues" market, which the major record companies had abandoned during World War II because of materials shortages. Occasionally, the independents, even with weak distribution systems were able to move their unique product into the larger pop market without being at a competitive disadvantage.[4]

The recording revolution was on and the results were devastating for the established record companies. In 1955, of the fifty-one records that appeared on *Billboard's* top-ten charts, only eight were rock records from the independent companies. Two years later, the independents had forty records on the charts. The majors were in trouble, but seeing the errors of their ways, fought back and won because they were in control of the market and moved quickly. For instance, Warner Brothers Records bought Reprise and Atlantic and through a merger acquired Elektra. The new firm had enough wholesale volume to make establishing its own distribution system economically feasible. Other majors even formed music publishing firms and bought retail record outlets.

By distributing their own product, the majors eliminated the middleman and profits increased. The independents wanted to do the same thing, but they moved into the national market less frequently than the majors, so it was not practical for them. Distribution is profitable only with volume; therefore, the independents had to rely on a loose network of independent distributors. Companies with their own distribution systems could emphasize which product they chose, exposing new talent that would help keep them on top of the corporate heap. Thus, controlling distribution increased the majors' profits by cutting out the middleman and helped their future potential by developing new artists. The rich got richer, and the internationalization of rock that came with the Beatles only continued this trend. For example, EMI, the largest European music conglomerate, had the right to repackage Capitol's records in its native territories, and Capitol held the American rights to EMI's products. The chief effect of such agreements was to increase the sales of American products abroad.[5]

Solid Gold

A technological achievement also contributed to the term "solid gold" referring to a record that makes a million dollars. The 33-rpm record album was originally produced to support classical and jazz works, whose natural flow had been interrupted by record changes on the phonograph. But, its major financial effect was felt in the rock and pop segments of the industry, whose audiences also were willing to pay more for better quality and fewer record changes.

By 1974, Warner and CBS controlled over half of the domestic recording market. A few other major companies accounted for another 40 percent. They were so strong that only the heartiest, most specialized independents like Motown could survive. Superstars tried to establish their own labels to break the monopoly, but always failed. The Grateful Dead, for example, left Warner to strike out on their own. All the records they released on their own failed to do as well as those they had recorded with Warner Brothers. They gave up and signed with United Artists. Their very first album with United Artists sold as well as their Warner records. The majors' control of distribution was the secret.

Tapes and Cassettes

By the early 1980s, this world of solid gold was turned upside down. The super musician, who had replaced the cinema star in the Hollywood firmament, was in trouble. The cost of going on tour, which was necessary to push records and keep their names and sounds in front of the public, was going up and ticket sales were going down. The cost of an album was nine dollars or more, and a lot of listeners were turning to buying blank tapes and recording off the radio. Retailers were offsetting dwindling record sales by selling blank cassettes and video accessories. A study done by CBS Records found that the record industry was losing over $700 million in sales annually to home taping on blank cassettes. Add on at least another $400 million in records pirated, counterfeited, or otherwise diverted from normal channels every year, and there is a burden not even a vigorous industry like the $3.7 billion record industry can sustain very long.

There were about 30 million fewer records sold in 1980 than in 1973. In that same period, the number of blank cassettes sold more than doubled, to over 250 million. Home-taped copies of long playing records are made from borrowed records or from albums broadcast over the radio. Radio stations advertise the uninterrupted play of soon-to-be-released recordings and the home-taping enthusiasts tape the entire record on one side of a ninety minute cassette. Half of a high-quality tape costs about two dollars versus the nine dollar album. To make matters worse, the recorded cassettes marketed by most record companies are usually inferior in quality to the cassettes made by home tapers.

Airplay is essential to record sales, so record companies cannot simply cut back prereleases of new records to stations. Trying to convince disk jockies to stop the uninterrupted play of albums has not worked. The pinch is beginning to hurt. Early in 1980, the major record companies unexpectedly eliminated their traditionally liberal 100 percent return policy designed to encourage distributors and retailers to keep large inventories and replaced it with a strict credit line and a new 20 percent return policy. Stores suddenly found themselves stuck with millions of dollars worth of unsaleable, unreturnable inventories; hundreds of small independent distributors were driven out of business.

Price reductions on catalogue items began in 1980; price reductions will probably happen soon with new releases. So far, the big record companies have managed to stave off red ink, but the distributors and retailers are not waiting around for another "Saturday Night Fever" album. With record sales declining, they're looking for the next new wave in the leisure industry—videotapes, video discs, and electronic game cartridges. Like films that are more often seen today on a television screen than in a movie theater, music will find new forms in the 1980s, and the beat will go on.

In late August of 1982, Kenny Rogers, the country-pop superstar, signed a long-term worldwide recording contract with RCA Records. At

ROCK HITS THE HARD PLACE

The Thrill Is Gone—Is it Bad Business or Middle Age?

Is there hope? This week, the J. Geils Band has settled itself onto the sunny snowy peak of the *Billboard* chart. Score one for the good guys. J. Geils has managed to nudge off Foreigner, which on and off occupied the top slot for eleven weeks. Score eleven for the bad guys. And these days, in rock and in the record business, the bad guys are winning.

Rolling Stone, a magazine that was once the most prominent and articulate forum for rock culture, divests itself of much of its music coverage and aims for a more general readership today. Record companies have cut back on corporate extravagances and are making a little money, mostly by kicking up prices. Punk is dead, New Wave is over, Disco moved out when your older sister left home. The Clash can't swing a major hit single, so its albums don't get high on the charts, and does anyone know there's a great new record by a great new group called the Blasters? Is anyone listening? Does anyone care?

The places to start looking for rock's real trouble are the ones that used to be the sources of its renewal: radio and records. What sells is what the radio plays, but the radio plays only what sells and, often, what sells out. Styx, Foreigner, AC/DC, Journey, REO are variously typical of what Columbia Records Executive Peter Philbin calls a "Madison Avenue approach to rock 'n' roll," a cunningly anonymous cruise down the mainstream. Telling any of these groups apart is like passing the Pepsi challenge: Even if you see any difference between them, what possible difference does it make?

"Record sales are flat," says an industry executive. "Everybody is making a nickel or a dime, but nobody is making millions."

For the first time, under the regency of radio programmers and the tyranny of marketing studies and demographics, rock 'n' roll has been successfully factionalized and fractionalized, smashed into a mass of splinters with few sharp edges.

The cultural fragmentation of rock is a melancholy sight for anyone who grew up with the magic waveband synthesis of Elvis Presley and Buddy Holly, Chuck Berry and Jackie Wilson, the Coasters and the Drifters, on through the Beatles and down to Creedence.

Source: Jay Cocks, *Time*, February 15, 1982, pp. 68-69.

a time when the industry was in a serious recession, the deal was reportedly the largest ever offered to a single act, in excess of $20 million. The deal was RCA's second major signing within a year. They wooed Diana Ross away from Motown in the fall of 1981, a deal interpreted by many in the industry as a signal that RCA, after a decade of lagging sales and many changes in management, was going to take on Warner Communications labels and CBS, the industry's two reigning giants.[6]

In the past, multimillion-dollar deals like the one for Mr. Rogers were often made for their prestige, rather than for expectations of huge profits. CBS, it is said, will be fortunate to break even on its eight-figure contract with Paul McCartney. Atlantic Records did not expect to break even on its comparably generous deal with the Rolling Stones until the sales of the "Some Girls" album surpassed all expectations. Every major label can point to its share of multimillion-dollar mistakes—RCA to Harry Nilsson and CBS to Stephen Stills and Chicago.[7]

RCA—GAMBLING ON KENNY ROGERS

When the recession struck the record business in 1979, RCA which had languished as the "sleeping giant" among major labels in the 70s was beginning to show new signs of health under the direction of president, Robert Summer. The floundering career of Daryl Hall and John Oates was resuscitated with a string of hit singles, and Rick Springfield and Alabama were developed into Platinum, or million-unit sellers.

The black oriented West Coast label Solar, now distributed by Elektra, scored with three best-selling groups—Shalamar, the Whispers and Lakeside. Diana Ross's debut on the label, "Why Do Fools Fall in Love?" sold Platinum.

The label's semi-autonomous Nashville division, which had always been profitable, continued to prosper with successful records by Waylon Jennings, Dolly Parton and Ronnie Milsap. Recently the novelty records "Hooked on Classics" and "Hooked on Swing" have done well.

No wonder RCA waxes optimistic about the Rogers signing. Mr. Summer says there is a huge untapped international market for Kenny Rogers, particularly in Australia, Germany, Japan and South America. But what if Rogers's audience shrinks? This is what happened to John Denver, Elton John and Barry Manilow in the 70s. Although all three still sell in the hundred of thousands and are huge concert attractions, the span of multiplatinum success for each lasted only about five years before there were precipitous dropoffs. Mr. Roger's streak began in 1978 with "The Gambler," which sold 4 million copies, is in its fourth year. After peaking with "Greatest Hits" (12 million sold worldwide and 9 million domestically), Mr. Rogers's next album, "Share Your Love," sold only 2 million domestically. Has Rogers already peaked? RCA is gambling otherwise.

Source: *New York Times*, July 28, 1982, p. C19.

Sound Waves of Tomorrow

■ New technologies in sound will produce better sound recordings for records and movies (digital recordings); the same can happen with television if audiences demand it. In the area of radio, FM will continue to be preferred by discriminating audiences.

■ The record business, which outgrew the movie business in the '70s, but hit a slump in the early '80s, may see a turnaround with the end of the recession. However, a new creative surge, a new sound as exciting as rock was at its beginning, will probably be required for major growth.

■ Records with moving pictures (video cassettes or records) have become a reality with great potential. There has been a mad rush to produce these "visual" records for cable and pay television. The industry hopes that, with more and more consumers owning video players, this will be the record of the future. Perhaps it will also replace the movie theater musical which has not been successful in recent years, as shown by *Pennies From Heaven* and *Annie*.

ADDITIONAL READINGS

McVay, Douglas. *The Musical Film*. Cranbury, N.J.: A.S. Barnes, 1967.

Sterne, Lee E. *The Movie Musical*. New York: Pyramid Publications, 1974.

Taylor, John Russell and Jackson, Arthur. *The Hollywood Musical*. New York: McGraw-Hill, 1971.

Vallance, Tom. *The American Musical*. Cranbury, N. J.: A. S. Barnes, 1970.

FOOTNOTES

1. Gerald Mast, *A Short History of the Movies* (New York: Pegasus, 1971), p. 26.

2. Ibid., p. 228.

3. Geoffrey Stokes, *Starmaking Machinery* (New York: Vintage Press, 1977), p. 4.

4. Ibid., p. 5.

5. Ibid., p. 7.

6. *The New York Times*, July 28, 1982, p. C19.

7. Ibid.

HOLLYWOOD: BUSINESS AND CENSORSHIP

Motion picture manufacturing in the United States was developed and controlled by businessmen, not artists. Motion pictures were products to be manufactured. Censorship, in the form of public protest, led to self-regulation only when profits were in danger.

The success of motion pictures brought competition, and Edison and his associates held most of the United States patents on motion picture equipment. They were furious that producers were buying their equipment from foreign companies to avoid paying fees to Edison. To stop the independents, Edison and other companies manufacturing motion picture equipment formed the Motion Picture Patents Company, whose sole purpose was to force producers to use the company's equipment. Most producers were unwilling to do this.

One of the independents who refused to pay was tough Carl Laemmle and his Independent Moving Picture Company,[1] which pirated Florence Lawrence, "The Biograph Girl," away from Biograph. He gave her a lot of publicity in 1910 and in doing so created the first film star. Prior to Lawrence, film actors and actresses worked anonymously. They were not identified on billboards or on the screen. By 1913, Laemmle's company had become Universal Pictures and the star system was firmly in place with stars like Mary Pickford. Actors became celebrities who were expected to promote and carry the picture.

The clash between Edison's Patent Company and the independents grew vicious.[2] To avoid lawsuits and find exciting locations and sun, many independents, including Laemmle, fled the East for a village near Los Angeles named Hollywood.

The Patents Company was dead by 1914, but a few eastern locations continued to attract producers. One of them was Ithaca, New York,

sidebar

AUDIENCE CENSOR-
SHIP?

The first thirteen-hour edition of *Intolerance* later was shortened to three-and-a-half hours and finally to two hours and fifty minutes. Not only did it fail to erase Griffith's reputation as a bigot, it bombed at the box office. So, still bothered by the racist tag, Griffith tried hard to apologize in his *Hearts of the World* (1918). In a death scene on a World War I battleground, he had a white soldier kiss a dying Black soldier who was crying for his mother. In 1919, Griffith, Charles Chaplin, Mary Pickford, and Douglas Fairbanks formed the United Artists Corporation. It was set up as a distribution/exhibition company. Each partner produced on her or his own. That was the year that Griffith made his last well-received film, *Broken Blossoms*, starring Richard Barthelmess and Lillian Gish. His film life and his personal life deteriorated quickly after that.

Source: Gerald Mast. *A Short History of the Movies.* New York: Pegasus, 1971, p. 127.

favored by serial producers for its natural, rugged beauty. A popular serial shot there in 1914 and 1915 was "The Exploits of Elaine."

EARLY MOVIE PRODUCERS

Although motion pictures were controlled by businessmen, from time to time a creative force like D.W. Griffith or Orson Welles had a great deal of power. However, their power was short-lived. Often the search for artistry would lead to overextended budgets, which in turn would revert to eventual control by the businessmen.

David Wark Griffith

In 1913, D.W. Griffith joined the Majestic/Reliance/Mutual film company at $300 per week, stock in the company, and a 50 percent interest in two films of his choice each year. In 1914, he started *The Clansman*, based on several novels by southern preacher Thomas Dixon. At its Los Angeles premiere the film's name became *The Birth of a Nation*, the story of the Civil War and Reconstruction as told from a southern point of view. At $110,000[3] *The Birth of a Nation* was an expensive film for its time. One reason the cost was so high was Griffith's inclination for the realistic and the spectacular. He used 1864 vintage cannons and mortars, an artillery train, a baggage train and 16,000 extras as soldiers. Billy Bitzer, the cameraman, shot 150,000 feet of film. *Birth of a Nation*, however, has paid its way, earning in excess of $20 million.[4] It is also one of the most controversial films ever made because of its negative treatment of Black people and its positive treatment of the Ku Klux Klan. Griffith was stung by criticism of the film and reacted by filming a *Plea for Tolerance* (1916). This epic film, whose name was shortened to *Intolerance,* cost $1.9 million, consumed 300,000 feet of film, used 60,000 players, and had a set of the city of Babylon that was so huge that an army of extras marched on its walls.

The high cost of a Griffith film gave rise to a new necessity in the motion picture field—money. Earlier films had been produced on low budgets with money provided by backers who were relatively unconcerned if one film failed, because others would surely succeed. But the $2 million Griffith projects required careful financial planning. After Griffith, bankers and financiers had to be satisfied that film projects would be successful. What was needed in Hollywood was a business manager of films.

Thomas Ince

This need was satisfied by Thomas Ince, who, when he became more interested in managing the production of films than in directing, became a film producer. He began his career as an actor-director at

American Biograph in 1910 and established "Inceville" (1912), which he built into the first "modern" Hollywood studio, complete with five self-contained shooting stages, in the Santa Ynez canyon. Ince's practice was to set up a number of production units on his lot, each headed by a director. Before Ince would approve a film, he required a script that satisfied him; there would be no more shooting from just an idea. Only after he had a solid script would Ince assign a director to film the story—in exactly the form it appeared in the script. During production, Ince remained involved. He made sure that actors, props, and all equipment were available on schedule.

Perhaps more than anyone else, Ince turned film production into a business. His methods were adopted by the large studios after his death in the early 1920s. In fact, MGM was created largely from Ince's property.

PROBLEMS OF EARLY FILM MANUFACTURERS

Competition and high costs were not the only worries of the early film manufacturers. Another was the nitrate film stock they used. It was made of nitrocellulose, the same substance used to manufacture gun powder. This material was so chemically unstable and highly flammable that it could even burn under water. Another drawback was its tendency to disintegrate quickly. Because of this self-destructive quality, approximately 50 percent of all films produced in the United States before 1950 have decomposed. Not until 1952, when the film industry accepted Eastman Kodak's acetate stock, did the disintegration of America's black and white film heritage stop. Today, the problem is color. Films shot in technicolor, like *Gone With the Wind*, are losing their original saturation and richness.

Mack Sennett

What Griffith was to drama, Mack Sennett was to comedy. In fact, they both started at Biograph at about the same time. People with talent moved up quickly in those days. Sennett, a former plumber's assistant, came to Biograph in 1909, and by 1911 was head of Majestic's Keystone Company.

Sennett's comics included Chester Conklin, Mabel Normand, Ford Sterling—chief of the Keystone Cops—Ben Turpin, Charlie Chase, and Roscoe Arbuckle. Gloria Swanson debuted for Essanay in 1915, slapsticked for Sennett in 1916, and then worked her way into drama with Cecil B. DeMille, Raoul Walsh, and Erich Von Stroheim. Harold Lloyd worked for a time with Sennett, but did most of his work with Hal Roach. Lloyd, a prolific comic who did nearly 100 films in two years, often appeared as a bumbling character or simulated a human fly.

CHARLIE CHAPLIN

Charlie Chaplin's character, the runt, sometimes the tramp, but always the man on the bottom, captivated audiences during the best years of the silent film. Never perfect, but always ready to protect the weak from those worse than himself, Chaplin was able to develop his character a great deal in his films. *The Tramp* typifies Chaplin's acting. In the tramp's travels, he chances upon a pretty woman being molested by meaner tramps and Charlie jumps in to protect her. His bravery results in a job on the farm of the young woman's parents where Charlie prevents the tramps from robbing the family. But all of his valiant fighting does not win the heart of the young woman, for her wealthy boyfriend returns and Charlie is a broke tramp once again.

Chaplin's films found him playing roles like an immigrant to the United States, a prospector, and a reformed sinner at a mission. In almost every film, Chaplin was somehow on the bottom trying to make good, and he sometimes did.

Source: Peter Klinge and Lee McConkey. *Introduction to Film Structure*. Washington, D.C.: University Press of America, 1982.

Charlie Chaplin

Charlie Chaplin came from Great Britain in 1910 with the Fred Karno Pantomine and Musical Comedy Company to tour the United States for three years. In 1913, he signed with Keystone for $150 a week. During thirty-five films with Keystone, Chaplin developed his famous underdog character. Chaplin, a small man, was physically well adapted to be on the losing side of every situation—the original film underdog.

In 1915, Chaplin signed with Essanay for $1,250 per week. Although he stayed with Essanay only a year, it was here that his tramp character blossomed and that Chaplin found the leading lady who would star with him in thirty-five pictures over the next nine years—Edna Purviance. She always played a pure, kind individual who perceived the redeeming characteristics buried within Chaplin.

Mutual offered Chaplin $670,000 a year in 1916, a deal that was topped in 1917 by First National's $1 million, eight-picture contract; but it was at Mutual that Chaplin made *Easy Street,* one of his better known tramp films. He did nine films at First National, one of which was *The Kid* with Jackie Coogan.

Chaplin helped form United Artists with Griffith, Pickford, and Fairbanks in 1919. By 1922, free of his other contractual commitments, Chaplin began working for the partnership. One of his best films for them was *The Gold Rush* (1924). He got the idea for the picture while looking at stereoscopic pictures of Alaska and the Klondike. The basic comic situations in *The Gold Rush* are built on hunger and cannibalism. Charlie is threatened with death by starvation or cold, with getting eaten or shot. The comic element here is deeply rooted in the terrifying. The shoe-eating sequence was inspired by a documentary account of the Donner Pass crossing. Chaplin's version of the great Yukon gold rush is a story of dire need. Greed for gold motivates others, but Charlie is looking for food, shelter, warmth, and human affection. The film took about fourteen months to make, cost about a $1 million and grossed $6 million.[6]

McCARTHY CENSORSHIP

Chaplin's last significant American film was *The Great Dictator* (1940). It received Academy Award nominations for best picture, best actor, best screenplay, and best supporting actor. The announcement of each nomination was booed, and none of these awards were won by Chaplin, because it was rumored that he was anti-American, and a Communist. Chaplin, angered by the personal attacks, rejected the New York Film Critics Award, but in the *New York Times* critic Bosley Crowther described the picture as "a truly superb accomplishment of a truly great artist—perhaps the most significant film ever produced."

Chaplin was barred from the United States in 1952, at the height of Senator Joseph McCarthy's anti-Communist purge. Chaplin said at the hearings, "I am not a Communist—I have no political persuasions whatsoever. My patriotism has never been to one country, one class, but to the whole world." In April, 1972, at the age of eight-three, after twenty years of exile, the United States and the film industry finally honored Charles Chaplin with a special Oscar in recognition of his great contributions to the art of film.

Source: Gerald Mast. *A Short History of the Movies.* New York: Pegasus, 1971.

Buster Keaton

Like Chaplin, Keaton was raised in vaudeville by his parents. When the family act broke up in 1917, the twenty-one-year-old was already a star, but he joined "Fatty" Arbuckle's Comique Studios as a supporting player rather than taking a starring role in the theater. Between 1917 and 1919, Keaton made fourteen two-reel shorts with Arbuckle.

Unlike Chaplin, Keaton did not play the same character over and over again, but the narrative situation in which his characters find themselves was always pretty much the same—a vulnerable but plucky human hero, as in *The Navigator,* is confronted with some vast and seemingly insurmountable problems, usually involving objects and machines rather than other humans. It is a classical absurdist situation, and the comic effect arises from the hero's spiritual but futile attempts to surmount the insurmountable, at which he ultimately—and for totally arbitrary reasons—somehow succeeds. Remarkably, Keaton never once repeated a narrative formula in his entire life.[7]

Unlike Sennett and his many imitators, much of Keaton's excellence stemmed from a strict adherence to the dramatic logic of his narratives and the use of gags that progressed according to the dictates of character and story.

In retrospect, he became an experimentalist. In *Sherlock Junior* (1924), Keaton plays a projectionist in a neighborhood theater who is accused of theft by his girlfriend's father. He falls asleep at work, slides down the projection beam, and enters the screen to become part of the action. The picture does not want to accept him at first, but once it does, he is able to solve the false charges against him as Sherlock Junior. He awakens to his girlfriend's embrace in the projection room. This and other films of Keaton's were widely admired by the European avant-garde: dadaists, surrealists, and absurdists.

In 1919, Joseph Schenck formed Buster Keaton Productions to manufacture two-reel shorts and acquired the former Chaplin studios for this purpose. Schenck handled all of the financing, but gave Keaton complete creative control in writing and directing, at a salary of $1,000 per week plus 25 percent of the profits. The resulting twenty Keaton shorts made between 1920 and 1923 represent, along with Chaplin's Mutual films, the high point of American slapstick comedy.[8]

In 1928, Keaton allowed his company to be absorbed by MGM with the promise that Joseph Schenck's brother, Nicholas, the newly installed president of Loew's Incorporated and the controller of MGM, would allow him to continue his creative mode of production. However, this was not realistic within the factory system of the world's largest film manufacturer. Although Keaton made several important films at MGM, including *The Cameraman* (1928), he began drinking and was eventually fired just as the sound era began. There is no question that Keaton's talent could have survived and even profited from the conversion to sound.[9]

THE CONVERSION TO SOUND

The introduction of *The Jazz Singer* in 1927 revolutionized the movie business. The film studios that were growing in Hollywood—MGM, Warner Brothers, United Artists—were changed forever. Still more money was needed to finance sound equipment, to build sound studios, to pay for the technicians to run the equipment, and to finance the actors with the beautiful voices. The movie barons had to rely more and more on banks, insurance companies, and Wall Street.

The deals were made, and the capitalists gained more and more control of the studios, but no one seemed to care at the time. This was the golden age of moving pictures. By the mid-1930s, people were streaming to the movie theaters whether the pictures were good or bad. They bought movie tickets in huge quantities—8 million a week in 1938. So popular were the movies of the day that all of the studios had to constantly produce at full steam to keep up with the demand. This was the

Depression. Audiences did not have much money, but by comparison, movies were very cheap entertainment. Audiences could forget their problems in ornate movie palaces built to complete the illusion, theaters that also cost a lot of money.

As their investments in equipment rose, the studios' need to keep the machines running became more and more important. Idle equipment was unproductive money and could not be tolerated. To keep the equipment rolling and to cut down on the cost of production, the studios conceived a two-layer system of making movies—the A and B movies.

Big budget, big name talent movies were called A movies. Into these productions the studios poured their largest sums of money, their best scripts, their best actors, and their biggest sets. Nothing was spared in making an A movie, and the audiences loved them.

Then there were the B movies: they got less money, unknown talent, inexperienced crews, and smaller sets. B movies became the training ground for new faces and mechanics. Out of the B sets came the A actors of later years. More importantly, B movies made it possible for the movie barons to keep the studios working most of the time. Their investment was working and earning money.

Why should viewers go to B movies when there were A films to be seen? Or more importantly, why would a theater manager risk a B picture on his theater's audience? Actually, the theater owner had little choice. Hollywood marketed its films by "blocks." For a price, a theater owner received a package of twenty-five or more films. About a third of these movies were A quality and the remainder were Bs. The studios simply did not sell A movies by themselves, so theater owners received a mixture or none at all.

Not satisfied that block booking would bring in enough income, the studios themselves purchased movie houses all over the nation. In time, the major studios owned all or most of the theaters in many cities. They were more easily able to dictate to their own movie houses which films to screen.

THE MOVIE MOGULS

As the United States hit the peak of the roaring twenties, the movies reached a pinnacle as well. They became one of the major industries of the country, right alongside the steel and automobile industries. The men who ran the major studios were moguls, courted by presidents and kings.

Louis B. Mayer

Louis B. Mayer, [10] vice-president and general manager of Metro-Goldwyn-Mayer for a quarter of a century (1924-1949), has been described as violent, stubborn, arrogant, rude, unmerciful, ruthless, senti-

FIGURE 9-1 Louis B. Mayer. (Movie Star News)

mental, spiteful, avaricious, pretentious, lustful, petty, savage, charming, and sincere. To actor Bill Haines, Louis B. Mayer was "a dyed in the wool sonofabitch, a liar, a cheat—despicable." To director Clarence Brown, Mayer was "the second coming of Christ." But few would dispute his reputation as one of the greatest packagers of film. He bought an eleven-acre Culver City studio in 1918, and throughout the twenties, thirties, and forties, he developed the MGM kingdom into the most powerful in film history.

Mayer used to say that the motion picture industry was the only one whose leading assets walked out of the gates at night. Through his MGM Culver City gates walked the greatest assemblage of stars of all time: Jeanette MacDonald, Nelson Eddy, Robert Taylor, Greta Garbo, Judy Garland, Norma Shearer, Joan Crawford, Jean Harlow, Elizabeth Taylor, John Gilbert, John Barrymore, Lionel Barrymore, Jackie Cooper, Wallace Berry, Spencer Tracy, Katharine Hepburn, Jimmy Stewart, Carole Lombard, William Powell, Kay Francis, Frank Sinatra, Gene Kelly, Mickey Rooney, and Clark Gable.

Mayer was born in Russia in 1885. His father, Jacob, became a junk collector in New Brunswick, Canada. Louis recalled gathering junk in his early years, and being taunted and teased by the other children. Junk salvaging led to ship salvaging, scrap metal sales led Louis to Boston. He arbitrarily picked the letter B as a middle initial and, patriotically, the fourth of July as his birthday. In 1907, Mayer bought a small theater in Haverhill, Massachusetts, followed by a new 1,600-seat theater in 1911. In 1915 he made $250,000 (some say $500,000), by securing the New England distribution rights to *The Birth of a Nation*.

Mayer went to California in 1918. In 1923 the Goldwyn Company consolidated with the old Metro Company to form Metro-Goldwyn. A year later Mayer became vice-president and general manager of the new company, Metro-Goldwyn-Mayer. At this point Sam Goldwyn withdrew to become an independent producer. He left only two things with MGM. One was his name, and only half of that was his; in 1916 Samuel Goldfish and Edward Selwyn had merged resources and names to form Goldwyn Pictures. The second thing Goldwyn left the new company was director Erich Von Stroheim,[11] who in 1923 was already filming *Greed*.

Actually, by the time Goldwyn left, the studio already thought Von Stroheim was over his head and certainly over budget. Perhaps that's why Goldwyn walked away with a smile on his face. Stroheim was attempting to shoot Frank Norris's novel *McTeague*, one sentence at a time. The original budget was a faint memory. Von Stroheim had learned extravagance from Griffith and he had learned it well. The final film was more than fifty reels—that's about eight hours of running time. He cut the picture to twenty-four reels, but Irving Thalberg,[12] MGM's gifted production supervisor, brought in scenarist June Mathis, who cut the show to two hours by substituting title cards for literally hours of footage. Thalberg destroyed the leftover film so Stroheim could not get his hands on it. Audiences actively disliked the movie and laughed at Zasu Pitts, who could not seem to break out of her comedienne personnae; but critics assigned *Greed*, even in its butchered version, a place in silent feature classic heaven.

Von Stroheim[13] produced *The Wedding March* (1928) for Paramount, part of which was filmed in a two-color technicolor process. It was a common practice in the early days of color experimentation to include a color interlude in an otherwise black and white film. It was not until the mid-thirties that directors shot feature films completely in color, however. *The Wedding March* was so long that Paramount had it cut in half; the first part ran fourteen reels, but Stroheim refused to permit the ten reels of the second half to be released in the United States. It was released in Europe as *The Honeymoon.*

Von Stroheim turned to acting and exiled himself in Europe. He returned in 1950 to be in Billy Wilder's *Sunset Boulevard* with Gloria Swanson and William Holden. The movie marked a comeback attempt on the part of silent screen star Swanson, whose first screen credit was in 1915. Billy Wilder congratulated Von Stroheim on his past films, "Von, you were always ten years ahead of your time." "Twenty," replied an unchastened Von Stroheim.

Sam Goldwyn left Mayer with another great problem. *Ben Hur* had been filming in Europe under the direction of George Walsh, and it was dragging. Mayer pulled the production back to the United States, scrapped most of the European footage and put director Fred Niblo in charge. In spite of Mayer's dramatic moves, *Ben Hur* ran up a phenomenal $6 million cost—and it was a silent film.

While Mayer was in Europe to cut off *Ben Hur* production, he stopped in Berlin to sign Swedish director Mauritz Stiller. Stiller refused to sign unless one of his actresses also was given a contract. Mayer was unimpressed by the shy, plump Greta Garbo, but offered her a three-year contract at $350 a week just to get the Swedish director. Garbo quickly caught fire in America. At the end of two years she demanded $5,000 per week. Mayer countered with $2,500. Garbo said, "I think I go home." She sat in her hotel room for seven months until Mayer capitulated. Mayer and Garbo never hit it off. Twice he came to the set to watch her and twice she refused to continue until he left.

Irving Thalberg

Irving Thalberg (1899-1936) and Mayer had a love-hate relationship, but Mayer deferred judgment to this thin, nervous right-hand man. Thalberg had a sixth sense about script material, knowing instinctively whether it would please the public. He could carry every detail of half a dozen productions in his head and hold three or four story conferences simultaneously. Mayer was both pleased and jealous of Thalberg's success. Without Thalberg, Mayer would not have produced more than 1,000 features between 1924 and 1949. Mayer was a ruthless businessman with little concern for the quality of art or entertainment; while Thalberg, the young production manager, maintained a consistently high level of achievement in MGM films until his early death.

sidebar

VON STROHEIM FIRED

Thalberg had the distinction of firing Von Stroheim twice. The first time both were at Universal where Von Stroheim's *Foolish Wives* (1921) had to be censored, which shortened it to two-thirds of its intended length. The picture that finished him, however, was *The Merry Widow* (1925) in which Von Stroheim's passion for authenticity showed up in such extravagances as providing silken underwear marked with a coat of arms for the soldiers and paying $10,000 for decorative medals.

Source: Jack C. Ellis. *A History of Film.* Englewood Cliffs, N.J.: Prentice-Hall, 1979.

TANGLES WITH ACTORS

In 1937, Louis B. Mayer's annual income was $1,296,503, and he was a hard-nosed businessman. But when Robert Taylor asked for a raise, Mayer demonstrated another side of his character. The MGM chief was an outrageous ham actor; to win an argument he would threaten, cajole, insult, bribe, flatter, even cry. The secretaries heard Taylor's loud voice followed by Mayer's persuasive tones. After a long interval, Taylor walked out misty eyed. "Did you get the raise?" asked a secretary. "No," said Taylor. "But I gained a father." In another instance, Mayer asked Buster Keaton to come to the studio on Saturday and run through some scenes for a group of visiting teachers. Keaton said no and Mayer asked again. The stone-faced comedian refused. On Monday Mayer fired him. On another occasion Mayer tangled with Chaplin. A Los Angeles newspaper described the fight: "Charles Chaplin entered wearing gray flannel and weighing 126. Louis B. Mayer entered wearing navy blue serge and weighing 168. Chaplin led with a remark to Mayer. Mayer countered with a crack. Mayer then led with his right and missed. Chaplin swung with his left and missed. Both fell down. The decision: a double technical knockout."

Source: Jack C. Ellis. *A History of Film.* Englewood Cliffs, N.J.: Prentice-Hall, 1979.

David O. Selznick

Mayer's son-in-law David O. Selznick[14] was practically born into the film industry. His father, Lewis, owned the World Film Company. From him, David and his older brother, Myron, learned distribution, merchandising, advertising, and finance. His first production opportunity was an assignment on a Tim McCoy western at MGM in 1926. Selznick capitalized on what might have been a dead-end experience by sending director Woody Van Dyke out with McCoy, two scripts, and two leading ladies. In effect, Selznick and Van Dyke made two pictures at the same time for about the price of one.

FIGURE 9–2 David O. Selznick. (Movie Star News)

In some respects Selznick was like Mayer. He was never considered a nice guy. He was characterized as overbearing, egocentric, aggressive, exhausting, and impossible. After two years at MGM, Selznick was fired by Irving Thalberg for fighting Hunt Stromberg's decision to send Woody Van Dyke and a Hollywood script along with Robert Flaherty to film *White Shadows in the South Seas.* Flaherty soon quit, leaving Van Dyke to complete the project.

Selznick went to Paramount (1928–31) where he worked on what was becoming an assembly line method of manufacturing movies. Although he would work for other studios, including another stint at MGM, Selznick hit his stride when he formed his own independent producing company, Selznick International, in 1935 employing United Artists as his distribution company.

With his obsession for detail work, Selznick got involved in every phase of each production beginning with story purchase, script writing, casting, costuming, set decoration, sound recording, and publicity. He was not above telling Marlene Dietrich that she was just about washed up as a star, but that he could be her salvation. Selznick would fire directors at the drop of a hat. He used three different directors to get the effect he demanded on *The Prisoner of Zenda,* which starred Ronald Colman and Madeleine Carroll. John Cromwell received directorial credit, but Woody Van Dyke directed the fencing scenes, and George Cukor directed just one scene, in which Madeleine Carroll's acting was critical. Selznick told Alfred Hitchcock, whom he brought to America to direct *Rebecca,* that the script treatment prepared under Hitchcock's supervision was distorted, vulgar, and cheap. When production began, he found Hitchcock's direction unacceptably slow. In later years, Hitchcock recalled the first lengthy memorandum he received from Selznick. With characteristic tongue-in-cheek humor, Hitchcock said that he started to read the memo in 1939, but hadn't quite finished it yet.

Even if Selznick had accomplished nothing else, his classic film, *Gone with the Wind* would stand as a monument to his creative drive and genius. He bought the screen rights to Margaret Mitchell's novel in 1936 for $50,000. The film cost $4.25 million to produce and when completed in 1939, won ten Oscars. It has been released six times and has grossed $177 million in the United States and Canada alone. It is now on 70mm film and has stereophonic sound.

MGM gave Selznick $1,250,000 and loaned him Clark Gable for Rhett Butler in return for the distribution rights and 50 percent of *Gone with the Wind*'s profits. Perhaps Mayer was thinking of twenty years earlier when another Civil War film, *The Birth of a Nation,* had earned him enough money to start production in Hollywood. Although Paulette Goddard had been a strong contender for the role, actress Vivian Leigh was finally signed to play Scarlett. Selznick received maximum publicity for his film by spending a year testing nearly every actress and nonactress on two continents. Olivia de Havilland was selected to play the second female lead, Melanie, and Leslie Howard was signed to play Ashley.

Essentially, the story was a love triangle surrounded by the Civil War. Scarlett yearned for the unattainable Ashley, while Rhett Butler managed to marry Scarlett O'Hara but never won her love. Shooting started on the back lot of Selznick's studio in December, 1938. Doubles were used for Gable and Leigh. In fact, Leigh had not been signed yet, when production began. They shot the burning of Atlanta first so they could build other exterior sets. For the fire, they used old sets with false fronts and profiles to simulate the Atlanta of Civil War days.

Selznick had director problems, too. George Cukor was at his best directing women, but Selznick did not like the way he was handling the action scenes in *Gone with the Wind.* He was taken off the picture and did not receive any directorial credit when the picture premiered

WHO WIELDS THE POWER IN HOLLYWOOD?

Directors Are Fighting Studios

Spiraling production costs, a slump at the box office, and, in some quarters, disillusionment with the wunderkind school of filmmaking, are causing strains these days in the economic-creative partnership that makes Hollywood run.

Francis Ford Coppola, the Oscar-winning director whose two *Godfather* movies are considered classics by some film historians, says again he may be facing bankruptcy and blames his problems on the fact that "the studios," not creative people control the movies.

Peter Bogdanovich, another prize-winning director, was forced to distribute his latest movie, *They All Laughed,* to theaters himself because he couldn't interest one of the major film studios to do so on acceptable terms.

And another celebrated director, Robert Altman, says that he can't even get studio executives to return his telephone calls.

Other filmmakers tell comparable stories. "It seems they want to say 'no,' whatever you ask," one disheartened screenwriter said recently after coming from a studio production meeting.

Studio executives acknowledge that they are saying "no" more often. But they blame their hesitation on the soaring cost of making and marketing movies, high interest rates and the profligacy of some directors recently as well as lackluster response to many of the movies they've made recently. "I think people are being very cautious," said Alan Ladd Jr., the former 20th Century-Fox executive who now heads his own company.

Mike Medavoy, the head of production at Orion Pictures, said things are likely to remain that way for a while, especially in trying to keep directors within their budgets. "I think people (at the studios) are going to get tougher," he said.

Like many other executives, Mr. Medavoy says he doesn't think much of Mr. Coppola's claim that it's unfair that filmmakers are beholden to the money men at the studios.

"The creative people have to be responsible not only to their craft, but to those people who make it possible for them to practice their craft," he said.

Source: Robert Lindsay. *The New York Times,* February 14, 1982, p. D1.

in Atlanta in December, 1939, and went on to become one of the top grossers in motion picture history.

Selznick dissolved his International organization after *Rebecca* (1940), but immediately formed David O. Selznick Productions. That company's first release was *Since You Went Away* (1944) starring Selznick's wife-to-be, Jennifer Jones. In 1945, he filmed *Spellbound,* his second film with Alfred Hitchcock. Then came *Duel in the Sun* with veterans Lillian Gish and Walter Huston. *Duel in the Sun* was directed by King Vidor. Vidor quit after some Selznick meddling on the set and William Dieterle finished the picture, but the Screen Director's Guild awarded all directorial credit to Vidor. Finally, there was *A Portrait of Jennie* (1948) and a few co-productions in the 1950s, like *A Farewell to Arms.* But Selznick had reached his peak when he made *Gone with the Wind* at the age of 37. He died of a heart attack in 1965 at the age of 63.

FIGURE 9–3 Orson Welles. (Movie Star News)

Orson Welles

Business and art do not always mix. Orson Welles[15] was born in Wisconsin in 1915 to a wealthy inventor father and a pianist mother. Welles was a child prodigy. At age twenty-two he formed the Mercury Theater. His radio players included Joseph Cotton, Everett Sloan, and Agnes Moorehead. The Mercury Theater Company frightened the wits out of people in the eastern half of the United States with its Halloween broadcast, "War of the Worlds," in the nervous pre-World War II year of 1938. Produced like a newscast, the show reported the invasion of the world from outer space. Phone lines at the studio were immediately jammed with calls asking for more information. Overnight, Orson Welles was a celebrity.

In 1939, at age twenty-four, Welles was given a contract with RKO Radio Pictures, which was in receivership. Stockholders Nelson Rockefeller and David Sarnoff first hired George Schaffer as president and then persuaded him to hire Orson Welles to save the company from bankruptcy. The sixty-page contract gave RKO script approval but gave Welles control over the final cut.

Early in 1940, Welles got writer Herman J. Mankiewicz to hole up in the Campbell Playhouse's Victorville, California, guest ranch for thirteen weeks. Mankiewicz was an accident-prone alcoholic. With him at the ranch were John Houseman, co-founder of the Mercury Theater Group, a nurse, and a secretary named Susan Alexander.

The script that came out of that thirteen-week confinement was first called *American,* then *John Citizen, USA,* and finally, *Citizen Kane.* The film was patterned on the life of William Randolph Hearst, owner of a media empire. Susan Alexander Kane was patterned after Hearst's mistress, Marion Davies, for whom Hearst built San Simeon and established the film production company Cosmopolitan. In real life, of course, Susan Alexander was the secretary to whom Mankiewicz dictated the script. Mankiewicz was a good man for the job: He had a background in journalism and had been a frequent house guest of Hearst and Davies.

Welles gave himself a crash course in film technique by studying the films of René Clair, King Vidor, Frank Capra, John Ford, and Fritz Lang. In her 1971 study *Raising Kane,* film critic Pauline Kael established a relationship between *Citizen Kane* and the German school of expressionism. Her line of development went like this: Robert Wiene made *The Cabinet of Dr. Caligari* in 1919. In 1924, German director

Fred Murnau used cinematographer Karl Freund and actor Emil Jan-
nings on *The Last Laugh.* In 1935 Karl Freund, by then a director in
America, did a remake of Robert Wiene's *Mad Love,* starring Peter
Lorre. Freund used a young cameraman by the name of Gregg Toland.
Six years later, Welles used Toland as director of cinematography on
Kane. Both the lighting techniques and Peter Lorre's make-up were
borrowed from the 1935 film.

Because of budget limitations, as well as some Wellesian psychology
and humor, materials from past RKO films were used in *Citizen Kane.*
Xanadu in long shot was similar in appearance to the castle in Disney's
1937 film, *Snow White and the Seven Dwarfs*—painted with the help
of Disney's former staff members. Kane also included a bit of *The
Hunchback of Notre Dame* and some animated bats reminiscent of
Son of Kong. Shooting began on July 30, 1940, and continued for seventy days at a final cost of $842,000.

HEARST CENSORSHIP

Film critic and columnist Louella Par-
sons, an employee of William Randolph Hearst, was convinced that
Citizen Kane blackened her boss's
name. Louis B. Mayer offered to buy
the negative at cost so he could
burn it. Welles and Mankiewicz were
sued by Ferdinand Lundberg, author
of *Imperial Hearst, A Social Biography* (1936) for plagiarism. The case
was settled out of court. Hearst
threatened to attack the entire film
industry.

Welles was delighted, but like Erich
Von Stroheim, he would soon become untouchable in Hollywood,
and would exile himself to Europe in
order to pursue a film career that
would never reach the same heights
again.

Hearst unleashed the power of forty-

five publications against the film.
RKO postponed its release. Nelson
Rockefeller, owner of Radio City
Music Hall, yielded to pressure and
refused to exhibit the picture. Although it finally opened at the Palace, the Hearst chain would not
even review the film. Chaplin liked it;
Bosley Crowthers liked it; but this
did not help it at the box office. Although the picture received several
Oscar nominations (1942), those attending the Academy Awards that
year booed because they were intimidated by Hearst and they sought
revenge on the precocious outsider.
Even so, the Academy voted Herman Mankiewicz an Oscar for best
screenplay.

Source: Pauline Kael. *The Citizen Kane Book.* Boston: Little, Brown and Co., 1971.

FIGURE 9-4 Darryl
Zanuck. (Movie Star
News)

Darryl Zanuck

Darryl Zanuck[16] broke into films as a scriptwriter. He had been writing
fiction for pulp magazines and after fifty rejections finally had a story
accepted in 1923. He pieced some of his short stories together and
managed to get them published as a book in 1923. From this small

success, Zanuck was hired as a gag writer for Mack Sennett. After an intense period of grinding out the screenplays for four dozen serials, Zanuck joined Warner Brothers in 1924 as a scriptwriter for a German shepherd—Rin Tin Tin. From the dog movies he graduated to writing for many other films that have long since dissolved into nitrate dust.

Jack Warner gave Zanuck a raise to $5,000 a week and made him head of production in 1928, but suggested that the twenty-six-year-old youth wear glasses and grow a moustache to look older. Zanuck was production supervisor of *The Jazz Singer*. Sam Warner advocated singing in the picture and Zanuck had the idea of having Al Jolson talk as well as sing. Harry Warner said, "Who the hell wants to hear actors talk?" As it turned out, next to Rin Tin Tin, talking actors were the biggest thing in Warner's history.

Warner Brothers netted $17 million in 1929, the same Depression year that the president of Union Cigar jumped to his death from the ledge of a New York City hotel. This act symbolized the trauma of a shattered economy, which had no ill effect on the movie industry. Over the next six years at Warner Brothers, Zanuck supervised or wrote twenty-one films including *Disraeli, Little Caesar, The Public Enemy,* and *I Am a Fugitive From a Chain Gang.*

Zanuck left Warner Brothers over a fight with Harry Warner in 1933, when Louis B. Mayer gave United Artists President Joseph Schenck and Zanuck a check for $100,000 to form the Twentieth Century Production Company. The one string Mayer attached to the check was the assurance of a job for his son-in-law William Goetz. In the new company Zanuck was production chief, Goetz his assistant, and Joe Schenck was president. Joe's younger brother, Nicholas Schenck, was Mayer's boss at MGM and also president of Loew's Incorporated, which was probably a major reason for Mayer's generosity.

In 1935, Twentieth Century merged with the Fox Film Corporation. So, at age 33, Darryl Zanuck became production head of Twentieth Century Fox. He had a ninety-six acre lot and a $20 million budget. Over the next twenty-seven years, Zanuck would personally produce or be intimately involved in producing some 126 films, including *Young Mr. Lincoln* (1939), *The Grapes of Wrath* (1940), *Gentleman's Agreement* (1948), and *All About Eve* (1950).

Zanuck eventually became president of Twentieth Century Fox and installed his son Richard as production chief. The company had its ups and downs: *Sound of Music* was a top grosser; *Hello Dolly* bombed; *Patton* was a hit; and *Tora! Tora! Tora!* was a $20 million turkey. Fox lost $77 million in 1970. Richard Zanuck was fired and Darryl Zanuck was booted up to chairman and retired.

TRANSITION YEARS

After Pearl Harbor, the film industry was officially mobilized to serve the war effort, but the business interests controlling the industry took an ambivalent attitude toward the war. They wanted films that stimulated patriotism and strengthened civilian and military morale, but they did not want to probe too deeply into the causes of the war or the meaning of fascism. The most effective films were action films that dealt with combat and the human attitudes of men under fire, defined in clear terms of duty and making decisions under the threat of death. When Hollywood was forced into thematic material, it remained timid. *Casablanca* (1943), with Humphrey Bogart, is representative. Bogart, the man with a shady past, finds he must commit himself to love and the struggle against fascism, but the movie does not really rise above the good guys versus the bad guys. Dorothy B. Jones, of the U.S. Office of War Information, said that only one out of every ten war pictures was really thematic, and this represented only 4 percent of the total number of films issued.[17] More than half of all film production was not directly concerned with the war at all.

After the war, Americans, feeling the war had solved little, turned inward. The Cold War was on, there was a recession, and many feared a new and greater depression. And people didn't go to the movies even if they did have the money because they also had television. Television, a conservative medium that avoids controversial issues, took the place of cinema as mass picture-sound entertainment. Records, and recordings on radio, took the place of the movie musical.

TV TAKES OVER AND MONOPOLIES BROKEN UP—A NEW ERA FOR MOTION PICTURES

Although the Attorney General's office had considered moves against the motion picture industry since the thirties, it wasn't until 1948 that *United States* v. *Paramount Pictures Inc., 334 U.S. 131* declared the industry, which owned both the production and theater distribution facilities, a monopoly that had to be broken up. Once the link between the two was broken, control over subject content became fragmented, and block booking was gone.

For the studios and the moviegoers, much good was lost. No longer could young talent learn in the B movie factory, hoping one day to break into the more prestigious A movie field. Nor could the studios any longer afford to produce specialty films with limited appeal, but great artistic value.

Whether the government's action alone could have dismantled the giant movie companies probably will never be known because television might have done it alone.

Just how significant those transition years in the late 1940s and the early 1950s were is demonstrated by statistics: In 1946, the film industry made an all-time high figure of $1.7 billion; but, in 1962 it made only $900 million —about half of what it earned in 1946.

How was the motion picture industry to cope with the change in its status and health? Quite literally, it tried everything. Some studios simply closed their doors. This group included Monogram and Republic, who were eventually followed by more. Other studios reduced production. Some of the big studios sold off their real estate. For example, in the 1970s, MGM's back lot was torn down to make room for a parking lot.

Besides idle equipment and props, most studios had contracts with now idle stars. These contracts required them to pay wages to actors and actresses for whom there was no work. Important as it was to reduce costs, most studios were very slow to extricate themselves from these heavy financial obligations. In the end, the largest studios suffered the most because they had the greatest investment in people and facilities.

In order to attract more people to theaters, the studios started to shoot everything in color. Then they tried different filmic techniques. One of their first experiments was in making three-dimensional films. In going beyond the usual two-dimensional screen, 3-D movies, as they were commonly called, could show herds of animals or trains rushing out of the screen into audience members' faces. The effect was electrifying—the first time or two. But the thrill soon wore off. To see 3-D movies, audience members had to wear awkward and cumbersome glasses that corrected the image for the eye. Most people found the glasses bothersome and movie after movie of rushing trains boring. After about a year, attendance at 3-D movies declined and producers concluded that they had only come up with a gimmick. The gimmick was tried again in 1981 with minor success, and it may be tried again. Smell-o-roma has been tried, too, without success so far.

Having failed with their 3-D venture, Hollywood turned to the "spectacular film"—a movie projected on a huge screen and filmed at great cost. Fox introduced the wide screen in 1953 with its biblical production *The Robe*. But, the new technique had problems. For example, close-ups near the center of the big screen were out of focus. Another problem was the wide horizontal format, which, said one critic, was great for filming pythons, but how would it be adapted to the vertical shape of a person? Nevertheless, audiences like wide screen spectaculars. Cinerama started making them in 1952, and the Todd-AO process followed shortly thereafter.

Marriage with Television

Working with television was not an easy decision for the movie industry moguls to make. Although they would have preferred to destroy the new medium, in about 1954, Warner Brothers decided to try selling shows made especially for television to ABC. Within a few short years, "Cheyenne," "77 Sunset Strip," and other Warner productions were weekly series on television.

In 1956, Hollywood began selling its feature movies to television at ever-increasing prices; prices were high because movies on television drew large audiences. In 1959, Columbia Pictures' Screen Gems subsidiary began producing films for television. Hollywood stopped fighting and became network television's major supplier of entertainment.

THE MAJOR MOVIE COMPANIES TODAY

The Motion Picture Association of America's (MPAA) membership is made up of the leading producers and distributors of motion pictures in the United States and throughout the world whose names follow:

Allied Artists Picture Corp.

AVCO Embassy Pictures Corp.

Columbia Pictures Industries, Inc.

Metro-Goldwyn-Mayer Inc.

Paramount Pictures Corp.

Twentieth Century Fox Film Corp.

United Artists Corp.

Universal Pictures, a division of Universal City Studios, Inc.

Warner Brothers Distributing Corp.[18]

These are the big nine, although many would add Orion, a breakaway group from United Artists, in the 1980s.
In 1939 the big eight were these:

Paramount Pictures

Metro-Goldwyn-Mayer (Loew's Inc.)

Twentieth Century Fox

Warner Brothers

RKO

Universal

Columbia

United Artists[19]

There are major differences between the companies on these two lists, even though seven companies survived decades of struggle. All of the corporations are diversified now, and own gambling casinos, parks, condominiums, and book companies, among other ventures. None of the pioneer moguls remain active in feature productions.

A strange, but certainly not new mixture of violence, sex, and music raised the movie industry's box office gross from 1968's $1.3 billion to 1972's $1.58 billion and it took fewer than 20 million weekly admissions to do it. This is a reflection of increased ticket prices,[20] but, it must also be remembered, film costs are way up, too.

In 1908, it cost about $200 to produce a one-reel film. In 1915, Griffith's *The Birth of a Nation* cost about $110,000 to produce. In 1916, Griffith's *Intolerance* production costs ran to $12,000 per day. In 1939, David O. Selznick's *Gone with the Wind* cost $4.25 million. By the early 1970s production costs could run to $75,000 per day, with the average cost of a film feature at a little more than $2 million. The average cost in the early 1980s is $6 million.

Actors' salaries have done much to boost costs; in 1912 they were paid only up to $50 per week. In 1973, Marlon Brando purportedly received $500,000 plus 10 percent of the gross to do *Godfather II*. In the 1980s, Brando gets $1 million up front, plus a percentage, plus a guarantee that he will only have to work a short time. When the studio system held sway, they were able to maintain a certain amount of control over stars' salaries. Now, everyone is independent—actors, producers, directors, and cinematographers. And their fees have gone through the roof.

Film for TV

When television turned to color in the 1960s, feature films turned up the sex, violence, ethnic, and social realism temperature. When television became a bit sexy and displayed a social consciousness in the 1970s, film's response was to show and say things that simply could not be publicly broadcast into people's living rooms because of Federal Communication Commission regulations. Where this escalation will end is anyone's guess.

With so much crossover between film and television personnel today (the MPAA supplies about 75 percent of prime time programming on the three national networks in the United States), it is unlikely that the end of motion pictures is at hand. Cinematographer Conrad Hall[21] says that cinema is actually about ready to enter its golden age. Hall thinks the future of film, or at least the home entertainment aspect of it, won't have any definite length; there won't be just one-hour films or two-hour films. There will be one-hour films, and ten-minute films, and five-minute films—however long it takes to tell the story. This would just about bring the industry full cycle—back to the one-and-two-reelers of the early 1900s.

This does not mean a reincarnation of the short subject, however. For in spite of its disappearance from movie theaters, the short film has been alive and well and living in places like television and education all along.

Television's commercial nature dictates a short format: it could be said that television, with its commercial breaks every reel, makes short subjects even of feature films. The longest regularly scheduled television film series are ninety minutes; most are thirty minutes. Not surprisingly, comedy shows are usually in the thirty-minute class; this harks back to the twenty-minute Mack Sennett, *Our Gang, Three Stooges,* and W. C. Fields comedies.

Whether the shorts of today, which are designed for commercial breaks, would work as well without these interruptions, is not known. Perhaps someday, some enlightened sponsor will do for comedy what some of the more secure image advertisers do infrequently for dramatic specials—very gently present their commercial message before and after the program. Only then will it be known if two reels of Bob Newhart and Susan Pleshette equals two reels of Laurel and Hardy.

Whether we have become a nation of people with limited attention spans (ten minutes), because of the conditioned rhythm of television programming may be a relevant question. It is interesting to note that the short-shorts like commercials hark back to the birth of cinema, when films or nonfilms were less than a minute in length (fifty feet) because of mechanical limitations.

THE MOVIE PACKAGE

Moviemaking in the eighties is a different business than it was in the thirties or even the fifties. But it is still a business, like all mass media.

The people who run Hollywood today—studio bosses, producers, directors, performers—are basically business people. They can talk about art versus entertainment, but the bottom line remains all-important. American moviemaking is a commercial venture. If it can be artistic and become true cinema in the process of making money, so much the better. The three *Rockys* of the seventies and early eighties are a success because they made money, not because the first version won critical acclaim.

THE $110,000 BLUNDER, OR THE MAN WHO COULDN'T WORK MIRACLES

Barry Jagoda arrived in Hollywood on December 1, 1980, with the screen rights to a novel, $110,000 to spend and a jaunty confidence that by the end of a year he would be a movie producer.

When the moving vans came on November 30, 1981, to take his furniture back to Washington, he was sadder but wiser. His option of *The Man Who Brought the Dodgers Back to Brooklyn* would expire the next day, along with his year's lease on the wrong house in the wrong neighborhood. The $110,000 was gone, and he was as far from producing a movie as ever.

The intense, 37-year-old Mr. Jagoda is not a hayseed with a dream. A 1967 graduate of the Columbia School of Journalism, a former CBS News producer and media advisor to former President Jimmy Carter, he was the proprietor of a small consulting concern in Washington.

His first mistake was leasing a four-bedroom house in Oxford Square, an aging neighborhood on the fringes of downtown Los Angeles.

His second mistake was "not really realizing the importance of an agent."

"It wasn't until February that we learned everything in Hollywood works off a screenplay and that we shouldn't have approached anybody before the screenplay was finished."

For $25,000 he had optioned the unpublished book about two friends who restore Ebbets Field brick by brick. The book was to be published in the spring of 1981, with Simon and Schuster printing 20,000 copies and spending $35,000 on promotion. His next mistake was hiring his friend, the author of the book, to do the screenplay. He had never done one. The script didn't grab you in the first ten minutes, it didn't have three acts, and the characters didn't develop. He was stuck with Mr. Ritz because he had given him the Writer's Guild minimum fee of $26,250 for two drafts and a polish; he couldn't afford to hire another writer. (Even if Mr. Ritz had been a fantastic writer, never hire an unknown.)

Mr. Ritz's second draft was, according to everyone who saw it, a "vast improvement." But the property was now somewhat stale and overexposed. Mr. Jagoda had shown it to too many people too early. By this time, it was September. The novel had been published without the supposedly promised $35,000 for promotion. It didn't sell well.

Mr. Jagoda was also in the process of learning that, by Hollywood standards, his novel was not a "commercial" subject. "It's a love story and a story of male bonding," he said, "but, to Hollywood, none of that mattered. To Hollywood, it was a sports story."

During his early months in Hollywood, he had thought if he could just get the novel and a script to Dustin Hoffman, his hoped-for star, and George Roy Hill, his hoped-for director, everything would be fine. A cynical producer said, "If old George is interested, he'll eat you up alive. He'll take over the project. As a matter of fact, anybody will. You have no track record, so I don't know how you expect to get the picture made."

George Roy Hill was not interested, Hoffman was dropped from the conversation, but Mr. Jagoda was, he said, strung along by a number of other people. But encouragement didn't translate into a developmental deal.

By November, a lot of people were telling him to make his movie for television, a polite brush-off. But he couldn't. "I had paid too much for the book and the script," he said in frustration, "So the numbers wouldn't work out for television."

"One looks around for a happy ending," Mr. Jagoda added, on his way out of town. "But then, this isn't a movie."

Source: *The New York Times*, January 4, 1982, C-13.

The Independent Producer

The movies produced in the new Hollywood come from a system that has been drastically revised in the last decade; the independent producer is king. Far fewer pictures are made on Hollywood sets; shooting on location is more common and desirable. The studios have chosen to become primarily financing and distribution agencies. Studio production facilities have shrunk; in fact, some major studios do not even have studios of their own anymore. They share the distribution systems and even the financing of pictures.

The idea of the independent producer is not new. Hollywood has always had successful independents like Roger Corman [*The Fall of the House of Usher* (1960), *The Wild Angels* (1966), *The Valentine's Day Massacre* (1967)], but it is only recently that the independent producers have begun to dominate. Today, men like Dino De Laurentis, Richard Zanuck, and Irwin Allen can pretty much write their own tickets as long as they are winners. Zanuck, who made *The Sting* and *Jaws,* has said, "It's a producer's business to think in terms of showmanship, not the director's. And since showmanship is the big thing in Hollywood today, producers are running shows." Irwin Allen, who produced the *Poseidon Adventure* and the *Towering Inferno,* said, "If there's an 'auteur' in movies it's the producer."[22] Producers are well rewarded for their contribution to the motion picture—they receive a sizable producer's fee, a percentage of the profits, and a large share of the control over the creative process. Actors like Warren Beatty have found production to their liking, and have invested as much time in producing as they have in directing and performing.

Generally, it is the producer's job to construct the package around which the movie is built. A production team of creative and technical people is formed—sometimes after the script or story is chosen, sometimes before. The production team includes the key people who will turn the story into a movie. Although the producer has great discretion in choosing the team, even at this early stage the system can impose limitations. Talent agencies, for example, which represent the creative people of the industry, can force a package on a producer. For example, say a producer wants to make a movie with Harry George in a leading role. When the producer talks to George's talent agency, they agree to the contract, but only if the producer agrees to use Joan Friend as a costar and Charles Russel as the director. The agency also represents these folks, and they need the work. If the producer wants George badly enough, he or she will take the rest of the group as well.

Once constructed, the package is then presented to a financing agency, often a studio. The studio can usually get financing and the means to distribute the movie when it is completed. If the studio likes the package, agrees to finance it or find financing for it, and will distribute the picture as well, it receives in return a percentage of the gross revenue the movie brings in. This money comes off the top.

Or, perhaps the studio puts together the package, hires an independent producer, performers, etc. The producer and performers may insist on a percentage of the gross revenue; they often do this in lieu of salary or flat fees.

It is not uncommon for the producer to secure the financing from multiple sources, especially if the picture has a big budget. The average movie made today costs about $6 million. Promoting, making prints, and distributing the film can cost another $6 million. Filmmaking is not a cheap way to make money.

Financing a Movie

Motion picture financiers are hardheaded. They look for a likely box office success. Although no one ever knows for certain whether a movie will be successful, there are some things the moneylenders evaluate: a bankable literary property, a best-selling novel, or a hit Broadway musical is something of value. *Jaws* was on the best-seller list for forty-five weeks before it became a movie. However, sometimes this strategy fails. *The Great Gatsby* was a popular novel but it did not do well in its screen treatment. (Apparently, the financial wizards did not bother to note that F. Scott Fitzgerald's work never translates to the screen very well.) But normally, a story's success as a book or play is a good indication that it will succeed as a movie, too.

The components of a movie package are another factor in its getting financing. Who is producing? Who is directing? Who is starring? Name value is everything. George Lucas or Francis Ford Coppala might be able to get money for a project that would never be funded without them. Even the star system is beginning to reemerge as a factor, after several decades of obscurity. There were always star pictures, but for a time, while audiences were interested in the antihero, stars were less important. Bankable stars can be insurance for a movie that lacks other assets. Many financiers think that a motion picture with an actor like Clint Eastwood, Paul Newman, Jack Nicholson, Robert Redford, or Marlon Brando has a decent shot at making money even if it's bad.

The cost of the film is another factor in whether it will be financed. The same package that might find support at $4 million might not find it at $6 million.

Finally, the producer of a film in the eighties had better be prepared to talk fast about the market for his proposed film. To get financing today, a producer has to have more than a "good feeling" about a script or a hunch that it is what the public wants. Computers with market research data are becoming more and more a part of the filmmaking process. Questions are being asked like "Who is the audience?" What are the demographics on its potential audience?" and "Where is your hard data?"

Movies are events. To lure the audiences away from their television sets a movie needs to be something special. It's tough for a movie that is not a big media-created event to find an audience, no matter how good it is.

COKE BUYS COLUMBIA IN 1982

According to *The New York Times*, a little understood accounting rule, once mostly an annoyance, is today masking millions of dollars in future profits at prospering motion picture companies. And it is these earnings that have been part of the lure for the Coca-Cola Company. According to Francis T. Vincent, Jr., president and chief executive of Columbia Pictures Inc., which agreed to be acquired by Coca-Cola for about $760 million, "There is more than $155 million on [future licensing] contracts . . . with commercial and pay television . . . which is largely profit, yet it is nowhere in our balance sheet or our income statement."

Vincent and other movie executives are not allowed to use such earnings to bolster their current bottom line because of an accounting rule adopted in 1973 by the Accounting Practices Board. The rule requires studios to record revenues from the sale of movies to non-theater outlets only when these films can be shown, which is typically a year or more after contracts are signed, because that is when the money actually changes hands. When first put into effect, the rule was intended to bring some comparability to the financial statements of motion picture studios, which had been logging the relatively small revenues generated by such contracts at different times. But with the rapid growth of the home entertainment industry, the amount of future profits from licensing contracts with commercial, and especially pay television rose sharply.

Perhaps 20 percent of a typical movie company's assets are off the balance sheet as a result of the accounting rule, and the figure is growing. Columbia, for example, last year signed one of the largest pay-television licensing agreements, for $6 million, for *Stir Crazy*. It will also get a minimum of $8.5 million for the network television rights to the film. Columbia licensed its 1979 hit, *Kramer vs. Kramer,* to ABC last year for more than $15 million. ABC is permitted to schedule the movie twice in the 24 months beginning September 1982. On January 7, *Daily Variety* reported that Columbia agreed to license *Only When I Laugh, The Blue Lagoon* and *Seems Like Old Times* to NBC for $18 million. Columbia has also sold the rights to *Stripes* to pay television for the summer of 1983, and the movie's network rights beginning in September 1983. And Columbia is syndicating rights to "Fantasy Island," now in its sixth year on network television to local stations around the country. What's more, the network television rights for its movie version of *Annie,* which did poorly at the box office, were sold to NBC for about $10 million long before the movie went into production.

The Other Side of the Coin

Not all film companies are doing as well as Columbia, according to the *Wall Street Journal.* Top executives of a major independent film company, Orion, and the nation's largest pay-television programming service HBO, have agreed to pump $26 million into financially ailing Filmways Inc. A series of transactions will leave the principals of Orion running Filmways. The transaction would lead to Orion's principals and their partners, Home Box Office, acquiring control of Filmways, if Filmways shareholders approve.

Filmways, which reported a $19.9 million loss from continuing operations in the nine months ended November 30, 1982, has been holding talks with potential suitors in recent months. Filmways produces motion pictures and television shows, and has interests in publishing and electronic manufacturing. Orion produces motion pictures.

For Orion, the investment could mean attaining long-sought control over distribution of its own motion pictures, currently distributed by the Warner Brothers unit of Warner Communications Inc. For Home Box Office, it is another step in tying up pay-television rights for motion pictures. Filmways signed a production-financing agreement with Home Box Office, which will receive certain pay-television and cable-television rights to Filmways movies in exchange for payment from Home Box Office.

CENSORSHIP

Since the early days of film, outcries have been heard regarding the content of movies. Objections were usually related to special themes. Not until recently has there been a major reaction against film violence. One *Chicago Tribune* article in March, 1907, called nickelodeons a compromise to "the lowest passions of childhood."[23] Titles of that year included *The Bigamist, Gaieties of Divorce,* and *Cupid's Barometer.*[24] Nickelodeons took up where vaudeville and burlesque had left off. The movie theaters, sometimes open all night, were said by a Chicago judge to "Cause indirectly or directly, more juvenile crime than all other causes combined."[25] In spite of the moralists' arguments, it is estimated that a million people attended movies each day in Chicago around 1907.[26] Filmmakers learned early that sex sells.

Hollywood was usually able to profit from publicity about sex in its films as long as it was not real-life sex. When the mishaps and misadventures of stars became headlines, the story was different. America had gathered Gladys Mary Smith to its bosom as Mary Pickford, but when she divorced husband Owen Moore and married Douglas Fairbanks within the month, she appeared to have betrayed her following. This alleged betrayal of American morality (an America that was rapidly losing its innocence in the Roaring 20s), was followed quickly by the 1921 death of starlet Virginia Rappe during a drinking party given by America's popular funny man, Roscoe "Fatty" Arbuckle. The scandal ended his career. In a similar fashion, the murder of director William Desmond Taylor destroyed the careers of Mary Miles Minter and Mabel Normand.

Voices of the nation's conscience had a field day. Moralists, who resented Hollywood's products, had been trying to get a shot at it since its christening in 1913. They resented Cecil B. DeMille's attacks on early 20th century mores in his *Male and Female* (1919) and *Don't Change Your Husband* (1919) and Eric Von Stroheim's mockery of their values in *Blind Husbands* (1919) and *The Devil's Passkey* (1919).

It did not matter to them that Mary Pickford had been involved in no illegal action or that Roscoe Arbuckle, Mary Miles Minter, and Mabel Normand were all found innocent; the reformers brushed these victims out of their militant path and continued in pursuit of the movie industry. Another victim in their sordid portfolio was Wallace Reid, who died in 1922 at age 30. It was soon revealed that he had been a drug addict.

States began to form censorship boards that were given the power of prior restraint—the ability to demand changes before a picture could be shown. The first censorship case was *Block* v. *Chicago, 239 Ill., 251, 87 N.E. 1011 (1909)*. The police, with the power granted by a municipal ordinance, refused to license *The James Boys* and *Night Riders*. The ordinance was upheld and the films were refused permits.

In 1915, Congress exerted pressure on the film industry by examining its financial activities, and censorship boards in Pennsylvania, Ohio, Kansas, Maryland, New York, and Virginia were declared legal in 236 U.S. 230.

What's more, this was the year of *Mutual Film Corp.* v. *Ohio 1915*. The Mutual Film Corporation was a Detroit company that purchased films from producers and leased them to exhibitors in Ohio and other states. In the case before the Supreme Court, Mutual had sought to enjoin enforcement of Ohio's prior-censorship law. The company claimed that the statute imposed an unlawful burden on interstate commerce, that it was an invalid delegation of legislative power to the board of censors because it failed to set up precise standards by which films were to be approved or rejected, and that it violated the free speech guarantees of the Ohio Constitution and the First Amendment.

A unanimous Court, speaking through Justice McKenna, ignored the federal free speech claim and rejected the other contentions. McKenna disposed of the commerce argument by saying that when films were in the hands of exchanges like Mutual Film, ready to be rented to exhibitors, they were mingled with other property in the state, at least as much as they could be considering their nature. At that point, they were subject to regulation by the state.[27]

Some critics say that the film industry never defended itself very hard against censorship, and allowed itself to be considered commerce rather than art or communication. Some even say that the industry asked to be censored. Perhaps it had something to do with Congressional examination of financial activities.

The industry responded by forming the National Board of Review, and later, the National Association of the Motion Picture Industry (1919).[28] This organization actually did little. Sex on the screen was thriving. By the 20s, 50 million people a week were turning out to see titles like *Luring Lips* and *Virgin Paradise*.[29]

Self-Censorship

By 1922, another two dozen legislatures were considering film censorship bills. The industry responded with self-censorship. Former Postmaster General Will Hays was appointed president of the newly constituted trade association called the Motion Picture Producers and Distributors of America (MPPDA). Through the next eight years, the organization tried various experiments with self-censorship, before hitting upon the code in 1930. (Unfortunately, it was a code with no teeth, because there were no penalties for noncompliance.)

In the summer of 1932, America was reminded of the movie scandals of a decade earlier when director Paul Bern blew his brains out after leaving a suicide note for his new bride, actress Jean Harlow: "Dearest Dear. Unfortunately, this is the only way to make good the frightful wrong I have done you and to wipe out my abject humiliation. I love you—Paul. You understand that last night was only a comedy." It was assumed that his "humiliation" was caused by his impotence, and the "wrong" he did her was his inability to consummate his marriage to MGM's "Platinum Blonde Bombshell." This was the topper. Jean Harlow's sexy role in *Hell's Angels* (1930) had already stirred the moralists and made her a star with its line, "Pardon me while I slip into something comfortable."

"Seal of Approval" Established

The moralists were restless. The Episcopal Committee on Motion Pictures, The National Legion of Decency (started in 1934), and other religious groups forced the Motion Picture Producers and Distributors of America to put teeth into their code.

But it wasn't until a required "seal of approval" was established that filmmakers really began to listen.[30] Joseph Breen headed a new department of the Hays office in Hollywood—the Production Code Administration. The new branch was authorized to levy fines. Producers were advised about what cuts were needed in their films in order to win the code's seal of approval. Twelve areas were involved: crime, sex, vulgarity, obscenity, profanity, costume, dance, religion, locations (e.g. bedrooms), national feelings, titles, and repellent subjects (e.g. torture). Deviant studies might find their products boycotted by exhibitors. The new code came too late to inhibit Mae West in *Night After Night,* but it crimped her style in *She Done Him Wrong* and *I'm No Angel,* which was originally titled *It Ain't No Sin.*

Will Hays's authority to regulate content rested more on influence than legality. Even though the major studios and distributors paid his salary, they wanted to make as much money as possible as long as the public did not balk. When it did, that was bad for business and they allowed Hays to regulate more. His office read stories and scripts, saw rushes, suggested cuts, and exercised veto rights over release prints. He introduced morality clauses into actors' contracts. He interceded with the press for a more factual, less sensational reporting of the film industry. Nudity, profanity, drugs, and racial and religious prejudice were forbidden as film content. Hays thought that crime shouldn't pay, be it robbery or prostitution. Sex, even between husband and wife, could be suggested, but could never be explicit. By these standards, Americans of the 20s and 30s would have been depicted in such a morally upright fashion that films would have been in danger of toppling over from top-heavy self-righteousness. Ingenious directors, however, found ways around the code. Cecil B. DeMille mixed lust and religion into a financially successful formula with biblical pictures. As long as the sinners were brutalized in the last reel and the sinned-against emerged victorious, an uncertain calm settled on the censorship battle.

No Hollywood film without a seal played the nation's theaters until 1953, and extensive changes were required of films on numerous occasions. The success of the movie industry's program of self-regulation before the 1950s can be attributed to the monopoly structure of the production-distribution-exhibition process—ownership of the entire process by a few major corporations.

The code became the pet peeve of censorship critics. Under the code, married couples were discouraged from sleeping in the same bed. Bedroom scenes were categorized into a nebulous category called special subjects. Certain terms were classified "vulgar," among them fairy, goose, and nuts.[31] Writers and other production personnel were soon to start a thirty-year campaign to bend the various restrictions. The censors cut references to athletic cups in a boxing movie and expressed concern over naked aborigines in a documentary.[32] Howard Hughes unsuccessfully tried to have the code declared illegal in his battle over the treatment of Jane Russell in *The Outlaw*.[33]

In 1945, Eric Johnson took over from Will Hays, and the Motion Picture Export Association of America was established to revive and expand the international commerce in films. To compete with television and an influx of "mature' films from Europe, Hollywood increased its films' violence and sex, and turned to more mature subjects. A new code was needed, but the ability to enforce it was lost when production was separated from distribution in the Paramount case (1948).

THE CENSORSHIP BATTLE MOVES TO THE COURTS

In the 1952 case *Burstyn* v. *Wilson,* which was the first censorship case to reach the court since 1915, the Supreme Court held what had been dictum in the anti-trust case. The Court announced that it now considered motion pictures a significant medium for the communication of ideas. This perception entitled movies to the protection of the First Amendment. However, governmental censorship boards were not dealt a fatal blow even though prior restraint was limited to exceptional cases, which came to mean those involving obscenity.

In 1952, in *Joseph Burstyn, Inc.* v. *Wilson, 343 U.S. 495, 497,* the New York Board of Regents was told that it could not stop the playing of the film *The Miracle* on the grounds that it was sacrilegious.

Although a measure of freedom from governmental censorship was gained in the *Miracle* case, the industry's own censorship scheme was weakened when United Artists released two Otto Preminger productions without that badge of code compliance, the seal. *The Moon is Blue* was denied a seal because it dealt with adulterous conduct, and *The Man with the Golden Arm* was disapproved because of its treatment of drug addiction.

With the more adult themes of films in the 50s and 60s came a rash of legislative proposals in various states, mainly in the form of obscenity statutes designed to protect children. But neither boards nor legislatures are completely self-starting. The Legion of Decency, now called the National Catholic Office for Motion Pictures, operates its own rating system designed to judge the suitability of various films for Catholic viewers. There are also the film boards of the Parents-Teachers Association, the Veterans of Foreign Wars, the Citizens for Decent Literature, the National Council of Churches, and those of other religious, ethnic, and professional organizations.

When significant changes began taking place in the movie industry in the early 1950s, eight states and close to ninety cities had licensing boards that reviewed all motion pictures exhibited in their jurisdiction. The demise of prior restraint of movies (which began in 1952) was complete by the mid-1960s, when all but a handful of the boards had been invalidated because of their unconstitutional standards, or effectively destroyed because of procedural defects.

Although the main reaction of state and local governments to this judicial emasculation of prior restraint activities has been a shift to reliance on obscenity prosecutions and extra-legal harassment, a few public officials did attempt to retain a vestige of prior restraint by implementing age classification systems. The Supreme Court, in *Interstate Circuit* v. *Dallas* (1968), invalidated the first such attempt by Dallas because of the vagueness of its classification standards. But, it left the path clear for future attempts by hinting that age classification systems with more tightly drawn standards might survive the application of constitutional tests.

Rating System Established

Following the Dallas decision on April 22, 1968, the Motion Picture Association of America, which is an outgrowth of the MPPDA, quickly came out with its own rating system designed to protect children and provide a guide for parents (May 1968): G, PG, R, and X.[34]

> *G—General Audience.* All ages admitted. This is a film, which in the judgment of the Rating Board, contains no significant material that would be objectionable or embarrassing for audiences of any age. A G-rated motion picture is *not* by definition a "children's" film, but it is a film which is generally regarded as being acceptable for viewing by the entire family.
>
> *PG—Parental Guidance Suggested.* All ages admitted. This film contains some material that may not be suitable for pre-teenagers. The rating alerts parents to the need for inquiry before allowing children to attend.

R—Restricted. Those under 17 must be accompanied to the theater by a parent or adult guardian. The R rating indicates a film that is significantly adult in theme and treatment. Parents may wish to view the picture with their children so they may discuss it together. A schoolteacher would qualify as an adult guardian.

*X—*The rating program provides that no one under 17 may attend. This is exclusively an adult film in theme and treatment, which is why no one under 17 may be admitted to the theater. The age limit may be higher in certain areas of the country.

This rating scheme does not guarantee that every theater will turn youngsters away from an R or an X film; it is merely a guidance system for parents. However, according to a poll by the Opinion Research Corporation (2,500 adults and teenagers polled), 55 percent of movie-going adults find the ratings very useful or fairly useful, 34 percent find the ratings not very useful, and 11% are undecided.

Obscenity

The battle over censorship continued, but the fight was now over obscenity. Neither the Constitution nor its subsequent 25 amendments mentions censorship, defines obscenity, or excludes obscenity and its sub-classification, pornography, from protection under the First Amendment. However, over the years, individual states have dealt with obscenity within their borders. Supreme Court Justice Brennan, with Justices Stewart and Marshall concurring, wrote in his *dissenting* opinion on *Paris Adult Theater 1 et al, Petitioners,* v. *Lewis R. Slaton, District Attorney, Atlanta Judicial Circuit, et al* (June 21, 1973) that:

> Obscenity laws have a long history in this country. Most of the states that had ratified the Constitution by 1792 punished the related crime of blasphemy or profanity despite the guarantees of free expression in their Constitution, and Massachusetts expressly prohibited the "Composing, Writing, Printing or Publishing of any Filthy, Obscene or Prophane Song, Pamphlet, Libel or Mock-Sermon, in Imitation of Preaching, or any other part of Devine Worship."[35]

The case involved two theater owners and managers in Atlanta, Georgia. The films in question were *Magic Mirror* and *It All Comes Out In the End.* A trial court judge found that obscenity was established but dismissed the complaints: "It appears to the Court that the display of these films in a commercial theatre, when surrounded by requisite notice to the public of their nature and by reasonable protection against the exposure of these films to minors, is constitutionally permissible."[36]

This opinion was reversed by the Georgia Supreme Court which held the films to be without protection under the First Amendment.

Chief Justice Burger delivered the prevailing opinion of the Supreme Court of the United States with White, Blackmun, Powell, and Rehnquist. The decision was that obscene material is not speech entitled to First Amendment protection, and that states have a legitimate interest in regulating commerce in obscene material and its exhibition in places of public accommodation, including "adult" theaters. Preventing the unlimited display of obscene material is not contrary to the free flow of ideas. The court said not all conduct directly involving "consenting adults" has a claim to constitutional protection.[37]

How powerful audio-visual symbology must be when light energy bouncing from a screen and sound waves coming from speaker horns can provoke an argument over the basic freedoms guaranteed citizens by the Constitution and the Bill of Rights.

Justice Burger said in his majority opinion: "Such laws (referring to "blue sky" laws regulating what sellers of securities may write or publish about their wares) are to protect the weak, the uninformed, the unsuspecting and the gullible from the exercise of their own volition. Nor do modern societies leave disposal of garbage and sewage up to the individual's "free will," but impose regulation to protect both public health and the appearance of public places.[38]

Justice Douglas, dissenting, noted that "People are, of course, offended by many offerings made by merchants in this area. They are also offended by political pronouncements, sociological themes, and by stories of official misconduct. The list of activities and publications and pronouncements that offend someone is endless. Some of it goes on in private, some of it is inescapably public, as when a government official generates crime, becomes a blatant offender of the moral sensibilities of the people, engages in burglary, or breaches the privacy of the telephone, the conference room, or the home."[39]

Strong words, indeed, generated by a couple of otherwise forgettable films whose niche in history is now assured. But the issues were so fundamental that they made the particular titles irrelevant.

Justice Brennan's dissenting opinion with Stewart and Marshall was twice as long as Chief Justice Burger's majority opinion with White, Blackmun, Powell, and Rehnquist. He expressed concern that after 15 years of experimentation and debate there still existed a vagueness between what constituted protected and unprotected speech. The meaning of such concepts as "prurient interest," "patent offensiveness," and "serious literary value," he said, . . . necessarily varies with the experience, outlook, and even idiosyncrasies of the person defining them. Although we have assumed that obscenity does exist and that we "know it when (we) see it," . . . we are manifestly unable to describe it in advance except between protected and unprotected speech.[40]

The problem is that one cannot say with certainty that material is obscene until at least five members of this Court, applying inevitably obscure standards, have pronounced it so.[41]
Where the state interest in regulation of morality is vague and ill

defined, interference with the guarantees of the First Amendment is even more difficult to justify.[42]

"I would hold, therefore, that at least in the absence of distribution to juveniles or obtrusive exposure to unconsenting adults, the First and Fourteenth Amendments prohibit the state and federal governments from attempting wholly to suppress sexually oriented materials on the basis of their allegedly "obscene" contents."[43]

In his separate dissenting opinion, Douglas concluded that ". . . our society—unlike most in the world—presupposes that freedom and liberty are in a frame of reference that make the individual, not government, the keeper of his tastes, beliefs and ideas. That is the philosophy of the First Amendment and it is the article of faith that sets us apart from most nations in the world."[44]

Another case decided on June 21, 1973, is also pertinent. *Miller* v. *California* resulted in a 5-4 split; Chief Justice Burger delivered the majority opinion for White, Blackmun, Powell, and Rehnquist. It reaffirmed that obscene material is not protected by the First Amendment.

The Miller case involved a mass mailing campaign used to advertise four books *(Intercourse, Man-Woman, Sex Orgies Illustrated,* and *An Illustrated History of Pornography)* and the film *Marital Intercourse.* Dissenting opinions were filed by Justice Douglas and Brennan with Stewart and Marshall. The following points were made by the court in the Miller Case:

1. A work may be subject to state regulation where that work, taken as a whole, appeals to the prurient interest in sex; portrays in a patently offensive way, sexual conduct specifically defined by the applicable state law, and taken as a whole, does not have serious literary, artistic, political or scientific value.

2. The basic guidelines must be whether the average person, applying contemporary community standards would find that the work, taken as a whole, meets the criteria for obscenity as specified under part 1 above.

3. The test of *utterly* without redeeming social value . . . is rejected as a constitutional standard.

4. The jury may measure the essential factual issues of prurient appeal and patent offensiveness by the standard that prevails in the forum community, and need not employ a national standard.[45]

Douglas opened his dissent by observing:

Today we leave the way for California to send a man to prison for distributing brochures that advertise books and a movie under freshly written standards defining obscenity which until today's decision were never the part of any law.

The court has worked hard to define obscenity and concededly has failed. . . . How under . . . vague tests can we sustain convictions for the sale of an article prior to the time when some court has declared it to be obscene?

The difficulty is that we do not deal with constitutional terms, since "obscenity" is not mentioned in the Constitution or Bill of Rights . . . there was no recognized exception to the free press at the time the Bill of Rights was adopted which treated "obscene" publications differently from other types of papers, magazines, and books.

. . . . we should not allow men to go to prison or be fined when they had no "fair warning" that what they did was criminal conduct.

Obscenity—which even we cannot define with precision—is a hodgepodge. To send men to jail for violating standards they cannot understand, construe, and apply is a monstrous thing to do in a nation dedicated to fair trials and due process.

The idea that the First Amendment permits punishment for ideas that are "offensive" to the particular judge or jury sitting in judgment is astounding, . . . To give the power to the censor, as we do today, is to make a sharp and radical break with the tradition of a free society. The First Amendment was not fashioned as a vehicle for dispensing tranquilizers to the people. . . . the tendency throughout history has been to subdue the individual and to exalt the power of government.

To many the Song of Solomon is obscene . . . . If it is to be defined, let the people debate and decide by a constitutional amendment what they want to ban as obscene and what standards they want the legislatures and the courts to apply. Perhaps the people will decide that the path towards a mature, integrated society requires that all ideas competing for acceptance must have no censor.[46]

But Douglas's dissenting opinion notwithstanding, state legislatures will be acting on the majority opinion, which holds that obscene material has no protection under the First Amendment; that exhibiting obscene material in places of public accommodation is not protected by any constitutional doctrine of privacy; that preventing the unlimited display of obscene material is not thought control; that not all conduct directly involving "consenting adults" has a claim to constitutional protection; and that a work is considered obscene if (1) the average person, applying contemporary community standards would find that the work, taken as a whole, appeals to the prurient interest, (2) the work depicts or describes, in a patently offensive way, sexual conduct specifically defined by the applicable state law, and (3) the work taken as a whole, lacks serious literary, artistic, political, or scientific value, in which case the jury may measure the essentially factual issues of prurient appeal and patent offensiveness by the standard that prevails in the forum community, and need not employ a national standard.[46]

Quite understandably the Motion Picture Producers Association of America is concerned, and not because they defend pornography. According to President Jack Valenti, "I don't know of a single sensible person who doesn't think obscenity is garbage. All of us detest obvious obscenity. But censorship is not the way to go about it. There are already sufficient laws on the books in the states to knock out the purveyors of pornography, if we are truly serious in doing that.[47]

By 1973, only one state—Maryland—maintained a censorship board. It still remains to be seen just what effect *Paris Adult Theatre 1* v. *Slaton, District Attorney* and *Miller* v. *California* will have on state legislatures and, ultimately, on all modes of expression. Creative artists, whether they be novelists, painters, poets, newspeople, musicians, actors and actresses, sculptors, or screenwriters cannot function under the strictures of unprotected expression.

The specter of Truffaut's *Fahrenheit 451,* in which the government burned books, forcing clandestine groups to memorize the world's literature in order to perpetuate culture, can be seen in Justice Douglas's chilling prediction: "What we do today is rather ominous as respects librarians. The net now designed by the court is so finely meshed that taken literally it could result in raids on libraries. Libraries, I had always assumed, were sacrosanct, representing every part of the spectrum. If what is offensive to the most influential person or group in a community can be purged from a library, the library system would be destroyed."[49]

TRENDS IN THE '80s

Hollywood's Challenges

- More theaters may close if there is not more product that will pull audiences away from their television sets.
- Producers have to find ways to reduce costs without a drop in quality.
- Sex and violence may reach a saturation point. What can replace them?

ADDITIONAL READINGS

Bluem, William. *The Film Business.* New York: Hastings House, 1972.

Brownlow, Kevin. *The Parade Gone By.* New York: Alfred A. Knopf, 1968.

Manvell, Roger. *The Film and the Public.* New York: Penguin Books, 1955.

Mayer, Michael F., ed. *The Film Industries.* New York: Hastings House, 1978.

FOOTNOTES

1. Gerald Mast, *A Short History of the Movies* (New York: Pegasus, 1971), pp. 55–59.

2. Robert Stanley, *The Celluloid Empire* (New York: Hastings House, 1978), pp. 11–20.

3. Thorold Dickinson, *A Discovery of Cinema* (New York: Oxford University Press, 1971), p. 18.

4. Ibid.

5. Mast, *History of the Movies,* pp. 107–09.

6. Leo Braudy and Morris Dickstein, *Great Film Directors* (New York: Oxford University Press, 1978), pp. 178–79.

7. David A. Cook, *A History of Narrative Film* (New York: W. W. Norton & Company, 1981), p. 203.

8. Ibid., p. 208.

9. Stanley, *Celluloid Empire,* pp. 34–36.

10. Kenneth Macgowan, *Behind the Screen* (New York: Delta, 1965), pp. 268–69.

11. Stanley, *Celluloid Empire,* p. 91.

12. Jack C. Ellis, *A History of Film* (New Jersey: Prentice Hall, 1979), pp. 149–51.

13. Rudy Behemer, ed., *Memo From David O. Selznick* (New York: Viking Press, 1972).

14. Pauline Kael, *The Citizen Kane Book* (Boston: Little Brown and Co., 1971).

15. Stanley, *Celluloid Empire,* pp. 59–60.

16. "Hollywood War Films, 1942–44," *Hollywood Quarterly,* (October 1945).

17. *A Review of the World of Movies,* (Los Angeles: Motion Picture Association of America, January 1973).

18. Lewis Jacobs, *The Rise of the American Film: A Critical History* (New York: Teachers College Press, 1939), p. 422.

19. *Variety,* Approximately mid January of each year there is an annual issue that recaps the previous year.

20. Leonard Maltin, *Behind the Camera: The Cinematographer's Art* (New York: Signet, The New American Library, Inc., 1971), pp. 185–218.

21. *Variety.*

22. Murray Schumach, *The Face on the Cutting Room Floor* (Toronto: William Morrow, 1964), p. 16.

23. Ibid.

24. Ibid.

25. Ibid.

26. Richard S. Randall, *Censorship of the Movies* (University of Wisconsin Press, 1968), p. 18.

27. Schumach, *Cutting Room Floor,* p. 16.

28. Ibid., p. 18.

29. Ibid.

30. Ibid.

31. Guy Phelps, *Film Censorship* (London: Victor Collanca, 1975), p. 218.

32. Schumach, *Cutting Room Floor,* p. 37.

33. Douglas Ayer, Roy E. Bates, Peter J. Herman, "Self-Censorship in the Movie Industry: An Historical Perspective on the Laws and Social Change," *Wisconsin Law Review* No. 3 (1970).

34. Paris Adult Theatre 1 v. Slaton, 413 U.S. 49, 104, 93 S. Ct. 2628 (1973).

35. Ibid., 413 U.S. 53.

36. Ibid., 413 U.S. 49, 59, 60.

37. Ibid., 413 U.S. 62–64.

38. Ibid., 413 U.S. 71.

39. Ibid., 413 U.S. 84.

40. Ibid., 413 U.S. 92.

41. Ibid., 413 U.S. 112.

42. Ibid., 413 U.S. 113.

43. Ibid., 413 U.S. 49.

44. Miller v. State of California, 413 U.S. 15, 93 S. Ct. 2607 (1973).

45. Ibid., 413 U.S. 40, 42–47.

46. Ibid.,413 U.S. 36, 37.

47. *A Review of the World of Movies* (Los Angeles: Motion Picture Association of America: January, 1973).

48. Paris Adult Theatre, 413 U.S. 72.

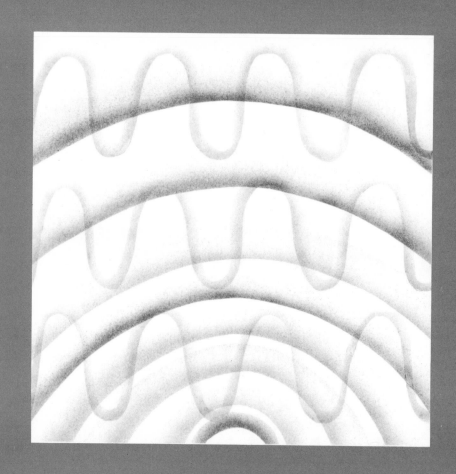

PART III

Broadcast/Electronics

10

BROADCASTING:
A BRIEF HISTORY

The process of developing a television newscast at Independent Network News (INN) requires split second timing, good intuition, financial resources and a team capable of working together professionally. Perhaps the managing editor has more to say about the final composition of a news show, but his judgment is informed and modified by the suggestions and knowledge of people throughout the newsroom and especially by the two anchorpersons Claire Carter and Marvin Scott (Midday Edition). Throughout the afternoon before the next day's 11:30 a.m. broadcast, Carter and Scott work with other reporters in writing stories or following up leads away from the newsroom. Wherever they go, a camera crew follows to document stories. The pace picks up the next morning as the 11:30 a.m. deadline approaches.

Independent Network News operated from the studios of WPIX in New York City illustrates the problems and challenges of a newsroom operating on a limited budget. Managing editor Frank Coffey supervises the overall flow of news and assignments. By late afternoon the day before the newscast, a list of proposed stories has been compiled on an assignment board. Reporters know what to cover during the afternoon and evening hours and stories recorded on videocassette tape filter back to the newsroom from Washington, New York, the Middle East—wherever a story is developing. One reporter continually covers activities of the President, including trips away from Washington. Camera crews for such stories are hired on location.

Sometimes the President, on one of his trips, decides suddenly to stop at an unscheduled place. When the side trip is only thirty minutes away, INN producers have just minutes to locate a crew in the unscheduled location—a task that requires telephone calls from INN headquarters in New York City to television stations and independent producers in the area to be visited. Then the contracted crew must reach the site to be visited, set up equipment and wait for the President to appear. Often the deadline is difficult to meet.

For Carter and Scott the days are filled with preparations for their broadcast, reading books and background material on upcoming guests to be interviewed, remote assignments, and writing and rewriting. The following accounts gives some indication of the moment to moment planning and changes that have to be made as developing stories change and new stories appear.

The Making of a Network Television Newscast

10:00 A.M.   The room, which measures no more than forty feet by forty feet, is filled with more than twenty typewriters, a maze of other equipment, and newspapers and books, to say nothing of the reporters, editors, producers, and others abuzz with frantic activity that belies the underlying organization.

The teletype equipment consists of two neat rows of machines lining one wall—the bottom with five machines, the top with four. Headline teletype machines are stationed at desks here and there. Four television sets line another wall—one tuned to CBS, one to NBC, one to ABC, and one to WPIX, which shortly will be showing Independent Network News (INN), the newest national commercial television network.

A videocassette machine and a monitor along one wall are just now playing back a story for two editors to review and select material from.

High on one wall a board shows assignments; on the opposite wall is an outline of all the stories to appear on today's newscasts.

In the middle of everything, a rectangular table sags under the weight of a dozen typewriters, and more papers and books than can be counted in an afternoon.

Meanwhile, the managing editor, Frank Coffey, is reading today's *New York Times,* reviewing stories of possible interest.

10:15 A.M.   Most of the news for today's 11:30 A.M. newscast already has been edited. Assignments were made long ago and news has been filtering into this tenth floor newsroom throughout the night and the early morning hours.

At 11:00 A.M., the morning stories from Washington will be sent up on cables, which connect the Washington Bureau to this crowded room.

The conversation deals with everything:

"Yankees look terrible . . ."

"Von Bulow sentencing tomorrow . . ."

". . . and it costs me $70 per month to rent a garage for my classic car . . ."

Coffey inquires of a nearby editor, "In discussions with Diane did you conclude she could push her 12:30 P.M. appointment back?''

No reply.

''I don't have a crew and need her.'' Coffey frowns.

Everywhere typewriters—the old manual kind—pound away, creating the copy for a newscast that is less than an hour away. Telephone: ''Iris, for you.''

10:45 A.M. President Ronald Reagan is to make an announcement about the compromise he got on the budget with Republican leaders on Capitol Hill. Announcement will be made in a few minutes. Panic time.

11:18 A.M. Three television screens show Reagan with a group of Republican members of Congress behind him. All regular programming is suspended. Coffey watches the screen closely as Reagan announces that Social Security retirees will get their cost of living adjustment this year and will continue to get benefits as scheduled. The President goes on to announce that limited changes will be proposed for those who are not on Social Security but are contemplating early retirement.

Other budget provisions follow; Reagan describes the new proposal as a $400 billion compromise.

The special news conference continues, but the time to go on the air is rapidly approaching.

11:29 A.M. In a crowded control room is a director who will supervise everything that goes out of the two rooms for the next thirty minutes; a technical director who will push the buttons that switch the picture from camera to camera to tape; an assistant director who will give time cues; an audio person who will control the complex arrangement of microphones and other sound sources. They, and others, wait.

''45 seconds.''

''30 seconds.''

''25 seconds.''

''Stand by. Go to black.'' All images on the television screen marked ''line'' disappear, but a dozen other television monitors show pictures of Marvin Scott and Claire Carter, the coanchors of the ''Midday Edition'' of INN's news program. There are also picture's of INN's symbol—a stylized world.

''Ready Chroma . . .'' The director's voice is the only sound in a control room that was noisy only seconds before. Everybody is ready for the instant when the program will begin.

''Ten seconds.''

''Five seconds.''

''Start cues for Marvin and Claire . . .''

''Four seconds.''

''Ready chroma.''

''Three seconds.''

Silence.

11:30 A.M.   "Take chroma . . . ready Marvin." At that instant, a signal travels from a satellite dish atop a building on East Forty-Second Street in New York City through a satellite to seventy-three television stations located from New England to California. Several million people watch the familiar INN logo as a voice announces the midday edition of Independent Network News.

Attention jumps to other television screens as Marvin Scott and Claire Carter introduce themselves and give background on the war in Argentina, which leads into reports gathered thousands of miles away. Then there is a studio interview with an Argentine representative at the United Nations. Another story deals with John Hinkley's trial for shooting President Reagan. Then there are stories about accidents, the President's budget compromise, and Soviet spying, including an interview with a Soviet spy that was recorded earlier.

The distance from the crowded control room to the studio where Scott and Carter are reading the news is just about the thickness of a wall. Inside the studio there are three sets: One used for the midday edition, another used for the evening edition, and a third used for interviews. Each is made of wood and painted with INN's stylized world. Television monitors and telephones cover the sets.

Three television cameras, each with a Teleprompter—a device for projecting the news on a screen in front of the camera lens so the anchorpersons can appear to be looking at the viewers while reading the news—are aimed at the anchors. At the edge of the studio, a young woman feeds news copy into the teleprompter pickup.

There is a break for commercials.

Then the three television cameras are moved to the interview set where Jeffrey Lyons interviews Michael Moriarty about his role in *Too Far To Go*.

The commercial break is over and Lyons wants to know what Moriarty would like to be remembered for.

The answer: "A poet." The light interview is launched.

Sometimes the cameras pick up the set where Scott and Carter sit waiting to finish the news program. Another commercial break and back to the two anchors, who round out the half-hour program. Then Carter and Scott close saying, "Hope your day is a good one," and the closing INN music with its animated world and floating logo bring the show to a close.

12:00   Camera people return their equipment to its original position. Carter and Scott leave their set. Conversation resumes—some stop to talk to Moriarty and others stream out of the studio.

Several people pause in the hallway to chat a moment. The frantic pace of an hour ago has slowed; everyone drifts off towards lunch and other assignments. The hall is vacant and quiet except for a reporter rushing toward the newsroom to write up an event she just covered.

INN is the only midday network television newscast offered directly to television stations. This nation's desire for news has made INN possible, along with a number of other cable news programs.

Two other news services recently developed for television are CNN (Cable News Network) and CNN-2. CNN provides news coverage with three-minute stories on events; CNN-2 is a headline service patterned after all-news radio stations. Both services are distributed by satellite to cable systems.

INN's success depends on the work of five news crews in New York City and two news crews in Washington (a news crew includes a reporter and the necessary technical personnel such as camera and sound persons). In addition, there are a number of reporters who operate throughout the world and hire local crews as stories develop. When Reagan made the surprise decision to go to Dayton, Ohio, to view flood conditions, INN had to find and hire a crew in Dayton while Reagan was flying there. A crew was found via long-distance telephone from New York and was on the scene in time.

Because INN does not have a full entertainment line-up to help support its news shows, the news must pay its own way. Consequently, INN has a news budget less than 3 percent the size of the news budgets of ABC, CBS, or NBC. Yet the network covers almost as much news as the other three networks. The INN news is produced by WPIX-TV, an independent television station is New York City, which is owned by Tribune Company Broadcasting which is itself owned by the Tribune Company, publisher of the *Chicago Tribune*. Without the low costs made possible by satellite communications, the service would not exist.

RADIO BROADCASTING

Radio came into the world just as the twentieth century was approaching, modes of travel were speeding up, business was diversifying, and international commerce was becoming a reality. Radio served a need for speedy communication, but before it was possible, many complicated electrical instruments had to be invented. The first step was taken by young artist Samuel F. B. Morris, who, on a trip across the Atlantic, fell into a discussion about the electromagnet and the possibilities of using it to communicate. Morris found the conversation so challenging that he spent the night working out the philosophy behind the telegraph. His first experiments in 1835 involved stringing 1,700 feet of wire around a workshop where, with his assistant, Alfred Vail, Morris sent out coded messages.[1] But it was not until Congress approved the financing of $30,000 that the famous electrical transmission "What Hath God Wrought" was sent from Washington to Baltimore in May, 1844. Although Morris continued his work with the telegraph, it couldn't transmit speech and it required a wire.

The next step was taken in Germany in 1861, where Philip Reis invented a crude telephone. But, it was Americans who invented the first telephone that really worked. Elijah Gray may have had the honor or inventing the telephone before Alexander Graham Bell, but Bell beat him to the patent office by a few hours; he filed his application on February 14, 1876.[2] Now that a talking wire had been invented, the direction was set.

The first wireless (radio) was the result of the work of many people—Joseph Henry, working in the United States, who demonstrated that metal objects could be magnetized at a distance; James Clerk-Maxwell, a Scottish physicist, who developed a theory on how radio waves might work (1873); and Heinrich Hertz, an experimental physicist in Germany, who demonstrated the existence of wireless waves.

But it was Guglielmo Marconi, an intense young Italian inventor, who rushed to invent the radio so that he would not be eclipsed by another inventor. Marconi was able to transmit coded information

BROADCASTING

1835	The telegraph is invented.
1844	Telegraph is demonstrated and installed from Washington to Baltimore.
1861	Philip Reis invents a crude telephone.
1876	Alexander Graham Bell asks for telephone patent.
1873	James Clerk-Maxwell creates theory of radio waves.
1896	Guglielmo Marconi applies for British patent on his wireless.
1901	Marconi transmits "S" across Atlantic.
1906	Reginald Fessenden transmits voice and music with his alternator.
1907	Lee DeForest patents the audion tube.
1912	David Sarnoff receives signals from the Titanic as it sinks.
1920	KDKA broadcasts election returns.
1922	AT&T's WEAF broadcasts first commercial program.
1926	NBC, the network, is formed.
1927	The Federal Radio Commission is formed to regulate radio.
1930	Forty-seven percent of homes have radio despite the Depression.
1934	Federal Communications Commission takes place of FRC.
1938	Radio tells the story of Germany's aggression in Europe.
1941	First FM station on the air with regular programs.

through the air without wires. He initially sold his invention in England, but soon took it to the United States. Others who contributed to the talking wireless were Reginald Fessenden, a Canadian-born physicist; Ernest Alexanderson, who worked for General Electric; and John Flemming, a British physicist.

Perhaps the first radio voice was transmitted by Nathan B. Stubblefield in Murray, Kentucky, in 1892, when he is supposed to have said "Hello Rainey," which was heard by a partner. Stubblefield's invention seems to have contributed little to the development of radio. Ernest Alexanderson, however, produced a giant alternator, which looked much like an oversized motor, to create radio waves. Working with him, Reginald Fessenden had a 200 hundred kilowatt alternator constructed to transmit voices and music in 1906—a transmission heard by several hundred people, although the alternator never became part of the American system of broadcasting.

Although Dr. Lee DeForest receives credit for inventing the important vacuum tube, his ideas grew out of the work of British physicist John Flemming, who invented a crude two-element tube. DeForest's tube made it possible to amplify sounds and impress them on a radio wave. Although he was a brilliant scientist, DeForest didn't have much of a business sense: He sold his invention to American Telephone and Telegraph Co. (AT&T) in the summer of 1913 for just $50,000. Using the vacuum tube, scientist Edwin Armstrong developed the hetrodyne circuit, which amazingly improved reception. A. N. Goldsmith simplified the receiver to one-knob tuning, making it easy for the most casual listener to control the radio.[3]

Until 1920, though, radio was for experimenters, the military, and business. Most private citizens had little opportunity to use a radio; it was thought of as an interesting toy. Then in 1920, Westinghouse employee, Frank Conrad, set up a transmitter on top of an East Pittsburgh building and began to experiment. On November 2, the station, which was licensed as KDKA, transmitted the Harding-Cox elections. Broadcasting had begun.

That early station received listener reports from amateur radio buffs all over the Pittsburgh area and from as far away as ships off the coast of Virginia. When Conrad began broadcasting music, the Hamilton Music Store of Wilkinsborough, Pennsylvania, saw an opportunity to promote itself by giving records to the station in return for free publicity. The trade-out or exchange of broadcast time for goods or services was born. Although KDKA is frequently cited as the first broadcast station still on the air, the government first licensed radio station WBZ in Boston.[4]

The telegraph, telephone, and radio came at a time when the entire western world was changing. Europe and the United States were being transformed from agrarian to industrial societies. The railroad was cutting the travel time from New York City to Washington, D.C., from forty-four hours to about four hours. Factories were being built and thousands of farm refugees found employment in the textile and heavy

FIGURE 10–1 An example of an early radio with audion vacuum tubes on top of set. (Culver Pictures)

machinery factories of the Northeast. The United States was trading with Europe, and the need for rapid forms of transportation and communication was becoming critical. Electrical inventions grew out of the same innovative spirit that characterized the entire industrial revolution.

Economic Realities of Radio Broadcasting

Although broadcasting had become a reality by 1920, many uncertainties remained. Because operating a station cost so much, broadcasters were confronted with questions about the sources of their operating funds. Radio programming had to be found. Radio came along before audio tape recording existed and before records were high quality, so early disc jockeys could not just sit at a control console and play records all day.

Young, energetic David Sarnoff was to contribute much to solving these questions brought about by the new medium. He spent more time at a transmitter; he was more interested in how the radio worked;

he asked many questions—he was, in a word, captivated. Sarnoff became famous when he reported the sinking of the *Titanic* in 1912.[5] Working at a Wanamaker radio transmitter in New York, Sarnoff was the first to hear distress signals from the sinking ship and from the S. S. *Olympic,* which was some distance from the Titanic. For hours the twenty-one-year-old youth was the United States's sole link with the developing disaster. And for the first time, the nation heard the details of a catastrophe as it happened hundreds of miles out at sea.

That transmitter in the Wanamaker store was installed by American Marconi—a company that later was bought by a group of American companies and operated as the Radio Corporation of America (RCA). The store secured the transmitter as a publicity move. It made the store and its young transmitter operator famous that day in April, 1912.

Sarnoff stayed in the center of radio's development. While his contemporaries in 1916 were thinking of radio as just a business and military communications instrument, Sarnoff wrote his boss a memo proposing some technical developments that would turn radio into a music box, bringing entertainment to millions of citizens. In his scheme, the sale of receivers to the public would produce a big profit and pay for sending out the music. (Sarnoff proposed a technically

FIGURE 10–2   David Sarnoff of RCA. (Culver Pictures)

simple receiver for nonmechanical customers, a device A. N. Gold-
smith achieved with his one-knob unit. Sarnoff did not conceive of
advertising to support broadcasting, and when it was later proposed,
he opposed it, believing that radio should be a public trust.)

Sarnoff tried to show Edward J. Nally how American Marconi could
make $75 million. Sarnoff said that in the first year the company would
make 100,000 receivers to make $7.5 million; in the second year, it
would make 300,000 receivers to make $22.5 million; and in the third
year, it would make 600,000 receivers to make $45 million. When a few
years later RCA began selling radios (1922), their first-year gross was
$11 million, their second-year sales matched Sarnoff's prediction, and
their third-year sales reached $50 million. Sarnoff became known as
something of a prophet because of his amazing predictions.[6]

Radio and the Military

Radio began as the work of experimenters and amateurs. Soon much of
the work had moved to laboratories, but amateurs or "hams" did not
lose interest. World War I revoked much of their freedom because the
government restricted hams from using the airwaves during the war—
the independent experimenters actually had to seal their equipment.
The restrictions came about because the government and the military
felt that amateurs were interfering with the military's use of the airwaves. Radio, it appeared, was to serve the needs of the U.S. Army and
Navy. Out of the military's desire to control the media, several companies—Westinghouse, General Electric, and Western Electric—were to
make fortunes.

Business and military circles perceived the same threat from the
American Marconi Company that they did from amateurs, because it
was owned by British interests. And U.S. companies wanted the radio
market. They argued, that in the event of war, a foreign concern might
take control of all the radio equipment in the United States, seriously
injuring the war effort. As a result, the Radio Corporation of America
was formed to control all radio manufacturing in the country. Several
companies had an interest in RCA—Westinghouse, General Electric,
AT&T, and United Fruit Company. Also, a representative of the U.S.
Navy was to sit on the board of directors of the new company.

RCA made radio music boxes, vacuum tubes, transmitters—in a
word—everything. RCA, incidentally, was largely the invention of
Owen D. Young, a young attorney at General Electric, who took the
suggestions of Admiral Bullard, that an American company should be
formed to take control of the wireless in the United States. Young secured an agreement from AT&T and Westinghouse to participate in the
formation of a new company that would take over American Marconi.
RCA was the result—a puppet company of the other three. However,
RCA eventually did become independent when internal fighting broke
out and the Department of Justice began considering antitrust actions
against the company.

RCA, of course, dominated the field of radio receiver and component manufacturing. And, Sarnoff's view that radio could be used to make money, by providing programming to home listeners prevailed in time.

Westinghouse and General Electric began making radio receivers for the home market as quickly as possible—all sold and distributed under the RCA name. Meanwhile, Western Electric, the partner authorized to build transmitters, was selling transmitters to radio stations around the nation. These early stations did not sell advertising as they do now. Rather, the broadcasters hoped to make money through the sale of receiving sets as Sarnoff had proposed.

Regulating Radio

Radio was getting a lot of public attention by 1922, so Secretary of Commerce Herbert Hoover convened a national radio conference with representatives from government, business, and education. That first conference led to three others; and with each passing conference, it became clearer that radio could not regulate itself. Broadcasters were clustering on the same frequencies, creating a rising level of pandemonium. It was apparent to those involved in broadcasting that something had to be done.

The direction that radio was to take was dictated in large measure by the AT&T's decision to engage in toll broadcasting—once called a telephone booth of the air. WEAF was the first toll station, and one of the characteristics quickly associated with it was the superior quality of its signal; another was its programs. Sponsors could purchase time to talk about their products, as the Queensboro Corporation did on August 28, 1922, paying fifty dollars to tell listeners about some real estate it wanted to sell in Jackson Heights, Long Island. Other advertisers soon followed.

AT&T claimed that it owned the sole right to engage in toll broadcasting, referring to the partnership agreement that had divided up the responsibilities of radio when RCA was formed. But, AT&T's view did not prevail.

Not all broadcast licenses belonged to commercial interests. Educational institutions owned about 90 of the 732 stations operating in 1927—the year the Federal Radio Commission was formed by an act of Congress.

Broadcasters, whether commercial or educational, increasingly competed with each other for limited broadcast space, creating such confusion that listeners had difficulty picking signals out of the air. Broadcasters realized they might be losing valuable listeners who might have an interest in purchasing an advertiser's product. The radio conferences led by Hoover provided a forum in which broadcasters, educators, and governmental officials could call upon Congress to impose a regulatory scheme to clear up the airwaves. During 1926, matters became so bad because of some adverse judicial opinions that Congress found itself forced to take some action.

The result of Congress's action was the formation of the Federal Radio Commission (FRC) through the Radio Act of 1927. Before the FRC could consider any other problems, it had to reduce the competition among stations. Because the educational broadcasters did not have the financial resources their commercial counterparts had, they constantly were urged to leave the airwaves to the richer commercial stations. In 1927, eight educational stations disappeared; in 1928, twenty-three stations disappeared; and in 1929, thirteen disappeared.

Much of the pressure to reduce the number of educational stations came from petitions from commercial stations asking the FRC to revoke educational licenses so that the airwave space could be given to commercial interests. Clearly, the commercial stations could afford to send expensive lawyers to Washington to lobby their interests while the educational stations lacked the same economic leverage.

As the years passed, still more educational stations gave up their licenses under intense FRC pressure until the *Harvard Business Review* was compelled to observe: "The point seems clear that the Federal Radio Commission has interpreted the concept of public interest so as to favor in actual practice one particular group . . . the commercial broadcasters."[7]

The First Radio Network

The number of stations operating in the United States grew rapidly—from 0 to 571 in five years. Anyone who had the skill to build a station or to buy the equipment seemed to be constructing a radio station. Some stations, like the one owned by Los Angeles evangelist Aimee Semple McPherson was not good enough technically to stay on the channel they were supposed to occupy. Other stations chose frequencies so close to competing stations that listeners had great difficulty in picking one station out of the maze.

But whatever the clutter, listeners were just as captivated by the new medium as were the entrepreneurs who built and operated stations. As the number of stations grew, the demand for programming also grew. In those early days almost everything was broadcast: election returns, boxing, live music and records, chatter, and more.

The 1920s were good years for business; employment was high, and people had money to spend on entertainment. It was time to build a network, or a chain as they were called then, to interconnect numerous stations so that they could carry live entertainment simultaneously.

Working with his usual intensity, Sarnoff was in the middle of the process that brought about National Broadcasting Company (NBC). Starting with a limited chain purchased from AT&T, NBC was founded on September 9, 1926. NBC acquired the exclusive right from the other partners to engage in broadcasting and networking. AT&T didn't give up much in the sale. It retained the right to provide interconnecting wires to hook up NBC's radio stations—for a toll, of course.

By the time NBC was formed, much of the basic structure of American broadcasting was in place. Although broadcasters hadn't yet heralded advertising as the financial foundation of the new medium, several advertising agencies were already selling broadcast advertising, many stations accepted advertising, and NBC, as a descendant of AT&T, had come into being as an advertising network. NBC quietly dropped the term toll broadcasting, which had been used to describe early AT&T advertising, but it retained the principle of advertising.

By 1926, radio had stations, networks, advertising agencies, and performers. About the same time, the organization that was to become Columbia Broadcasting System (CBS) was born, in part because Sarnoff had given the cold shoulder to two businesspeople.

Other Networks

George A. Coats and Arthur Judson ran a talent agency that supplied musicians and actors to NBC and other broadcasters. Their agency became a weak competitor of the broadcasters when Sarnoff stopped using their services and they turned instead to supplying programming directly to stations. Coats and Judson were not particularly good at operating their network, so they invited others to join the company and provide funds and management. After several reorganizations and bailouts by interested people, the Paley family, who produced La Palina cigars in Philadelphia, bought the network which was to become CBS for young William S. Paley. Ambitious and bored with Philadelphia, twenty-six-year-old Paley was looking for new opportunities.

When Paley took over the ailing network, he wrote an affiliate-network contract that gave the network great control over its affiliates. Many stations willingly signed up, making CBS a strong competitor to NBC.

The difference between NBC's affiliate contract and CBS's contract was important. NBC paid its affiliate stations for running the network's sponsored programs (those with advertising)—initially thirty dollars, later fifty dollars—no matter how large or small the station. Stations that wanted to use NBC's sustaining, or unsponsored programs, had to pay the network a fee. Stations were free to select just one type of programming, both, or none at all. Paley didn't think that this arrangement worked well. To make matters more comfortable for affiliates, Paley wrote a contract allowing affiliates to use any, all, or none of the sustaining programming without cost. How much of the sustaining programming that stations used was up to them. In exchange, Paley required that stations accept and broadcast any programming that the network sold to sponsors. In this way, Paley could guarantee sponsors that their ads would be heard on stations from coast to coast. Each station was paid for commercial time based on its established rates: large stations with many listeners received more than stations with fewer listeners. Paley's contract proved to be a bonanza for most stations, and it eliminated many sources of friction between the stations and the network that had been experienced by NBC. Many stations willingly signed contracts with CBS.

Meanwhile, NBC had two networks—NBC-Red and NBC-Blue— named for the color of ink used on their scripts and advertising copy. Years later, the Supreme Court (1943) forced NBC to sell its Blue net- work. Edward Noble, the purchaser, renamed the Blue network Ameri- can Broadcasting Company (ABC).

THE GOLDEN AGE OF RADIO

During the Depression, even nature was hostile—a drought created a dust bowl in the nation's heartland. Banks closed, and people lost for- tunes big and small. But most of broadcasting was booming. The net- works fared well, even though some little stations across the land could barely keep their utility bills paid to keep the transmitters run- ning. Some stations gave up; others sold out to chains or newspapers; a few resorted to playing records; and most signed with a network that provided programming.

The advertising agencies in New York and Chicago were doing a booming radio business, hiring bright young persons from Ivy League universities to write copy, create advertising, produce dramatic pro- grams, and sell products. When agencies could not keep up with the volume of business, they hired free-lance writers like Harry Herrmann, who worked for advertising agencies writing scripts for programs like "Mr. District Attorney."

Before the networks, most radio programming was music, with a lit- tle talk and a little news. The variety of programs began increasing in the late 1920s and was slowed down only slightly by World War II. Whatever one's taste, the programs were there. Ellery Queen solved mysteries; Jack Benny made the unemployed laugh with remarks about his stinginess; Superman jumped over the tallest buildings; Gene Autry entertained with songs from his "Melody Ranch"; and Lamont Cran- ston (the Shadow) disappeared without any double shots in the minds of millions of children and adults.

Radio helped people to imagine all sorts of things during a time when the Depression seemed to press an unforgiving reality upon them from every side. Audiences weren't disappointed, because their imaginations could produce pictures far superior to any film or televi- sion picture. Young children might thrill with fear under the bed- clothes on a dark night while listening to the "Whistler"; parents might spend their evenings sewing or playing cards, while listening to live music from New York City.

By 1930, 47 percent of all homes had at least one radio and by 1940, that number had risen to 81 percent. Meanwhile, between 600 and 850 stations were on the air serving the nation. People everywhere in the United States had access to one or more radio stations; some stations boasted 50,000 watts of power—quite enough to reach the most re- mote midwestern farm-house.[8]

Although listeners received their programs from local outlets, most of these programs originated in New York City and Hollywood, and were sent by telephone cables to stations. All of the radio programs were live, and they made people like Bing Crosby, Kate Smith, and Bob Hope famous.

The networks were in the driver's seat, providing programming, advertising, and income for local affiliates. In fact, a network contract almost assured a local station that it would be able to survive. But, how were networks able to be so powerful during the Depression? After all, they had been formed only a few years before, and while other, better capitalized businesses were going broke, the networks were making millions of dollars.

Albert D. Lasker

Much of the networks' success can be traced to the advertising agencies. Leading the advertising agencies into radio was Albert D. Lasker, owner and president of Lord & Thomas, a large Chicago advertising agency, and a man who was described as combative, sharp, and a shrewd salesperson. Although Lasker started in the newspaper business, he quickly found that his real talent lay in selling everything from cardboard hearing aids to tobacco products. His remarkable advertising talents bloomed just as network radio was presenting itself to advertisers, and Lasker quickly saw its potential. Before long, Lasker, who had started at Lord & Thomas as a staff salesperson, was able to buy out both senior partners. Soon, Lasker found himself selling Pepsodent, Palmolive, Kotex, Kleenex, and Lucky Strike over the radio. The line that made Lucky Strike so popular with women, previously an untapped market for cigarettes, was, "Reach for a Lucky instead of a sweet." Lasker's pre-1929 income of $1 million rose to as much as $3.5 million during the early years of the Depression. And as Lasker prospered, so did the networks.[9]

Lasker never could have been as successful as he was without the cooperation of advertisers who wanted to sell their products. Chief among these was George Washington Hill, who headed American Tobacco Company. Hill's open Cadillac decorated with Lucky Strike packages became a landmark on the avenues of New York. Every waking moment found Hill devising new strategies to increase the sales of Lucky Strike cigarettes—a task that Lasker wholeheartedly joined in. Together, Hill and Lasker brought the Lucky Strike Orchestra under the baton of B. A. Rolfe to millions of listeners. As the popularity of the orchestra grew, so did the length and stridency of the commercial interruptions. Yet NBC, with its strict policy on advertising, acquiesced. Clearly, the advertiser and the advertising agency were in charge of the programming they sponsored. Network officials grumbled, some critics complained, and occasional government officials objected, but the die was cast. Like it or not, the advertising agencies made radio what it was.

Agencies and networks made their money selling entertainment programs as vehicles for advertising; but agencies like Lasker's didn't limit their interests to entertainment. Lasker actively tried to influence government, as well. When the Food and Drug Administration developed a bill to require food, drug, and cosmetics products to list ingredients on their labels, (then known as the Tugwell bill), Lasker proclaimed that the bill would be a "menace [to] human welfare." With Lasker leading them, advertisers and broadcasters declared war on the bill, — a campaign that led to the passage of a watered down measure. Over time, the Federal Trade Commission has even become watchful about false advertising claims.

Early News Programming

While they were successful at providing entertainment programming like "Gangbusters," "The Shadow," or "Lux Radio Theater," networks engaged in little journalistic programming for some years. NBC's sole news effort was A. A. Schechter, who created a daily news broadcast from telephone calls he made to newsmakers. It seemed as if anyone would accept a call from Schechter in Lowell Thomas's office. (Thomas was the network's newscaster.) The governor of Iowa, who had refused a battery of journalists at his door, answered a call from Schechter to talk about a threatened milk strike among farmers. When the persuasive powers of his office didn't work, Schechter offered people free tickets to Rudy Vallee broadcasts in return for cooperation— and the tickets seemed to have just the right value. Schechter was so successful, that he was able to fill a daily Lowell Thomas program and still provide an occasional item for Walter Winchell, a print journalist with a weekend gossip program.

To compete with Schechter, CBS established its own news service and hired Paul W. White, a former UP editor, to head it. White began building a regular news organization with reporters and stringers, who were paid for occasional stories.

All of this network news activity scared the newspapers and the wire services. Consequently, representatives from the American Newspaper Publishers Association (ANPA), the wire services, and newspapers met with NBC, CBS, and the National Association of Broadcasters in an attempt to stop the news take-over that journalists were convinced that broadcasters were attempting. In the resulting treaty, called the Biltmore program (for the hotel in New York where the meeting occurred), CBS and NBC agreed to leave the news-gathering business. Moreover, the wire services would supply only short bulletins or news summaries to broadcasters through a new Press-Radio Bureau.

The Press-Radio War and Others

Called the Press-Radio War, the battle that took place between print and radio interests before and after that December, 1933, meeting was an attempt by the newspapers to protect their industry from a threat they probably did not fully understand. Yet, the effort amounted to an attack on the freedom of speech and press that the newspapers had so long championed. But, the feud did not last—partly because newspapers owned many broadcast outlets; partly because radio was growing powerful; and, partly because newspapers began to realize that broadcasting would never take away newspapers' business.

Then in 1934, another battle began brewing. Educators still were smarting from the defeats they had experienced under the FRC's total enthusiasm for commercial stations. The new administration of Franklin D. Roosevelt gave dissident educators hope when the new President called for a law to control broadcasting. Roosevelt's interest stemmed from his desire to cluster the regulation of telephone and radio communication under a single agency—rather than under the purview of several agencies as they had been.

Senate leaders like Senator Robert F. Wagner of New York and Senator Henry D. Hatfield of West Virginia proposed an amendment that would declare all radio licenses null and void 90 days after the passage of the new law. When new licenses were awarded, one-fourth were to go to "educational, religious, agricultural, cooperative" and other non-profit groups. The amendment also required that the channels given to noncommercial users be as desirable as those given to advertising-based stations.

The commercial broadcast industry was shocked. It rallied its best spokespersons—as did the educational interests. One former advertising copywriter wrote the book *Our Master's Voice,* which attacked advertising in general and radio advertising in particular. Although James Rorty's book garnered much attention, it was only one of many voices demanding attention.

Meanwhile, the procommercial interests magazine *Broadcasting,* said it believed that powerful interests were threatening the foundation of broadcasting. Perhaps they were, but there was a flaw in the armor—some educators, strapped for funds, wanted the right to engage in advertising to help support their enterprises. Senator Clarence C. Dill, seeing the opening, attacked educational interests for wanting more advertising—not less—a cry that became standard for commercial broadcasters. In time, the Wagner-Hatfield bill was defeated.

When the new Federal Communications Commission emerged from the Communications Act of 1934, commercial interests had gained the right to their nearly exclusive monopoly on the broadcast channels, but they also had given up something. During all the debates over the Communications Act, broadcasters had pointed to the unsold time they had and proposed to provide some of it free to educators, who could then offer courses and cultural and other programming not usually offered on sponsored broadcasts.

Some stations and networks were already offering educational and informational programs before the act passed. There were NBC's programs "University of Chicago Round Table" and "America's Town Meeting of the Air," and CBS's "American School of the Air." And, broadcasters promised more.

Educators held broadcasters to their promises—not always too successfully, but with some small gains. Commercial stations' educational, informational, religious, and other nonprofit programs diffused critical comment and garnered new listeners—who sometimes stayed around for the commercial programs. And, the educators gained an outlet for their programs.

If one were keeping a scorecard, it might look like this: educators lost most of their own stations, but gained a tenuous right to provide programming over commercial outlets; commercial broadcasters gained broadcast channels, but had to promise time to noncommercial programming—a promise that was at least partially kept. Years later, when television stations were licensed, some of the same fervor would surface again over who should get the channels.

Political and Social Uses of Radio

The New Deal, brainchild of Franklin D. Roosevelt and his administration, was sold on radio as a means to take America out of the Depression, a period when twenty-five percent of the nation's work force was unemployed. Bread lines abounded; farm produce wasn't making it to the city; manufactured goods seemed destined for nowhere.[10] FDR, who was elected in 1932, proposed an alphabet soup of agencies to cope with the problems—AAA, NRA, WPA. Even more important than all the new agencies he planned was the personality of FDR himself. On radio, Roosevelt's voice seemed to console millions of people. His home "fireside chats" conveyed an intimacy that even through the radio made 40 million people feel that they were talking privately with their president—their friend. So intimate were the chats that one hot summer day Roosevelt asked his listeners to wait while he took a drink of water.

Father Charles E. Coughlin in Detroit had an equally captivating radio style—a style, which, when combined with his political views, made him a very popular radio personality during the Depression. His church had assigned Coughlin to the Shrine of the Little Flower in Royal Oak, near Detroit, where he discovered the power of radio to communicate his messages, which were not always religious. Early broadcasts were designed for children, but Coughlin soon turned his attention toward adults.

A powerful speaker, Coughlin attacked "unregulated capitalism" because it was trampling human rights. Those with wealth had responsibilities to those without, he said. Listeners, burdened with the problems of unemployment and underemployment, greeted Coughlin's messages with enthusiasm. Contributions flowed in. Coughlin damned international bankers and President Hoover, but by now Coughlin was on CBS and the network became concerned. Edward Klauber, the network's executive vice president, asked Coughlin to tone down his messages. He received the reply—which came on the air January 4, 1931—that he was trying to censor Coughlin. Although CBS gave up trying to change Coughlin's message, it slowly eased him off the air. Undaunted, Coughlin turned unsuccessfully to other networks and finally to syndicating his program to stations.[11]

Coughlin was an open supporter of Roosevelt's programs throughout 1933. During the next year, he alternately supported and opposed the President. After 1934, Coughlin usually opposed Roosevelt's policies, and many in the Roosevelt administration openly opposed the minister. Some tried to link Coughlin to a powerful Louisiana senator named Huey Long, another fiery radio speaker—a man who exercised dictatorial powers over the state legislature using patronage, corruption, and a flamboyant personality to get his way. Although Coughlin and Long never had any formal relationship, some of their views paralleled each other. Long formed Share-The-Wealth clubs with the view that the great wealth that was clustered in the hands of the few should be spread among the population. Long was assassinated in September, 1935. When news of the assassination reached Roosevelt, he was entertaining two visitors—Coughlin and Joseph P. Kennedy, who was trying to heal the division[12] between the president and the radio personality.

The 1920s and 1930s produced many people who were skilled at using radio for political and social purposes, good and ill. One in the latter category was Dr. John Brinkley of Kansas, who operated a radio station to sell worthless medical cures. His most popular product was a supposed restorer of men's sexual powers, which relied on a goat's gland.[13] Although the Federal Radio Commission took Brinkley off the air, he later went to Mexico and got a license there.

Journalists in Radio

The Press-Radio Bureau had done little to stop the rising interest in radio news, and World War II did everything to propel it—on-the-spot radio accounts of events became nationally prominent. To make these newscasts, Paul White at CBS was recruiting bright young journalists to work with H. V. Kaltenborn.

CBS did not consider Kaltenborn commercial material; the network hired him on fringe time with a salary of $100 per week. But 58-year-old Kaltenborn took news seriously, spending more than he earned at CBS to travel to the sources of news: to Spain for the Franco rebellion; to Washington, D.C., to talk to the President; to Czechoslovakia to visit with the President of that nation; to anywhere in the world to interview a world leader or cover a developing situation. Kaltenborn's travel allowed him to sprinkle his newscasts with statements like, "Two weeks ago, I was flying over the locks of the Panama Canal . . ." or "Politically they are as the President of Czechoslovakia said to me . . ."[14]

Although Kaltenborn may not have been taken seriously by CBS, his popularity on the lecture circuit brought financial rewards that helped him in his diligent attempts to cover the news of the world. Kaltenborn's aggressive and expensive pursuit of the news led him to the first live broadcast of a war in Europe, using shortwave broadcasts to the United States. America heard the fighting along the Spanish/French border, complete with planes flying overhead and bullets passing close by. Done largely at his own expense, and broadcast on unsponsored time, Kaltenborn's newscast of the Battle of Irun made history.

Another young reporter who made history during the late Depression and who was active for many years afterward, was Edward R. Murrow, also of CBS. When he worked as CBS's director of talks, Murrow was described as lean, young, and handsome. He also was aggressive and fully prepared to perform his new job. Shortly after being named director of talks, Murrow went to Europe as CBS's person in charge of cultural events. On a tip from William L. Shirer, Murrow chartered a twenty-seven-seat plane to Vienna to broadcast the fall of that city to the Germans in 1938. Murrow and Kaltenborn were attracting attention and World War II was shaping up. News programming at CBS was to change quickly.

Edward R. Murrow, William L. Shirer, Edgar Ansel Mowrer, and Frank Gervasi became the voices of a distant war, which was soon to touch America. From those 1938 broadcasts the news round-up came about, featured these reporters in various cities who, described events as they saw them. Shortwave broadcasts in which reporters were heard live from throughout the world, became commonplace on CBS, NBC, and the young Mutual Broadcasting System. These broadcasts featured not only reporters and the sounds of fighting, but also interviews with the principal characters of war—Hitler, Mussolini, Chamberlain, and others.

From September 2 to 19, 1938, the nation listened breathlessly as Germany gobbled up more and more of Czechoslovakia. Much was changing in radio: Networks added commentators like Dorothy Thompson on NBC-Red, and General Hugh S. Johnson on NBC-Blue. Even more startling, sponsors began to pay for news and commentary broadcasts—news was becoming a saleable commodity. During Germany's invasion of Czechoslovakia, Kaltenborn did more than anyone else to bring a new status to the radio reporter; even the White House staff asked reporters for their views on the world situation.

Just as the Depression gave entertainment radio a much needed boost, so the war in Europe gave broadcast news a boost—making stars out of unknown reporters in unsponsored time slots.

But the rising popularity of the news commentator created its own problem—news censorship. General Mills canceled an advertising contract for Kaltenborn's program when he discussed Spain on the air—against the company's wishes. To cope with criticism, CBS decided to relabel commentators news analysts, and to remove some of their freedom. Frequently, CBS Vice-President Edward Klauber had friendly chats with Kaltenborn in an attempt to restrict his expression of controversial views over the network, but to no avail. Kaltenborn saw no distinction between the roles of analyst and commentator.

Even the government, through the FCC (which had replaced the Federal Radio Commission) thought stations should not carry editorial opinions. The FCC wrote the Mayflower Doctrine in 1941 when it reprimanded WAAB in Boston for its one-sided presentation of the news. But, the broadcast industry, through the National Association of Broadcasters, derided the FCC decision as tyrannical.

A new style of reporting was developing in 1941, and the leading proponent of that style was Edward R. Murrow. Characterized by a quiet dignity that was neither stuffy nor folksy, the new style allowed the reporter to speak with directness yet without frenzy. Young reporters like Erik Sevareid learned that they were not to display the emotion of a reporter at a prize fight during their newscasts, and the big test of broadcast journalism was about to come in the form of World War II coverage.

World War II and Radio

On December 8, 1941, President Roosevelt asked Congress to declare war on Japan because of Japan's attack on Hawaii. Germany and Italy quickly declared war on the United States and Congress reacted by voting a state of war with all the Axis partners.

Because of the war and military leaders, fears for national security, the Office of Censorship was created on January 15, 1942. Established as a voluntary system whereby broadcasters could submit their scripts for approval, the new office was opposed by the military precisely because of its voluntary nature. The new office did exercise an important influence on news and commentary programming, however. A few programs, such as Time's "March of Time," submitted scripts for approval. Others exercised voluntary restraint until, on his "Confidentially Yours" program, Arthur Hale noted that atomic research was being conducted at Pasco, Washington. Then the military insisted on tighter controls.

Still another agency, the Office of War Information (1942), was established during World War II to provide programming that would promote the Allied cause. Some of the films this office produced have remained a rich source of information on the war to this day.

By 1944, reporters were using new wire recorders to report their personal accounts of events along the battle lines—this was in conflict with network rules that no programs were to be recorded. As it turned out, this was the first chink in the ironclad rule, a rule that was abandoned completely with the development of television.

RADIO'S CHANGING ROLE

With the end of the war, radio news declined, along with radio entertainment. The best performers—at least the performers who looked best on television—were leaving radio for the new medium. Although the move to television didn't really reach a feverish pitch until the 1950s, some new radio elements already arriving foreshadowed the change—rip-and-read newscasts and the disc jockey. The rip-and-read newscast amounted to tearing copy from the AP, UP, or INS wire, and reading the stories just as they came from the teletype machine. Gone was radio's former pride in exhaustive reporting and serious attention to detail.

Most radio station owners felt abandoned and were unwilling to accept the new popularity of television. Fortunately, a program format that had its roots in Al Jarvis's 1930s program, "Make Believe Ballroom," saved the day. Essentially a recorded music program with information sprinkled between records, this format became radio's mainstay, replacing dramas, comedies, and live music. Cheap, entertaining, and always available, the new radio shows appealed to station managers who were barely able to cope with rising costs and decreasing revenues.

In time, the disc jockey radio show began to target certain audiences. Radio categories like Top-40, middle of the road (MOR), ethnic, and easy listening crept into the broadcasters' vocabulary. The trend was for each station to try to sell commercial time to local advertisers who sought to focus their messages on specialized audiences. National advertisers were sold time on the stations by representatives with offices in the major cities.

In time, the new formats worked and radio came back from the brink of bankruptcy to a new, highly profitable position. These formats were brought to their seemingly ultimate conclusion in the 1970s, when computer devices were used to fully automate recordings of announcers, commercials, music, and news.

FREQUENCY MODULATION (FM) BROADCASTING

FM broadcasting came along at about the same time that interest in television was reaching a peak. Consequently, the two media were frequently in conflict. Here is how FM developed:

1902   First FM patent is issued.

1940   FCC authorizes fifteen FM stations at about the same time. The first of these on the air is WSM.

1941   Edwin H. Armstrong gets FCC authorization and puts first commercial FM station on the air.

1955   FCC allows FM to carry background music on special "piggyback" FM channel that was not heard by most listeners. This helped stations financially.

1961   FM stereo broadcasting is approved.

Source: "A Short Story of Electrical Communications" (Washington, D.C.: FCC, 1979).

AM and FM Radio

AM radio—a term that stands for amplitude modulation—is a means of broadcasting that is subject to static from storms and electrical devices such as kitchen mixers. Edwin Howard Armstrong had invented several circuits that improved the capabilities of AM radio—the regenerative feedback circuit and the continuous-wave oscillator, but he was never satisfied with the sound that AM broadcasting produced. Armstrong loved music and began looking for a better form for transmitting music during the late 1920s and early 1930s. In 1933 he found the answer—frequency modulation or FM radio. The new invention varied the frequency of the radio waves as the means for sending information, whereas AM varied their strength or amplitude.

The same year, Armstrong demonstrated his invention for his friend David Sarnoff—a demonstration that Sarnoff found impressive indeed. Still at RCA, Sarnoff was more interested in television and AM radio, and ordered Armstrong to dismantle his transmitter. Although rebuffed by RCA, Armstrong decided to demonstrate his invention for the Institute of Radio Engineers in 1935—with astonishing success. But, Armstrong still needed a license.

Armstrong had little luck with the Federal Communications Commission. His first bid for a license was refused in 1936, but he finally received approval to erect an experimental station at Alpine, New Jersey.

By 1939, Armstrong's station in New Jersey was broadcasting successfully. General Electric had built some sets for Armstrong and was enthusiastic. FM radio appeared to have a bright future. Applications for 150 stations came rolling in and the FCC converted channel 1 that had previously been set aside for television to FM broadcasting. But World War II brought commercial FM to a temporary stop—FM was taken over by the military during the war, and all civilian manufacturing ceased.

After the war, the FCC reassigned FM to a different frequency band—the one it currently uses—making obsolete all previous FM transmitters and receivers. By some estimates the conversion costs would reach $75 million—a crushing blow to a medium that was just getting started. The television forces rejoiced because buyers of receivers would not be confused over choosing FM or television. Then the FCC made another decision that slowed the growth of FM—it allowed owners of both AM and FM stations to duplicate programs on both stations—further reducing the public's incentive to purchase new radio sets.[15]

These early defeats so slowed the growth of FM that it was not until the late 1950s that matters finally began to improve. In 1955, the FCC permitted FM stations to add a background music service that could be sold to stores and increase FM station profits. This music channel was added to the regular broadcast signal in such a way that home radios could not pick it up. Stations that had been operating with marginal revenues now could show a profit by selling music to stores. Then in

1961 the FCC began licensing FM stereo broadcasting—something AM stations had never been allowed to do. The main differences in FM and AM broadcasting are: FM provides clear, static free reception; FM can offer stereo programs; and FM broadcasters can sell a separate music channel that provides only music—no talk—to stores. Both AM and FM offer about the same kinds of programs to home listeners—music, news and talk. The two services are licensed to different parts of the radio spectrum however—thus the difference in numbers on the two radio dials. Besides the absence of static inherent in the way FM works, the FCC allows FM stations to broadcast a wider spectrum of tones (audio frequencies) than AM, therefore providing a hifi sound unavailable on AM radio.

A BRIEF HISTORY OF TELEVISION

The principle behind television was patented by Paul Nipkow, a German, in 1884, but his invention was developed slowly. The growing technology of television is illustrated in the following summary.

1890　Charles F. Jenkins begins the first U.S. study of television.

1900-1905　First French experiments with television are carried out.

1915　Marconi predicts picture telephone.

1922　Philco T. Farnsworth develops idea for electronic television.

1925　First mechanical television is demonstrated.

1926　More television experiments are carried out by E.F.W. Alexanderson, Philco T. Farnsworth, John L. Baird.

1927　Farnsworth demonstrates his system of components.

1927　Television picture is sent by wire between Washington and New York by Bell Laboratories.

1928　First color television experiments take place in England.

1929　Bell Telephone Laboratories experiments with color television.

1937　Seventeen experimental television stations are operating in the United States. (1937)

1938　CBS builds a television studio; NBC acquires a mobile van.

1939　President Franklin D. Roosevelt appears on television at the New York World's Fair.

1940　Twenty-three television stations are on the air.

1940　FCC revokes licenses of limited commercial operations.

1940-1945　Freeze on new television construction during World War II.

1945　FCC allocates experimental color channels.

1948　FCC freezes all television licensing.

1950　FCC adopts color system.

1952　FCC adds seventy Ultra High

Frequency (UHF) channels to the existing twelve Very High Frequency (VHF) channels and renews licensing for television stations.

1952   First noncommercial educational television station, KSAC, is authorized.

1953   First noncommercial educational television station (KUHT) on air.

1953   FCC adopts current color system.

1950   FCC authorizes pay television. (Rules are later amended in 1959 and 1960.)

1961   First pay television station, WHCT, begins in Hartford, Connecticut.

1982   FCC authorizes the licensing of up to 4,000 low power television stations.

Source: "A Short History of Electrical Communication" (Washington, D.C.: FCC pamphlet, 1979) and Erick Barnouw's (1966, 1968, 1970) trilogy on broadcast history.

TELEVISION

Although the development of television was delayed by World War II and the FCC's indecision in the late 1940s, it experienced a great creative burst in the 1950s. During the years 1953 through 1955, anthology drama made such an impact that many television historians look back on that period with a fondness rarely shown for any other period of television. The period is admired for its great drama programs like "Kraft Television Theater," "Studio One," "U.S. Steel Hour," "Medallion Theater" and "Robert Montgomery Presents." Before the television networks even started, Kraft was on New York television with its program which employed material from the theater. In those first days, length was unimportant because networks had not developed and stations did not have to worry about the division between network and station. Soon, however, networks developed and stations and networks demanded smooth transitions and programs that were exactly long enough to fit with commercials in 58½ minutes.

Those early television programs were created by a small number of highly talented individuals who worked not so much for the money as for the stimulation of a new medium. Thirty-three of the first thirty-five Kraft programs were directed by Stanley Quinn, and all the scripts were found and edited by Ed Rice.[16] When the heavy burden of directing a live television show every week became too great, Harry Herrmann joined the Kraft program as a second director. Herrmann also wrote the first script for "Kraft Television Theater," which was probably the first dramatic script ever written for television. About a corrupt member of Congress, the script created so much consternation that Herrmann was summoned to Washington to explain it. Some members of the committee who questioned Herrmann suggested that perhaps Congress should exercise stern control over the new medium.

Quinn did thirty-three of the first thirty-five Kraft shows in 1947 under this incredibly tight schedule. At the end of 1947, director Harry

sidebar

ERA OF TALENT

The era of anthology drama spawned many talented individuals, including writers like Rod Serling and Paddy Chayefsky, and actors like Sidney Poitier and Rod Steiger.

THE MAKING OF "KRAFT TELEVISION THEATER"

The early days of television just after World War II when directors, producers, actors, and owners were traveling over untested ground, was a period when resources were few and everyone worked hard. One product of this early period was "Kraft Television Theater" (1947). During its first year, the show had but one director and one scriptwriter-selector for its weekly program. The director-producer was Stanley Quinn; the scriptwriter was Ed Rice. Here is how Quinn and Rice divided their time for a weekly show, which was aired Wednesday nights.

Wednesday 9:00 P.M.: This week's show finished.

Thursday A.M.: Quinn reviews scripts with Ed Rice for three weeks hence; they make selections. Rice has gone through dozens of scripts to give Quinn perhaps six from which to select.

Thursday P.M.: First reading with actors for next week's show.

Friday: Select costumes and fit cast for next week's show. Select cast for the show two weeks hence.

Saturday: Rehearse script, iron out the rough spots.

Sunday: Study day for cast; day off for Quinn.

Monday: Rehearse with cast; work out set with set designer, making sure everything will fit in the television studio. Work out floor plan. (Preliminary work had been done Friday.) Rehearsals this day are done without scripts as much as possible. Production assistant coaches.

Tuesday: Make adjustments on scenes that are not going well; polish those that are. Rehearsals to date have been done with chalk marks on the floor and chairs instead of scenery. The final rehearsal today is done with the camerapeople standing in the locations where their cameras will be the next night.

Wednesday: This day was devoted to insuring that the scenery is in place and that all necessary props are ready. The final rehearsal is in the afternoon. The dress rehearsal comes one hour before air time—director, camera persons, and actors have one final chance to get everything correct—then its air time at 8 p.m.

Herrmann joined the Kraft show so that Quinn had to direct only one show every two weeks.

All of the shows were live. Although the actors and settings changed from week to week, every show had to fit in a large television studio. In those days, television cameras were large and cumbersome and had no zoom lens. The amount of light required to light a studio was great and everyone was uncomfortable before the production was over.

Then two events changed the nature of television—the invention and development of video tape, and the first use of motion picture film on television. Ampex developed video tape to a point where it could be used in broadcast work by 1956, and ABC was using film for broadcast. These two developments permitted networks to go on location for programs, and to preserve shows for rebroadcast—which allowed for reruns, so disliked by many people.

Blacks on Radio and Television

Although in the prenetwork days of the 1920s radio waves were filled with music, the radio networks of the thirties and forties catered to comedy and drama. During the days of radio music, Black entertainers received fair treatment. The Southernaires had a Sunday program filled with spirituals; Marion Anderson, Dorothy Maynor, and others appeared on an occasional program. But the later dramatic programs seemed intent on casting Black people in the stereotype made famous on the program "Amos 'n' Andy." These Blacks talked in an idiom that white people thought was Black English. This style of speaking became so accepted that Black actors were consistently squeezed out of jobs because they didn't sound Black. When Black people did get acting roles, they were usually servants, like Rochester on Jack Benny's program.

Infrequently, Black musicians received recognition, as the great vocalist Paul Robeson did for singing "Ballad for Americans," which spoke of a better world in which there was no intolerance. Another highpoint for racial tolerance came when CBS broadcast the program "Open Letter on Race Hatred," which many southern stations refused to carry even after it had been toned down by the writers. The program closed with a call for a new understanding of people with nonwhite skins, which was made by Wendell Wilkie, a Republican presidential candidate in 1940. Although the program featured Black and white performers working together, they could not dine together in New York restaurants between performances.

Racial intolerance and segregation existed in military as well as civilian ranks. World War II military recruits found themselves trained in separate groups, and transported to camp in segregated trains. Even the AFRS (Armed Forces Radio Service) did not carry programs that treated Black citizens respectfully.

Yet, there were signs that things might change. After World War II, change came even to the broadcasting business, once again dictated by business. *Ebony Magazine* had shown itself to be an effective advertising medium, reaching a public untouched by the white media. As a result, a number of Black radio stations started in the late 1940s. Although the stations were usually owned by white people, the entertainers were Black and the programming featured rhythm and blues music. And, a few stations, like WSOK in Nashville, had at least some Black shareholders.

In many cities, Black radio stations found that they had white listeners, and white applicants for station jobs. WERD, a wholly Black-owned station, found itself in that position. On the other hand, some communities opposed the new Black stations so much that they destroyed antenna towers or radio equipment. Nevertheless, Black radio was here to stay, as was the longstanding racial intolerance that gave rise to the need for ethnic stations. It was to be expressed in new ways during the 1950s and 1960s, and legal reforms were to follow.

The 1950s saw changes in how Black people related to their communities. There was unrest among Blacks, over their unequal treatment regarding voting, education, media coverage, and work opportunities. Then in 1955, the United States Supreme Court declared separate education to be "inherently unequal." About the same time, young Martin Luther King began rallying Blacks in nonviolent protests, and media awareness of Black people began to change. Although news reporters covered King's activities in the South, Edward R. Murrow gave King no attention in 1956. The Black movement still had far to go in influencing the media.

Some Southern governors and citizens were quick to use means to defy Supreme Court orders giving equality to Black citizens. Black churches were burned, demonstrators were driven back, and southern stations refused to carry programs with Black performers.

The 1960s brought a new change in media attitudes, again dictated by economics. More attention was focused on the buying power of the Black community. The box office success of movies about interracial matters and a few highly successful commercials featuring Black actors, like the one for Manufacturers Hanover Trust Company, which featured Diahann Carroll, made the point effectively. Not everyone was happy about the trend, however, Senator Strom Thurmond of South Carolina accused CBS president Frank Stanton of swallowing the NAACP line. Governor George C. Wallace of Alabama complained when NBC refused to carry the Blue-Gray football game (1963) from which Black players were barred. And, many sponsors remained unwilling to pay for programs that dealt with racial issues.

While the commercial networks handled racial issues as carefully as possible to avoid losing sponsors or viewers, the public broadcasting network carried many interviews, dialogues, and news footage accounts of Black activities, juxtaposed in some cases with activities of the Klu Klux Klan.

One racial event, however, was lost on no one. Even the networks carried Martin Luther King's speech before 200,000 people at the Lincoln Memorial in 1963, when the Black leader proclaimed, "I have a dream. It is a dream deeply rooted, the American Dream . . . I have a dream that even the state of Mississippi . . . will be transformed into an oasis of freedom and justice."

COMMUNISM AND TELEVISION

For a brief period following World War II, America launched into a paranoid search for Communists in every quarter of life from entertainment to politics. Promoters of this paranoia included persons like Senator Joseph McCarthy of Wisconsin, broadcasters Fulton Lewis, Jr., and George Sokolsky, and supermarket executive Laurence Johnson. The anti-Communists were so impassioned that they formed the group Aware, Inc., in late 1953.

One of the most powerful weapons available to the leaders of the anit-Communist movement was economics—the anti-Communists' mere threat of taking actions that might reduce sales was enough to lead some companies to drop actors or directors from their programs.

Block Drug Company, manufacturer of Amm-i-dent toothpaste, which had found television to be a most effective sales medium, was one of the anti-Communist targets. Laurence Johnson, the supermarket executive from Syracuse, New York, wrote Leonard Block a letter, noting that the program Block sponsored, "Danger," sometimes employed persons suspected of Communist leanings. The letter went on to propose a test in which Lever Brothers toothpaste would be compared with Block's toothpaste in markets. Over Lever Brothers products, stores would post signs noting that "pro-American actors" appeared in Lever Brothers-sponsored programs, while a sign over Block's products would proclaim that his programs employed "Stalin's little creatures." In the letter, Johnson agreed to wait for a response from Block before starting the campaign.[17]

Block saw his newly built empire crumbling and immediately took steps to comply with Johnson's blackmail. Block had the political affiliations of casts, writers, and directors checked. Many other sponsors found themselves in the same position, and most buckled under the threats and pressure.

The persons targeted by the anti-communists were "blacklisted," that is, they appeared in one of the published lists of persons suspected of being affiliated with Communist organizations. To be blacklisted, a person needed only to have been seen at a meeting that Communists may have attended. Some people were even blacklisted for having the wrong friends or for having attended a group that was later associated with Communists in their youth. Others made the list for having visited Moscow. The reasons for blacklisting people were many and thin.

One leader of Aware, a long time staff member from the crime drama series "Gangbusters," Vincent Hartnett, knew no limits in his enthusiasm for finding Communists. His search led him to closely scrutinize photographs and articles from any event even remotely connected to a Communist cause. He wrote and called well-known people, warning them to stay away from anything associated with Communism. Meanwhile, Senator McCarthy used every legal (and perhaps, many illegal) means at his disposal to pursue Communists. Possible Communists were called to Senate hearings, inflammatory speeches against Communism were delivered to arouse the nation, and an ever expanding list of supposed Communists was developed. To be listed as a "known or suspected Communist" was the kiss of death to a performer, writer, or producer. Network executives stood in fear of the anti-Communist movement.

Two publications, *Counterattack* and *Red Channels*, were established, to further the goals of the anti-Communists.[18] Importer Alfred Kohlberg, a leader of support for greater United States involvement with China, financed the two publications, which attained considerable significance during the anti-Communist years of the early 1950s. Anti-Communist adherents were to be found at all levels of government. John Foster Dulles, President Dwight Eisenhower's secretary of state, appointed Scott McLeod to direct security and personnel. McLeod was an FBI person and a McCarthy supporter. Robert E. Lee, also a friend of McCarthy's, was named FCC commissioner.

But who were these supposed Communists? Although an official congressional list was never published, McCarthy aides offered various unofficial lists, which included people like Stephen Vincent Benet, Elmer Davis, John Dewey, Archibald MacLeish, and Arthur Schlesinger, Jr. That many powerful people in the media did not like these lists could be seen from their party guests, which included many blacklisted people. But the blacklisted people were still refused work. Even reporters and producers of news shows failed to report the damage that was being done for fear of damage to themselves.

As the 1950s wound down, so did McCarthyism, but its disappearance was no quick or easy matter. McCarthy died in 1957, but a case involving John Henry Faulk, vice-president of the New York chapter of the American Federation of Television and Radio Artists, and a WCBS disc jockey, lasted several years beyond that. During the trial, the outright lies and half-truths upon which McCarthyism had been based became painfully apparent; but, Faulk lost his WCBS job anyway and became unemployable. His career was ruined by the misrepresentations of an over-zealous group. Although no public records exist proving how many entertainers' careers were destroyed by the malicious actions of the anti-Communists, the number must have been considerable.

Although McCarthyism was an important development of the 1950s, much else was occurring in television at that time as well. The anthology programs had given way to series programs like the comedy "I Love Lucy," and the police show "Dragnet" a trend that has accounted for the core of television entertainment ever since.

NONCOMMERCIAL BROADCASTING

Whether called educational, noncommercial, or public television, the noncommercial channels in the United States exist today because educators and some active FCC members believed that some of the valuable television air space should be devoted to educational, cultural, and informational programs. During the television freeze imposed by the FCC between 1948 and 1952, one of the issues most hotly debated, and kept very much alive by Commissioner Freida B. Hennock, was the allocation of educational channels. Out of the freeze and its hearing came FCC regulations requiring educational channels. Here's how it developed:

> 1941—FCC allocates first five channels for noncommercial broadcasting. All are FM radio channels.

1945—Twenty additional FM educational channels are allocated.

1949—FCC invites comments regarding noncommercial television.

1952—FCC reserves 80 UHF and 162 VHF television channels for noncommercial broadcasting.

1953—KUHT, University of Houston's first educational television station, goes on the air.

1965 and 1966—FCC amends allocations to include 107 VHF and 508 UHF channels for noncommercial television.

1982—1,112 educational FM stations and 1,071 educational TV stations on air.

At present, educational broadcasting uses all the technologies that are employed by commercial broadcasters: AM, FM, television, cable, microwave, translators (small television stations that rebroadcast signals from an originating station), and satellites.

As the 1980s begin, educators are offering courses for academic credit via satellite, cable, and broadcast. But noncommercial offerings are hardly limited to courses. The FCC estimates that about 20 percent of educational programming goes to classrooms, and the remainder includes such diverse fare as Shakespearean plays, other English dramas, concerts, news, and public affairs programs. About half of the population views noncommercial television stations once a month, and 78 percent of all Americans can tune in to a noncommercial television station. The future of educational broadcasting may depend on finding new financial resources.[19]

TELEVISION AND FILMS

For some time after the advent of television, the major film studios did not want to release their films to the new medium, fearing that that would mean the death of the movie theater. Jack Warner of Warner Brothers held to that view until his son-in-law William Orr returned from a trip East to describe the number of television antennas growing from houses. Then Leonard Goldenson, a former film executive who had become an ABC executive, began wooing Warner and others. The first to give in to the networks was Walt Disney, who started his Disney television series in 1954. Jack Warner liked the terms that Disney had won, and decided to produce films for ABC under a deal in which Warner could spend ten minutes of each hour program focusing on its releases to theaters—free advertising. Warner's series started in the 1955-56 season; each one-hour program cost $75,000. The series title was "Warner Brothers Presents" and the little ten-minute insert went under the name "Behind the Cameras." The ten-minute sequence was short-lived because of audience disapproval, but the big Hollywood film houses were finally on television.

Film studios' contributions to television production resulted in a se-

BROADCAST PSYCHOLOGISTS?

In 1970, it was sex talk shows; today, the hot radio shows feature broadcast psychologists. They feature professionals like clinical psychologist Toni Grant giving advice over KABC radio (Los Angeles) to a distraught listener worried about his fetish for getting into his wife's lingerie and fear that he will be found out. In Boston, Dr. Joy Browne dispenses advice over WITS-AM on her program "Up Close and Personal." Even public television has its Dr. Tom Cottle, who talks to audiences over WGBH-TV in Boston. Whether they are talking to a male homosexual dealing with how to tell his relatives, a woman with a history of abusive boyfriends, or a mother who lets an 11-year-old boy babysit a younger girl only to return home and find them watching a pornographic videocassette together, the psychology programs trade long private sessions in psychologist's office for three-minute telephone conversations heard by thousands. Grant's program is so popular that it is distributed by satellite from Los Angeles to New York and elsewhere. Grant's Los Angeles program typically has 122,000 local listeners. These pop-psychology call-in programs differ from earlier advice programs in that all the hosts are trained and licensed psychologists or medical professionals. Qualifications aside, some critics are asking if the programs really provide a worthwhile service or simply improve ratings and make hosts rich. In mid-1981, Grant was a $100,000 a year media star, called Dr. Toni by her admirers.

The American Psychological Association plans to review the whole area of media psychology to determine the ethics of such programs. Whatever their decision is, for now, broadcast psychologists have found a place in listeners' hearts.

Source: Barbara Braustark. "On-Air Psychologists . . . Healers or Exploiters?" *The New York Times* (August 9, 1981), pp. 4-23.

ries of westerns and other violent programs like "Cheyenne," "Sugarfoot," "The Untouchables," and "Dragnet." Jack Warner learned that television series could be produced cheaply using stock footage from Warner's own film libraries. Other networks made alliances with film producers like MCA, United Artists, and Universal. Moreover, old feature films were revived from dusty storage vaults and shown on television. The film companies had found a new gold mine.

Meanwhile, television stations were becoming wealthy; an affiliation with a network helped, but independents like WOR-TV in New York were doing well. Also, television formats shifted in the fifties and sixties with the demands of each season—one year westerns were in, the next year it was police dramas, or spy shows, and so on. Situation comedies were always popular.

But in the early 1970s, a young man decided that television was not treating issues that were important to the citizens of the nation. All that violence, while entertaining, did little to help individuals understand the issues that had begun to be debated during the 1960s—racism, women's rights, television violence, assassinations of public figures, the war in Viet Nam, and world hunger. Norman Lear set about to produce a program that would freely treat these matters, despite their controversy. His program, "All in the Family," was not received well by the networks initially. In fact, Lear approached executive after executive before CBS finally agreed to give the program a try in 1971. It was immediately successful, and Lear found himself besieged with requests to produce more programs, which he did. Each Lear program was produced before a live audience and recorded on video tape. All of his programs used comedy to press home the program's point about bigotry, abortion, black-white relations, and other issues. Lear's success led other producers, such as MTM productions, to embark upon new areas of television programming with similar success.

Of course, the crime drama and traditional comedy programs did not fade from the screen. There are still programs like "SWAT," "Kojak," "The Streets of San Francisco," and "Hawaii Five-O."

CABLE TELEVISION

In 1948, the FCC imposed a freeze on the licensing of television stations so it could contemplate the future of the medium. Up to that time, the FCC merely granted licenses based on the order in which requests came in without any consideration of need. This led to an abundance of stations in communities where television had been developed or manufactured, and little or none in many other communities. When the freeze was imposed 108 stations had been licensed, however only 24 cities had two or more stations.

Cities like Houston, Milwaukee, and St. Louis had only 1 station; Denver, Little Rock, and Austin had none. The freeze lasted until 1952, maintaining the unbalanced distribution of stations for nearly four years. Large cities like Philadelphia that are surrounded by mountains had television service, but nearby communities had no service. Palm Springs, only a few miles and one mountain range from Los Angeles, had no television service, while Los Angeles had 7 stations.

The demand for television service was just as great in outlying communities as it was in large, well-served cities. So, because the FCC was not providing for the demand through its licensing powers, small entrepreneurs—often owners of appliance stores—decided to fill the void. Community antenna television, later called cable television, began to emerge. The first cable systems were made up of television antennas mounted on top of mountains or high hills where they could pick up the signals from nearby television markets. By running cables from the antenna and amplifying the signal every so often, the new cable owners were able to connect a number of households to their central antennas.

Those first cable systems were crude by modern standards. Often the cables were nailed to trees and houses; the service was limited to one, two, or at the most three choices, and the picture often was distorted. But, people subscribed to the new service, mostly because the choice was between no television or the new, crude service.

A cable television system is made up of four basic elements: the master antenna or receiving system, the headend, the cable grid, and the drops to homes.

Although early cable systems had antennas much like the ones people install on their roofs, modern cable systems use much more elaborate means to secure program services. The traditional antenna still receives nearby transmissions, but today, microwaves and satellites also deliver programs to cable systems. The pay services like Home Box Office and CBS cable reach the subscriber through a satellite link. Both satellite and microwave connections deliver superstation signals to cable systems. Superstations are television stations like Ted Turner's station in Atlanta that send signals to cable systems all over the United States. Most cable systems also have some form of local origination.

The headend, housed in a central building, contains all the necessary electronic equipment to amplify signals and arrange them for delivery on the cable grid. Also, any local origination facilities probably exist at the headend. These might include a studio, tape recorders, cameras, and similar equipment.

The cable grid is the elaborate network of cables and amplifiers that distributes signals through the community served by the cable system. An amplifier must be placed in the cable line about every 1,500 to 3,000 feet to keep the signal strong enough for home television sets.

The drop is a short section of cable running from the cable grid to the home set so subscribers may receive the cable service. To be connected, the subscriber must pay an installation fee that ranges from nothing to $100.00, and a monthly rental fee that averages about $8.50. To secure Home Box Office or other pay services, the subscriber must pay an additional fee.

Here is a chronology of the development of cable television:

> 1948—First cable system is instituted.
> 1950—Cable is working in seventy communities.
> 1962—FCC becomes interested in cable.
> 1966—First cable regulations issued by FCC.
> 1968—Supreme Court affirms FCC's jurisdiction over cable.
> 1968—FCC revises and expands cable rules.
> 1972—FCC creates new cable rules.
> 1977—FCC deletes many franchise standards.
> 1978 and 1980—FCC amends or eliminates other cable rules.

By 1980, some 4,250 cable systems were serving more than 16 million subscribers in 10,000 communities. The largest technically connected system is in San Diego; it serves more than 170,000 subscribers. The average system has about ten channels, but a few systems are capable of offering sixty channels or more. Cable service includes retransmission of regular broadcast television, subscription movies and sports, two-way special channels, shopping services, and more. The United States has cable systems in every state. Many other countries also have cable systems, including Austria, Canada, Belgium, Germany, Great Britain, Italy, and Japan.

TELEVISION—ALWAYS A BUSINESS

Broadcasting has always depended for its revenue on the number of people watching television programs. To dominate the evening hours, networks will resort to all kinds of devices. In the next chapter we will talk about how television, radio, and cable pay their way.

ADDITIONAL READINGS

Archer, Gleason L. *History of Radio to 1926*. New York: The American Historical Society, 1938.

Barnouw, Erik. *The Golden Web: A History of Broadcasting in the United States 1933–1953*. New York: Oxford University Press, 1968.

Barnouw, E. *The Image Empire: A History of Broadcasting in the United States from 1953*. New York: Oxford University Press, 1970.

———. *The Sponsors: Notes on a Modern Potentate*. New York: Oxford University Press, 1978.

———. *A Tower in Babel: A History of Broadcasting in the United States to 1933*. New York: Oxford University Press, 1966.

Bower, Robert T. *Television and the Public*. New York: Holt, Rinehart & Winston, 1973.

Cogley, John. *Report of Black Listing*. Reprint New York: Arnold Press, 1971.

Dunlap, Orrin E., Jr. *Radio's 100 Men of Science*. New York: Books for Libraries Press, 1944.

Steiner, Gary A. *The People Who Look at Television*. New York: Knopf, 1963.

FOOTNOTES

1. "A Short History of Electrical Communication" (Washington, D.C.: Federal Communications Commission, 1979), p. 2.

2. Orrin E. Dunlap, Jr., *Radio's 100 Men of Science* (Freeport, N.Y.: Books for Libraries Press, 1944), p. 64.

3. "A Short History," p. 10.

4. Gleason L. Archer, *History of Radio to 1926* (New York: The American Society, 1938), p. 28.

5. Erik Barnouw, *A Tower in Babel: A History of Broadcasting in the United States to 1933* (New York: Oxford University Press, 1966), p. 76.

6. Elliot N. Sivowitch, "A Technological Survey of Broadcasting's Prehistory," *Journal of Broadcasting*, 15, no. 1 (Winter 1970-71): 16–17.

7. E. Pendelton Herring, "Politics and Radio Regulation," *Harvard Business Review*, 13, no. 1 (January 1935): 173.

8. Lawrence W. Lichty and Malachi C. Topping, *A Source Book on the History of Radio and Television* (New York: Hastings House, 1975), p. 521.

9. Erik Barnouw, *The Golden Web: A History of Broadcasting in the United States 1933–1953* (New York: Oxford University Press, 1968), p. 10.

10. Sheldon Marcus, *Father Coughlin: The Tumultuous Life of the Priest of the Little Flower* (Boston: Little, Brown and Company, 1973), pp. 48–49.

11. See the Rev. Chas. E. Coughlin, *Father Coughlin's Radio Discourses: 1931–1932* (Royal Oak, Mich: The Radio League of the Little Flower, 1932).

12. Charles J. Tull, *Father Coughlin and the New Deal* (Syracuse: Syracuse University Press, 1965), p. 101.

13. *KFKB Broadcasting Association, Inc.* v. *Federal Radio Commission* 47 F. 2d 670 (D.C. Cir. 1931).

14. Barnouw, *The Golden Web*, p. 75.

15. Hans Fontel, "Recalling The Genius Who Devised FM Radio," *The New York Times*, December 27, 1981, II p. 23.

16. Interview with Stanley Quinn, September 13, 1979.

17. Erik Barnouw, *The Sponsor* (New York: Oxford University Press, 1978), p. 48.

18. Walter Gellhorn, ed., *The States and Subversion* (Ithaca, N.Y.: Cornell University Press, 1952), p. 35.

19. "Educational Television" (Washington, D.C.: FCC, 1979).

11

THE BUSINESS OF BROADCASTING AND NEWER TECHNOLOGIES

Unlike magazines, books, or newspaper publishers, broadcasters usually cannot sell their product to the subscribing public, although there is a limited form of subscription television in this nation. Consequently, broadcasters earn their income from advertisers, who want to win the attention of a television audience that numbers in the millions in order to sell their products. Those advertisements that appear daily on television programs and radio shows pay the bills for the system of "free broadcasting," as it has sometimes been called.

Behind the programming is a vast array of people and companies that have been established to make the system work, including companies owning local stations, network organizations, advertising agencies, audience research firms, station representatives, program packagers, and advertisers.

The mass media are supported in three different ways—by subscriber payments, advertising, and a combination of advertising and subscriptions. The subscription media include records, books, pay television, pay cable (like HBO), motion pictures, and basic cable service. Media that rely on a combination of subscription and advertising are newspapers and magazines. Radio, television, some cable services (like local origination stations), direct mail, billboards, and specialty items (such as buttons and bumper stickers) are supported only by advertiser payments. Earlier chapters have discussed the cinema and print media. This chapter will discuss how radio, television, and cable businesses are financially supported.

FIGURE 11-1   Advertiser Supported Media

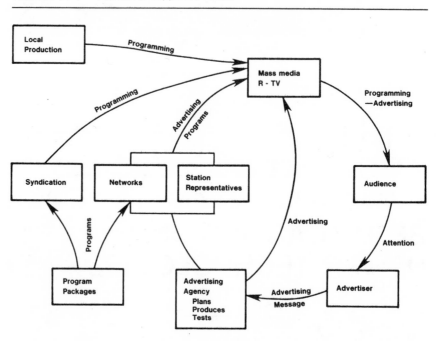

Some media, like radio and television stations, receive their income from companies who wish to promote their products to the public. The result is a circle (illustrated in Figure 11-1) of giving something to receive something. The audience is entertained by programs, but in return, they give their attention to sponsors who hope to induce them to buy products. Stations are paid to broadcast advertisements; advertisers pay for the audience's attention. Within this scheme are the program producers who receive money for their productions, the networks, who send programs and advertising to stations, the representatives, who sell station time, and the syndicators, who sell programs to stations. Stations also produce some of their own programs.

Media like magazines, newspapers, and to some extent, cable television, receive revenue from both advertisers and subscribers. Newspapers, for example, charge readers a fee for each newspaper. That fee covers about 30 percent of the cost of printing the newspaper. The remainder of the cost is paid by advertisers who want exposure for their products. On cable television some advertising revenue is obtained to support local productions, but the rest of the cost of service is made up through subscriptions. Figure 11-2 shows the relationship between subscribers—who pay a fee for entertainment and news—and the media. In addition, the media must acquire their content from diverse sources, for which they pay a fee.

A third group of media—books and pay cable (HBO)—receive all their income from subscribers. When they buy these media, subscrib-

FIGURE 11-2   Subscription—Advertising Media

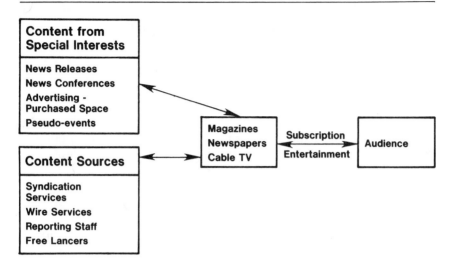

ers are paying for entertainment and information uninterrupted by commercial messages. The means of distribution and the flow of products and revenue of subscription media are suggested in Figure 11-3.

THE STRUCTURE

The advertiser-supported businesses of radio and television must rely on their income to come from manufacturers, retailers, and other businesses who wish to expose their products and services to the public.

FIGURE 11-3   Subscription Media

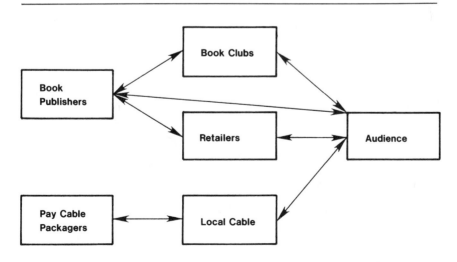

Whether the product is a small, inexpensive item like a bottle of cola or an expensive item like an automobile, advertisers must convince the public to try it and then to continue using it. To achieve their goal of maximum sales, advertisers must rely on a complex system of organizations to bring their products to the public's attention.

THE ADVERTISER

The advertiser provides the funds that make much of the mass media work, but advertisers also want something in return—the attention of large numbers of people. Consequently, the advertising-supported mass media are selling advertisers public attention that will come through the broadcast and print media that run ads and the advertising agencies, creative services companies, program packagers, and ratings services that make them up.

Every night on television or in the newspapers, advertising appears for automobile companies like Ford and Chrysler, packaged food corporations like General Foods, and personal care products companies like Revlon. These companies rely on a kind of odds game. If enough people are told enough times about their products, then sponsors will be able to make the huge number of sales that will be necessary for them to cover their investment in the product and earn a reasonable profit. Clearly, the media have been effective sellers, or advertisers would not continue spending so much money on advertising. However, not every advertising campaign has been successful. The ill-fated campaign for the Edsel, Ford's mid-priced luxury car, is a good example. Just because the media say buy, does not mean the public is going to passively fall in line, especially when it's costing them. Advertisers spend large sums on radio, television, newspaper, magazine, and other forms of advertising to persuade audiences to purchase products. The funds for that advertising come from the sale of products. Part of the final cost of an advertised product is the expense of advertising it. In the end, therefore, it is the customer who pays the cost of the advertising-supported media.

ADVERTISING AGENCIES

At the heart of the advertising side of broadcasting, is the advertising agency. (For a list of the ten largest, see Table 11-1.) Whether in a small town or a large city, advertising agencies try to get a sponsor's messages before the public in the most appealing way, using a mix of mass media that fits the advertiser's needs.

Although the largest advertising agencies are in New York City, most cities of any size have a number of advertising agencies that provide services to local firms and often to regional firms. The agencies provide a variety of services for their clients. They help plan an advertis-

TABLE 11-1   Ten Largest Advertising Agencies with Billings (1982)

NAME	BILLINGS IN MILLIONS (WORLDWIDE)
1. JWT Group, Inc.	$2,384.2
2. Young & Rubicam	2,273.2
3. McCann-Erickson	1,792.1
4. Ogilvy and Mather	1,661.0
5. Ted Bates W.W. Inc.	1,600.0
6. Leo Burnett Co.	1,331.0
7. BBD&O Intly., Co.	1,330.1
8. Foote Cone & Belding	1,228.0
9. SSC and B	1,220.1
10. D'Arcy-MacManus & Masius	1,120.0

Source: *Standard Directory of Advertisers* (Skokie, Ill.: National Register Publishing Co., February-March 1982) p. A5.

ing campaign, design the messages, select the media to be used, buy the time and space, test advertising ideas to determine the likelihood of their success, produce the finished layouts for magazines, newspapers, billboards, and direct mail, and the finished films or video and audio tapes for broadcast.

To perform these services, advertising agencies have a variety of departments to deal with each specialized task. The full-service advertising agencies have departments and staffs to handle all the advertising needs of clients, but some smaller, more specialized agencies concentrate on only some of these services, subcontracting the others out to other firms.

Some terms commonly used by advertising agencies and media need to be defined at this point, to help the reader understand later parts of this chapter.

Some Advertising Terms

ROS, a shorthand term for run of schedule, refers to purchasing advertising that stations can drop into convenient spots, as long as the advertisement appears in the class of time purchased.

Spot advertising is placed by advertising agencies or advertisers directly with the local stations (or through their representatives), bypassing the networks. One type of spot advertising is those short announcements that come between television programs. Some spot advertising, however, is placed within programs, particularly within syndicated programs.

Network advertising, by comparison, is placed by an advertiser or its representative directly with a network in order to reach the audiences of many stations.

Program length commercials. Although some may deny the exis-

TABLE 11–2   Cost of a Typical Network 30-second Commercial (in thousands)

	JAN-MAR '82			APR-JUNE '82		
	Cost	Household Rating %	Household Cost/1000	Cost	Household Rating %	Household Cost/1000
Daytime (Mon.-Fri.)	10.3	7.0	1.80	11.2	6.1	2.25
Prime Time (Mon.-Sat.)	71.2	18.6	4.70	76.3	15.6	6.00
Fringe Time						
Early Morning	8.2	4.9	2.05	9.0	4.4	2.50
News	27.0	14.4	2.30	27.2	11.3	2.95
Late Night	12.1	4.5	3.30	13.7	4.3	3.90
Weekend Children's Programs	7.0	5.6	1.54	9.8	4.8	2.51

Source: A.C. Nielsen Rating Service

tence of program length commercials, these programs, if they exist, are programs of five minutes or more in which the sponsor is directly or indirectly selling to the audience throughout the program. An example of a program length commercial is the behind-the-scenes look at a movie being made.

CPM or cost per thousand is the cost of reaching 1,000 readers or viewers. The CPM for television is higher than that for radio, and the CPM for a specialized magazine like *Sports Illustrated* is higher than that for a newspaper. CPM is the figure used to determine the efficiency of advertising dollars.

Trade-outs, long a part of the advertising business, is a practice in which a station or newspaper trades advertising time or space for some product or service of the advertiser. For example, an automobile dealer may trade a car for television advertising. Trades only work when both sides want the products or services to be traded.

Rate cards. Rate cards are printed by stations to show the prices they charge for advertising at different times of the day. Rate cards also list costs by lengths of time and spell out discounts for large orders.

Time classifications. Some times of the day attract more listeners or viewers than other times. Because of this, stations try to equalize the CPM somewhat by charging different rates for different time periods. Prime time, the most watched or viewed time, costs the most, while fringe times cost less. Many stations have as many as four rate or time classifications. Table 11-2 illustrates this time/rate classification structure.

Drive time. Prime time for many radio stations is the period when people are driving to and from work because car radios are on and stations have nearly captive audiences.

Advertising agencies employ *account executives* to deal with the

TABLE 11-2   Cost of a Typical Network 30-second Commercial (continued)

	JULY-AUG '82			SEPT-DEC '82		
	Cost	Household Rating %	Household Cost/1000	Cost	Household Rating %	Household Cost/1000
Daytime (Mon.-Fri.)	10.2	6.6	1.90	12.6	6.1	2.45
Prime Time (Mon.-Sat.)	53.0	13.4	4.85	88.9	18.3	5.75
Fringe Time						
Early Morning	7.4	3.7	2.45	10.4	4.4	2.80
News	20.8	10.4	2.45	31.6	13.1	2.85
Late Night	11.9	4.1	3.55	16.1	4.7	4.05
Weekend Children's Programs	8.1	4.0	2.48	14.5	5.3	3.24

vertiser. Account executives have from a few to many accounts, depending on the accounts' size. The account executive's job is to anticipate every client's need, to help the client with decisions, to insure that the other divisions of the agency are following the client's requirements, and to solicit new business. An inept account executive can lose a good account through poor communication.

Elsewhere in an advertising agency, the *research department* tests advertising ideas and the success of campaigns, the *creative services* department creates ideas, writes scripts, designs graphics, secures music, and lays out print advertising. *Time and space buyers* purchase time and space from broadcasters, newspapers, magazines, and other media.

The advertising agency is as important to the media as it is to the advertisers. About 60 percent of newspaper space is devoted to advertising; just over half of magazine space is filled with advertising; and 25 percent of broadcasters' time is filled with advertisements. Consequently, the symbiotic relationship between advertisers and the media is important. Although many broadcasters and newspapers have their own advertising departments, much advertising is handled by agencies, making them an important link between the media and the sponsor.

The Advertisers' Audience

When companies started advertising, their primary objective was to reach as many people as possible as many times as possible with their advertising message. Soon, there arose the term "r and r," which stands for reach and reinforcement. Reach refers to the number of people who are reached by the message and reinforcement refers to the number of times each receiver is exposed to the message.

HYPE

A word that has crept into our vocabulary with new meaning is hype—it means to sell something so hard that the item achieves a status far beyond that which is warranted. So common has hype become that NBC's Edwin Newman devoted an hour to "Land of Hype and Glory," a 1978 documentary on the subject. Years earlier, historian Daniel Boorstin conceived the term "pseudo events" to refer to events that are created to get media attention and coverage. Hype carries that notion a bit farther.

Newman pointed to the rock music group "Kiss" as an example of hype—a group packaged for television and film. Clever costumes served to cover an average musical ability and propelled the group into national attention.

Hype exists in every area of the media—in selling products using sex appeal where none exists, in promoting persons into "stars." Newman got down to specific examples of hype—Liberace, Muhammad Ali, the *Little Red Book* of Chairman Mao, and Jimmy Carter's *Why Not the Best?*

Hype is not solely a product of the 1970s and 1980s. Although early broadcasters said much about the ills of advertising on radio during its first years in the 1920s, when the stigma vanished, radio unabashedly promoted almost anything—patent medicines that had little desirable effect, trinkets of every sort—the list was endless. A Kellogg boxtop offer got some 14,000 responses every day it was offered. Dr. John Brinkley sold millions of his drug potions. So extensive was the abuse that the government tried to stem the tide.

Source: Arthur Unger, "Frighteningly Entertaining Look at Hype," *The Christian Science Monitor*, January 9, 1978, p. 15.

In recent years, advertisers have begun to refine their advertising strategies to focus on those people who are most likely to buy their products or services. Most groceries and household products traditionally have been purchased by women, so manufacturers of these products have chosen to advertise in places and at times where they can expect to reach large numbers of women.

At the same time, automobile buying decisions traditionally have been more the responsibility of men, and advertisers have focused their advertising accordingly. However, with the rising number of single parent families and the blurring of the traditional male and female roles, many buying patterns have changed, and advertiser strategies have had to keep up. The point is that advertising directed to a group not interested in buying a product is wasted effort. Middle income persons, for example, do not normally buy $60,000 fur coats or $100,000 diamond rings.

Because of the need to focus advertising, the media have prepared their products to appeal to specialized audiences, such as the young, the rich, etc. But, that kind of special programming is useless unless advertisers know how many people in each category are listening, watching, or reading. To tell them this, a rating industry has arisen.

Rating companies divide the people watching television programs or listening to radio programs into income, sex, education, ethnic, geographic, and age categories. These audience composition categories are the *demographics.* Thus, the advertiser interested in reaching middle-aged persons earning annual salaries above $20,000 may look at a station's demographic information to find out how many people in that category are watching television and what shows they are watching. One example of specialized programming is the Saturday morning cartoons on television, which appear at a time when the audience is made up largely of children. The products advertised during that time slot are predominantly toys, soft drinks, candy, and sweetened cereals. Advertisers have matched their advertising time purchases to the audience.

Radio and television stations do not conduct their own audience surveys. Ratings are conducted by independent ratings companies established for that very purpose. These firms include Arbitron, Nielson, and others who conduct ratings surveys throughout the nation.

HOW TELEVISION RATINGS WORK

With more than 70 million television households in the United States, it is impossible to count if every household is watching a program. Therefore, for national counts the ratings services rely on surveys of 1,500 to 2,500 households. Using statistical concepts, the services are able to use these small samples to project how many households have their televisions tuned to various programs. This gives networks and stations an estimate of the viewership of each program. The word *estimate* is important. As statisticians will point out, statistics rely on samples to estimate how the larger population is behaving. But statistics also permit one to estimate how accurate the sample results are likely to be, and rating services do publish information about the possible errors in their samples. These estimates of accuracy are important because a sample may not perfectly represent the population from which it is drawn.

Because there are no truly national radio programs, Arbitron, the radio company, does not need to come up with estimates of national audiences. But, it does have to produce information on how well a local station is competing with the other stations in its market.

Because radio and television ratings must be based on the area or market served by stations in a particular community, the rating services have chosen to divide the nation into geographic areas served by clusters of radio or television stations. Arbitron calls these regions "areas of dominant influence" (ADI) and Nielsen calls them "designated market areas" (DMA). The divisions tend to follow county lines and they correspond roughly to the reach of the stations in an area. Table 11-3 shows the ten largest markets as an example of the markets surveyed. Market size, of course, is figured from the number of house-

TABLE 11–3 The
Ten Largest Television
Markets

1	New York, N.Y.
2	Los Angeles, Calif.
3	Chicago, Ill.
4	Philadelphia, Pa.
5	San Francisco, Calif.
6	Boston, Mass.
7	Detroit, Mich.
8	Washington, D.C.
9	Cleveland, Ohio
10	Dallas-Fort Worth, Tex.

Source: *Standard Rate and
Data Service: Spot Television*
(Skokie, Ill., SRDS, March 15,
1982) p. A19.

holds in each community, thus New York has more households than Los Angeles does. The ratings services have divided the nation into 209 rating regions. Obviously, bigger markets are more important to advertisers than smaller markets because of the greater number of television households. Some advertisers seem most interested in the 100 largest markets, much to the irritation of the stations in smaller markets.

The ratings companies gather information about the public in several ways. The A.C. Nielsen Company uses electronic monitors called Audimeters that are connected to television sets. Arbitron and Nielsen both use diaries in which viewers and listeners record their viewing or listening over a specified period. Some ratings services use telephone interviews to record *coincidental ratings*—what that person is doing at the moment of the call, and *recall,* what that person viewed over a certain past period. Finally, some personal interviews are conducted, but because they are very expensive, they are not used often. Although variations of the above methods have been developed, these techniques reflect the basic means ratings companies use to collect audience data.

The collected data is used to produce two types of information: program ratings and share of audience ratings. A rating is the ratio of homes tuned to a program to the total number of television households. This number is expressed as a percentage. A rating of 20 means that 20 percent of the homes with television sets in the sample are watching the program. Share of audience is the ratio of homes watching a program to all homes watching television in the sample. Again the number is expressed as a percentage. A program having a share of 25 means that 25 percent of the current television audience (all television sets in the sample turned on) is tuned to the program. If 80 percent of the television households in a sample are watching television, a rating of 20 would be the same as a share of 25. Since there probably never is a time when 100 percent of the television households are watching television, the share of audience figure is always larger than the rating—consequently television broadcasters prefer the share numbers while advertisers are more inclined to look at ratings.

All of this information about radio and television audiences is printed in large reports and sold to stations, advertising agencies, and others who are interested in viewer and listener habits. These reports are very important to the advertising industry because they form the basis for deciding how much money stations should get for carrying an advertiser's messages. The information also helps advertisers select the media they will advertise in.

BROADCAST STATIONS

In the United States (1982), there are 9,116 radio stations and 1,057 television stations. These local stations spread across the nation can be thought of as the retail outlets of broadcasting. The stations send en-

FIGURE 11–4   Nelson Audiometer used to record television viewing.

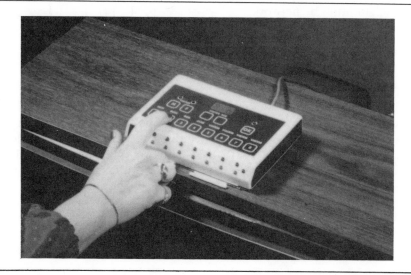

tertainment, news, information, and sales messages through the air. Those who wish to watch must purchase television or radio sets. Later in this chapter the ownership patterns in broadcasting will be discussed, but for now, the broadcast outlets' function will be dealt with.

Television Stations

Television stations receive a large portion of their programs from the major networks—ABC, NBC, CBS, PBS—and some specialized or regional networks. Each of the major commercial networks has about 200 television stations that take programs regularly, including comedy, drama, news, documentary, sports, and talk shows. Whatever the time, some programming is available. Talk shows like "The Tonight Show" and prime time reruns dominate the late night hours. Prime time refers to the most popular evening viewing hours, when most people are home and have leisure time to watch television. Reruns are programs that have been shown on television before and are appearing again. Reruns are what permit networks to make money on their big investment in costly productions.

Prime time, the most important hours for networks, are between 8:00 and 11:00 P.M. (an hour earlier in some time zones), when there is fierce competition between networks for viewers.

Local stations have a big stake in how popular their networks are, since an affiliation with a well-watched network can mean that more people are watching their local station programming as well. Stations seldom change from one network to another, since the network-affiliate relationships they developed long ago have proven profitable for both.

Networks also provide news programming during the early evening hours, daytime programming, and late night programming. Competition exists at every time period. In recent years, the early morning shows, aimed at people getting ready for work, have been paid considerable attention by networks.

Local stations take programming from sources other than networks, too. In fact, networks do not provide a full twenty-four hour a day of programming, leaving time open for local stations to fill. That open time is filled with local news, local talk shows.

The other source of nonnetwork programs is syndicated programs. Syndication companies offer stations film or videotape programs for a price. Within the syndicated program there is time for local advertising. Typical syndicated programs include "PM Magazine," "The Merv Griffin Show," "Let's Make A Deal," "Hollywood Squares," and "The Lawrence Welk Show." Other shows, like "I Love Lucy," originally ran on networks and now are syndicated to local stations. Whatever the programming source, the syndicator agrees to a contract and sends tapes or films to the station on a prearranged schedule. Incidentally, some feature-length film producers syndicate motion pictures to local

---

THE CHANGING NEWS CLIMATE

For many television stations, news has become the most profitable program in the entire schedule, even more profitable than network shows and syndicated series. Not long ago news programs were short, to the point, and produced mostly to satisfy the FCC. Now that they have proven their profitability, many stations are turning their news programs into a form of dramatic entertainment in order to attract more viewers.

WCBS reporter Arnold Diaz, using hidden cameras and recorders, filmed a dramatic little feature showing people gambling illegally. Some of the bettors did not even use OTB (State Off-Track Betting offices) to handle their business. Even though no one ever really thought that all betting was strictly legal, the feature did make good drama.

All over the country, similar features are popping up and ambitious an-

chor persons are making $50,000 to $100,000 a year following their trades at local stations in moderate-sized markets. In the top markets, salary figures rise to $500,000.

It almost sounds like television journalism has come of age. But has it? Today's local station *is* trying hard—not for good journalism but for ratings and the additional revenue those ratings will generate. Some say the drive for ratings leads stations to an obsession with lurid and titillating details rather than to thoughtful, critical analyses of major stories. Action is substituted for information.

The debate over television news is far from over. In the meantime, television viewers find themselves exposed to a new form of television journalism.

Source: Tony Schwartz, "When News Goes Show Biz," *The New York Times*, August 9, 1981, pp. 4–23.

stations, usually films that ran earlier in theaters or on network television.

About two-thirds of a station's programs come from networks, another 25 percent or more come from syndicators, and the remaining 10 percent come from local productions. In part, the local programs exist because stations must show the FCC that they are serving the needs of their community through local programming. A few stations have no network affiliation; they are called independents. These stations acquire all their programs from syndication, local production, or specialized networks.

Radio Stations

Radio programming originates mostly at the station level in the form of record and talk shows—the records provide the music and an announcer ties everything together. Like television stations, radio stations take some programming from syndicated sources, such as religious programs.

Radio differs from television in more than the absence of a picture. Whereas television programs are distributed to the general population much as shotguns spread pellets across the land, radio stations aim their programs at selected audiences. That's why a community will have top-forty, soul, ethnic, all-news, all-talk, and religious stations. Each of these formats reaches a special portion of the population. In the larger markets, the range of specialized radio stations is vast.

Most radio programming comes from local sources—taped, recorded, or live. The national networks, like Mutual Broadcasting system, ABC, NBC, and CBS provide short hourly newscasts for member stations. Sometimes the networks also provide short news features that stations may work into their own local productions. These are sent through the network wire or cable between regularly scheduled newscasts, with accompanying information to help the stations when they use the segments.

ABC has gone beyond the other networks by establishing four radio networks (all sent on the same line) to serve the specialized formats of radio stations. They have an FM format, a rock format, an easy listening format, and an adult format. Because in a 1943 case the Supreme Court had prohibited one organization from owning multiple networks, ABC had to get a special ruling from the FCC before it started its four networks. The ruling allowed an interpretation that called the four services one network, since they all went out on the same line. Recently ABC added two additional services, Rock Radio and Directions.

Because radio stations are so specialized in their programming, advertisers with products that appeal to specific segments of the buying public can select just those radio stations whose listeners meet their particular needs. This focused advertising saves dollars, because the advertiser does not pay for advertising to people who do not usually buy their products.

A portion of each hour of radio or television time is devoted to entertainment, information, or other programming designed to interest audiences enough so they'll listen. Once people are tuned in, stations can fill the remainder of the hour with advertising messages, hoping that its audience won't go to the refrigerator for another beer while the advertising is in progress.

The amount of time devoted to advertising varies from station to station, between television and radio, and during different parts of the year. However, the National Association of Broadcasters has adopted recommended time standards, shown in Table 11-4.

Many stations have their own standards of good programming practices that guide their advertising and programming departments in filling hours with advertising and entertainment programming. Demands for station advertising are higher during the Christmas and political seasons, times when some broadcasters exceed their own standards for quantity of advertising.

Station Representatives

Many stations hire national sales representatives to solicit regional and national advertising that is beyond the reach of their local sales staff. Groups of stations owned by the same person or business sometimes form a representative firm to help all the stations in the group get national and regional advertising. Whether a station hires an outside representative firm or sets up its own, sales representatives use all possible means to secure advertising for their stations. Representatives call on advertiser or advertising agencies in person, use the trade press (such as *Broadcasting* magazine) to promote their stations, and use telephone calls and mail to reach advertisers.

TELEVISION NETWORKS

Much has already been said about networks. In fact, television networks and stations hardly can be discussed separately because they are so mutually dependent. All three of the major television networks have headquarters in New York City and production and office facilities in southern California. Most of the networks' programming comes from the Los Angeles-Hollywood area.

Most network programs originate with independent packagers such as Columbia Pictures, MCA, Orion, and MGM. Each year, many producers approach the networks with ideas, scripts, and pilots for television shows, hoping to sell programs that will appear on the networks a few months to two or more years later. A pilot is an episode produced so that network executives can test audience response and see how the series will look. Sometimes a pilot is run as a television movie of the week.

Those programs that receive approval for network run lead to contracts to produce a limited number of programs—from three to thir-

TABLE 11–4 National Association of Broadcasters Guidelines for Non-Program Material

MEDIA	NUMBER OF MINUTES PERMITTED/CLOCK HOUR	
	PRIME TIME	NON-PRIME TIME
Independents (TV)	14	16
Network affiliates (TV)	9'30''	16
Children's programs (TV)	12	12
Children's weekend programs (TV)	9'30''	12
Radio	18	18

Source: *The Television Code (NAB), Broadcasting Cable Yearbook 1981* (Washington: Broadcasting Publications, 1981) pp. D15-D22.

teen. In recent years the cost of producing even a half-hour program has become so high that the number of new original shows per season has declined from about 35 to no more than thirteen.

With thirty seconds of prime television time costing up to $100,000 in some cases, ratings translate directly into vast sums of money.

Networks, when reduced to their basic functions, serve as a sophisticated means of getting programming from producers to stations, while selling thirty-second pieces of time next to those programs to advertisers. Revenue from advertisers is divided between the network and its affiliates, and is based on a fraction of member stations' usual rates for advertising.

When a network selects a show, it hopes that the show will be very popular, ideally one of the five or ten most popular programs on television. Needless to say, not every show can please audiences, and as each new season progresses, some shows are dropped from the line-up.

The bottom line for each network is to have the largest evening audience. For most years before 1976-77, CBS was the most popular television network, followed by NBC, and as a distant third, ABC. Suddenly, with the mini-series "Roots," ABC took over first place, pushing CBS and NBC to second and third places. Not until the 1980-81 season did CBS regain its first place with audiences, pushing ABC to second. NBC now clamors for a higher rating. Ratings mean more than prestige to networks. The higher their ratings, the more the networks can charge for their advertising time.

PUBLIC TELEVISION

Having learned that neither the FRC nor the FCC were likely to defend very strongly the interests of educational and nonprofit radio broadcasters, the educational community was ready to fight for its television and radio channels. Moreover, many educators still remembered the promises of commercial broadcasters to provide free time for education on AM radio—time that was provided in quantities smaller than educators had expected. During the television freeze (1948–1950), educators readied themselves to fight for their portion of the new channels. Although there was little support for the educator's position at the FCC, one member, Commissioner Freida B. Hennock, defended the educators in their fight. Indeed, Hennock's position became somewhat of a rallying point. To promote the educational point of view, the Joint Committee on Educational Television (JCET) was formed by the National Association of Educational Broadcasters and the U.S. Office of Education in 1950. JCET was able to show that commercial broadcasters were not providing adequate educational service, and by the end of the freeze, some 80 VHF and 152 UHF channels had been set aside for educational and noncommercial uses. However, some large markets, notably those in New York, Philadelphia, and Washington, did not receive any educational channels.

But channels alone couldn't create educational broadcasting. Without funds, educational television or radio could hardly have become the reality it is. One of the prime movers to obtain funds to support educational television was the Ford Foundation. Early on, the foundation provided $1 million to set up a small network for sending tapes and films from station to station. Located at Ann Arbor, Michigan, the Educational Television and Radio Center (ETRC) soon moved to New York City and became National Educational Television (NET) in 1959. NET was a key to the growing prestige of educational television.

In 1962, the federal government began providing funding for educational television through the Educational Television Facilities Act, which authorized the Department of Health, Education, and Welfare to grant money to build or expand facilities. The grant program helped many stations go on the air.

Studies commenced by the Carnegie Commission on Educational Television in 1967 led to a recommendation that federal, state, and local agencies provide permanent funding for educational television. Moreover, the commission recommended the formation of a permanent organization through which federal funds could flow into educational broadcasting. The Public Broadcasting Act of 1967 amended the Communications Act of 1934 to create the Corporation for Public Broadcasting (CPB) as a nonprofit corporation. CPB was to help develop programs, distribute grants to station, and help interconnect stations. Out of CPB's encouragement came the Public Broadcasting Service (PBS) and later, National Public Radio (NPR) as interconnecting networks. Ultimately, these networks were to use satellite interconnections.

After the 1967 law, a number of new television stations were able to go on the air. By 1966, 99 licenses had been granted. In 1967, there were 111, and by 1970, 130 licenses authorized. By 1973, the number was up to 152, and by 1976, 160 licensed stations were on the air. About 10 percent were licensed to local public schools, 30 percent to higher education, 25 percent to community organizations, and 35 percent to states and municipalities.

In 1975, Congress passed for the first time a long-term, five-year educational broadcasting funding bill; previously, funding had been on a year-to-year basis. Although some of the funding for public television stations comes from federal sources, other funding sources include local boards of education, local governments, state boards of education, state governments, universities, foundations, businesses, and industries, subscriptions, and auctions. Because they operate on such limited sources of funds, a significant drop in any area can lead to near disaster for public broadcasting stations. Moreover, their ties to sources of funds are quite frail.

During the school day, much public television and radio programming is directed to the primary and secondary classroom. From this programming, stations are able to receive some support from education. In evening hours, public broadcasting is more cultural in nature.

The public stations face criticism from all sides; they are called too liberal or too conservative, too probusiness or too anti-business, too hard on the administration in power or too soft on it, providing too much educational programming and too little cultural programming or vice versa.

WHO OWNS WHAT—MEDIA OWNERSHIP

Based on the history of broadcasting, it is not surprising that companies like General Electric and RCA still have major investments in the field. That Rockwell International and American Express are high on the list of broadcast investors might raise an eyebrow, however. Table 11-5 is a list of some major investors in electronic communications.

Broadcast stations, much like other business enterprises, are owned by a wide variety of companies and individuals. Some stations are still "mom and pop" one or two station operations. These single owner-single station companies have become rarer in recent years, with more and more stations held by large group owners. Some of the group owners have holdings in broadcasting, newspapers, books, and other media.

The New York Times Company, for example, owns book publishing companies, newspapers, magazines, educational film companies, radio and television stations, educational recording companies, a news service, and a data bank. ABC, CBS, and RCA (owner of NBC) have both station and network holdings in broadcasting, as well as a variety of publishing holdings.

The networks might own even more stations were it not for a restriction imposed by the FCC limiting the number of television stations one organization may own to seven, of which no more than five can be VHF (very high frequency stations that operate on channels two through thirteen). The same limitation applies to AM and FM radio

TABLE 11-5   The Largest Companies With Electronic Communications Holdings

OVERALL RANK	COMPANY	TOTAL GROSS REVENUE	ELECTRONIC COMMUNICATION REVENUE
1.	General Electric Co.	$26,599,000,000	$ 106,396,000
2.	Getty Oil	12,719,752,000	63,598,760
3.	Eastman Kodak Co.	10,372,501,000	103,725,010
4.	Westinghouse Electric Corp.	9,366,313,000	533,879,841
5.	RCA Corp.	7,985,500,000	2,785,475,000
6.	Rockwell International	7,039,700,000	1,759,925,000
7.	American Express	6,914,500,000	65,000,000
8.	3M Co.	6,436,000,000	533,000,000
9.	Gulf & Western Industries	5,702,476,000	171,000,000
10.	Signals Cos.	5,299,900,000	476,991,000

Source: "Tabulating the Fifth Estate's Top 100," *Broadcasting*, January 4, 1982, pp. 40-41.

stations—a single owner may have not more than seven of each type of radio stations. In addition, a single owner may not own more than one station in a single market. ABC, CBS, and NBC own the legal limit of VHF television stations. Stations owned by networks are called O&Os—owned and operated stations.

The variety of broadcasting holdings of some large corporations is surprising. General Electric Company, for example, owns radio and television stations, cable systems, and film and television production facilities. During the diversification years of the 1960s and 1970s, many companies not traditionally connected with broadcasting entered the field, while some broadcasters acquired holdings in other industries.

One area that has been a cause for concern for FCC and Department of Justice officials over the years has been newspaper ownership of radio and television stations. The FCC has even promulgated regulations imposing restrictions on cross-ownership of the two media, but has allowed existing arrangements to continue. Some of the companies with holdings in both industries include Newhouse Newspapers, The Hearst Corporation, Combined Communications Corporation, Meredith Corporation, Media General, The Washington Post Company, Times-Mirror Company, Time Incorporated, and Cox Broadcasting Corporation.[1]

As Table 11-6 shows, the top fifteen group media owners cover a large number of homes in the United States.

The three television networks, through the television stations they own, reach 65 percent of all television homes each week. No other owners come close to that proportion of viewership. Of course, the television networks have wider circulation than even these impressive figures suggest, because of their affiliated stations. The reason the network O&Os have such large weekly audiences is because all three networks own stations in the three largest television markets—New York, Los Angeles, and Chicago. Moreover, some of the networks also own stations in the next largest markets, including Philadelphia (4), San Francisco (5), and Detroit (7), plus other markets.

But what is the trend in media holdings? The number of television stations controlled by group owners has risen from 37.5 percent in 1948 to 58 percent in 1976, as Table 11-7 shows. Moreover, the number of group owners has increased from 3 to 119; therefore, the number of companies with wide holdings in the media industries has been increasing over the past thirty-five years.

A growing interest has focused on the cross-media holdings of companies with interests in broadcast, print, and other media areas. Although little research has been done in the area, some attention has been given to compiling lists of companies with multi-media holdings.

Although a solid growth in group and cross-media ownership can be seen from the foregoing data, the question that naturally arises is this: What is so bad about the trend? With larger and larger companies owning broadcast and other media outlets, one might conclude that more funds would be available for documentary programs, educational offerings, and serious art. And indeed, some revenue from large stations or groups has been used for high quality production. Westinghouse Broadcasting's "PM Magazine" (or "Evening Magazine") may be pointed out as a reasonable attempt to both entertain and inform.

TABLE 11–6 The Television Reach of Large Broadcast Units

OWNERSHIP UNIT	NUMBER OF STATIONS OWNED	NET WEEKLY CIRCULATION (MILLIONS)	PERCENT OF HOUSEHOLDS
1. CBS	5	15.1	22
2. RCA (NBC)	5	14.5	21
3. ABC	5	14.5	21
4. Metromedia	6	11.7	17
5. RKO	4	8.7	13
6. Westinghouse	5	8.6	12
7. WGN-Continental	4	7.3	11
8. Kaiser	7	6.2	9
9. Capitol Cities	6	5.1	7
10. Storer	7	5.0	7
11. Cox	5	4.5	6
12. Taft	6	4.3	6
13. WKY-System	6	3.4	5
14. Scripps-Howard	5	3.3	5
15. Post-Newsweek	4	3.3	5

Source: Television Factbook.

TABLE 11-7 Group-Owned Television Stations in the United States, 1948-1976

YEAR	NUMBER OF GROUPS	NUMBER OF GROUP-OWNED STATIONS	TOTAL COMMERCIAL STATIONS	PERCENT OF GROUP CONTROL
1948	3	6	16	37.5
1950	17	52	98	53.1
1955	62	165	411	40.1
1960	84	252	515	48.9
1965	109	310	569	54.5
1975	115	405	711	57.0
1976	119	415	710	58.0
1982	184*	—	784*	—

* Television-Cable Yearbook (1981).

Source: Sterling and Haight, *The Mass Media: Aspen Institute Guide to Communication Industry Trends* (New York: Praeger, 1978), p. 100.

Shown nightly on many stations across the nation, this syndicated program has features on travel, cooking, exercise, and medical self-help. A review of documentary shows reveals programs dealing with education, political issues, and special events.

Media critics, on the other hand, say that the early evening period between network news and prime time (set aside by the FCC) is a television ghetto filled with syndicated game shows of questionable social or aesthetic value, rather than the wide array of local offerings that the FCC intended. Many critics also think that concentration of media control stifles free speech and innovative programming. A city that critics point to is Atlanta, where much of the local media is controlled by the Cox family. Within the city the family owns Cox Cable Communications, Cox Broadcasting Corporation (WSB-AM, FM, TV), and Cox Enterprises, holder of the two largest Atlanta newspapers. Because its broadcast and print properties are Atlanta's most widely viewed, listened to, and read media, Cox holds virtual control over the formation of local public opinion. Said the Department of Justice:

> The combination of Cox's almost total dominance of the Atlanta newspaper market, of Cox's first-ranked television station, Cox's superior radio facilities and the enormous potential for development of Cox's Atlanta Cable television system, creates a *prime facie* case that there is at present greater concentration of media control in Atlanta than in any other top-twenty market in the country.[2]

In an extended study of the Cox empire in Atlanta, Bill Cutler found that Cox had a cozy relationship with Rich's, the city's largest department store, a relationship that sometimes led to killing stories that were unfavorable to the store chain. This cozy relationship benefits the Cox business which, according to one petition, controls 83 percent of the advertising business in the city.[3]

Cox's control of the news was illustrated when the American Civil Liberties Union and the National Association for the Advancement of Colored People filed a petition with the government requesting that the Cox media monopoly be broken up. The petition was big news in newspapers elsewhere and in the non-Cox newpapers in Atlanta. Some newspapers ran large stories with huge headlines. Cox newspapers, however, only could find enough space to run very small one-column stories with obscure headlines far removed from the front of the news-papers. One critic observed that any other media holder probably could better serve Atlanta.

While the Cox story is unique in the top twenty markets, multimedia domination exists in many smaller cities.

In 1977, the Star Company, owner of the *Kansas City Star,* sold out to Capital Cities Communications, a New York-based firm that owns broadcast stations, other newspapers, and a magazine.[4] The company paid $125 million for the newspaper—perhaps the largest price ever paid for a newspaper up to that time. Table 11-8 shows how newspa-pers' ownership of broadcasting stations has grown.

Why do companies want to own newspapers and broadcast outlets? Broadcasting, traditionally, has been very profitable. Newspapers can be if they are run efficiently and if the city has only one daily newspa-per, or one morning and one evening newspaper. Newspaper acquisi-tion has been so rapid that by 1976, the top twenty-five newspaper chains controlled over half of all daily circulation.[5]

As columnist and lawyer Kevin Phillips pointed out, the mass media companies have monopolistic tendencies that reflect both horizontal integration—control in various media such as books, television, maga-zines, and radio, and vertical integration—control over the production,

TABLE 11-8   Newspaper Ownership of Broadcasting, 1922-1980

YEAR	AM	PERCENT TOTAL AM	FM	PERCENT TOTAL FM	TV	PERCENT TOTAL TV
1922	48	12.6	—	—	—	—
1930	36	5.8	—	—	—	—
1940	250	32.7	—	—	—	—
1950	472	22.6	273	37.2	41	41.8
1960	429	12.4	145	21.1	175	33.9
1970	394	9.2	245	11.2	189	27.9
1980	314	6.9	267	6.2	226	22.2

Source: Sterling and Haight, pp. 95-96, except 1980 data compiled from *Broadcasting-Cable Yearbook, 1981.*

distribution, and retailing of one medium. Horizontal integration refers to one company which owns several companies at the same level
in the production, distribution and retailing cycle. In broadcasting, local radio or television stations are the retailers and a firm owning several radio or television stations is involved in horizontal integration.
By contrast, vertical integration means that the company owns businesses engaged in two or three levels of production, distribution and
retailing. Thus a television network that owns a program production
house (production), a network (distribution), and stations (retailing)
is vertically integrated. To protect the public's right to know what is
happening, and to insulate the media from establishing cozy relationships with the government that should regulate them, Phillips believes
the formation of many small media establishments must be encouraged rather than allowing a few large corporations to control the entire
flow of ideas and information.[6]

Phillips is not the only person frightened by the growing concentration of power among media industries. Media scholar Ben Bagdikian,
former FCC commissioner Nicholas Johnson, and others have agreed
that changes must come.

To deal with media concentration problems, the FCC has created
rules over the years that are intended to restrain the amount of control
any single owner can exercise over the electronic media. Those rules
include the one-to-a customer rule, which prevents the owner of a
television station from owning newspapers in the same market; the
rule allowing no company to own more than seven FM and seven AM
radio stations and seven television stations (owning fewer than seven
stations in one class does not permit the owner to own more than
seven stations in the other class), and the duopoly rule, which prevents companies from owning two or more stations of one class in one
market. For example, one company could not own two television stations in St. Louis.

> No renewal of license shall be granted for a term extending be-
> yond January 1, 1980, to any party that as of January 1, 1975, di-
> rectly or indirectly owns, operates, or controls the only daily
> newspaper published in a community and also as of January 1,
> 1975, directly or indirectly owns, operates or controls the only
> commercial television station encompassing the entire commu-
> nity with a city-grade signal. The provisions of this paragraph
> shall not require divestiture of any interest not in conformity with
> its provisions earlier than January 1, 1980. (FCC 73.636 (c))

These ownership rules prevented wealthy Texan Joe L. Allbritton
from buying and keeping WMAL-AM-FM-TV and the *Washington Star*
in Washington, D.C. The FCC did permit Allbritton to buy the package
on the agreement that he would sell off some of the media properties
in a short time. But, the broadcast properties had been keeping the
Washington Star going, and without those stations, the newspaper

couldn't make it. It ceased publication in August, 1981. The rules, therefore, have not been all good, nor do they apply to agreements that existed before their creation.

At best, the evidence is conflicting. Media monopolies have engaged in unethical and illegal practices, but sometimes the co-ownership of various media has made survival possible. One proposal that has merit is to separate, perhaps legally, the editorial and business functions of the media. The government still cannot regulate freedom of speech and the press. But, it can exercise some control over the business side of the mass media, just as it can regulate the business practices of other industries, particularly when monopolistic or restraint of trade practices are evident. If the government did this, there would be fewer opportunities for the business side of a media organization to pressure the editorial side.

There is another group of media owners that needs to be mentioned, largely because of their small representation in the total ownership picture—minorities. As of 1977, only one VHF television and only seven UHF television stations were owned by minorities. Thirty-two AM and nine FM radio stations were under minority control. This does not include two noncommericial radio stations owned by minority firms. Matters were not much better in the cable business, where just six operating cable systems and thirty nonoperating franchises were held by minority groups. Because of this considerable underrepresentation, the FCC has proposed new regulations that would permit the establishment of a number of low power television stations in the United States. As of September, 1980, the FCC was accepting applications for low power stations; it continued to accept applications through February, 1981. If the FCC grants these new licenses, a number of nonrepresented groups would have the opportunity to start stations representing special points of view,[7] although the major operations have taken most of the low power stations already.

Public Television Ownership

Most writers focus on the implications of large corporations owning many of the commercial media outlets in the nation and ignore who owns the nearly 300 public television stations in the nation. Public television stations are prohibited by law from engaging in editorializing and the news carried on most of these stations is fairly limited. Although some special programs like the "McNeil-Lehrer Report" and "Wall Street Week" treat current topics, most public television falls far short of selective editorializing. Therefore, some of the problems commonly identified in commercial broadcasting do not exist in public television. However, it is interesting to examine who owns public television stations.

The largest number—ninety-seven—are owned by state or municipal authorities; colleges and universities own seventy-eight; community organizations own seventy-three; and public school systems own

THE SPIN-OFF

What does the name *Roots* conjure up: a television mini-series or a book? Both, of course. The *Roots* syndrome symbolizes what has been happening throughout the mass media system in the United States. *Rich Man, Poor Man* was both a television series and a book. Other stories have been both books and movies; still others like "M*A*S*H," have been a movie and then a television series. One property might be first a hard-back book, then a paperback book, then a movie, and finally, a television series.

Not even Broadway is exempt. The cost of producing a play or musical on Broadway is so high (perhaps over $1 million) that some of the costs must be recouped through other means. Consequently, *Grease,* which was originally a Broadway musical, later became a movie released to theaters. But its life was not over yet—the movie was then released on video disk and video cassette. And of course, there was the sound track record and the television showing.

The spin-off has become an important part of any property's life—so important that writers negotiate book, movie, paperback, television, and other rights when they sell their creative output. These rights can amount to millions of dollars, as was the case with *Jaws,* the movie, and *Jaws,* the book.

---

nineteen. The community organizations are frequently nonprofit corporations set up to build and operate the stations.

WITF, owned and operated by the South Central Educational Broadcasting Council in South Central Pennsylvania, is typical of the community organizations that own public television stations. WITF gets money from the state public television network, the school district, fund raising, the state Department of Education, and grants. Elsewhere, Connecticut Public Television is an independent television network that owns and operates its own television stations. Although the network receives much money from the state of Connecticut, other funds come from production grants and contracts, federal funds, and private gifts.

Unlike their commercial counterparts, public broadcasting stations operate on severely limited sums of money. The closest that public television comes to advertising are those announcements like "Funds for the following program were provided by . . . ," that accompany most public television programs. Some funds come from the wealthy oil companies and other corporations interested in improving their public image.

ECONOMICS OF BROADCASTING

AT&T may have led the way into toll or advertiser supported broadcasting, but modern broadcast advertising has moved far from its original pattern—both in terms of style and revenue generated.

FREE TELEVISION IS NOT FREE

In 1979, consumers spent $4.2 billion on television receiving equipment and approximately $1 billion on 40 million radio receivers.

By comparison, television broadcasters had a depreciated investment in their facilities of $1.32 billion (new cost $2.7 billion) and radio broadcasters had a depreciated investment of $829 million (new cost $1.5 billion) at the beginning of 1979. During 1978, television broadcasters spent $1.37 billion and radio broadcasters spent $1.079 billion on labor costs. All of these figures include investments and expenses incurred by the networks.

Not included in the above information is data on the amount of money spent on electricity or other utilities used by broadcasters and audiences. In any event, it is evident that the audiences have very large financial stakes in broadcasting—larger, in fact, than those of broadcasters who earn large profits from the business.

Sources: *Broadcasting and Cable Yearbook*, *1981* (Washington: Broadcasting Publications Inc., 1981) pp. D110-D111 and *FCC Annual Report*, *1979* (Washington: Government Printing Office, 1980), pp. 104, 105, 110.

The rising cost of television production in recent years has greatly increased the cost of television advertising, as Table 11-9 demonstrates. Yet, the effectiveness of the medium has brought advertisers back again and again. Most advertisers, however, believe that using a mix of media is more effective than using a single medium. Consequently, the same advertiser may choose to use newspapers, magazines, television, and radio (or some other combination) to reach the public with its advertising messages. Just because television has such large revenues does not mean that other media are left behind. In fact, newspapers' advertising revenue exceeds television's by a sizable margin.

All of the foregoing suggests that nonsubscription broadcasting is supported solely by advertisers, however audiences of the electronic media do have a substantial investment in television and radio sets, in repairs, and in electricity or batteries to keep those sets going. These hidden costs represent the price citizens must pay to be entertained and sold to. For example, during the five-year period beginning in 1975, consumers of broadcasting spent about $3.6 billion annually on television sets, as compared to the approximately $7 billion annually spent by television advertisers. But these figures do not include service to the consumer's equipment nor do they include the cost of electricity to run the sets. Clearly, the public has a large stake in the broadcast industry.[8]

Not only do audiences have a substantial financial investment in broadcast receiving equipment, they also have a large time investment in listening to radio or viewing television. During the 1930s, 1940s, and early 1950s, radios were on in the home between four and five hours daily; but by 1955, use was down to just over two hours daily.

TABLE 11-9
Broadcast Advertising

Year	Average Yearly Expenditure
1930-34	$57,640,000
1940-45	285,980,000
1950-55	1,075,600,000
1960-65	2,649,260,000
1970-75	5,691,600,000
1976-79	10,080,600,000*

* Averages taken in 1976-1978 for radio and 1976-1979 for television.

Source: Data from FCC Annual Reports

TABLE 11–10   The Thirteen Most Popular Television Shows

DATE	PROGRAM	PERCENTAGE OF VIEWING HOUSEHOLDS
March, 1981	Academy Awards	58
March, 1981	Masada, Part IV	42
January, 1981	Superbowl	63
January, 1977	Roots, Part VIII	51
January, 1977	Roots, Part VI	46
January, 1977	Roots, Part V	46
January, 1977	Roots, Part III	45
November, 1976	Gone With the Wind, Part II	47
November, 1976	Gone With the Wind, Part I	48
January, 1971	Bob Hope Christmas Show	45
January, 1970	Bob Hope Christmas Show	47
August, 1967	The Fugitive (final episode)	46
February, 1964	Ed Sullivan (first Beatles appearance)	45

Source: A.C. Nielsen Company

Although radio listenership declined after the advent of television, it began to grow again during the 1960s.

Television, meanwhile, has always enjoyed strong audience use. As early as 1950, people in cities with television stations had their home sets on about four-and-a-half hours a day—a figure that rose to over six hours a day by 1975, a figure that continues into the 1980s. Thus, by 1975, people at home during the day watched television, the whole family watched television during the evening, and some hardy souls even watched television into the late night hours.[9]

Ninety-eight percent of all homes and 95 percent of all cars in the nation have radio sets, while almost 98 percent of all homes have television sets. In many respects, television is the most mass of the mass media, because it commands the largest audience attending to one program at a single time. In fact, some programs have captivated as much as half of all the television homes. Table 11-10 has a list of the most popular television shows ever broadcast.

The advertising potential in reaching such large groups of people at one time is tremendous.

Some of the most popular television series have included "Bonanza," "All in the Family," "The Beverly Hillbillies," "The Andy Griffith Show," "Gunsmoke," and "Wagon Train."[10] Certain news events have attracted more than 90 percent of all television households. Among this select group of news events was the assassination of Kennedy, the Gemini IV space walk, the Apollo 11 moon landing, the Ford-Carter debates, and the Kennedy-Nixon election returns.

Yet with all the attention given to television, there has been some evidence that television's popularity is on the wane. Two important studies published in 1963 and 1973 suggest that fewer people in the later study considered themselves "super-fans" of television than had in the earlier study. The number of people who preferred television without advertising had increased from 43 percent to 48 percent, and the number who were willing to pay a price for television without advertising had risen from 24 percent to 30 percent.[11] In the 1980s the networks experienced declines in total viewership as video games and other services became available.

THE SUPER MEDIA FIGURE

Without the media, some people who have become household words would never be known to most Americans. The ability of the media to take an unknown nine-year-old girl and convert her into a household name, earning her over $2 million a year by the age of sixteen, shows the incredible power of the media. By that youthful age, the young woman had sold Calvin Klein jeans on television, magazines, newspapers, and billboards, had starred in *The Blue Lagoon* and *Endless Love* (her eighth film), and was receiving more than one thousand fan letters weekly, while modeling for $10,000 a day.

Although young Brooke Shields first appeared in an Ivory soap advertisement as an infant and on occasional other assignments, her mother turned down most assignments until Shields reached the age of nine and appeared in *Alice, Sweet Alice*. Other assignments quickly followed. Film, television, and print media provided the forum to make Shields famous, and her mother provided the encouragement and management needed to bring everything together.

Source: John Duka, "Brooke Shields and Company —Manufacturing a Superstar," *The New York Times*, August 2, 1981, 2:l p15.

The changing viewer attitudes toward television (and perhaps other mass media) has required the advertising community to change its means of reaching the public. One of the most important shifts in advertising in the last thirty years has been its flexibility in appealing to the changing age and attitudes of the American population. During the 1950s, the children of the famous post-World War II baby boom were quite young, and advertising for the candy bar Snickers featured cartoon elephants and children. During the 1960s and into the 1970s, Snickers commercials focused on the nutrition of peanuts but kept children, with an occasional parent, in the commercial. Since the late 1970s, Snickers ads have featured adults, homemakers, hardhats, and others. The baby and childhood images were gone because the baby boom generation had reached adulthood. As executives at the advertising firm of Ted Bates believe, every product has a U.S.P.—unique selling position—and for Snickers, that position is now with adults. Incidentally, the candy bar is the largest selling candy snack in the nation.

Other advertisers have followed similar paths. Pepsi has moved from advertisements featuring young teenagers on motorcycles to advertisements featuring middle Americans in family settings. Gerber is now so successfully selling its oil, powder, and shampoo to adults that more adults than children are using its products.

This adjusting to a new market has a name—repositioning. Sometimes the repositioning is to wider audiences than were originally sought; at other times it is to an older or younger audience, depending on the changing demographics of the population. Perhaps by the year 2000, McDonalds will be featuring 65-year-olds munching on french fries and Big Macs.[12] Of course, this does not mean children and young teens are now ignored completely, but they are certainly not emphasized as they once were.

BUSINESSES' HIDDEN MEDIA INFLUENCE

Every year, nearly 33 billion dollars is spent by business to sell its products through direct advertising in the nation's mass media. The public sees the direct results of these expenditures through identifiable advertising messages. Although many people claim the advertising is in poor taste or runs too long, those who object may at least tune out the messages. However, there is a more subtle form of advertising called advocacy advertising on which companies spend an estimated $500 to $1,000 million yearly. Advocacy advertising does not come in the usual advertising formats, rather it appears as "op-ettes" editorial advertisements, often near the editorial page of large newspapers. Mobil Oil Company spent approximately $10 million during the mid-1970s on editorial advertising to rebut oil industry critics.

In 1964, Ben Bagdikian noted that the National Association of Manufacturers had prepared editorials printed by some 600 newspapers, often without citing the source. Mobil Oil Company produced a series of creative cartoons supporting their point of view on issues. Often the cartoons and editorials appeared without any indication that they came from interest groups who wanted to influence public opinion.

Modern Talking Picture Service, created by AT&T during the 1920s and spun off during the 1930s under antitrust pressure, places sponsored films in schools, television stations, and civic groups. Modern's pictures are sent free to requesting organizations—the cost of production and distribution is covered by business, industry, government, and other entities interested in communicating their messages to the public. Most television stations use Modern's films to fill unsold time. Moreover, thousands of churches, schools, and other groups have used the company's films.

Sponsors willingly cover the costs of producing and distributing films because they know they can quietly circulate their views on issues—airlines sponsor travelogues designed to make viewers want to travel, government agencies sponsor nature films to promote their views on ecology, and manufacturers sponsor films on the modern uses of chemicals, plastics, or other products in which they have an interest.

Modern's program has been so successful that a competing company, Association-Sterling, arose. Clients for both companies include foreign governments, U.S. agencies, industries, businesses, and nonprofit agencies like the Salvation Army.

Many other forms of corporate selling exist that do not credit the sources. For example, the Tobacco Institute has provided pro-tobacco speeches for physicians sympathetic to their cause and has paid some reporters $1,000 a week for stories favorable to tobacco interests. Many firms prepare lengthy feature articles that quietly advertise their interests. Ortho, a garden supply manufacturer, produced a sixteen page supplement for newspapers that was carried free in many places.

The simple threat by a company to withdraw advertising from a medium can be enough to kill media stories that present that company or industry in an unfavorable light. A few years ago a series on supermarket abuses was abruptly dropped when supermarkets in the area threatened to withdraw their advertising.

Public television has been another area fruitful for corporate manipulation. As Congress has shown increasing unwillingness to contribute to public radio and television, business has stepped in to underwrite public television to the tune of some $14 million a year. Because many people perceive public television to be a prestige medium, some of that image rubs off on the companies underwriting the programs. A review of viewership statistics on public television shows a large number of upper middle-class viewers, a key group in influencing opinion. Moreover, the underwriting company sometimes reviews scripts to insure that there are no segments damaging to their image. Although there is no clear indication that corporate underwriters are manipulating public television's content, the question must arise when script reviews are a reality.

Another area where business influences the media needs to be mentioned. Back in the 1960s, International Telephone and Telegraph Company (ITT) tried to take over ABC. To suppress unfavorable comments in *The New York Times,* representatives from ITT visited a *Times* reporter. Other indications of media control also became evident during the hearings that would have led to the takeover. Although the FCC approved the merger, later the Justice Department threatened legal action. This incident and many others like it raise the specter of industry seeking its own media outlets so that their corporate messages can be funneled directly to the public. And indeed, RCA Corporation owns NBC, and other nonmedia companies also own media interests.[13]

Although the extent to which business manipulates or controls the news and opinions reaching the American people can never be accurately assessed, the issue needs to be explored from time to time. As

John Kenneth Galbraith observed, the advertising media provide the mechanism to create demand for a huge number of mass-produced products in an industrial country. That fact makes the business community interested in the mass media.

CABLE TELEVISION

Since 1975, there has been an incredible growth in the number of cable systems, the variety of services they offer, and the number of people that subscribe to them. This vigorous interest in cable comes at a time when the economy generally is in a recession. The reasons for cable television's recent success arise from the changing patterns in regulation, the willingness of investors to enter the field, and a public interested in an alternative to commercial network television.

In 1982, some forty-four hundred cable systems are providing service to more than ten-thousand communities in the United States. These cable systems have 17.2 million subscribing homes and reach 48 million people, giving cable television access to approximately 30 percent of the nation, according to Broadcasting (Jan. 4, 1982, p. 82). Not only has the number of systems and subscribers increased, but the variety of services has increased as well. Besides broadcast programming, cable systems offer movie channels, sports programming, FM music, and other services.

Although cable television started with small "mom and pop" operations, today's cable system is more likely to belong to a large corporation that owns several or many cable systems. These companies, called multiple system owners (MSOs), range from modest operations to Fortune 500 companies like Teleprompter and American Television and Communications, which have 1.4 million subscribers each and systems in many communities. Time, Incorporated owns AT&C.

Cable operators derive their income from selling their services to subscribers, charging both installation and monthly fees. Monthly fees, main source of cable income, average $8.50 per customer, while connection fees range from nothing to $100. Most systems now offer one or more pay channels (featuring commercial movies and sports for example) at an average cost of $10 per channel per month. These pay channels are called enhanced services.

In return for their cable investment, subscribers receive expanded choices—twenty or more channels of television programming, and often FM music, plus an improved television picture and sound. Types of cable services include the four broadcast networks, movie, sports, religious, ethnic, and other specialized channels; and channels printing out time, weather, and news. A few cable systems even permit subscribers to play games with a central computer or register attitudes on questions and other events—viewer "talk back" to the cable system.

The wide variety of new services have induced people to subscribe to cable television services even in markets that already have extensive broadcast services, such as those in New York, Chicago, or Atlanta.

One distant service comes from "superstations," which are television stations that sell their services to many cable systems. Their service is delivered by satellite or microwave.

According to *Broadcasting Yearbook* (1982) some nine superstations were providing programming to cable systems in 1982. The best known is WTBS, a station owned by Ted Turner in Atlanta. That station uses a satellite link and is carried on 2,100 cable systems, and can be viewed by 9.5 million subscribers. Other superstations include KBMA in Kansas City, KSTW in Tacoma, Washington, KTVT in Dallas, WGN in Chicago, WOR and WPIX in New York, WSBK in Boston, and one FM station—WFMT in Chicago.

Satellites also bring both free and subscription services such as Black Entertainment Television, ESPN, Cinemerica Satellite Network, Home Box Office, and a number of other services. Some of the services provide general interest programming without commercial interruptions, while other services focus on specialized audiences such as Blacks, Hispanics, older people, sports enthusiasts, and old movie buffs.

More recently, one system in Ohio started the QUBE, which allows viewers to register their attitudes, play games with a central computer, take tests, and participate in television shows using a home console. In Florida, Knight-Ridder has begun experimenting with facsimile newspapers over cable; others have sent letters over cable; some cable systems have emergency warning services (available in Harbison near Columbia, S.C.) or news-sports-weather services; and other systems provide opportunities for citizens to go on the cable.

In summary, cable television has made possible the following range of services: (1) expanded broadcast services including NBC, CBS, ABC, PBS, independent stations, and superstations; (2) pay services like HBO, Showtime, Movie Channel, and Cinemax; (3) free specialty services such as ESPN, MTV (rock music in FM stereo); (4) local access for the public, government, education, and paying clients; (5) crawls, which are words rolled across the screen that carry advertising, sports, news, weather, or other information; (6) newspapers available on a screen or in some cases via a printer; (7) two-way services such as polling, computer access, and electronic mail; (8) emergency services such as home security systems connected to a central computer and city street surveillance; and (9) educational programs from schools.

To provide all these services, cable must interconnect with microwave systems, satellites, computers, local studios, and specialized equipment. In addition, the cable system usually makes itself available to community service groups wishing to reach its subscribers, such as educational institutions, cultural institutions, or governmental agencies.

How Cable Works

The basis of any cable system is the network of wires conducting signals to subscribers from a central point. The wire is actually a coaxial cable (Figure 11-5) composed of a wire surrounded by an insulator, which is itself encased in a shield made of wire braid. The entire assembly is then insulated from the elements by one or more layers of protective materials.

Because signals get weaker as they travel down the cable, amplifiers are spaced about every 1,500 to 3,000 feet to bring the programs back up to a strength that can be used by television sets. The amplifiers are called wideband because of their capability of handling many channels; the actual number of channels they can handle depends on the quality of the amplifiers, with many of the newer amplifiers capable of handling nearly fifty. Sometimes voice and data are substituted for regular television programs. When this is the case, some 2,000 voice channels will fit in the space of a single television channel.

From the cable grid, drops run to subscribing home television sets. To insulate the drop and the subscriber's set from the cable, the cable operator uses an insulation amplifier. This amplifier prevents electrical interference created by television and radio sets from reaching the trunk cable. Like the trunk coaxial cable, the drop uses coaxial cable to a small unit next to the television or radio where a piece of regular television antenna wire makes the final connection. The shield around the center wire keeps outside interference away from the cable signals and prevents the cable signals from interfering with outside communications.

The headend, as it is called, feeds the cable grid and includes a

---

FIGURE 11–5   Cable used in cable television system.

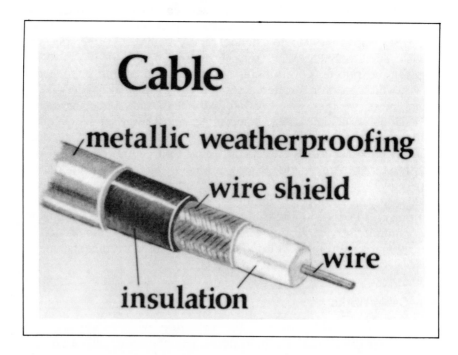

FIGURE 11-6   Programming for cable systems is secured in various ways.

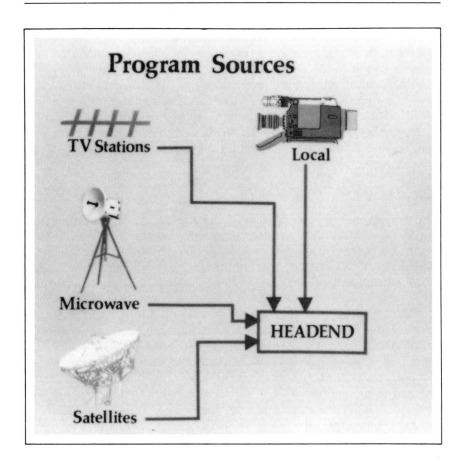

building and all the necessary electrical equipment to send television, radio, data, and voice communications to subscribers, and to receive communications back. The equipment includes small television transmitters, control equipment, receiving equipment (to obtain satellite and other programs), and monitoring equipment to insure that all is working well.

Cable headends receive signals from several sources: (1) from television stations; (2) from satellites using special dish-shaped antennas; (3) from microwave links using systems like those owned by telephone companies (in fact many times telephone companies provide the microwave signals); (4) from their own cable studios; (5) from local studios operated by educational institutions, citizens groups, government, or other interested groups; (6) through the mail from program suppliers; and (7) from special electronic origination equipment including computers. As technology now stands, a cable system amounts to a giant party line with all subscribers connected to the same line (Figure 11-6). (A few systems now use two lines to expand capabilities or a second line for talk-back from consoles.)

FIGURE 11-7 A typical amplifier used to maintain strong television signals.

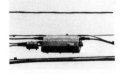

Limitations

A primary limitation of cable systems is the number of amplifiers that may be connected together in a line before the noise level at the ends becomes intolerable. Each amplifier inserts some noise during the process of bringing the signals back up to an adequate strength. Once noise is added to the signal it never leaves, and with each additional amplifier adding more noise, eventually the signal becomes unacceptably distorted. Although the practical length of a line varies greatly based on the quality of the amplifiers and cable, the usual practical limit may be about fifteen miles. To extend the reach of a cable system, some operators have used multiple headends connected by microwave systems.

Optical Fibers

A recent invention—optical fibers—contains the most promising possibility for expanding the already impressive capabilities of cable television. Comprised of strands of glass about the size of a human hair, optical fibers can carry far more than the 50 or so channels available on a conventional cable. Estimates suggest that a single optical fiber may carry 600 to 1,000 channels of television.

Instead of using electrical waves for carrying information, optical fibers use light waves—waves that are transmitted through that thin fiber of glass. Like the wire cable, however, the optical fiber does cause some loss in signal strength, so the light wave also needs to be amplified every so often. To do this, a small laser is used. It is placed in the line just as an amplifier for an electrical cable is. Using this technology, much longer lines may be used than are permitted by electrical cables. Teleprompter has been using an optical fiber system for some of its headend operations in Manhattan with much success. In addition, telephone companies have been installing optical fibers for some of their telephone circuits. When a person makes a telephone call over any distance, there is a great likelihood that that person's voice is converted into light at some point.

Satellites

Another component in cable communications is the reception of programs through satellites. An outgrowth of the aerospace program of the United States, satellites have evolved quite a bit since the first experiments in the 1950s. Today, satellites permit the beaming of voices, computer data, and television signals around vast distances of the earth. An uplink—or transmitter—sends program information up to a receiver mounted in a satellite. The satellite in turn accepts the information, amplifies it, and sends it back to earth using a transmitter. The whole transmitter-receiver system has come to be known as a transponder. Back on earth, a downlink accepts the signal sent from the satellite. Finally, the signal is placed on the cable system for subscribers to view.

The Future

One of the people who forsees better times for cable is Mike Dann, once affiliated with CBS-TV and later with Children's Television Workshop, the producer of shows like "Sesame Street." Dann sees a day when the nation will be wired with strands of cable that will bring many services by video to American households. He predicts that cable will have as much impact on Americans' lifestyles as automobiles and cheap gasoline did when they created the suburbs. By the 1990s, Dann sees as many as 220 channels being available to home and business users. Combined with satellites and videodisc and videocassette, entertainment, business, education, and shopping all could be handled through wires. Because so many matters could be handled at home, traffic jams would disappear, or at least be reduced significantly.

Eventually, Dann says, cable channels could become highly specific—channels for tennis, bridge, chess, cooking, home decorators—almost anything. There could be channels in French, Japanese; indeed, there already is a Spanish channel. But, all of these services will cost the consumer: Dann predicts fees of up to $500 per month—a frightening cost until one realizes how much is spent on newspapers, magazines, gasoline, theater admissions, and other services that cable could help reduce.[14]

Cable: Who Pays?

A trend developing recently is the production of 'informercials," or commercials with more than the usual minimal product information. Offered as a means of defraying some of the cable program and distribution costs, informercials may be appearing more in the near future. Unlike regular commercial television networks, which broadcast commercials during programs, the informercials will not be sprinkled through a program, but will be run before and after entertainment shows.

COMPUTERS

At the heart of interactive cable, or the two-way cable communication system, is a very small computer at the viewer's home, which can talk to a much larger computer at the system's headend. This is one example of how computers have become an increasingly important part of the total communications environment. In fact, almost no communications medium functions without some computer involvement.

Many radio and television stations use computers to help program their stations. In fact, some radio stations use entirely automated programming. Newspapers, because of their rising production costs, have been forced to adopt computers in many parts of the production cycle such as storing stories until use and handling some layout chores. Reporters use video display terminals connected to computers, which are themselves set to produce camera-ready copy. In time, computers will

FIGURE 11-8   An example of microcomputers used in homes and schools.

be used to lay out full pages, replacing the old method of cutting copy, headlines, and pictures, and pasting them on a page.

Not all computers are used by the media producers themselves. Individuals have found increasing uses of computers in the home. In fact, many computers found in home use display information on a television set. The result is increasing competition for the television set. Manufacturers like Radio Shack, Apple, and Atari, among others, sold some $120 million in computers in 1980—a figure that is expected to rise to $475 million in 1985.

Home users find that computers can help with family finances, offer challenging new games to play, and help with educational needs. Some of the new home computers function much like big office and industrial units—they have keyboards and display numerical and verbal information on a television screen.

Not all computers look like their larger industrial cousins. Atari has built a number of electronic games, some of which are displayed on television screens. Other companies build computers into dolls, toy trucks and cars, and little talking plastic boxes. Although a recession hit the nation during late 1981, sales of toys were up some three percent (after correction for inflation) over 1980. Much of that increase was based on the sales of video games and other computer toys. The bulk of the video market has been supplied by Atari, a division of Warner Communications, and Mattel, which makes the game Intellivision.[15]

Obviously, not all computer business is directed at the mass media—or at home use—small businesses and larger businesses use computers for all kinds of accounting chores such as billing, payroll, tax

INVITED COMPUTERS

Some landmarks look so large you walk by without noticing. Take two recent mileposts of the computer age. One is the estimate that the population of computers is about to reach 5 billion, outnumbering humans. Will it matter?

Of course the 5 billion figure includes computers of all kinds, from the micro-processor in your digital watch to the Cray-1 mainframe that simulates global weather or nuclear bursts. Neither kind is likely to jump out and grab you, or demand your vote. No, the threat comes from the computers you invite home, the so-called personal computers. They come in quietly, politely, and you entrust them with your correspondence and bank records. Then you patch them in to your telephone lines so they can rap with data banks and "mode" with one another.

Next they offer to run your household, waking you up in the morning and turning out the lights at night. They ask for speech modules and learn to imitate your voice. A whole industry is out there trying to satisfy their burgeoning demands. The latest thing is mechanical arms. It will be legs next, then a checking account and then a computer of its own . . . .

The other milepost? Last fall, a Japanese worker, Kenji Urada, became the new age's first victim: he was crushed to death by an industrial robot he was trying to repair.

Source: *New York Times*, April 25, 1982, p. 22.

---

records, and projecting future patterns. In addition, scientific enterprises have long been users of computers.

Estimates suggest that 1980 computer sales of $590 million to small businesses will rise to $2,700 million by 1985. Computer sales to offices of word processors—machine assistance in writing letters and compiling word reports and similar chores—will rise from $90 million in 1980 to $1,450 million in 1985. Scientific computer sales should rise from 1980 sales of $220 million to sales of $1,020 million in 1985. The companies who stand to reap the greatest rewards from these new sales include Apple, IBM, Commodore, Xerox, Zenith, and Hewlett-Packard.

One other market—the educational field—has been making increasing use of computers. Again, a striking sales growth—from $35 million in 1980 to some $145 million in 1985—is expected.

Interestingly, all the above figures deal with sales of small computers—those that sell for under $10,000. In addition, there are the much larger computers sold by companies like IBM and Digital Equipment Company. These markets have been strong as well and will continue to grow.[16]

But computer hardware, (all the equipment, terminals, and printers), is only part of the story. The other part is software—the programs that make computers perform various functions. Software packages, as they are called, range from accounting and business programs to sophisticated scientific and mathematical programs, and from games like Pac Man to home business programs.

Another important function performed by special purpose computers and some general purpose computers is word processing. A word processing computer has a keyboard and VDT, video display terminal, or box with a television screen, for viewing the results of the keyboard operator. The program in the machine makes it easy to edit, rearrange, delete, or add copy. Some word processing computers can store whole books in their memories. When the manuscript or letter has reached the desired state, the push of a button produces a typewritten manuscript on paper—all without error if keyed correctly. Some word processing machines even have dictionary programs to help with spelling. As the price of word processors continues to decline, the traditional electric typewriter will be threatened with obsolescence—just as it made the mechanical typewriter obsolete.

The data coming out of the computer may take many forms, from typewritten information to charts and graphs. To produce the output information, manufacturers have developed plotters to make graphs, high speed printers to print out information quickly, and letter quality printers to print out letters and longer documents that look like custom-produced letters.

The central processing unit of the computer is where the calculations take place; it must be able to accommodate any information or calculation demanded by the operator. In recent years, the speed of the processors, which are called CPUs, has increased dramatically. All the operations of the CPU are guided by programs instructing the computer what to do in various circumstances.

Closely allied to the CPU is the memory. Computer memories have gotten smaller in recent years, while their capacity has increased dramatically. The basis of the computer's memory is the RAM or random access memory chip. By 1982, a new chip was capable of storing 256,000 bytes of information. Previous memory chips were limited to 128,000 or 64,000 bytes. A byte is one character of information such as a letter or number. These little silicone chips are not much larger than a postage stamp. The term random access means that any information may be reached without going through any other point in the computer memory.

Storage may be increased by adding memory disks such as floppy disks, small flexible disks that look very much like records but record like audio tape, Winchester drives (a specialized hard disk), and hard disks that can store millions of bytes of information. Today's home computers have the capacity of the large industrial computers of an earlier era.

The future of computers seems bright indeed. Just how the systems will be used depends much on the initiative of users and the responsibility they bring to the task. It seems clear, however, that the merging of fiber optics, cable, telephones, computers, television, and other

THE COMPUTER GOES TO SCHOOL

From graduate school laboratories to elementary school classrooms, computers have moved into education in a big way. The machines have become so popular that some educators have even invested their own money in computers to teach their students with. By 1982, more than ninety thousand computers were in use in the nation's classrooms—a number that will increase 300 percent by 1985.

Contrary to the usual notion, teachers do not seem intimidated by computers—in fact, most teachers want computers in their classrooms. Some teachers even write programs for their students, while others buy prepackaged programs. Scott Foreman and Company distributes a program to help young children learn to read by using sound, color, and a voice synthesizer.

Computers have been used to teach math, language arts, reading, social studies, science, special education, business, art, and music, as well as computer science. Computers can be used to drill and practice students—the machine does not mind repeating a question or concept as many times as needed for a student to learn—so that the teacher can perform other duties. The computer can provide the catch-up work that slow learners need. Also, computers can be used to test and interact with students to describe what they are doing wrong, and how their errors were committed.

Meanwhile, a debate goes on in schools over what are the best uses for computers. How that debate will turn out is unclear, but one thing is certain—classroom computers are here to stay.

means of electrical communication will continue, and the final mix will have much to do with the uses made of the new media. The computer revolution of the 1980s is just as dramatic an occurrence as the coming of the automobile, the printing press, or the radio.

Electronic Files

For centuries, the book was the basic form for storing information. Today, that has begun to change; now there are computer files on every conceivable subject. One such file is the New York Times Information Service (NYTIS), an index of everything that has appeared in *The New York Times* up to 48 hours before the present. The information file is distributed through a satellite network anywhere in the world. Users can send key words back to the NYTIS system and view relevant abstracts or summaries on their own VDTs.

Teleconferencing

Because the price of gasoline and transportation have increased so much in recent years, business travel has been curtailed. One solution is video teleconferencing aimed at large associations and companies.

Through teleconferencing, people all across the country can sit in front of their large projection television screens and communicate with other groups of people hundreds of miles away. Teleconferencing uses satellites and microwave systems to provide immediate communication among groups. One of the large teleconferencing organizations is Holiday Inn Corporation. The company provides conference rooms and all the necessary equipment in its hotels to those who wish to lease its facilities. In addition, the Bell System has its Picturephone Meeting Service. Other services no doubt will follow.[17]

| TRENDS IN THE '80s | A Summary of the New Communication Technologies |

The range of electronic communications services available to both the consumer and business has been growing rapidly during the 1980s. Here is how some of the major areas look in early 1982:

■ Cable television serves 30 percent of all homes, forty-seven cable-satellite programmers including Home Box Office, are operating with some seventeen additional programmers scheduled to begin operation during 1982. About 4,700 systems are serving 12,900 communities.

■ Interactive (talk-back) cable experiments with 350 households in Southern California show possibilities for other parts of the country. Subscribers can pay bills, check ski conditions, order from retailers—all with a small instrument connected to their cable and television set. QUBE, A Warner Amex operation in Columbus, Ohio (1978), provides subscribers opportunities to vote on various issues. Some systems provide security, medical, and fire alerts. Interactive techniques such as banking, electronic mail, and newspapers at home are being tested in many cities.

■ Three thousand to four thousand new low power television stations that will open up opportunities for women and minorities without interrupting regular service are planned by the FCC. At least one such station was operating in 1982.

■ Large screen projection television sets that produce five- or six-foot images have existed for several years, but new screens that can hang on the wall have been invented and are being developed for home use.

■ Video cassette units made by several manufacturers will allow people to produce their own television shows at home. Programs made in one format cannot be used on the other. Nevertheless, video cassette units have become very popular.

■ New television sets adapted for cable can tune into more than 100 different channels.

■ Direct satellite broadcasting to homes appears to be likely in the near future. Such service would make it possible for a national television station to be available to all properly equipped homes.

■ Video and electronic games continue to proliferate in both homes and businesses, with Atari and similar companies leading the way.

■ Video disks, shaped like records, opened the way for the low-cost purchase of motion pictures and other programs for home use.

■ Small, portable television cameras and recorders easily carried by journalists and other producers for field work make their job easier. Everything necessary for recording a program can be carried on the back of one person.

■ Digital television, that is, converting the television picture into numbers, has arrived, making it possible to get an improved picture quality on smaller recording tapes. Digital recordings for music have arrived also.

■ Using satellite interconnections, television networks can offer news programs with stories originating all over the world.

■ Computers for home and business use have grown in variety and capacity while prices have dropped. Basic machines can be purchased for $100 in 1982. And, some of the more sophisticated machines have capacities equaling the giant business machines of an earlier period.

■ Typewriters are changing from the old mechanical and electrical machines to largely electronic or computer machines called word processors that can remember pages, correct spelling (with a dictionary program), and perform other functions.

■ Small desk top computers can handle typing, accounting, taxes, scientific calculations, and many other functions in both offices and homes. Many computers also can accept programs for playing games.

■ Robots are becoming more sophisticated, capable of handling most assembly line operations, and the newer machines can be reprogrammed when the manufacturing operation changes.

■ The electronic communication developments mean jobs for computer programmers, engineers, creative programming talent, and managers with technical backgrounds. Indeed, while other fields are shrinking, telecommunications will continue to grow in the 1980s.

■ A video section (1981) and a computer section (1982) were added recently in *Time* magazine, illustrating the growing impact of video and computers.

■ Radio is still important to national networks—at least to ABC, which added two more radio networks in 1982—Rock Radio and Direction. Rock Radio features music from rock albums; Direction focuses on lifestyles. This brings to six ABC's radio networks.

■ Some technologies are threatening cable television. Among them are pay television—television stations that offer movies to subscribers without commercials. The viewer pays a fee to use a machine that descrambles the television signal that was scrambled before broadcast. Another system called multipoint distribution system (MDS) uses low power television stations operating outside the usual channels to send pay movies and programs to subscribers. Instead of one large transmitter, a group of low power transmitters cover an area.

ADDITIONAL READINGS

Bluem, A. William. *Documentary in American Television: Form, Future, Method.* New York: Hastings House, Publishers, 1965.

Cutler, Bill. "Cox Controls Our Media: Covering Atlanta Like a Wet Blanket." *Atlanta Gazette,* July 20, 1977, p. 8.

————— "How the Cox Media Monopoly Affects—Part III," *Atlanta Gazette,* August 3, 1977, p. 6.

Gibson, George H. *Public Broadcasting: The Role of the Federal Government.* New York: Praeger Publishers, 1977.

Guimary, Donald L. *Citizens' Groups and Broadcasting.* New York: Praeger, 1975.

Hall, Claude and Hall, Barbara. *This Business of Radio Programming.* New York: Billboard Publishers, 1977.

Quinilan, Sterling. *The Hundred Million Dollar Lunch.* Chicago: J. Philip O'Hara, Inc., 1974.

Span, Paula. "*Madison Ave. Chases the Baby Boom.*" In The New York Times. Dubuque, Iowa: William C. Brown, Co., Publishers, 1977.

Steiner, Gary A. *The People Look at Television: A Study of Audience Attitudes.* New York: Alfred A. Knopf, 1963.

FOOTNOTES

1. Christopher H. Sterling and Timothy R. Haight, *The Mass Media: Aspen Institute Guide to Communication Industry Trends* (New York: Praeger, 1978), pp. 65–70.

2. Bill Cutler, "Cox Controls Our Media: Covering Atlanta Like a Wet Blanket," *Atlanta Gazette,* July 20, 1977, p. 8.

3. Bill Cutler, "How the Cox Media Monopoly Affects Us—Part III," *Atlanta Gazette,* August 3, 1977, p. 6.

4. "Printing Money," *Time,* February 21, 1977, p. 52.

5. Ben H. Bagdikian, "Newspaper Mergers: The Final Phase," *Columbia Journalism Review* (March-April 1977).

6. Kevin Phillips, "Busting the Media Trust," *Harper's* (July 1977): 23–34

7. "Low Power Television: A Fact Sheet" (Washington: FCC, 1980).

8. *Broadcasting-Cable Yearbook, 1981* (Washington, D.C., Broadcasting Publications, Inc. 1981).

9. Sterling and Haight, "Communication Industry Trends," p. 366.

10. A.C. Nielsen Company, "Television Audience," 1976, p. 71.

11. Robert T. Bower, *Television and the Public* (New York: Holt, Rinehart & Winston, 1973); Gary A. Steiner, *The People Who Look at Television* (New York: Knopf, 1963).

12. Paula Span, "Madison Ave. Chases the Baby Boom," *The New York Times Magazine,* June 14, 1981, pp. 55–57.

13. Mark Green, "How Business Is Misusing the Media," *The New York Times,* December 18, 1977, p. 14.

14. Carey Winfrey, "The Cable TV Revolution: How it Affects the Arts," *The New York Times,* July 5, 1981, pp. 1, 21, 22.

15. Sandra Salmans, "Christmas Is a Video Game," *The New York Times,* December 6, 1981, p. 1.

16. Andrew Pollack, "Next, a Computer on Every Desk," *The New York Times,* August 23, 1981, p. 1.

17. Allan Zullo, "Update: Telecommunications," *Sky* (December 1981): 21–27.

12

REGULATION OF BROADCASTING AND NEWER TECHNOLOGIES

The mass media, whether it be print, broadcast or film, trades in ideas—ideas that are sometimes titillating, frequently controversial, often commercial, but always there posing some thought. In the 1980s, United States journalists and other mass media practitioners enjoy considerable freedom of expression, yet many other countries on both sides of the Iron Curtain exercise stern control over their media. In centuries past, journalists had to fight vigorously through the printed page for even the most limited freedom. Sometimes this fight cost them dearly in the loss of printing presses, jobs, or favor from their political rulers.

Freedom was gained slowly from the time of the invention of the first printing press, through the years of licensing in England and through that country's repressive policies toward the early settlers in America, to modern times. Even now, reporters occasionally find themselves behind bars for something they have written. Despite the First Amendment to the Constitution, the freedom to speak or print anything is never complete, absolute, or permanent; therefore, the fight continues.

Perhaps more than any other group, journalists and printers have battled for freedom from authoritarian governments and repressive laws—freedom that once gained, has allowed many other citizens to express their views or seek the truth as they choose.

Traditionally, the mass media have been guardians of their hard won freedom. They do this by serving as watchdogs on government and anyone else who would take away their individual liberties. Consequently, every newspaper and broadcaster feels an obligation to provide detailed coverage of the workings of government. That coverage is not limited to simply recording the daily facts of government, but extends to include free and frank criticism of the evidence. Through reporting and criticism, journalists hope to make the public aware of government actions that might have deleterious effects, not only on journalists, but on the public.

The workings of journalism may be seen in the resignation of Richard Nixon from the presidency in the 1970s or the treatment of nuclear power in the 1980s. Public opinion, informed by the work of reporters, continually revises its posture and, many hope, influences the direction of government.

Only in a society where reporters have broad freedom to seek and report can such a dialogue take place among political leaders, journalists, and the public—a dialogue that everyone hopes will lead to the best solutions.

It would have seemed natural for freedom of the press to have been extended to radio, because the new medium served the same journalistic purposes that newspapers and magazines have long performed. However, in the United States, a nation committed to freedom from government interference, some radio and television stations are operated by local school boards or state universities—both part of the government—and all stations, regardless of who owns their equipment, are regulated by the United States government. So it is that broadcasters have imposed on them many regulatory restraints unknown to their print counterparts. And, indeed, in every nation of the world broadcasting is either regulated by the state or owned by the state. Less than the ideal condition anticipated in the First Amendment.

Should the strong arm of government intervene as it does, using authoritarian restraints? This question is still debated today in journalism classrooms, in courthouses, and around cocktail tables. That the answer seems elusive is not enough reason to stop the debate.

REGULATING RADIO

Regulating radio was not an idea that sprang spontaneously into the mind of some government bureaucrat. In fact, radio regulation seemed quite unnecessary for the first few years. The first law simply required that ships at sea have radio receiving and transmitting equipment on board—there were no requirements that the equipment even be turned on. That 1910 law seemed to be a good idea because with radios, disasters could be communicated to other ships, or to the shore so that help might be dispatched. Two years later, when the Titanic sank, many ships in the vicinity were completely unaware of the disaster because their radio operators were off duty, yet ships several hundred miles away heard the distress signals and headed toward the sinking ship only to arrive too late.

Sarnoff's spectacular reporting of the catastrophe and the failure of nearby ships to hear the call for help jolted Congress into enacting a second radio law (1912), which required that ships sailing under the U.S. flag have their radio equipment staffed and operating at all times. The law also set aside special channels for emergency and government services. Both laws failed to anticipate the vast array of radio services that would develop in the following decades: they omitted any discussion of land communications, amateur services, or broadcasting.

The trend established in those first two radio laws became the dominant mode for creating radio regulations and laws—wait until an apparent, often critical need arose, then seek legal means for dealing with it. Although the Radio Act of 1912 designated the Secretary of Commerce as the enforcer of the law, little was said about the secretary's authority to penalize those who violated the laws.

Congress's unwillingness to enact radio laws grew quite naturally out of its libertarian views of the media and the First Amendment prohibition of laws restricting free speech. Libertarians had kept government from regulating the press—newspapers, books, and magazines—with considerable success. Now there was radio, with its own special problems, not the least of which was the confusion produced by the unrestrained broadcasting of the 1920s. What should be done? Should government exercise its powers and revert to some of the authoritarian principles that had dominated England centuries before when licenses were issued to printers? In general, Congress viewed regulating radio as hazardous.

It was clear that radio regulation would have to steer a course between the essentially unlimited freedoms called for by the First Amendment and the uniquely limited qualities of radio and television channels. Unfortunately, how Congress and its agencies have traveled this perilous course has not always been consistent, nor has it honored every guarantee of the Constitution.

Congress first gave authority over radio licensing to the secretary of commerce, then to a group of five commissioners called the Federal Radio Commission (FRC), and finally to seven commissioners named the Federal Communications Commission (FCC). Whatever the agency or its name, each has been restricted by statute, judicial interpretation, and Constitutional guarantees.

The Radio Act of 1912 remained the cornerstone of radio regulation for a number of years; however, it was based on ships' needs for shore communication and not on the wider dimensions that radio took on after World War I. When nonmilitary radio use resumed after the war, broadcasting was one of the first civilian uses, a use that was dominated by the consortium of radio companies—Westinghouse, AT&T, RCA, and General Electric. These companies had the money and facilities to construct stations. Moreover, they were the nation's manufacturers of radio equipment.

But, soon other companies and organizations took an interest in stations and began building their own facilities. Secretary of Commerce

Herbert Hoover used the 1912 law to grant radio licenses and to specify channels, power, and time of operation. Although there were difficulties, matters worked all right until a court told Hoover he could not refuse a license to any applicant (1923).[1] Then Hoover's powers were further eroded when another court told him he could not designate time, power, or channel of operation.[2]

Frustrated, Secretary Hoover asked the attorney general for an opinion on the powers lodged in the Department of Commerce. The resulting opinion, issued in 1926, said that Congress, not an administrative official, had the authority to assign regulations, specify transmitter power, and the like. The secretary of commerce was left powerless.

THE EVOLUTION OF RADIO REGULATION

1910   First U.S. radio law requires the installation of radio equipment on ships bearing the U.S. flag.

1912   New law requires that ship radio equipment be turned on and staffed while at sea.

1923   Secretary Hoover receives word from the courts that he cannot deny a license to a station.

1926   In a case involving Zenith Radio Corporation, Hoover finds he cannot designate channel, power, or time of operation of stations.

1927   The Radio Act of 1927 became law.

1931   FRC is supported by the courts in its decision to revoke Dr. Brinkley's license.

1934   The Federal Communications Commission replaces the FRC.

1943   NBC has to sell one of its networks to Edward Noble—Noble names his network ABC.

CBS has to revise its contract with affiliates to give them more control over their programming.

1966   Citizens are given standing before the FCC when a station's license is under consideration.

With the repeal of all government restraints over broadcast channels, almost total chaos filled the airwaves. Although listeners may not have shown much concern over this dreary state of affairs, broadcasters and manufacturers, along with government officials, saw many problems. Some day, they said, the tolerant listener would lose interest in buying receivers capable only of picking up noise. Industrial concern over the state of radio had been evident in conferences called by Hoover each year from 1922 to 1926. In most years, the conference participants called for self-restraint, or lacking that, for government regulation aimed at bringing order to the airwaves.

The problem was simple: more people wanted to broadcast than there were channels to accommodate them. For signals to be received clearly, some who wished to broadcast had to be kept off the air so that those who remained could be heard clearly. Yet to restrain some people from broadcasting while others were free to do so is contrary to the First Amendment, which guarantees *all* the right to speak and write freely. Must one right give way to another? Years later, the Supreme Court was to comment:

> Freedom of utterance is abridged to many who wish to use the limited facilities of radio. Unlike other media of expression, radio inherently is not available to all. That is its unique characteristic; and that is why, unlike other modes of expression, it is subject to governmental regulation.[3]

Using the scarcity of radio channels as the basis for creating a new regulatory body, Congress enacted the Radio Act of 1927—a law that established a five-member commission—initially unpaid—to bring order to the radio waves. The new Federal Radio Commission (FRC) started business in 1927 with 732 stations on the air. To reduce the clutter, the FRC revoked the right of the least powerful—that is the least rich—stations to broadcast. The least rich stations usually belonged to educational institutions and other nonprofit entities. Consequently, within three years forty-four of the roughly ninety educational stations were off the air—and in time, were joined by others.

The remaining stations were the rich and powerful ones owned by companies like Westinghouse, RCA-NBC, and General Electric. Educational radio—at least radio stations owned by educational institutions—virtually disappeared. Indeed, the FRC pressured educational stations to give up in favor of commercial stations. Incidentally, the FRC itself was pressured by powerful industrial groups. (Later, the Federal Communications Commission devised new ways to accommodate more stations and the number began to rise again after 1934.)

Besides taking stations off the air for technical violations or economic inadequacies, the FRC occasionally revoked a license because a station had failed to provide programs in "the public interest, convenience or necessity," a phrase neatly included in the Radio Act to cover matters not anticipated by Congress.

One such unanticipated matter was broadcaster, Dr. J.R. Brinkley, who had a radio station and a hospital in Milford, Kansas, where he sold cures for all kinds of ailments. Using the radio as a soap box, Brinkley could be heard to recommend:

> Here's one from Tillie. She says she had an operation, had some trouble 10 years ago. I think the operation was unnecessary, and it isn't very good sense to have an ovary removed with the expec-

tation of motherhood resulting therefrom. My advice to you is to use Women's Tonic Number 50, 67, and 61. This combination will do for you what you desire if any combination will, after three months use.[4]

Brinkley carefully failed to describe the contents of his medication. He also concealed the fact that his "medical degree" was a mail order diploma for which he had paid $100. Neither the American Medical Association nor the local medical associations approved of Brinkley's cures or procedures; and they demanded that the FRC take some action. At issue was not a station competing with other stations, but a station engaging in broadcasting that was not serving the public good. The FRC was asked to act on an issue that few had anticipated, and act the FRC did, ordering the station off the air.

Brinkley promptly appealed to the court, but received a ruling that supported the right of the FRC to revoke licenses of stations that did not program in the "public interest." Agreeing with the FRC, the court found that Brinkley was using the station solely for his own good. Although Brinkley lost his license, he continued his medical practice.

The quack medicine of Brinkley was but one of many cases confronting the FRC that were unrelated to technical matters. More and more, the agency found itself regulating programs.

The FRC went out of business when Congress formed the Federal Communications Commission in 1934—an agency that had permanent status from the day it was created. The FCC has a seven-member commission and can employ a staff to assist it.

The Federal Communications Commission was formed at the insistence of President Franklin D. Roosevelt, who wanted to deal with the monopolistic tendencies he saw in the broadcast industry. Networks were becoming bigger and more powerful, newspaper corporations were gaining control of many broadcast stations, and some extremely powerful radio stations were reaching a disproportionately large audience. The small family-owned station was being squeezed out on every side.

THE COMMISSION

Much of this chapter will sound like a treatment of legal cases, rules, and laws that appeared out of a machine without human aid. Nothing could be further from the truth. While it is necessary to examine some of the rules and laws, the FCC really is composed of individuals with special interests. Indeed, the FCC's history is very much the result of the commissioners who have served on it. Some have had vigorous interests in increasing the government's role in the regulatory process; others have tried to keep the government out. FCC regulatory patterns follow the political climate as much as any other government agency— a natural result of the appointment process.

During the Jimmy Carter and Ronald Reagan administrations, regulation was out and a laissez faire attitude was in. Consequently, people like FCC Chairman Charles D. Ferris were appointed to the commission (1977). More interested in bringing some order to the commission's complicated processes than in adding layers of regulation to broadcasters and cable operators, Ferris became a deregulator during a time when all of government was withdrawing restrictions on industry.

Nicholas Johnson, who came to Washington during President Lyndon Johnson's administration, was very different in his approach to regulation. Johnson, a bright young lawyer from Iowa, reached the FCC after working for the Maritime Commission, and as a law clerk for a Supreme Court justice. Never very popular with the broadcasting industry, Johnson frequently criticized what he saw as ineffective regulation. Once, when ABC and International Telephone and Telegraph (ITT) were contemplating a merger, Johnson's research found evidence that ITT was trying to mislead the FCC and influence stories in *The New York Times.* Nevertheless, the commission approved the merger, leading Johnson to observe that the FCC was "making a mockery of the public responsibility of a regulatory commission that was perhaps unparalleled in the history of the American administrative process."[5]

To be unloved by his colleagues on the FCC and by the industry it regulated may not have been a pleasant experience, but Johnson was a kind of folk hero to citizen groups, and his frequent dissents became the basis of many judicial opinions regarding FCC actions.

Some FCC commissioners have used public speeches to bring the industry into line, as Newton Minnow did in 1961 when he declared that the typical television schedule was a "vast wasteland." Others, like Richard Wiley, used group meetings in which major broadcasters proposed their own means of reform—the family viewing period—a time when television violence and sex would be minimized.

Early in the history of the FCC, James Lawrence Fly came to the agency as its chairman. A New Deal Democrat appointed by President Roosevelt, Fly had a vigorous antitrust philosophy. His enthusiasm found immediate focus in an ongoing investigation of radio networks and an investigation of cross-ownership between newspapers and radio stations. Roosevelt encouraged Fly in his new endeavors.

Fly pursued the network investigation, concluding that NBC ought to sell one of its networks and that CBS should revise its network-affiliate contract. CBS's contract gave it almost total control over the commercial programming carried on affiliate stations—an unwarranted transfer of control from the station to another party. But, the FCC couldn't regulate the networks directly, so Fly proposed a regulation that said "No license shall be issued to a standard broadcast station affiliated with a network organization which maintains more than one network." In other words, Fly was regulating the stations, not the networks, but the effect on the networks was obvious.

These new regulations were announced just before the National As-

FIGURE 12–1
James L. Fly, a controversial FCC chairman in the 1940s.

sociation of Broadcasters (NAB) annual convention in 1941, and immediately the broadcast industry was thrown into an uproar. Fly had been scheduled to give an address at the convention, but as he stood to speak, the membership walked out of the convention hall. Fly responded by returning to Washington that evening, despite a commitment to speak the next day. He remarked of the NAB, "It's like a dead mackerel in the moonlight, it both shines and stinks."

Some business publications headlined stories about Fly and his work with titles such as: "Fly in the Broadcasters Pie." But strong language and, later, hostilities from Congress notwithstanding, Fly's regulations withstood a Supreme Court test.[6] NBC sold its Blue network to Edward J. Noble, chairman of the board of Life Savers Corporation, who renamed it American Broadcasting Company (ABC), and CBS revised its network-affiliate contract.

Freida B. Hennock, an FCC commissioner during the late 1940s and early 1950s, did much to make educational channels available to nonprofit entities such as school districts, nonprofit corporations, communities, and universities. Her diligent work during the three-and-a-half years of television hearings (1948–1952) provided a rallying point for educators everywhere.

Licensing Broadcasters

Both the FRC and the FCC were, and the FCC remains, empowered to issue licenses for the operation of radio and television stations. In fact, its powers are not unlike the licensing powers of the English censors who licensed printers. However, the FCC has to balance the interests of broadcasters with the interests of listeners. English censors were not terribly concerned with the interests of readers. Secretary of Commerce Herbert Hoover put the role of broadcasters and the public in perspective by observing:

> The main consideration in the radio field is, and always will be, the great body of the listening public, millions in number, country-wide in distribution. There is no proper line of conflict between the broadcaster and the listener . . . Their interests are mutual, for without the one the other could not exist.[7]

It was this need to protect the public that led to regulation in "public interest, convenience, or necessity" as the frequently appearing phrase from both the Radio Act of 1927 and the Communications Act of 1934 says. The Communications Act specifically directed the FCC to ". . . regulate interstate and foreign commerce in communication by wire and radio so as to make available, so far as possible, to all the *people* of the United States a rapid, efficient, nation-wide, and world-wide wire and radio communications service" (emphasis added). Radio includes, as far as the law is concerned, television or any other form of communication through the air.

When the FCC started business, it could have been directed to sell channels to the highest bidders or to distribute radio channels by lottery, thereafter limiting itself to insuring that the channel owners did not drift out of their assigned regions. But instead, the law retained federal ownership of the radio waves. The FCC loaned the use of radio channels to broadcasters on the basis of the legal, technical, financial, and *programming* merits of each applicant. The government was in the business of regulating programming or content, a very sticky area in view of the First Amendment and the generally libertarian views that have dominated United States legal thought for more than 100 years.

Although the courts have generally upheld the right of the FCC to award and revoke licenses on the basis of the public interest and the licensee's qualifications, the course the FCC has followed has sometimes run afoul of public sentiment, broadcaster attitudes, and judicial views. When the FCC decided a broadcaster could not engage in editorializing,[8] broadcasters expressed such strongly negative sentiments that the FCC eventually revoked the decision.[9]

The FCC licenses radio and television stations, cable television, and common carrier communications sent by wire and through the air, such as telephones and ship to shore communications, but it only licenses these media when they are international or interstate. State commissions and boards license intrastate communications.

There are some communication means over which the FCC has little or no control—networks, closed circuit systems such as those found in department stores or apartment complexes, and program events like baseball games and dramas.

Moreover, the FCC has no control over the production, distribution, or rating of movies; the publication or sale of newspapers, books, or magazines; or the recording or distribution of records and tapes. And, the commission does not administer copyright laws.

The FCC does regulate about 10,000 broadcast stations (television and radio) of which some 1,300 are noncommercial educational stations operated by schools, municipalities, and nonprofit corporations. Noncommercial educational stations are frequently referred to as public stations. The FCC also regulates interstate telephone lines, satellites, microwave equipment, aircraft and ship communications, and other special services.

A broadcast license from the FCC is usually for three years, although the FCC may shorten the length of a license for stations that it believes have not operated as they should. To get a license, a station must file an application showing how it will operate the station, or how it has operated this station, and how it plans to operate the station in the future.

The application requires that the station conduct a study to ascertain the problems, needs, and interests of people in its coverage area. Then the applicant must show how its programming has and will serve those ascertained needs. Using this information, the FCC tries to determine if the station has been serving the "public interest, convenience and necessity." When such a determination is made, the license is renewed. Of course, the application also must show that the operator is financially, technically, and legally qualified to operate a station.

The legal qualifications are that the applicant is a United States citizen, or that most of the major stockholders are U.S. citizens and have not committed any major crimes. The technical qualifications require that the station has equipment that meets FCC standards and engineering personnel with the proper FCC licenses. The financial qualifications require that the applicant has enough money to operate the station for a reasonable length of time.

In recent years, the FCC has taken greater interest in involving the public in the licensing process. To inform the public of their application, stations must broadcast announcements about the expiration of their licenses on the first and sixteenth days of each month for the last six months of their license term. These announcements must tell the public about the expiration of the license, the deadline date for comments to the FCC, the availability of public files at the station that people may examine, and the location of additional information regarding license renewal.

The public file that stations must keep available to citizens includes applications filed with the FCC, data on station ownership, employment practices, an FCC manual entitled "The Public and Broadcasting—a Procedure Manual" (if the station is commercial), letters from the audience, and a list of the ten problems needing service in that community and how the station's programming meets those needs.

The Citizen's Broadcasting Rights

In Chapter 11, an examination of the relative investment of citizens and broadcasters in equipment showed that citizens have a bigger financial stake in broadcasting than broadcasters do. Yet over the years, the FCC consistently has limited itself to resolving disputes among broadcasters, and has promulgated regulations dealing with the industry directly. Little or no attention has been given to citizens—apparently because the FCC did not see the audience as a "party at interest," that is, someone who has a sufficient financial interest in the practice of broadcasting to merit attention.

Two cases during the 1960s changed the legal climate in which citizens were to be viewed. The first involved a television station in Jackson, Mississippi, which, although about half of its audience was Black, avoided carrying network programming dealing with Black issues; employed no Black person other than janitors; and, had on-air personnel who frequently took positions negative to Black people. When Black politicians tried to buy time on WLBT-TV, they were refused or threatened with harm.

Because of this poor performance, the United Church of Christ, the Rev. L. T. Smith, and Aaron Henry, along with the NAACP, filed petitions with the FCC to deny a renewal of the station's license. In preparing their case, the petitioners collected vast amounts of evidence showing the biased nature of the station's performance, which included transcripts of station programs.

The FCC refused to grant the petitioners standing in a hearing involving the station because citizens do not have a "substantial interest." The FCC did give some attention to the complaints about programming, however, and gave the station a one-year temporary license to clean up their schedule. The citizens, by this time, believed that the FCC was not seriously considering their claims, and so appealed to the Court of Appeals in Washington, D.C., asking that it grant the petitioners standing before the FCC, and that it revoke WLBT's license. After some legal maneuvers, the court directed the FCC to seek another applicant for the channel and to deny WLBT's request for a license renewal. This case established the right of audiences to participate in hearings involving a station. In granting citizens standing, the court noted that citizens have a much bigger investment in broadcasting than broadcasters do.

Another case, this one in Boston, involved the *Herald Traveler,* a newspaper that owned WHDH, AM and FM radio stations, and a television station in the same market. Station owners had been involved in some illegal contacts with members of the FCC during the 1950s. Because each of these properties was among the most powerful media forces in Boston, the situation may have been in violation of antitrust law.

Competing applicants came forward for the channel and the hearings dragged on throughout the 1960s. In 1969, in a four-to-three vote, the FCC granted WHDH-TV's (Channel 2) license to another applicant—one that promised better local programming. The four commissioners who voted to award the channel to a competing applicant had differing reasons for their votes—some wanted to foster diversity among media voices, others were offended by the illegal FCC contacts during the 1950s. But whatever their convictions, the FCC tempered their decision by taking great pains to tell the broadcasting industry that the WHDH decision did not foreshadow a new direction in commission policy.

Indeed, neither of these cases really changed the FCC's basic desire to protect the industry it is called upon to regulate. Although citizens may now have standing in hearings, they still must work against the economic power of the industry and the FCC's friendly attitude toward broadcasters.

And how did the FCC's decision to award channel 2 in Boston to another applicant turn out? When WHDH gave up broadcasting, WCVB took over. In February, 1982, one reviewer observed that WCVB might be the best commercial television station in the United States. Others, such as television producer Norman Lear and ABC News president Roone Arledge, have agreed with that assessment.

WCVB is one of the few twenty-four-hour stations in the nation; but more importantly, it devotes some 30 percent of its schedule to local programming—programming that also has been of a consistently high quality. The average amount of locally produced programming by television stations is only 10 percent. When it got the Boston license, WCVB promised a new era in local programming—and it delivered. Perhaps television stations should be awarded to new groups more often.[10]

The right of citizens to participate in hearings involving their community stations focuses mostly upon economic control of broadcasting. However, there is another matter that must not be overlooked—the First Amendment issue. When government assumed the right to regulate radio in the 1920s, it did so in order to protect the public's right to hear a diversity of voices. The legitimacy of the fairness doctrine and most other program regulations rests, at least, in theory on this right. (See discussion of Fairness Doctrine later in this chapter.)

Ascertainment

Because the FCC does not prescribe how stations are to be programmed, it relies on an assessment of community need through the "ascertainment" procedure it requires. The first guidelines for the ascertainment procedure appeared in 1960 and were approved by the courts in the Suburban (1962)[11] case, and were later revised through a *Primer* published in 1976, and amended that same year. The new *Primer* requires that stations continuously monitor their community to identify its important problems. For stations in communities with populations below 10,000 and for educational stations, the ascertainment procedure does not need to be continuous.

The ascertainment must solicit information from two sources: community leaders and the general public. The FCC has gone to some lengths to spell out some nineteen categories of community leaders who must be interviewed, including people in agriculture, business, charities, consumer services, culture, education, and labor. Station personnel must make contact with the community leaders to hear their views.

The second part of ascertainment—a general public survey—is similar to the usual survey in which a random sampling of the public is contacted and asked their views. The results of the surveys become part of the license application and part of a public file kept at the station.

Types of Stations

The FCC licenses both radio and television stations. Within both of these groups there are subcategories. Radio has both AM (amplitude modulation) and FM (frequency modulation). Each operates on different channels and the terms refer to how sounds are placed on the radio wave. Besides AM and FM, the FCC has distinguished between local and regional radio stations. Local stations have less power and may be restricted in operating power or in the directions that their signals may go.

For example, some stations are not allowed to operate at night—because AM radio waves go further at night and if all stations stayed on the air, too much confusion would result.

All FM stations may operate twenty four hours a day, but some stations cannot use as much power or have their antennas built quite as tall; therefore, there are also local and regional FM stations.

Television stations can be either UHF (ultra high frequency)or VHF (very high frequency). VHF and UHF stations differ only in the band of frequencies they occupy—UHF uses higher frequencies than VHF. The consequences of the different frequencies are great. First, the higher UHF waves do not have as wide a range as the VHF stations. The higher waves begin to take on some of the characteristics of light, and the energy from the waves is more easily absorbed by the earth's atmosphere. Second, UHF waves are more susceptible to signal obstacles like buildings. Consequently, VHF signals reach out farther into the community than UHF signals do. In communities with both UHF and VHF stations, the VHF stations have a considerable advantage.

The FCC's rules have created a hierarchy of stations based on how far their signals reach. Stations with greater reach can charge more for advertising because they can reach more people.

Programming

Although the First Amendment to the Constitution says "Congress shall make no law . . . abridging the freedom of speech, or of the press," and the Communications Act of 1934 prohibits the FCC from censoring broadcasters (326), the commission still finds itself in the business of regulating some aspects of programming. In fact, the Communications Act spells out areas where the FCC *must* regulate. Because of the tenuous nature of program regulation, a huge body of cases has developed over the years. The cases are tangled and require close scrutiny to be understood, but the general pattern can be described well enough to serve the purposes of this book.

Forbidding censorship actually means that the government may not impose any prior restraint on the broadcasting of any program. But, some limited exceptions may exist to this general rule. Licensees may select advertisers, programs, religious offerings, news, sports, public affairs, and network shows they wish to broadcast. Advertisers, listeners, and the FCC may not substitute their judgment for that of the licensee. When asked to give their judgment on the amount of control the FCC should have over licensee programming practices, the courts have usually voted on the side of restraint—keeping the government out.

All of the foregoing sounds very libertarian, but these wide ranging freedoms have limitations. The FCC's program regulations, or other federal laws reach into the following broadcast areas:

1. Duplication of AM/FM programming

2. Station identification

3. Discussions of controversial issues

4. Personal attacks

5. Broadcasts by political candidates

6. Defamation

7. Obscenity, indecency, and profanity

8. Contests and lotteries

9. Sponsor identification

10. Loud commercials

11. Cigarette advertising

12. False or misleading advertising

13. Subliminal advertising

Duplication

Frequently, a single owner holds both AM and FM stations in the same community. When the community has more than 25,000 people, the FCC prohibits the FM station from duplicating the AM station's programming for more than 25 percent of its air time weekly. The FCC says that duplication has occurred if the identical program is carried on both stations within twenty-four hours.

Station Identification

Stations must identify themselves once each hour—as nearly as possible on the hour—by giving their call letters and the community in which they are licensed. On television the announcement may be either spoken or pictured. The FCC is firm in telling stations that they may not misrepresent their community of license. For example, a station licensed to operate in the smaller town of East St. Louis, Illinois, may not say simply W___, St. Louis, because that would give listeners the impression that the station is licensed in the larger city across the river in Missouri.

Obscenity, Indecency and Profanity

The prohibition against obscenity, indecency, and profanity appears in the law as part of the United States Criminal Code, not the Communications Act, so the law is of consequence, to more than just broadcasting.[12] The code imposes a fine or imprisonment upon convicted violators. Over the years, a number of cases have arisen dealing with obscenity and related matters.

For example, the FCC refused to renew the radio license of WDKD because an announcer was accused of frequently repeating off-color jokes—a practice the commission did not consider to be in the public interest.[13] On another occasion, the commission chastised two non-commercial stations (KPFA and WUHY) for airing materials that appeared to be indecent or inconsistent with the stations' program representations.

One of the most interesting obscenity cases involved a national phenomenon of the late 1960s and early 1970s in which radio stations broadcast programs commonly called "topless radio." Call-in programs in which the radio host encouraged callers to discuss their sexual hangups, these "topless radio" programs became both popular and explicit. Although the format was widespread, WGLD-FM in Oak Park, Illinois, was the station called to task over its "Femme Forum," and ultimately fined $2,000 in 1973. Although the Sonderling Broadcasting Corporation, the station's owner, was encouraged to appeal to the courts, it chose instead to pay the fine, avoiding a judicial test to determine if the FCC had overstepped its authority.[14]

A recent case involving obscenity, indecency, and profanity occurred when WBAI in New York City broadcast a George Carlin record containing seven four-letter words of a questionable nature. The program dealt with society's attitude toward language. The case went all the way to the U.S. Court of Appeals, which decided against the $2,000 fine the FCC had imposed on the station for broadcasting material that was "patently offensive to . . . community standards . . ."—not on the basis of the commission's power to regulate indecent speech, but because "the order sweepingly forbids any broadcast of the seven words irrespective to context."[15] By 1980 the FCC was trying to sidestep making rulings on indecent material (*NAACP* v. *FCC*, 1979).

The FCC's occasional decisions regarding obscene, indecent, or profane programming amount to only token broadcasting censorship in practical terms. The commission hardly has the staff to police every broadcast or react to every complaint. Its actions reflect more of a guideline for those broadcasters who wish to be guided. Nevertheless, the commission sometimes has issued pronouncements on record lyrics or other elements of a station's programming in documents such as *Licensee Responsibilities to Review Records Before Their Broadcast* (1971), which dealt with drug-oriented record lyrics. This notice was amended slightly only a month later, but its intent was to put the burden of responsibility on the licensee rather than on the commission.

One important extra-legal regulatory development in broadcasting was the NAB's family viewing period between 7:00 and 9:00 each evening. The notion of a family viewing period arose out of conversations between the chairman of the FCC, the networks, and the NAB. Not a federal regulation, Congressional statute, or court opinion, the family viewing period nevertheless became an effective tool in the hands of television network censors, or continuity acceptance staff, as they are called, who tried to remove violence and sex from the early evening hours. Program packagers accused the networks of conspiring to censor program producers and went to court in the *Writers Guild* v. *FCC* (1976) case. The networks, naturally, claimed otherwise. To date, the family viewing period has prevailed.

Contests and Lotteries

Certain types of lotteries and contests on TV or radio are illegal. While that seems clear enough, closer examination raises some questions of interpretation. For example, what exactly is a lottery or a contest? That question was left partly unresolved until the FCC tried to declare two national programs illegal in 1954 and the networks appealed to the courts.[16] That decision defined lotteries and contests as having three elements: a prize of value for the winner, a winner chosen in whole or in part by chance, and a participant who furnishes something of value. The shows in question did not require participants to pay anything to play—one of the three necessary parts of a lottery.

Although the lottery provision was transferred to the United States Criminal Code (18 USC 1304), it was originally part of the Communications Act. To restrict the broadcast of lotteries, the FCC has denied licenses, failed to renew license applications, and imposed fines. The commission also has used the technique of the "raised eyebrow"— letters or telephone calls to stations to inquire about their practices.

So long as the contest or lottery does not involve all three of the elements listed above, stations are free to advertise them or sponsor them on their own. After listening briefly to most radio and television stations, it becomes readily apparent that many stations hold contests and announce others. Incidentally, state lotteries and certain other lotteries are exempt from the prohibition against broadcasting lottery information.

Some television and radio programs depend on contests for success. Such programs include "The Newlywed Game," "Name that Tune," "The $64,000 Question," and others. During the 1950s, some game show producers tried to control who won and who lost by priming some contestants and not others. In January, 1959, the lid blew off this practice through revelations made by contestants like Charles Van Doren and Herbert Stempel. The results of their revelations led to new regulations and congressional hearings. Also, the networks made their program censorship departments stronger and took much of the control over programs away from the advertising agencies.

Advertising

From time to time, the FCC has considered the possibility of regulating the amount of advertising permitted during each broadcast hour, but each time they've considered it, broadcasters have put up so much resistance that the FCC has backed down. Instead, broadcasters have used the NAB Code and individual station and network codes of programming practices to impose their own voluntary limits on advertising time.

The FCC does regulate some aspects of advertising. Sponsored announcements or programs must include identification of the sponsor at the time of broadcast. This provision would prohibit for example, a new department store from purchasing a sponsored message like, "Remember July 27," unless the name of the sponsor is also included.

The FCC has issued a policy statement warning licensees that airing loud commercials can get them into trouble. Loud commercials are those played at louder volume than the programs surrounding them.

Although the FTC exercises primary responsibility in this area, both the FCC and the FTC have been interested in false or misleading advertising. The FCC can fail to renew an offending license for repeated violations.

The Food and Drug Administration (FDA) regulates matters related to food and drug advertising; it sometimes cooperates with the FCC or FTC.

An amendment to the Communications Act of 1934 prohibits radio or television advertising for cigarettes and small cigars. Interestingly, no law exists to control the advertising of alcoholic beverages.

Subliminal advertising is advertising that passes before the viewer so fast that the message cannot be perceived consciously. The technique is to flash one or two frames of movie film on the screen, naming the sponsor's product or showing a picture of it. Although the effectiveness of such advertising has long been debated, the FCC prohibits it on the grounds that people cannot consciously reject the advertising.

FAIRNESS DOCTRINE

The Fairness Doctrine, one of the best known FCC rules, has been the topic of much debate in and out of legal circles. Along with the equal time rule of the Communications Act of 1934, no other FCC policy has received so much attention. Because of considerable public interest, the FCC produced a book entitled *The Law of Political Broadcasting and Cablecasting: A Political Primer* to guide the public, broadcasters, and cablecasters. Containing some 100 pages, the book covers all the details of the fairness and political doctrines. Some still argue that the Fairness Doctrine violates the First Amendment and Section 326 of the Communications Act of 1934 which prohibits censorship.

The Fairness Doctrine deals with the discussion of issues—on news shows, in advertising, during public affairs programs, or any time *controversial issues of public importance* are discussed on the electronic media. The FCC has held that reasonable time must be devoted to the treatment of controversial public issues and that contrary opinions must be given a fair hearing. Questions immediately arise: What is a controversial issue of public importance? How much time is reasonable? What constitutes opposing viewpoints?

The Fairness Doctrine was created by the FCC with a little help from the FRC. The doctrine started with the idea of balance in a 1929 FRC[17] decision and was more fully developed in the *United Broadcasters* case (1945) when the FCC pointed out the need for making "sufficient time available, on a nondiscriminatory basis" for the discussion of controversial issues. The fairness doctrine was finally established in 1949,[18] when the FCC really made known its desire to impose balance in programming issues. Then, in 1959, Congress amended Section 315 of the Communications Act of 1934 to include a statement that "reasonable opportunity for the discussion of conflicting viewpoints on issues of public importance" be afforded. In a 1969 case, *Red Lion* v. *FCC,* the U.S. Supreme Court acknowledged that Congress had amended the Communications Act of 1934 to give congressional force to the commission's Fairness Doctrine.

During the years since that decision, the FCC has periodically reviewed the fairness requirements and issued updates or clarifications on it. Undoubtedly, the doctrine will be reviewed again and again, not only by the FCC but by Congress and the courts as well.

FAIRNESS DOCTRINE

1929   FRC requires some balance on the part of licensees when carrying controversial issues.

1938   FCC reinforces the balance requirement in a case involving the Young People's Association for the Propagation of the Gospel.

1941   In the Mayflower case of the FCC declares its opposition to editorializing.

1949   FCC reverses its position on editorialzing and issues an elaborate booklet detailing its requirements for balance.

1959   Section 315 of the Communications Act is amended to include the Fairness Doctrine.

1969   The U.S. Supreme Court gives judicial support to the Fairness Doctrine in the Red Lion decision.

1973   U.S. Supreme Court holds that Fairness Doctrine applies to *issues* not to *persons* when defining who has access.

Let's look at how the doctrine works. In determining if an issue is of sufficient public importance to warrant coverage, station personnel or concerned members of the audience should look at the following: (1) the quantity of media coverage given the matter; (2) the interest shown by governmental officials; and (3) the potential impact on the community at large. Final determination on when or how to apply the doctrine usually rests with station managers.

If a viewer wishes to complain to the FCC, the complaint must contain these items: 1) the name of station, 2) the statement of the issue, 3) the date and time of the alleged violation, 4) the basis upon which the claim of one-sidedness rests, and 5) the plans of the station to treat other sides of the issue.

Personal Attack

An aspect of that Fairness Doctrine for which the FCC has written specific regulations is personal attack. The personal attack rules cover those situations when a program dealing with "controversial issues of public importance" carries "an attack . . . made upon the honesty, character, integrity or personal qualities of an identified person or group." Under these conditions, the licensee is expected to send a letter to the attacked person within one week detailing the circumstances of the attack and offering the person time to reply.

Some programs containing personal attacks are excluded from the rules. These include attacks that occur on broadcasts made by legally qualified political candidates or their supporters or attacks that occur during bona fide newscasts, news interviews, and on the spot coverage of news events.

The FCC's first regulations regarding personal attacks came in 1962 and were clarified in 1967. The rules came under judicial review when right-wing minister Billy James Hargis attacked liberal journalist Fred Cook on radio station WGCB, owned by John M. Norris in Red Lion, Pennsylvania. Cook wanted air time to reply to the attack and asked the FCC to help him get it—for free. As a result, a series of strongly worded letters flowed back and forth between the FCC and Norris. Finally, the letters changed to arguments before the courts, and ultimately reached the U.S. Supreme Court, where in 1967 the decision went in favor of the FCC's rules on personal attack. At the Supreme Court, a case involving the Radio and Television News Directors Association (RTNDA) was combined with the Norris case.

The situation was particularly interesting because lower courts had decided in favor of Norris and RTNDA. In his opinion for both cases, Justice Byron White, speaking for the majority of the Supreme Court, found that both the Fairness Doctrine and the personal attack provisions were constitutional. White used as a basis the fact that not everyone could hold a broadcast license:

> A license permits broadcasting, but the licensee has no constitutional right to be the one who holds the license or to monopolize a radio frequency to the exclusion of his fellow citizens. There is nothing in the First Amendment which prevents the government from requiring a licensee to share his frequency with others and to conduct himself as a proxy or fiduciary with obligations to pre-

sent those views and voices which are representative of his community and which would otherwise, by necessity, be barred from
the airwaves.[19]

Yet the Supreme Court did not stand by its Red Lion decision without reexamining the issue. In a 1973 case,[20] the Supreme Court concluded that editing was what news editors did and while they may err,
it was not for the courts or the FCC to intervene in the process—a
principle long established in newspaper law. But a year later,[21] the Supreme Court stood by the requirement that broadcasters provide programming that deals with public issues and that the programming be
balanced.[22]

Licensee Responsibility

To secure a license from the FCC, an applicant must show that the
programming proposed for the station will satisfy the public interest,
need, and convenience. To meet this vague standard, the FCC requires
information about the quantity of news, sports, entertainment, agriculture, public affairs, religious, educational, and instructional programming to be carried. Although the FCC has never done much to regulate the quality of programming over the years, those program
regulations that do exist arise from the view that a licensee has a responsibility to citizens—regardless of their age, color, or other demographics. Perhaps the nearest that the FCC came to program regulation
was when it created in the 1940s the *Blue Book*—a publication that
detailed the FCC's program standards. Because broadcasters' complaints were so violent, the document was never enforced.

Citizen Broadcast Activist Groups

Because the FCC is concerned about First Amendment conflicts, and
more recently, with deregulation, citizens have little hope of reform-
ing broadcast programming through appeals to the FCC. However, other avenues have proven fruitful—direct challenges to licenses, negoti-
ations with station managements, and establishing citizens groups
concerned with broadcast practices. Two of the most successful citizens reform groups have been Action for Children's Television (ACT)
and the National Citizens Committee for Broadcasting (NCCB). ACT, a
Boston-based group, has focused its attention on advertising that occurs during children's programming as well as on children's programming itself. ACT has appealed to the FTC, the FCC, broadcasters, and
advertisers. After their appeal, the FTC went so far as to consider regulations directed at children's advertising.

NCCB, a group affiliated with Ralph Nader's organization, has challenged various broadcast actions before the FCC, has published newsletters and other materials describing abuses in broadcasting, and has
served as a rallying point for several causes.

Besides national groups, many communities have started their own groups, focusing on broadcast and cable causes of interest to their particular community. Because local groups may hold considerable economic leverage over broadcasters in their area, they have had considerable influence. For example, one group in Missouri was able to persuade a television broadcaster to carry "Sesame Street."

Equal Time

Actually the notion of equal time as a synonym for the Fairness Doctrine is incorrect. Equal time is actually a legal principle embodied in Section 315 of the Communications Act of 1934, which requires stations to give *equal opportunities* to all candidates for an office when the station provides time for one candidate for that office. The doctrine does not require stations to sell time to every candidate or to give time to any candidate, but if a station chooses to sell or give time to one candidate, it must make the same opportunities available to all other legally qualified candidates for the same office.

Equal opportunity has a legal definition—candidates invoking Section 315 have a right to buy an equal quantity of time; buy a time that is likely to reach about the same number of people reached by the first candidate's time (equal quality); and buy a time for the same price per unit as that paid for by the first candidate.

Of course, this means that if the second candidate doesn't have enough money to buy as much time as the first candidate, tough luck. The law will not help; but the law also will not let a station put one candidate in a poorly watched or listened to time if the other candidate received a popular time slot.

These equal time provisions have some exceptions. If a candidate appears on a bona fide newscast, a news interview, a documentary, or an on the spot coverage of a news events, then section 315 does not provide equal opportunities for other candidates. This exclusion has made possible debates between the major party candidates for the presidency without affording time for minor party candidates for the same office. It works like this: An organization like the League of Women Voters plans a legitimate news event—a debate between two or three candidates for the presidency. Then the national television and radio networks can cover the "news event" without having to fear that the law will force all the other candidates on them.

The networks could not offer the debates free, according to Section 315, because then the event would be considered to be staged by them (an outside organizer like the League of Women Voters must handle the event). The distinction is thin, but the law seems able to detect the difference.

In addition, many conditions about notification, payment, maximum charges, and other topics have been written into the equal time regulations or interpreted in later legal cases. The *Political Primer* mentioned earlier explains all the conditions; it may be acquired from the FCC in Washington, D.C.

Employment Opportunities

A provision of the FCC's regulations requires that broadcasters must provide equal employment opportunities to all persons regardless of race, color, religion, national origin, or sex. The regulation also demands that stations have an aggressive equal employment opportunity policy, seeking and training people for positions within the station.

Although federal regulation, spurred by laws passed by Congress, requires that stations use persons of all races, religions, and sexes on and off the air, a major study released by the U.S. Commission on Civil Rights in August, 1977, found that minorities and women, particularly minority women, continue to be underrepresented on the staffs of local stations, and are almost totally excluded from decision making and important professional positions at those stations. Furthermore, it found that minorities and women—again, particularly minority women—are underrepresented on network dramatic television programs and on network news. When they do appear, they are frequently seen in token or stereotyped roles.[23]

As of 1977, then, the rules, or at least their enforcement, had not had the intended effect. While a comparable major study of more recent origin does not exist, it is doubtful that much has changed.

Licenses and the Public

Earlier sections noted that the FCC awards, renews, revokes, and penalizes licensees on the basis of findings it collects from many sources. Its primary source of information, however, is the application submitted by each licensee or applicant.

But, the application is not the only form of information. Interested members of the public may submit information, as members of the United Church of Christ (1966)[24] did. After the FCC held that residents living near WLBT in Mississippi did not have legal standing to appear at the hearings solely on the basis of their membership in the station's viewing audience, the court disagreed and told the FCC that viewers had a strong legal interest and standing. Although citizens have always submitted comments to the FCC, they had little influence on its decisions before the United Church of Christ case. Although both the broadcast industry and the FCC objected, the case decided, that citizens injured by the programming practices of a television station could challenge the license of the offending owner and could win a short-term license or a refusal to renew the license.

CABLE TELEVISION REGULATIONS

When cable television was young, no one wanted the task of regulating it—the FCC took no interest, and state public service commissions evaded the issue. Although municipal governments may have been uninterested, too, they were thrust into the regulatory business because they had to grant authority to use public easements. Some of that early cable regulation amounted to little more than an exchange of letters authorizing the stringing of cables. In other cases, bribery took place and city officials lost their positions; but whatever it was, municipal cable regulation was uneven.[25]

Then, as cable began to enter markets with television stations, the FCC began showing an interest in the new medium. For the FCC could see the potential competition between cable and network television.

CABLE TELEVISION REGULATIONS CHRONOLOGY

1959 FCC concludes it has no right to regulate cable under the Communications Act of 1934.

1962 In the Carter Mountain Transmission Company case, the FCC exerts some control over cable by regulating microwave companies that supply programming.

1965 FCC promulgates first regulations regarding cable saying that cable systems using microwave to receive signals must not duplicate programming available on local stations (except for carrying the local station's signal).

1966 FCC modifies rules to apply to cable systems with or without microwaves and prohibits importing signals into the top 100 television markets.

1968 In the Southwestern Cable case the U.S. Supreme Court declares the FCC regulations are valid.

1969 FCC creates rule requiring cable systems to provide local programming if they have more than 3,500 subscribers.

1972 In the Midwest Video case the Supreme Court upholds the 1969 rule.

The same year the FCC promulgates its most comprehensive set of cable regulations which are restrictive to cable development.

1974 FCC revokes the local originating rule (1969).

1976 New copyright law requires royalty payments from cable television.

1977 Appeals court overturns FCC regulation requiring cable systems to carry non-broadcast services.

1978 Access channels for government and others overturned in Midwest Video case.

1982 FCC has overturned most of its own regulations and provides little more than housekeeping tasks for cable television.

During the 1950s, the FCC considered regulating cable as a common carrier—like telephone and microwave—under provisions of the Communications Act of 1934, but it rejected the idea in 1956. By 1959, the FCC had concluded that it had no authority under the Communications Act of 1934 to regulate cable television, and asked Congress to amend the act to provide that authority. Although some bills were considered in committee, Congress never passed any new provisions.

In the absence of congressional action, the FCC reconsidered the Communications Act, concluded that it had misjudged its authority, and decided to exert limited regulatory authority over the cable industry. It did so by using its power to regulate microwave companies, in the Carter Mountain Transmission Company case (1962). The FCC ruled that Carter Mountain could not carry programs to a cable system from a distant station when the same network programs were available from a local television station. This amounted to indirect regulation of what the cable system could carry.

A series of reports in 1965, followed by another in 1966, and a final comprehensive report issued by the FCC, in 1972, were used to exercise more extensive control over cable television. In these pronouncements, the FCC regulated cable as if it were an ancillary service to broadcast television—a junior partner. According to the new regulations, the FCC regulated only those cable systems that carried signals from broadcast television stations. However, that included all cable systems because broadcasting was the source of most early cable programming.

Although the line of authority that the FCC derived from the Communications Act is questionable at best, the U.S. Supreme Court decided to support the FCC in a 1968 decision involving Southwestern Cable. The FCC's regulatory posture restricted the free development of cable television—in fact, its regulations virtually stopped cable development in the largest television markets, except in places like San Diego where some cable television already existed.

With the 1972 regulations, the FCC reached its most restrictive level. Those regulations survived nearly unchanged until 1976 when, through a series of commission actions and judicial decisions, they began to fall.

In 1976, the FCC withdrew the requirement that local authorities must approve cable rates and conduct hearings to award or change franchises. The next year, the commission eliminated standards requiring cities to impose a timetable spelling out how fast a new cable system was to wire different parts of the community. Also in 1977, the rule (called an antisyphoning provision) that prohibited a cable system from carrying films and sports that were also carried on broadcast television was dropped. This decision was a result of a case involving HBO (*HBO* v. *FCC,* 1977), an entertainment and movie network.

Then in 1978, in the Midwest Video case, the FCC gave up its requirement that cable systems provide channels for use by government, education, citizens, and others.

COPYRIGHT AND TECHNOLOGY

With the rapid growth of videocassettes (as well as home audio recording devices), the question had to be asked: Does the home recording buff have the right to record a movie or other program without paying the producer a copyright royalty? An answer came in 1981 in a case between Sony Corporation and Universal City Studios and Walt Disney Productions, when the U.S. Court of Appeals in San Francisco decided that home users did not have the right to reproduce or record films or other materials off the air. The decision was a sweeping victory for copyright owners and a disaster for producers of home recording devices.

But the copyright owners' victory may have been hollow. Purchasing reproduction equipment, using the equipment to illegally record material, and then hiding the resulting tapes has become easy—so easy that prosecution of in-home video cassette users is virtually impossible. To offset this, one possibility being considered is to add a royalty fee to the price of blank tape.

The court's decision affects not only films and video tapes, but computer programs, records, and printed material. That creators of audio, video, and print materials wanted such a decision is an understatement. According to estimates, some $100 million of illegally duplicated movies, and some $600 million in illegal sound recordings were produced in 1981.

But, the San Francisco decision is hardly the final word—opponents have promised both legislative and judicial fights. In fact, bills already are being considered by Congress.

The copyright issue pits two conflicting interests: the right of creators to be rewarded for their efforts, and the right of the public to use today's recording technology in their own homes.

Source: Philip Shenon, "Copyright v. 'Reprography' Revolution," *The New York Times*, October 25, 1981, IV, p. 7.

By 1982, virtually all the cable regulations had been dropped. The FCC's Cable Bureau was engaged in little more than housekeeping chores—keeping annual reports of cable activities, enforcing affirmative action regulations, and the like. So, although the FCC had started without specific authority from Congress to construct an elaborate matrix of regulations to protect broadcasters from cable operators, the deregulatory fever of the late 1970s and early 1980s led to the almost complete revocation of those regulations.

Whether cable television should be regulated at a national level is a matter open to debate. Some think that state and local regulation is best. Some eleven states regulate cable at the state level. Public utility commissions have authority over cable television in Alaska, Connecticut, Delaware, Hawaii, Nevada, New Jersey, Rhode Island, and Vermont. Separate cable commissions exist in Massachusetts, Minnesota,

---

AT&T

A longstanding legal dispute between the Department of Justice and AT&T came to an end in early 1982 when AT&T agreed to a consent order with the Department of Justice in which the huge company agreed to sell off its local service companies such as New York Telephone, Southern Bell, and others. AT&T will retain its long-distance telephone lines, microwave equipment, satellite interests, and manufacturing plants. In addition, AT&T will receive the right to enter some of the new technology areas such as cable and computers.

The effect of the decision is to relieve AT&T of its interests in an old communication enterprise that has reached near total saturation—local telephone service—while permitting the company to enter some undeveloped areas that may grow greatly in the future.

AT&T was given eighteen months to sell off its local service companies—giving it until late 1983.

---

and New York. Most other states have nuisance regulations or general business laws that regulate cable to some limited extent. In those states that have exercised specific authority, state regulation falls into three categories:

1. State has all the power and municipalities act only as interested parties in any regulatory action (Connecticut is an example).

2. State serves as mediator between cable system and municipalities (New York and Massachusetts are examples).

3. State serves in an advisory role, aiding municipalities on regulatory matters (New York and Massachusetts are examples).

Finally, many local governments still regulate cable television. In states where regulation is on a state level, the local authorities have somewhat more restricted powers. The character of local regulation ranges from cities with whole regulatory agencies such as New York City, to municipalities that exercise little or no control. There are advantages and weaknesses to local regulation. Some advantages are that:

Local regulatory officials are closer to the people they serve;

Changes in regulation can be effected quickly;

Officials understand the needs of their communities.

Some of the disadvantages of local regulation are that:

Local officials often are inadequately trained for the task;

Insufficient local funds are available to do the job well;

Local officials may be more susceptible to political influence or bribery;

National regulatory standards are unlikely to occur using this form of regulation.

The regulatory environment of cable television is still very much in flux in the early 1980s as the industry's and the citizens' demands vary. Undoubtedly, much will change in the next decade.

CAMERAS, REPORTERS, AND COURTS

Although reporters long have been permitted into the courtroom to view proceedings, usually they have had to leave their cameras, cables, flash equipment, and tape recorders at the door. But even though the American Bar Association's Canon 35 closed courtrooms to media equipment, not every state adopted the canon. Friction between lawyers and reporters grew in the 1960s when the news media were permitted to cover the financial dealings trial of Billie Sol Estes—they made fools of themselves because of the chaos they created in the courtroom. (See also print regulation, chapter 6.)

Television cameras at the pretrial hearing and still cameras throughout the trial created such clutter and confusion that the U.S. Supreme Court, when reviewing the case, saw several hazards caused by cameras in the courtroom: interfering with the jury, interfering with witnesses, creating problems for the trial judge, and disturbing the defendant.[26] Moreover, Justice Tom Clark, author of the majority opinion, did not believe that reporters with their equipment had an automatic right to access.

Revising the *Canons of Judicial Ethics* in 1972, the American Bar Association created section 3A (7) as part of the new Code of Judicial Conduct that prohibited "broadcasting, televising, recording, or taking photographs in the courtroom." The code did allow the use of television equipment for presenting evidence or sending television signals to other rooms where reporters might follow trial events.

But, the issue of television in courtrooms was not closed by the 1972 code. In 1981, the U.S. Supreme Court approved a Florida plan permitting television camera people to cover criminal trials. Under the experimental Florida plan, one unobtrusive television camera and one still camera were to be allowed in the courtroom. Footage from either camera could be used by the news media.

In a trial involving two Miami Beach policemen who had robbed a store, the Florida rule was put to the test. Only about three minutes of prosecution footage was shown on television, however, Chief Justice Warren Burger, speaking for the Court, held that the defendants' rights had not been abridged and that the Florida regulation should be permitted to stand. Although Burger disliked television, he and a majority of the court felt that federal intervention into state matters would not serve the cause of justice; federal courts can still ban cameras.

The decision opened the way for other states to initiate or continue tests of cameras in the courtrooms. Presumably, any regulations should include safeguards as the Florida law does—children, sex victims, government informants, and timid witnesses all have protection. At present, some twenty-seven states permit cameras in courtrooms under varying conditions.[27]

BROADCAST'S SELF-REGULATION

The government, no matter how hard it tries, cannot regulate every aspect of broadcasting. Some areas, such as news, programming, and advertising, appear to be out of reach of government intervention, while others may be of no interest to the government. Yet, the public has a legitimate interest in the programming and advertising practices of broadcast and cable outlets. Moreover, most broadcasters have a deep interest in the concerns of their viewers and listeners—failure to accommodate audience interests can quickly lead to a declining audience. That audiences might abandon traditional favorites has become increasingly clear in the early 1980s.

Although television network revenues increased during 1980, 1981, and 1982 (estimated), the rate of increase lagged behind inflation, so that in real terms the networks were experiencing hard times. Total revenue in 1980 for the big three networks was $5.1 billion, which rose by 8 percent in 1981 to $5.5 billion, and is expected to rise about 10 percent in 1982 to $6 billion. Although these increases appear significant, the three national television networks built their industry on 11 to 15% yearly revenue increases.[28]

This decline is a result of audiences abandoning commercial television networks. The reduced growth has resulted from two areas: increasing numbers of women in the work force who are not home to watch daytime television, and teenagers who were tuning out commercial television entirely. Also, the increasing use of pay cable, cable in general, video tape, and other media, diffused audiences for commercial television networks. The bottom line is that as the number of choices available to audiences continues to grow, audiences are becoming more selective about the programs they watch.

Broadcasters have long known that they must balance their desire to sell ever more advertising time against the public's willingness to sit through commercials in order to see the entertainment programming. Moreover, networks have always known that they must provide programming that large numbers of people are willing to watch, despite the interruptions created by advertising.

Balancing commercial interests against the public's willingness to sit through commercials has been a large part of the impetus for broadcasters to impose restrictions on their business and programming practices. The other variable that has stimulated self-regulation has been the ever present threat of increasing outside—government—regulation. Self-regulation, which broadcasters find preferable, comes in several forms: industry-wide restrictions through the National Association of Broadcasters (NAB), individual station or company codes of good practice, network controls, and advertiser restrictions.

The NAB and individual network or station codes of programming and advertising practices create the framework within which continuity acceptance (network censors) and station programmers make decisions on what programs audiences will see and hear. The codes change yearly to reflect changing trends in broadcaster and public attitudes. Moreover, interpretations of codes change periodically. In the 1930s, writer Harry Herrmann was resoundly censored for writing a fist fight into an episode of the radio show "Mr. District Attorney"—in the 1980s, fights in all forms are routine. In the 1950s, dramatic presentations on abortion never would have appeared on the screen; in the 1970s, "Maude" and other programs dealt with all aspects of abortion.

Although trends may suggest a liberalizing tendency, appearances can be misleading. The 1920s had quack physicians, the 1930s had misleading advertising, the 1960s had "topless radio," and the 1980s have pop psychologists. Other eras have had their rigged quiz shows, smut announcers, rigged baseball games, lotteries, and misleading editorials. In every season, one can point to offensive practices. Yet the public still enjoys broadcasting.

The most widely used broadcast programming code is the NAB Code, which has separate codes for radio and television. The NAB explains the origin and role of its codes:

> As a means of self-regulation and in order to maintain the highest possible programming and advertising standards, the Radio Code (1937) and the Television Code (1952) were established by broadcasters for broadcasters. These codes of ethics are administered by the Code Authority, an arm of the National Association of Broadcasters. Over the years, the Codes have moved from simple, prescriptive documents to complex combinations of prescriptive and proscriptive language which comprise rules, amendments, guidelines, and interpretations—all reflecting the growth and complexity of the broadcasting industry and that industry's response to the public interest.[29]

The NAB has offices in Hollywood, New York, and Washington, D.C. The Hollywood office reviews packaged programs and commercials. The New York office reviews commercial practices, because of its proximity to the major advertising agencies that serve large national and regional accounts. The Washington, D.C. office is the center of review and enforcement, dealing with the government when the industry requires representation.

Some 2,700 radio stations and 470 commercial television stations subscribe to the NAB Codes. All three commercial television networks and four of the five major radio networks also are members. Subscribers agree to maintain code standards; there are no sanctions that the NAB can impose on stations, other than revoking their NAB membership. A vice-president and general manager, along with a staff, supervise compliance with code provisions and respond to complaints or questions from the public or broadcasters. To secure information on subscriber activities, the code authority maintains a monitoring program, including film and video tape of programs and advertising. The monitoring includes over 30,000 hours of radio and 70,000 hours of television yearly. A review panel at the NAB examines complaints, and withdraws the station's code seal and the right to be identified as a code subscriber when willful and continued violations are found.

Because the code seal appears infrequently on most stations (usually at the beginning and end of the broadcast day) the public probably does not know if a station is a code member. Consequently, the value of stimulating public reaction to a station that is not a code member is questionable.

Perhaps the networks, because of their greater visibility with the government, the industry, and the public, may value code membership more than stations do. If this is true, stations experience a strong code influence quite apart from their own membership.

Besides its code, the NAB publishes loose leaf binders of interpretations of the code and legal actions. Taken together, these two works give stations a view of the practices and trends in programming, and other aspects of stations as seen from Washington, D.C.

Whatever the views of the government or the NAB are, in the end, the public has much more control over broadcasters. As the entertainment choices available to the public increase with videocassette, video disc, more cable channels, and outside entertainment like movies, theater, sports, and leisure activities, public attention to commercial broadcasting is bound to wane. When that happens, the television networks will be forced to rethink their product, just as auto makers have been forced to redesign their product to comply with changing public tastes and foreign imports. In the end, the buying public holds all the cards, and when the public plays its cards, industry must listen or fail.

COPYRIGHT ROYALTY TRIBUNAL

When Congress revised the Copyright Act to take into account the new communications industries, it created the Copyright Royalty Tribunal (1976) to collect copyright fees from the nation's cable television systems (now numbering about 4,300) and to forward that revenue to producers of copyrighted programs. Most of the copyright money goes to the Motion Picture Association of America, the Christian Broadcasting Network, sports groups, the Public Broadcasting Service, music composers, and local television stations.

Not everyone has been happy with the tribunal's methods. Recently, former director, Clarence L. James, Jr., resigned because he felt that the agency was underworked, unnecessary, and slow. Although the agency has a budget of $450,000 (modest by Washington standards), it has been an important element in the developing cable industry. Many copyright owners, however, feel that the tribunal is ineffective. Robert W. Kastenmeier of Wisconsin, who heads the House Judiciary subcommittee on courts, civil rights, and the administration of justice, now has the responsibility of reviewing the tribunal.[30]

Regulatory Directions of the Future

TRENDS
IN THE '80s

At best, the future of communications regulation remains clouded. The deregulatory climate that has pervaded Washington during the last 1970s and early 1980s has opened the way for a vast array of new communications services—services that may have been offered to the public without adequately researching whether there is any need or desire for them. At present, cable television is largely unregulated, broadcast television has fewer restrictions (and more channels), and everyone is jumping to enter the cable television field. In the computer area, there are few, if any, regulations other than some basic business laws.

Both the business community developing the new technologies and the citizens using them are being exposed to many unknowns, which may later prove to have negative consequences. Here are some of the questions:

■ Today, cable television is virtually unregulated at the national level. Should regulation develop, and if so, should it develop at the national, state, or local level? Earlier industries that were initially unregulated, such as radio and railroads, eventually came under national regulation—demanded in large measure by the industries themselves.

■ Before the creation of the FRC, radio stations competed with each other, creating confusion on the radio waves. Cable television is now following a course not unlike that of early radio—many new services are being developed willy nilly, everyone seems willing to invest money in cable programming networks and local companies. Will the new services create problems that injure subscriber and investor? If so, regulation will follow.

■ Copyright issues will continue to dominate cable, satellite, computer, and other services for some time. Where does the right of the citizen to "fair use" of a work stop, and where does the producer's right to be reimbursed begin? The Sony case may ultimately be reviewed by the Supreme Court before a determination is reached.

■ Privacy is an issue that will continue to become more important. As the marriage between computers, cable, and other technologies becomes more extensive, cable operators will be able to search their lines to determine who is watching what. With small talk-back computers in our homes, central computers will know everything we order, request, or do with that little machine. What stops government or other interested parties from examining that information to learn about our lives? Such possibilities raise "big brother is listening" questions. Eventually, legislation or case law will have to resolve these conflicting rights.

■ As cable television adds more X-rated programming on pay channels, children increasingly will have access to programming considered inappropriate by many parents. While some may argue that parents must assume control over their own sets, that argument does not ring true. Even theaters refuse to admit children to certain films, and require parental accompaniment for others; in the home parents are not always available to control the television set. If the cable companies do not provide adequate protection, some regulation is bound to be devised.

■ A bill that would assess annual fees of broadcasters ($150 to $7,500), change procedures for renewing licenses, and permit some institutional advertising over public stations, among other things, is being considered in the Senate. The House of Representatives has considered bills that would deregulate much of broadcasting and raise fines for violations of the Communications Act (from $2,000 to $100,000). Changes, however, are still far from receiving Congressional approval. In fact, for much of the FCC's history, Congress has had before it bills that would change the FCC's powers.

■ The Department of Justice and AT&T entered a consent order in 1982 in which AT&T agreed to sell off its local telephone operating companies such as New York Telephone and Southern Bell. In return, the order would permit AT&T to enter into many new technology areas like computers.

■ Television and radio code authorities have been established by the NAB to police various aspects of broadcasting, including advertising time and content standards. One of the standards prohibited multiple product advertising in spots less than one minute long, but District Court Judge Harold Greene ruled that that provision violated antitrust laws. The case raises the question of whether a national association can prescribe standards for the broadcast industry—even standards established to stave off federal regulation.

■ Provisions permitting AM stations to broadcast stereophonic programs (as FM broadcasters long have done) have been under consideration by the FCC for five years. The problem has not been whether to approve AM stereo, but which system to use—five manufacturers have offered systems for FCC approval. The FCC has been sidestepping the issue by proposing to let market forces make the selection—a decision manufacturers and broadcasters are opposed to. By 1982, four of those systems were ready for use and the decision was still pending.

■ President Ronald Reagan signed into law (1982) a bill that made it a crime to disclose the identity of covert agents. Disclosure is illegal even if the identities had been made known previously. Both government officials and members of the press may be subjected to a fine and a jail term for violation. Objections to the law center on the belief that it violates the First Amendment to the Constitution. Proponents believe the law will protect United States intelligence activities.

■ The deregulation of cable television has been an important issue since the FCC promulgated its first major restrictions in the late 1960s and early 1970s. Deregulatory fever reached a high pitch during the early 1980s. One FCC regulation requires cable systems to carry certain television stations depending on the proximity of the station to the cable system. Ted Turner (owner of superstation WTBS, which is carried on many cable systems) asked the FCC to repeal this restriction. No decision has been made yet.

■ Rules preventing cable systems from carrying programs from distant television stations and syndicated programs duplicated on local stations were lifted by the FCC in 1980. To right the inequity they saw, broadcasters asked the FCC to approve a "retransmission consent" that would give them some control over programs carried by cable. The FCC refused. Malrite Broadcasting and other broadcasters have asked the courts to overturn the FCC.

ADDITIONAL READINGS

Emery, Walter B. *Broadcasting and Government.* East Lansing: Michigan State University Press, 1971.

Gillmor, Donald M., and Barron, Jerome A. *Mass Communication Law: Cases and Comment.* St. Paul: West Publishing Co., 1969.

Kahn, Frank J., ed. *Documents of American Broadcasting.* 3rd rev. ed. Englewood Cliffs, N.J.: Prentice Hall, 1978.

Krasnow, Erwin G., and Longley, Lawrence D. *Politics of Broadcast Regulation.* New York: St. Martin's Press, 1973.

Nelson, Harold L., and Teeter, Dwight L., Jr. *Law of Mass Communications: Freedom and Control of Print and Broadcast Media.* 3rd ed. Mineola, New York: The Foundation Press, Inc., 1978.

Schmidt, Brenno C., Jr. *Freedom of the Press vs. Public Access.* New York: Praeger Publishers, 1976.

FOOTNOTES

1. Hoover v. Intercity Radio Co., Inc., 286 F.1003 (D.C. Cir., 1923).

2. United States v. Zenith Radio Corporation et al., 12 F2d 614 (N.D. Ill., 1926).

3. National Broadcasting Co. v. U.S. 319 U.S. 190, 63 S.Ct. 997,1014 (1943).

4. KFKB Broadcasting Association, Inc. v. Federal Radio Commission, 47 F.2d 670 (D.C. Cir., 1931).

5. Leonard Zeidenberg, "Seven Years and Five Months: A Look Back at the Tenure of Nick Johnson," *Broadcasting,* December 10, 1973, p. 26.

6. National Broadcasting Co., Inc., et al. v. United States et al. 319 US 190 (1943).

7. Walter B. Emery, *Broadcasting and Government* (East Lansing: Michigan State University Press, 1971), p. 33.

8. In the Matter of The Mayflower Broadcasting Corporation and The Yankee Network Inc., 8 FCC 333 (1941).

9. In The Matter of Editorializing by Broadcast Licensees, 13 FCC 246 (1949).

10. Tony Schwartz, "Some Say This is America's Best TV Station," *The New York Times,* February 15, 1981, p. 2–1.

11. Suburban Broadcasters v. FCC, 302 F. 2d 191 (D.C. Cir., 1962).

12. United States Criminal Code 18 U.S.C. 1464. (1948).

13. In re Palmetto Broadcasting Co., 33 FCC 250 (1962).

14. Sonderling Broadcasting Corp., 27 R.R. 285 (1973).

15. Pacifica Foundation v. FCC, 556 F. 2d 9 (D.C. Cir., 1977).

16. FCC v. American Broadcasting Company et al. 347 US 284 (1954).

17. Great Lakes Broadcasting, 3 FRC Ann. Rpt. 32 (1929).

18. In the Matter of Editorializing by Broadcast Licensees, 13 FCC 1246 (1949).

19. Red Lion Broadcasting Co., v. FCC, 395 US 367 (1969).

20. CBS v. Democratic National Committee, 412 US 94 (1973).

21. Miami Herald Co. v. Tornillo, 94 SCT 2831 (1974).

22. The Fairness Doctrine (and subsequently the personal attack rules) grew out of the following decisions and cases: Great Lakes Broadcasting Co., 3 FRC Ann. Rep. 32, 33 (1929), 59 App. D.C. 197, cert. dismissed, 281 U.S. 706 (1930); Trinity Methodist Church, South v. FRC, 61 App. D.C. 311 (1932), cert. denied, 288 U.S. 599 (1933); Young People's Association for the Propagation of the Gospel, 6 F.C.C. 178 (1938); Mayflower Broadcasting Corp., 8 F.C.C. 515 (1941); In the Matter of Editorializing by Broadcast Licensees 13 F.C.C. 1246 (1949); 47 U.S.C. Sec. 315 (amended 1959); CBS v. Democratic National Committee, 412 U.S. 94 (1973); Miami Herald Co., v. Tornillo, 94 S.Ct. 2831 (1974); and other cases including those cited earlier. As can be seen, the Fairness Doctrine has had a long administrative and judicial history.

23. "Window Dressing on the Set: Woman and Minorities in Television," (A Report of the United States Commission on Civil Rights, Washington, D.C., 1977), p. 3.

24. Office of Communication of the United Church of Christ v. Federal Communications Commission, 359 F.2d 994 (D.C. Cir., 1966).

25. Subcommittee on Communications, U.S. House of Representatives, "Cable Television: Promise versus Regulatory Performance" (Washington, D.C.: Government Printing Office, 1976), p. 9.

26. Estes v. Texas, 381 U.S. 532 (1965).

27. Bennett H. Beach and Evan Thomas, "Blind Justice Gets a Seeing Eye," *Time,* February 9, 1981, p. 51.

28. "TV in Transition," *The New York Times,* August 16, 1981, 3–1. See 3, p. 1.

29. "Functions and Procedures of the Code Offices (Memorandum)" (Washington, D.C.: National Association of Broadcasting, 1978), p. 1.

30. Philip Shenon, "Cable TV's Benefactor Comes Under Fire," *The New York Times,* August 9, 1981, pp. 3–6.

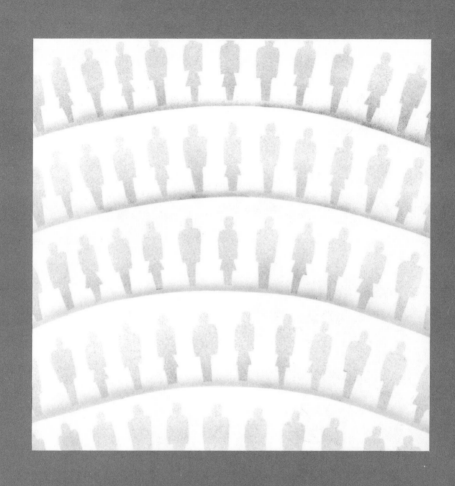

PART IV

Audience/Futures

13

MEDIA EFFECTS

Anything that interferes with effective communication can be called noise. Most noise is caused not by the information source or the channel of communication, but by the audience. People are enormously proficient at ignoring, misinterpreting, and misremembering communications that for one reason or another do not appeal to them. Audiences use at least three psychological strategies to distort or eliminate undesirable information.

First, people are selectively attentive to communications they like. If they are not interested in buying a washing machine, they will not read washing machine ads. If they are interested, they will probably read many ads. Second, people practice selective perception—when exposed to a communication, they tend to interpret it in a way that coincides with their preconceptions. They see what they want to see. Finally, people practice selective retention. Even if they understand a communication, they tend to remember only what they want to remember. If they are against an issue, they will readily see all its disadvantages and none of its advantages.

Most communications are controlled by the source. When a teacher lectures to a class, it is the teacher, not the class, who decides what will be said. Selective attention, selection perception, and selective retention, then, are the principle methods the audience can use to control the message. If a student is bored or offended by what the teacher is saying, he or she may tune the teacher out and think about something else. Or, the student may unconsciously misinterpret the lecture, perhaps hearing that there will be one term paper when the teacher actually said there would be two; or, the student may simply forget the least appealing parts of the message.

Selective attention, perception, and retention are universal. They add a tremendous amount of "noise" or interference to nearly every communication. The source can control what is said, but the source cannot control what the audience hears, or thinks it hears.

Audience noise is most potent when the message is controversial; simple and unthreatening messages tend to be received similarly to how they are sent. As a result, it is almost impossible for any communication to convert an audience from one point of view to another. It is much easier to create a new viewpoint where none existed before, and it is easier still to communicate information that tends to support the audience's established viewpoint. All communicators—advertisers, politicians, reporters, even teachers—must work within these constraints.

THE ELEMENTS OF MEDIA RESEARCH

Despite the fact that the mass media play such an important role in the culture today, their impact is largely undocumented. Research on communication is a relatively new development compared to research in fields like chemistry or history. Wilbur Schramm[1] has estimated that more than half of all research on human communication has been undertaken since 1952.

Communication research can best be explained using Harold Lasswell's[2] description of the act of communication: "Who says what in which channel to whom with what effect?" By breaking this description down into its basic parts, it is possible to see the various sub-areas of communication research.

"Who" is the speaker or the reporter. There has been a considerable amount of research on the who's in communication: demographic studies of reporters and broadcasters, studies of how journalists become socialized into accepting the values of the news organizations they work for, studies of the political biases of reporters

"What" is the content of the messages. There has been a significant amount of information collected about the content of messages, too. Researchers have studied the content of election campaign stories, for example, to determine if one candidate was given more space or more favorable treatment than another. Studies of television advertising by people like William Melody[3] at Pennsylvania State University have focused on the content of both programming and advertising aimed at children.

The next area is the source or channel. When the economic structure of the newspaper industry is outlined, the ownership patterns of television stations are tabulated, or the financing of motion pictures is discussed, communication "channels" are being examined.

To whom do these channels communicate? Communications researchers rarely think of the audience as a "mass." They perceive audiences as being composed of individuals. Not all of these individuals respond in the same way to the same communication. Philip Davidson[4] said that the audience is not a passive recipient, not a lump of clay to

---

WHERE WE GET NEWS

The newspaper is the oldest and traditionally the most important source of current information. Even today, the average daily paper contains far more news than is available on television or elsewhere. But most of that news is not read, and the newspaper appears to be growing less influential every year. This is a source of profound dissatisfaction for many publishers and reporters, and a possible threat to American society.

Newspaper reading is a firmly entrenched habit. A 1972 survey found that more people read a paper every day than drink coffee, drive a car, or go to work. But what do they read? Most people turn to the least taxing, most entertaining sections first. Nearly twice as many read the comics as the editorials.

Most newspaper readers are not very interested in news. When a strike deprives them of their daily paper, what do they miss most? They miss the ads, the news of supermarket sales, apartments for rent, and new movies in town. And they miss the service announcements—weddings, deaths, and weather.

Television is, in fact, the preferred source of news for most Americans today. In 1959, Roper Research Associates asked a sample of Americans where they got their news. Newspapers were mentioned by 57 percent of the respondents; television by 51 percent; radio by 34 percent; and magazines by 8 percent. In 1972, Roper repeated the study. This time 64 percent mentioned television; newspapers were down to 50 percent; radio to 21 percent; and magazines to 6 percent.

The decline in newspaper credibility at the expense of television is even more dramatic:

	1959	1972
Television	29%	48%
Newspapers	32	21
Magazines	10	10
Radio	12	8

Students of journalism believe that the newspaper is the best available daily source of news. But many newspaper readers prefer to get their news from television, which actually covers very little news. That's a problem for a democracy based on the public's right to know.

Source: Roper Research Associates 1959, 1972

---

be molded by the master propagandist. Rather, the audience is made up of individuals who demand something from the communications to which they are exposed, and select those communications that are likely to be useful to them. While this description defies what we know about how some people watch television from early evening to sign-off regardless of what it offers, Davidson's concept of the audience is probably fairly close to reality.

Finally, what are the effects of the media? The audience is people. Not only do people use the media for different purposes at different times, they also have different personalities, which greatly affect how they respond to persuasive arguments. Passive people are more easily persuaded than independent thinkers, especially by a high status source. People with high IQs are more influenced by logical arguments and less influenced by emotional ones than people with low IQs. Some psychologists have even suggested that being easily persuaded is in itself a personality trait. Age, sex, social class, occupation, and many other demographic variables also influence people's responses to persuasion. Even the groups to which one belongs, or wishes to belong, affect one's persuasibility. The mass media audience is made up of real people who lead real lives, not robots who do whatever the media tells them.

Most Americans are happy with their mass media. They have complaints, of course—too much depressing news, too many commercials—but on the whole, they are quite satisfied. When survey researchers go into the field and ask people what they would like from the media that they are not getting, the response is almost invariably—nothing. Undoubtedly, there are public needs not adequately served by the mass media. The public, however, is largely unaware of these needs or how the mass media can serve them.

WHY PEOPLE USE THE MEDIA

What public needs do the mass media serve? Play is obviously one of the most important ones. From the first time a parent reads a story to a child, that child is taught that media use is fun. And for most people, the media *are* fun—and not just the explicit entertainment part of the media either. Many people watch commercials and read newspapers for pleasure, but then advertisers and reporters work hard to make their products pleasurable. Providing pleasure or fun is a public service and the media's greatest contribution to its audience, claims scholar William Stephenson. Other observers disagree, complaining that the media make people spectators rather than participants in leisure time activities, turning them apathetic about the serious problems of the day.

Media as a time filler is related to media as play, but is more passive. When New York's newspapers went on strike in 1945, Bernard Berelson[5] asked people what they missed. Most readers talked about the importance of newspapers as part of their daily routines, not as an information source. They resented the disruption in their lives caused by the strike, and many resorted to scanning cereal boxes or subway ads just to have something to read. People listen to the radio while driving and the television while doing chores mainly to fill time.

Media use also serves a number of social needs for the audience. People are social beings. They like to talk—to their friends, coworkers, and families. To feed those conversations, they need information. The media are reliable, current sources of information and they provide information on a tremendous range of topics. Many magazines are purchased strictly for the social status they confer when mentioned in conversation or seen on the coffee table. Television gives families a chance to spend some time together peacefully. People go to movies to get away from their kids, or to get away from their parents, or to get close to someone else.

Psychological needs are met by the media, too. For example, studies have shown that when family fights break out, children turn to television for solace; when their egos are bruised by failure, they read more comic books. Many women read serials for the vicarious enjoyment of open emotion, while many men read racy magazines for the vicarious enjoyment of open sex. The catharsis of Shakespearean tragedy, the violence of a shoot-em-up western, and the self-confidence of a news commentator all serve psychological needs in the audience.

psychol. needs met

Information seeking is another reason why people turn to the media. Not just news, but also quiz programs and advertisements capture attention in part because they offer information. One early study even found that one reason people went to movies was to learn how higher status Americans dress, behave, and make love. Sometimes people seek information for its own sake; our society considers it a civic virtue to be well informed. Sometimes people just want information that is reassuring. Someone who just bought a Ford, for example, will read Ford ads to collect information showing why they made a wise decision. And, sometimes, information is just useful. Why else does one read the weather forecast?

Info.

Finally, people use the media for guidance in problem solving. When a decision needs to be made, they seek out not only relevant information, but also relevant influence, looking for someone to tell them what to decide. Self-help books, editorials, advice columns, and how-to articles obviously meet this need. Other media content also helps them solve problems, but is less obvious. For example, a classic study of radio soap operas found that many listeners used the soaps for guidance in their everyday activities.

guidance in prob. solv.

Audiences use the mass media to meet social, psychological, and functional needs. How people respond to media persuasion depends largely on what they are looking for, be it fun, status, information, reassurance, guidance, or just a time killer. There's nothing covert or manipulative on the part of media; it's apparent that people get from the media what they seek.

More recent research has shown that Lazarsfeld's two-step flow theory is oversimplified. A more accurate concept might be the multi-step flow. For every field of interest—politics, fashion, economics, movies—there are apparently certain people who make great use of the media for information and guidance. These opinion leaders then communicate with each other, their views crystallizing in the process. Later, they transmit their views to lesser opinion leaders, who also use the mass media but not as frequently. These recipients compare what they get from the media with what they get from their opinion leaders, then pass the combination on. Eventually, the message reaches the largest

OPINION LEADERS

When people sit down to chat, the things they talk about and the attitudes they express are often derived from the mass media. In 1940, Paul Lazarsfeld and his colleagues studied the voting behavior of a group of citizens in Erie County, Ohio. However, they discovered that very few people decided how to vote on the basis of information they had learned directly from the mass media. Instead, most voters made up their minds as a result of interpersonal communications—conversations with a friend, a neighbor, a union leader, or a spouse.

Lazarsfeld found only a minority of Erie County's citizens made significant use of the media to obtain voting information. Members of this minority then transmitted the message of the media through interpersonal communication to their friends and neighbors. Lazarsfeld called these minority members "opinion leaders." He concluded that ideas often flow from media to opinion leaders and then from opinion leaders to less active members of the population. This process is known as the two-step flow theory of mass media influence.

Source: Paul Lazarsfeld, *Continuities in the Language of Social Research.* New York: Free Press, 1972, and *Personal Influence: The Part Played by People in the Flow of Mass Communications.* New York: Free Press, 1964.

segment of the population—those people who make little or no direct use of the media.

Opinion leaders are a minority in any population, but they establish the issues for the majority. The two main characteristics of opinion leaders are that they pay greater than average attention to the mass media, and that they are respected by their followers. Like any other kind of leader, an opinion leader must not get too far ahead of the group. If an opinion leader's distillation of media content conflicts too strongly with the group's customs and norms, the group is very likely to find itself another leader.

In the field of labor relations, the multi-step flow might run something like this: A group of union leaders, all inveterate newspaper readers, find that they are opposed to the president's plan for wage and price controls. They pass this information on to the shop stewards, who have followed the issue casually on television. The shop stewards then pass it on to the rank and file, who have only a hazy understanding of the problem. Then the rank and file pass the information on to their friends and families.

The information chain for birth control methods would be quite different. A male union leader is unlikely to read about the medical hazards of the pill and then pass the information on to his shop stewards. He is far more likely to hear about it from his wife, who heard about it from a woman friend or coworker, who read about it in the newspaper. The principle, however, is the same. The direct effect of the mass media on labor relations and contraception is comparatively minor. But the indirect impact is huge.

INFORMATION TRANSMISSION

By the time people enter kindergarten, they have already been exposed to hundreds or even thousands of hours of radio and television. They have attended dozens of movies and browsed through scores of children's books. They have cut pictures out of magazines, and scowled at the newspaper in unconscious imitation of their parents. All these experiences have taught them something about literacy, something about violence, and something about America. Already, they are in a very real sense children of the mass media.

Meanwhile, for most adults, the mass media constitute the only advanced education they receive after high school or college. It is obvious that the media offer every American a continuous course in modern world history, but it is not so obvious that the very basics of community living come to people through the media—births, weddings, deaths, weather reports, traffic accidents, crimes, sales, and elections.

It is hard to imagine an efficient system of democratic government without an equally efficient system of mass communication. Citizens would learn of new legislation only after it passed, and then only if they visited their representative in Washington, D.C. Incumbents would probably serve for life, because no challengers could make themselves known to the electorate. Political corruption would go largely unchecked. News of foreign affairs would remain the monopoly of the president and the State Department. And on the local level, mayors would be free to run their cities as personal fiefdoms. The point is clear: Political information is political power. Without the mass media to transmit such information, the American people would be powerless.

PERSUASION AND PROPAGANDA

People have thought about the effects of communication on attitudes and behavior at least since the time of Aristotle, and the special power of mass communication to change the way people think, feel, and behave has been a source of concern, especially to governments, since the invention of the printing press. The modern science of communication, however, was born out of psychology, sociology, and political science in the 1930s. There were two immediate reasons for its quick development at that point in history. First, advertisers wanted to know how to spend their money more effectively, and second, American intellectuals were worried about the propaganda efforts of Nazi Germany.

The research tradition that developed over the next thirty years was devoted to answering one basic question: What factors determine how much impact a particular piece of communication will have on the attitudes of its audience? What persuades, causes someone to do or believe something? Hundreds of books and thousands of journal articles have been written on various aspects of this question.

By way of example, here is a more or less random list of six findings from this type of research:

1. It is usually better to state conclusions explicitly than to let the audience draw its own conclusions.

2. Arguments presented at the beginning or end of a communication are remembered better than arguments presented in the middle.

3. Emotional appeals are often more effective than strictly rational ones.

4. When dealing with an audience that disagrees with your position, it helps to acknowledge some validity to the opposing view.

5. Attitude change may be greater some time after a communication than right after it.

6. High credibility sources, such as doctors, provoke more attitude change than low credibility sources such as patients, even if the reason for their credibility has nothing to do with the topic of the communication.

These findings, and hundreds more like them, were very helpful to advertisers, who used them to design more effective ads. They also were very helpful to organizers of the World War II effort, who used them to counter Nazi propaganda and later to produce Allied propaganda. They are still helpful today to marketing experts, political candidates, and anyone else interested in using communication to change people's attitudes.

But as the studies accumulated, attitude change turned out to be a more complicated phenomenon than the early findings had seemed to imply. Later researchers had to specify the conditions under which the various principles of attitude change did or did not hold true. As time went on, and more and more conflicting findings turned up, it became harder and harder to specify which principles were valid under which conditions.

Researchers began to suspect that there was something fundamentally wrong with the way they were studying the effects of communications. In fact, there were at least four things wrong with it.

First, the majority of the early studies were conducted in the laboratories of academic social scientists, using students as subjects. Whole theories of communication emerged from the unpaid efforts of undergraduates in introductory psychology courses. This was convenient for the researchers and made for neat, methodologically controlled studies, but it made for unreal results. The occasional field research that was done almost invariably showed much less attitude change than the lab studies had led everyone to expect. The complexities and counter pressures of reality just could not be duplicated in controlled laboratory experiments.

Second, most of the early communication studies dealt with topics like dental hygiene, currency devaluation, or the future of movie theaters, which, though of some intellectual importance, stimulated practically no audience involvement. The way attitudes are changed regarding topics like these has turned out to be almost irrelevant. Most propagandists were interested in more gut grabbing topics, such as racial prejudice, the welfare state, or the upcoming presidential election. Audiences already had strong emotional commitments on those issues, and a speech on race relations yielded a lot less attitude change than one on the future of movie theaters. Advertisers, on the other hand, were interested in topics of no intellectual interest to the audience, like the choice of a breakfast cereal. By 1965, Herbert E. Krugman was arguing that people are motivated to buy products through advertising without paying attention to the message and without changing their attitudes at all.

Third, most early attitude change research was based on oversimplified models of how attitudes are related to information and behavior. Many studies assumed that if the audience learned the message, its attitudes would necessarily be changed. Even more studies assumed that if attitudes as expressed on a questionnaire had changed, behavior would inevitably change, too. But, by the 1960s, these assumptions were falling apart. In 1964, Jack B. Haskins had surveyed twenty-eight different studies of information, attitudes, and behavior, and had concluded that there was no relationship between what a person paid attention to, understood, or recalled on the one hand, and what he did or how he felt on the other. In that same year, Leon Festinger reviewed the meager research literature on how attitudes affect behavior, and found no evidence of a consistent relationship there, either.

The fourth problem with the early research on attitude change was that it virtually ignored the audience. All the care and creativity went into figuring out the effects of different sources, channels, and styles of presentation. The audience was viewed as just being there—passive, receiving the message, and then changing or not changing, depending on the source's skill and know-how. But in fact, people are not just sponges who soak up media content. They use the media for their own purposes, and therefore they are active participants in the communication process. How the media affect them depends very largely on who they are and how they are using the media.

In a sense, everything that was wrong with traditional communication research resulted from underestimating the audience. It is known that people respond differently to an experiment in a psychology class than to an editorial on television. It is also known that their views on currency devaluation are more thoughtful than their views on breakfast cereals, and less emotional than their views on racial prejudice. It has also been found that people can learn things without believing them, believe things without doing them, and do things without learning or believing them. It has taken communication researchers thirty years to acknowledge these truths fully, because for thirty years they concentrated on the source and the message and virtually ignored the audience.

Today, with the audience in mind, researchers are working to uncover the effects of specific kinds of media content, such as violence or political advertising. But, because different people tend to use the media differently, it is difficult to come up with theories in these limited areas. Professor Raymond Bauer of the Harvard Business School, a public opinion research specialist, has said that given a reasonably large audience, communication varies in its impact. It affects some one way, some in the opposite way, and some not at all. Bernard Berelson, a communications research pioneer, years ago stated the same proposition—that some kinds of communications on some kinds of issues, brought to the attention of some kinds of people, under some kinds of conditions, have some kinds of effects.

Researchers know that if ten people watch the same motion picture on television at the same time, there will be considerable variation in their reports of the movie's content. This variance would increase if their questioning was delayed for a week or more. In looking at the same picture or reading the same story, people see and remember things differently. This is selective attention, selective perception, and selective retention at work.

Given the same communication or the same event, different people will emphasize different things. This can make it extremely difficult to resolve situations in which witnesses' accuracy is crucial. After one of the University of Wisconsin's first large-scale war protests in the late sixties, at which police used tear gas and clubs to disperse a large crowd, the university formed a research team to uncover what had sparked the violence. After a considerable amount of research, which included questioning hundreds of people involved in the melee, researchers were still unable to determine exactly what had triggered the turmoil. They discovered that the people present had seen many different versions of the events. Police and other officials tended to see unruly students; students tended to see aggressive police.

Reporters and commentators face the same problem. Everyone has attended an event that was subsequently reported in the press. It often seems remarkable how the journalist could have gotten the facts so fouled up. But, of course, he or she probably just perceived the event differently. Public officials, political candidates, and especially presidents frequently are furious at press reports of a speech they have given, believing that the news media have distorted it. Former President Nixon lashed out against the instant analyses of his nationwide televised speeches because he claimed that the commentators misrepresented what he had said. Presidents frequently prefer talking directly to the people via television to avoid having their speeches reported as they are perceived by the press. They would rather take their chances with how the American people perceive what they say.

Everyone has some control over the information they receive, and most people seek out information that interests them. At least this is what those who subscribe to the concept of selectivity suggest. Norman Felsenthal asserts that people try to avoid messages they consider boring or messages that conflict with their predispositions. Theoretically then, when people turn to the editorial page of the newspaper, they will read the columnists with whom they normally agree. Liberals will look for Tom Wicker, Nicholas Von Hoffman, or Garry Wills, while conservatives will seek out William Safire or James J. Kilpatrick. Research has demonstrated, however, that this is not always true. Some people do read materials with which they disagree. They do this to develop counter arguments, to reassure themselves that their position is indeed the correct one, or to see what the opposition is saying. But, as a general rule, selectivity is a concept that works. Generally, people will subscribe to a newspaper or magazine that reflects their own point of view, although today it is frequently difficult to determine exactly where newspapers and some magazines stand politically. People will buy books with which they expect to agree. People will also expose themselves to new ideas because of curiosity or peer pressure. But, more often than not they do this for the purpose of selecting enough information to reinforce their opposing view. "It's just as I thought. They're crazy!" is a commonly heard reaction. Media cannot change people's already established opinions, but it can form their opinions in areas where they have no preexisting point of view.

Because people tend to remember those things that support their beliefs, confirm their prejudices, and maintain their predispositions, it becomes important to know what factors influence their opinion development. It has been determined that such things as self-assurance, upbringing, intelligence, sense of humor, and level of tolerance play important roles. Associates, families, and friends also determine to a very large degree how the selectivity process works within an individual. Social scientists call these "reference groups." Age, education, sex, marital status, and other demographics also play a part in selective attention, selective perception, and selective retention.

If what is believed about selectivity is true, it is easy to see why it is so difficult to develop theories regarding the effects of mass media. Not only does research have to take into account the tremendous variance in the kinds of communication that people receive, but it must also attempt to account for the tremendous difference in the way in which people receive the communication.

Melvin DeFleur and Sandra Ball-Rokeach[7] suggest that there are really three levels of communication effects. The first level is what they call cognitive effects, or how mass media can affect the thinking process. They argue that mass communications can assist people in forming attitudes, can set the agenda for things that people will think about, can resolve ambiguity, and can even have an impact on values.

The second level of media effects is an impact upon people's feelings and emotions. Mass media can make people cry or laugh. It can frustrate them and alienate them or it can reassure them and give them confidence. Too much communication can numb people, having what

Paul Lazarsfeld and Robert Merton[8] call a narcotizing dysfunction. The vast supply of communications may elicit only a superficial concern with the problems of society, and this superficiality often cloaks mass apathy.

AGENDA SETTING

The general notion of agenda setting—the ability of the media to influence the salience of events in the public mind—has been part of our political culture for at least half a century. Recall that the opening chapter of Walter Lippmann's 1922 book *Public Opinion* is titled: "The World Outside and the Pictures in Our Heads." As Lippmann pointed out, it is, of course, the mass media which dominate in the creation of these pictures of public affairs.

More recently, this assumption of media power has been asserted by presidential observer Theodore White in *The Making of the President, 1972.*

The press does more than bring these issues to a level of political awareness among the public. The idea of agenda setting asserts that the priorities of the press, to some degree, become the priorities of the public. What the press emphasizes is in turn emphasized privately and publicly by the audience of the press.

Source: Donald Shaw and Maxwell McCombs, *The Emergence of American Political Issues: The Agenda-Setting Function of the Press.* St. Paul: West Publishing Co., 1977, pp. 5–6.

It is argued that mass communication can have an effect upon behavior, but this is hard to prove. At one time there was great concern over the manner in which television networks might be influencing the electoral process by the way they reported election returns. Shortly after the polls closed in the East, the networks began projecting which presidential candidate had won the states where voting was already completed. In 1964, when Lyndon Johnson won such a sweeping victory over Barry Goldwater, the tide against Goldwater was evident almost immediately. But while the networks were projecting the winner in the East, people were still voting in the West, where it was only 5:30 P.M. At first it was argued that these media reports would discourage people in the West from voting. Later, others argued that what really happened was that the reports did not deter anyone from voting, but rather they pushed to the polls more people who wanted to vote for a winner, in what was called the bandwagon effect. How can a question like this really be answered? How can one really find out what goes on in people's heads, what impels people to vote or to stay home? One can ask them, but they often don't know why they do things, or they may not want to answer the question honestly for fear of embarrassing themselves. This is the problem that the researcher investigating mass media effects usually faces.

Voting data can establish correlations. People who did this also tended to do that. There may be a close relationship, but what do the correlations really mean? An example could be the 1980 presidential election. Let's imagine that NBC projected Ronald Reagan the winner when it was just six o'clock on the West Coast. The other two networks did not project Reagan to be the winner until it was eight o'clock on the West Coast. The researcher's survey has indicated that 37 percent of the people questioned said they had planned to vote, but decided not to in the early evening. Of that 37 percent, let's imagine that 70 percent watched the election returns on NBC. That correlation—that most of the people who changed their minds about voting were watching the network that projected the winner at six o'clock—is a pretty strong one and could lead one to suspect that projecting winners on television before the polls are closed does have a serious impact on voting behavior.

But are there other explanations for this behavior? There might be. It might just be coincidence. Or it might have something to do with the personalities of the people who watch NBC. One could hypothesize that the commentators on NBC appeal to people who tend to be procrastinators, who frequently plan to do something that they ultimately do not do. If this is the case, projecting the winner has nothing to do with voting behavior. It just happened that viewers who were procrastinators about voting tended to watch the network that projected the winner early. This is clearly less plausible, but it could be the real explanation. Usually, the most a researcher can do is to establish a high correlation between the suspected cause and the resultant behavior and then attempt to demonstrate why every other conceivable explanation for this behavior is implausible. But to jump from correlation to causation, a definitive motive or reason, is a very dangerous move, and is not often done.

MEDIA VIOLENCE

The question of whether violence on television and in films incites violent behavior in viewers, ultimately producing a more violent society, is a terribly important question, but one that still defies a conclusive answer. The question has been around since the late 1940s, when the first studies were done that counted the number of violent acts committed on television during an average evening. People were appalled at the results of those content analyses then, and they are appalled now. Despite the outcry against violence on televison, television networks and programming syndicates have been slow to respond, because ratings suggest that many people seem to enjoy violent shows. Although not every program in the top twenty can be considered violent, many of the most popular programs have contained a considerable amount of killing, maiming, and beating. Because there are so many nonviolent programs that also are successful, it would be misleading to suggest that violence alone can make a program popular. At the same time, however, viewers do not seem to avoid a program they like because it contains violence.

Television network executives must be exceedingly cautious in their public pronouncements regarding the controversy over television violence. They could argue that television cannot put ideas in people's heads or motivate them to do things, and therefore, there is little reason to be concerned about televised violence. But, supporting this argument makes it extremely difficult for them to turn around and tell potential advertisers that the medium can sell a product.

At the same time, the position of many people who vigorously insist that television violence directly affects audience behavior is also sometimes ambiguous. Many of these same people reject the notion that obscene movies and books should be banned because they have an effect on their audience.

Research on Violence

Because the problem of violence on television is still being debated, it offers an appropriate case study of mass media research and theories.

Some of the difficulties of researching a question like the impact of television violence seem almost insurmountable. How does one define violence or differentiate between fantasy violence in a Bugs Bunny cartoon or a detective show, and real life violence in the news? If the violence is justified, does this make a difference? For the purpose of comparison in the study, how can people be found who have not been exposed to violence? How can the full effects of media violence on a human being be measured? It is fairly easy to measure the short-term impact of violent programming, but it is difficult to measure the impact of viewing violence over twenty or thirty years. Does watching violence over a long period have an accumulative effect, or does it have a diluting effect? In other words, if people watch violent programming for ten years, does the potential impact build up in them, or does continual exposure to television violence mean less as time goes by? And how does one accurately determine what is cause and what is effect?

Two types of research have been conducted in an effort to answer questions about television violence—laboratory experiments and field surveys. Two kinds of lab experiments have been conducted—those that look at whether children (and most research has been done on children), will imitate what is seen on television, and those that attempt to determine whether televised violence will instigate violent behavior in subjects. Experiments show that children *can* imitate televised violence. Some researchers claim that televised violence can increase the likelihood of aggressive behavior in a child, as well. These studies have been criticized, however, on the grounds that an experimental laboratory setting does not reflect real life closely enough. In these experiments, children are generally shown a violent film or television program, and after viewing it, are taken to another setting where their behavior is observed and compared with a second group of children who watched a nonviolent film. Critics of these studies complain that in the laboratory setting, factors that normally inhibit violence are absent. Social norms seem somewhat suspended, and there appears to be little risk of disapproval or retaliation for the child.

Field surveys have been conducted to uncover any correlation between exposure to television violence and aggressive tendencies. People were asked to view violent programming and then were asked how they might respond in various situations. The responses of those who watched the violent programming were compared to the responses of those who watched the nonviolent programming. Most of the surveys have shown a modest relationship between exposure to television violence and aggressive tendencies.

Some recently completed long-term research studies on the impact of violent television programming on aggressive behavior have suggested that there indeed appears to be a correlation between the two, but the studies also suggest that there is a blurring of the effects over time.

This is clearly not a comprehensive discussion of the research on television violence, but the outline is sufficient to show the kinds of studies that have been undertaken. From research, three theories or hypotheses of television violence have evolved. These are the catharsis hypothesis, the modeling hypothesis, and the catalytic hypothesis.

The catharsis hypothesis is based on the principle that emotions and feelings can be purged through indirect or vicarious experience. For example, a little boy might really want to hit his sister. While watching television he sees the hero of a program hit the villain. This gives the child a feeling of satisfaction and reduces his desire to strike his sister. People who believe in the catharsis hypothesis suggest that exposure to television violence allows media users to discharge in fantasy what they might otherwise act out. Watching violent television shows, they say, provides a harmless outlet for human frustrations and hostile impulses in much the same way as hitting a punching bag. There is some research to support this hypothesis, but it has been criticized. But then, all research on television violence has been criticized by someone.

The modeling hypothesis suggests that symbolic violence on television, whether in a real or fantasy setting, will increase aggressive behavior, harden viewers to pain and suffering, and lead them to accept violence as a way of life and a solution to personal and social problems.

It is ironic that in responding to criticism, television has sought not to eliminate violence but to sanitize it. When someone is shot or beaten up on television, there is usually little evidence of blood or suffering. It is common to show a killer point the gun at a victim and pull the trigger, but less common to see the victim hit or die. If one subscribes to the modeling hypothesis, this sanitary violence is probably worse than the bloody kind, because it does not show the awful results of violence. The thought of shooting someone one dislikes is not nearly as bad as the thought of them dying. Pain, blood, agony, and death, the true results of violence, can be impediments to the use of violence. When this aspect of violence is eliminated, it can become all the more attractive. There is considerable research supporting the modeling thesis, but it, too, has been criticized. Based upon research, however, this hypothesis seems to be more plausible than the catharsis hypothesis.

The catalytic hypothesis is the one which has gained the most supporters in the debate. A catalyst is an agent that brings about a reaction or change between certain substances. The catalytic hypothesis suggests that most people are unaffected by television violence. But, there are unstable individuals in the world who can be triggered into action by watching violence, or who are likely to imitate the violence they see on the small screen.

In 1966, NBC aired a movie called *The Doomsday Flight,* which was about an individual who placed a bomb aboard an airplane and then contacted the airline and agreed to tell them the location of the bomb in exchange for money. Several airlines received similar threats in the days following the film's broadcast. When it was reshown on television years later, the same thing happened again. Not everybody reacted that way, obviously, just a small group of presumably unstable persons to whom the television show was a catalyst. Research tends to give this hypothesis the strongest support. This hypothesis also seems to be much closer in line with the theoretical conception of the audience that was discussed earlier: the audience as a diverse group of individuals who attune themselves to the mass media in different ways and therefore react to the same communication in different ways.

It is probably unfair to summarize in a few pages the scores of research studies about the effects of television violence on viewers. Yet, these pages reflect the essence of what social science has revealed about this problem. The entire controversy over televised violence has generated far more heat than light. It is an emotional subject. Some say that violence on television and in the movies is merely a convenient scapegoat for the increasing lawlessness in American society.

While social scientists try to discover the effects of violence on the audience, others speculate on the reasons why both American television and American movies seem so violence prone. Television probably mirrors America more than many people like to admit. Although the typical shoot-out between the marshal and the outlaw is no doubt exaggerated, violence in the American West was very real. And, although "Hawaii Five-O"'s people used their guns more than most cops do in real life, police, criminals, and frequently innocent citizens are killed every day on American streets. The violent parts of society cannot be erased by altering only the picture in the mirror.

In an article in *TV Guide,* television writer-producer Gene Roddenberry, the creator of "Star Trek" and other programs, offered another

THE MISSING EFFECTS

Can clever advertisements persuade people to buy products they do not want or need? Does violence on television provoke violence in television viewers? Can a candidate win votes by flashing a smile on the screen in thirty-second units several times a day during the two weeks before an election? There is little evidence votes are won. Evidence is lacking to confirm that most advertising has a significant impact upon most consumer purchasing decisions, as well. Most advertisers will report, however, that when they stop advertising, sales dip. On this basis they believe that advertising has some kind of effect on consumers.

Source: Melvin DeFleur and Sandra Ball-Rokeach, *Theories of Mass Communication:* New York: McKay, 1976.

explanation for television's emphasis on physical confrontation and violence. Roddenberry blames it on the people who control the networks—the station owners and managers, and the advertisers—who are reluctant to allow ideological controversy on the small screen. Roddenberry argues that plays must have conflict, which is the source of the drama. If writers aren't allowed to write shows about ideological conflict, they'll write shows about physical conflict. If writers cannot show moral struggles over controversial issues, they'll show life and death struggles over noncontroversial issues. The excessive reliance on physical violence was caused by censorship, says Roddenberry, who has concluded that further censorship of television—banning violence from the airwaves—is not the solution.

DIFFERENT KINDS OF RESEARCHERS HAVE DIFFERENT APPROACHES

Melvin DeFleur and Sandra Ball-Rokeach present the kind of dilemma that faces researchers in mass media: scientists say the media have few effects; historians and other analysts of the broader picture say that the mass media have sweeping effects. These two statements are probably not as contradictory as they sound. The historian, who sees a radical change over time in the American way of life, government, and people can suggest that the growth and development of the mass media have had a profound impact on society. For example, the introduction of printing, the first mass medium, radically changed the world. It broke the monopoly the government had on information. This was of major importance to the development of new relationships between people and government, including this country's constitutional democracy. On a somewhat smaller level, the reporting of war by the press has had an impact on the way people look at war. Vietnam was the most recent example. Uncensored press reports on the frustration of American forces clearly had an effect over time on public opinion.

The introduction of television in the late forties and early fifties changed the way people lived, as radio had changed people's lifestyles in the twenties and thirties. When looking at the big picture, only the terribly naive would argue that the mass media has no effect upon people's lives.

But, communication researchers are, for the most part, social scientists. They have generally concentrated on documenting specific results, rather than the more general results viewed by the historian. These kinds of effects are not easily detectable in laboratory experiments, where a realistic environment is lacking. The field study survey approach has not really worked either, because of the many variables involved. There is a need for new methods of doing communication research.

What, finally, can be said about the impact of the mass media on attitudes and behavior? Can there be an improvement on Bernard Berelson's truism, "some kinds of communication on some kinds of issues, brought to the attention of some kinds of people, under some kinds of conditions, have some kinds of effects?"

Opinion conversion through the mass media is extremely rare. Hundreds of social philosophers have worried about it, hundreds of researchers have looked for it, but it just does not happen very often. In fact, the opposite is far more likely. Regardless of the issue, the mass media usually reinforce the existing attitudes and lifestyles of their audience rather than changing them. Far more often, the media are a force for stability rather than a force for change. However, when there is no existing point of view, an opinion or attitude *can* be formed by the media.

The fact that the media tend to reinforce attitudes is itself an important effect. Views are strengthened by ammunition from the media. They give new facts to cite, new sources to quote, and, above all, a sense that the individual is right and that others agree with him or her. In this way, the media set the agenda for what people will discuss. Imagine a hot local debate over a school bond issue, where the bulk of the news happens to favor the supporters. Most opponents probably will not be converted, but that really is not necessary. If the supporters are getting lots of reinforcement from the media, they'll be much more likely to speak up in conversations with their friends, and to vote on election day. Lacking this reinforcement, opponents of the bond issue are more likely to keep quiet and forget to vote. A crucial piece of every persuasion strategy is to increase the fervor of one's allies and dampen the enthusiasm of one's enemies. This the media do very, very well.

Advertisers know that people rarely seek out information or guidance on breakfast cereals, but they don't resist it either. They barely pay attention to it, but through repetition, an advertiser can build in people's minds a sense of the product's appropriateness. So, when they go to buy a cereal, a detergent, or anything else they don't care much about, they usually buy an advertised brand. They do this not because they believe it is better (nothing really is believed about it), but just because the brand is familiar and it somehow seems like a good one.

In some cases, however, attitudes can be changed through peer pressure, a friend's recommendation, or a bad experience with the product. Also, the desire for esteem within the peer group should never be ignored. If none of this has taken place, however, chances are that mere repetition in the media, resulting in brand name recognition, will be enough to determine what people buy without their giving it any further thought.

Advertisers do not have to rely only on low involvement and repetition for their impact, however. They know that people use the media to satisfy their needs, and they know that the media are good at reinforcing values. Nothing is easier than tying a product to people's needs and values. People get the toothpaste that promises social and sexual success in return for their purchase. Of course, the needs triggered and reinforced by the ad—sex, status, and the like,—are not really satisfied by switching toothpastes. People do not really believe that Ultra Brite gives them sex appeal, but unless there's an opposing influence somewhere in their social environment, the connection made by the advertiser between the product and the sexual needs and values is often enough to motivate the switch to Ultra Brite.

Once the switch is made, people may begin to feel a bit silly. They like to have solid reasons for what they do. Suddenly they are reading Ultra Brite ads with unusual interest to rationalize their decision. In the case of Ultra Brite, as with so many products, it probably will not work. It has never been proven that one toothpaste is better than another. Finally, the only thing that keeps people using Ultra Brite is habit and the constant repetition of those sexy ads.

Suppose a new behavior is something a little more defensible—like recycling used newspapers, cans, and bottles. Here the new behavior may signal an attitude change. Many people start recycling ·for the same sorts of irrational reasons that determine their choice of a toothpaste—peer pressure, pressure from their children, etc.,—but once they start, they begin looking for information to make sense of what they are doing, and they find it in the media. News about the value of recycling probably does not do much to get people started, (for that they need the sort of manipulative persuasion found in toothpaste ads), but news is absolutely essential to help people make sense of what they are already doing, and thus to keep on doing it because they can now believe in it.

Information in the media also helps people apply existing attitudes to new circumstances. News of the Watergate scandals, for example, did not create opposition to political corruption, but it did strengthen it by focusing opposition on the behavior of Richard Nixon. Similarly, the news that a product contributes to pollution cannot create an attitude against pollution, but if people are already worried about it, the information can reinforce that attitude, while at the same time turning them against the product. As early as 1948, Lazarsfeld and Merton acknowledged this role of the media. They call it canalization.

To review, there are five ways that media content can affect people's attitudes and behavior:

1.   The media can provide reasons to support existing attitudes, thus increasing commitments to them.

2.   The media can directly change behavior on low involvement issues, where there are no competing influences, by mere repetition.

3.   The media can get people to act without changing their attitudes by catering to their existing needs and values and linking them to a new behavior.

4.   The media's information can be used to justify or rationalize behavior initially based on needs, building attitudes to support that behavior.

5.   The media can relate an existing attitude to a new object, by providing information that ties the two together.

None of these five premises are inconsistent with the general principle that the media are more a force for stability than a force for change. Mass media involve reinforcement, not conversion.

There may be a sixth premise that is *not* based on reinforcement. Although it is true that when a communication conflicts with current attitudes, there is a tendency to ignore or reject it, psychologists have found that every attitude has a "latitude of acceptance" around it. A communication that falls within this latitude of acceptance is not ignored or rejected. In fact, people see such a communication as closer to their own views than it really is, and as a result, their own views move in the direction of the communication. A piece of information that is just barely consistent with an original attitude will thus shift the attitude slightly, and a more extreme piece of information then becomes acceptable. With careful planning and a thorough knowledge of the audience, it is thus possible to slowly guide people toward a whole new value system.

Long-term exposure through the media to unpopular points of view or radically different lifestyles within society can gain a kind of tolerance, if not acceptance, by the majority. To this extent, attitude change has taken place. It is then possible that tolerance can be moved toward acceptance, as the fear of the unknown diminishes. However, the entire process requires the nonopposition or passive resistance of peer groups, opinion leaders, and the media. If the resistance is active, original attitudes are usually hardened.

MEDIA-INDUCED APATHY

We have talked a lot about things that the media make people do. But what about the things that the media *keep* people from doing?

At the most obvious level, most people spend more than four hours a day passively watching television, reading newspapers or magazines, or listening to the radio. One of the most common criticisms of the mass media is that they replace genuine participation with a kind of vicarious passive pseudo-experience. The result, it is charged, is an apathetic and uninvolved public.

This argument is usually made about media entertainment, especially television, but it may apply to news as well. News in the media is mostly raw, uninterpreted information. In their effort to be objective, reporters seldom tell people what they should do with the information, or even what they could do with it. The speed of modern mass communication and the complexity of the world's problems encourage people to conclude that informed action is impossible, and perhaps even inappropriate. Let the government handle it.

The very format of media news presentations is aimed at rewarding the reader, listener, or viewer for the mere act of reading, listening, or viewing. Reporters are taught to round out their stories, to work at creating the impression that all relevant questions have been asked and answered; that the job—reporter's and audience's—is done. The result may be a redefinition of the obligation of a citizen. Instead of feeling obliged to do something about the world's problems, people may come to feel that it's enough just to know what the world's problems are. Some researchers call this the syndrome of well-informed futility. Most call it apathy.

Agenda setting, in which the media pick the issues and thereby the norms and culture, results in cultural apathy. It has little to do with persuasion, but a lot to do with people's lives, and media's impact on their lives.

MEDIA AS ENVIRONMENT

Every waking moment of people's lives, they learn from their environment. Some of this learning is through their rational faculties; some of it is through sense, intuition, and feelings. They learn from the smell of the air in a meadow or on a city street, from the conversations, glances, and half-glances of the people they meet. They learn from the feeling in their muscles after a hard workout. All of these experiences provide educational material for input into the human biocomputer.

Before the invention of the printing press, and later the television, people spent nearly all of their time experiencing life in these ways. Even today, very few people live their lives entirely in the mass media, but more and more of their time, especially leisure time, is devoted to the pseudo-reality of the media instead of the genuine reality all around them.

This must make a difference. Think about watching television for four hours a night—just sitting there, eyes wide, body still, room dark, other people reduced to vague shadows, images pouring into the brain. Regardless of what's on the tube, all those hours spent in front of it must have some kind of impact on a person, if for no other reason

FIGURE 13-1
Marshall McLuhan. (UPI Photo)

than that individual's exposure to other activities is drastically reduced.

Communication researchers have seldom studied these sorts of questions, because there was and is no methodology by which to study them rigorously. Until the 1960s, what little was known about the effects of media, irrespective of content, had come from anthropologists, who recorded the reactions of primitive cultures to new communication technologies. Edmund Carpenter,[9] describing his experiences in the village of Sio in New Guinea, suggests that the introduction of photography and then motion pictures rapidly changed the village. Within a short time, several houses had been remodeled in a new style and men wore European-style clothes. They carried themselves differently and acted differently as a result of polaroid pictures and home movies taken of them.

Except for anthropologists, for a long time no one wrote very much about the impact on culture of the very existence of mass media. Then in 1964, a Canadian scholar named Marshall McLuhan[10] published his book *Understanding Media*. McLuhan's thinking relied heavily on the ideas of another Canadian scholar, Harold Innis, [11] but it was McLuhan who first popularized these ideas.

Trained in engineering and English literature, McLuhan was an intellectual eclectic. He ignored the findings of social science even when they supported his ideas. He did not bother to prove his statements with evidence, but rather illustrated them with examples drawn from such varied sources as James Joyce and professional football. The reaction of traditional scholars to these tactics is summed up by critic Dwight Macdonald,[12] who said that the parts are greater than the whole in *Understanding Media*. The whole is an accumulation of contradictions, nonsequiturs, distorted facts, nonfacts, exaggerations, and chronic rhetorical vagueness.

These accusations did not seem to bother McLuhan, who claimed that his unrigorous style is ideally suited to the world of television. Nor do they bother his disciples, who number in the thousands.

McLuhan's central assertion was that "the medium is the message." The customary distinction between the two, he argued, is mythical. What a medium communicates, quite apart from its content, is the nature of the medium itself. The conventional response to all media—namely, that it is how they are used that counts—is the dumb stance of the technological idiot according to McLuhan. In *The Medium Is The Massage,* McLuhan purposely turned the title into a pun in order to emphasize that the real "message" of a medium is the way it pokes, jabs, and kneads its audience, not what it says.

Media for McLuhan were extensions of one or more of the five senses. Face-to-face speech, the oldest of the media, extends all five senses—hearing, seeing, touching, smelling, and tasting. Print extends only the eye, radio only the ear. Television is an extension of both the eye and the ear. The impact of a medium is determined by which senses it extends and the way it extends them. Elsewhere, McLuhan

insisted that television is primarily a tactile medium, but he never clarified the meaning or significance of that assertion.

Media, said McLuhan, are either "hot" or "cool." This was a crucial
distinction for McLuhan. A hot medium is one that extends a single
sense in "high definition," which means a medium filled with data or
information. A photograph is visually high definition. A cartoon is low
definition because it provides little visual information. Radio is a hot
sound medium because of the intensity of the information; the telephone is a cooler sound medium because of the pauses and what goes
unsaid but is filled in by the listener—background, attitudes, etc. A
movie is a hot medium because of its large screen, which provides
more information than the cool television set.

Hot media do not leave as much to be filled in or completed by the
audience as cool media. Therefore, hot media are low in participation
and cool media are high. Naturally then, a hot medium like radio has
very different effects on the user than a cool medium like the telephone.

McLuhan wanted to know only two things about any medium in order to examine what it really does: which senses it extends, and
whether it does so in high definition (hot) or low definition (cool).

History, for McLuhan, was divided into three stages. The first may be
called the "tribal" stage. It is characterized by local, oral communication within each tribe or community. Person-to-person speech is, in
McLuhan's view, a cool medium, involving all the senses. It thus requires the maximum amount of participation.

The second stage begins with the invention of the printing press.
Print, of course, is the hottest of McLuhan's media, and extends only
one sense—the eye. Instead of participation and involvement, it requires dispassionate attention to the words on the page. Print aug-
ments the tendency to consider reality discrete units with casual relations and a linear serial order. The search for order by structure in
nature can be traced to the influence of print.

In an oral culture, one acquires knowledge only in contact with other people, via communal activities. Print allows individuals to withdraw, to contemplate and meditate outside of communal activities.
Print thus encourages the development of private, individual points of
view.

McLuhan said that print created the price system because it made
uniform costs feasible. Before print, the price of an article was subject
to haggle and adjustment. Print is also responsible for the growth of
nationalism, because it permitted visual comprehension of the mother
tongue and, through maps, visual comprehension of the nation. All
these effects taken together McLuhan called detribalization.

McLuhan's third stage begins with the invention of television. Television, he said is a cool medium; it requires its audience to participate.
Through television, involvement has once again become a fundamental part of the communication process. Instead of the "tribal village" of
the first stage, we are faced now with a "global village," mediated by

television (television will reach the entire world eventually). We are in the process of being "retribalized" by television said McLuhan.

In McLuhan's view, people born after 1950 do not need retribalizing. They grew up with television, and hence they have always been members of the tribe. According to Thomas Wolfe, literate people always have the feeling that no matter what anybody says, they can go check it out, look it up. The new person, not so much of an individualist, is more a part of the collective consciousness. The literate person is as unable to cope with the new age as the tribal native of Ghana is able to cope with literacy. The desire of students for involvement and participation, for talking rather than reading, for seminars rather than lectures, for action rather than reflection, are the results of the reorchestration of their senses by television.

The impact of television is so enormous that McLuhan did not hesitate to assert that it has begun to dissolve the very fabric of American life. He recommended, apparently quite seriously, that television be banned in the United States before it destroys the country by eliminating serious, print-oriented thought.

Was McLuhan right about this? Certainly he was right about some things. The mass media do have far-reaching effects on society, effects too broad to be measured in the experiments of social scientists. And at least some of these effects, it seems, stem from the nature of the media themselves, irrespective of content. McLuhan looked at the history of civilization from a new perspective—much of what he saw no one else has seen. However, the concept of the global village is based on the idea that television is an active medium and most research indicates that it is actually a passive medium. Furthermore, the global village may have been created not by television but by European imperialism. The class society, overwhelmingly pre-electronic, is based on private property. The actual use made of media like television in our society may simply reinforce the materialism of capitalism.

McLuhan's concept that the medium is the message is also questionable. The fifth rerun of "The Twilight Zone" is a considerably different television experience from a presidential address. Yet, many people watching the president will turn on Rod Serling when he appears. Why, if the medium is the message? Perhaps even on the medium which probably has the narrowest range of content, the answer is simply one is entertainment and the other is not.

McLuhan and his disciples share a complete disdain for evidence. One of the distinctions between print and broadcasting, according to McLuhan, is that print follows a linear one-thing-at-a-time logic, while broadcasting is global, everything at once. As a result, McLuhanites claim that western civilization is now undergoing a change from a linear lifestyle to a global one. In the language of social science, this is a testable hypothesis, but McLuhan and his followers have not bothered to test it, or even to find out whether it has already been tested. Instead, they simply point out that baseball, a linear game, is now less popular than football, a global game. If you want more proof than that, you are obviously a linear personality, unfit for the television age.

Evidence for McLuhan's propositions turns up in unexpected places, however. For example, Professor John Wilson of the African Institute of London University, tried to use a movie to teach African villagers how to read. He found, to his surprise, that these people did not "see" the film in the same way he did. In each scene of the movie, they picked out a familiar object like a chicken and fastened on that, switching to a different object only when the scene switched. There was so much information in the film that they concentrated instead on just a part. They made no effort to connect the scenes or to follow the story line. (They are therefore nonlinear.) Several studies of children watching television have produced intriguingly similar results. The children did not focus on the whole screen as their parents did; instead, they scanned the screen for details to fasten on. Perhaps television is retribalizing us after all.

In conclusion, McLuhan has brought attention to possible effects of media that were not even considered before. Research on the effects of media is still in its infancy, and has yet to acquire enough data to base any assumptions on, much less to draw any firm conclusions with.

Media for the Future

Because large segments of the population cannot be put in experimental laboratories, it is difficult to compute media effects precisely. New methods of research will have to be found. Because the world is changing rapidly, research of today may have little value by the time it is published. Somehow, research will have to project into the future. McLuhan has shown us that the environment plays a major role in media effects. New research should test these ideas.

■ One recent study of diffusion found that dozens of factors influence a decision to adopt a new way of doing things. The study conducted in the Republic of Korea, examined how women adopted or refused to adopt birth control methods. One community in time wholeheartedly accepted the techniques government workers were promoting—but hardly for the reasons anticipated. True enough, the women heard the ideas of government workers, saw billboards, and read literature, but other factors had just as important a part. A pig won by the women made possible free discussion of family planning when it had litters of only two twice and got the name of "family planning pig." Changing power structures in the community were important and the growth of strong farming and retail businesses had an impact. Researchers concluded that a complex "network" of influences led to the dramatic change—and no social worker could hope to control the environment as completely as would be required to duplicate the change elsewhere.

■ In the past advertisers decided how to spend their fifteen billion dollars on television on the basis of relatively crude demographics: income, age, and sex distributions of viewers. Thus an advertiser wishing to reach women between eighteen and thirty-four years of age making more than $15,000 per year could examine a station's ratings in that area. Little more was known of each group's reasons for purchasing. Now the Stanford Research Institute offers VALS (Values And Life Styles). The new research technique describes the audience along lines of their attitudes on very basic issues. At present the research has divided the U.S. population into eight groups: *Belongers* (33%), *Achievers* (25%), *Emulators* (10%), *I-Am-Me* (5%), *Experiential* (7%), *Societally Conscious* (9%), *Survivors* (4%), and *Sustainers* (7%).

Sentimental and traditional by nature, the Belongers are patriotic. The Achievers, successful middle-aged persons, concern themselves with material accumulations. Meanwhile, Emulators are trying to follow the lead of the Achievers, but are somewhat younger. Impulsive young adults fall in the I-Am-Me group, while more people-oriented people belong to the Experiential. Mature people, who have rejected material luxuries, receive the title of Societally Conscious. Survivors are older people who have little enthusiasm

for life, and Sustainers, who have trouble making ends meet, are bitter over their circumstances.

For advertisers, these groups have well-defined buying habits that may be used in the hands of a skilled practitioner to further selling goals. The new research, therefore, not only influences the stations or networks selected, but the means used in advertisements to stimulate buying activity.

■ Started as a means for determining what respondents read in newspapers, eye tracking research long labored under suspicion. Now, however, new computerized means for gauging eye movements are changing attitudes. Eye research works like this: People are brought into a theater and asked to view a screen where advertisements are flashed. Unknown to the respondent, a videotaped record of their eye movements is being made. Then the computer takes over, producing a bouncing ball over an image of the advertisements to show researchers where the viewer's eyes look. The result shows what consumers see and miss. The studies have been used by R. J. Reynolds, Seagram, Anheuser-Busch, Du Pont and other large corporations to discover if their advertisements are working.

ADDITIONAL READINGS

Blumler, Jay G., and Katz, Elihu, eds. *The Uses of Mass Communications: Current Perspectives on Gratifications Research*. Beverly Hills, Calif.: Sage Publications, Inc., 1974.

Cater, Douglas, and Strickland, Stephen. *TV Violence and the Child*. New York: Russell Sage Foundation, 1975.

Chaffee, Steven H., ed. *Political Communication: Issues and Strategies for Research*. Beverly Hills, Calif.: Sage Publications, Inc., 1975.

Comstock, George; Chaffee, Steven; Katzman, Nathan; McCombs, Maxwell; and

Roberts, Don. *Television and Human Behavior.* New York: Columbia University Press, 1979.

Kraus, Sidney, and Davis, Dennis. *The Effects of Mass Communication on Political Behavior.* University Park: Pennsylvania State University Press, 1976.

Rogers, Everett M. and Kincaid, D. Lawrence. *Communication Networks: Toward a New Paradigm for Research.* New York: The Free Press, 1981.

Schramm, Wilbur, and Roberts, Donald F., eds. *The Process and Effects of Mass Communication.* 2d rev. ed. Urbana: University of Illinois Press, 1971.

Stephenson, William. *The Play Theory of Mass Communication.* Chicago: University of Chicago Press, 1967.

Winick, Charles, ed. *Deviance and Mass Media.* Beverly Hills: Sage Publications, Inc., 1978.

Winick, Mariann P., and Winick, Charles. *The Television Experience: What Children See.* Beverly Hills: Sage Publications, Inc., 1979.

FOOTNOTES

1. Wilbur Schramm, *Communications Research: A Half-Century Appraisal* (Hawaii: University Press of Hawaii, 1977); *The Process and Effects of Mass Communication* (Illinois: University of Illinois Press, 1971).

2. Harold Lasswell, *Lasswell on Political Sociology* (Chicago: University of Chicago Press, 1977); *Propaganda and Communication in World History* (Hawaii: University Press of Hawaii, 1979).

3. William Melody, *Communications Technology and Social Policy: Understanding the New Cultural Revolution* (New York: Wiley, 1973).

4. Philip Davidson, *Propaganda and the American Revolution* (North Carolina: University of North Carolina Press, 1981).

5. Bernard Berelson, *Reader in Public Opinion and Communication* (New York: Free Press, 1966), *The People's Choice: How the Voter Makes Up His Mind in a Presidential Campaign* (North Carolina: University of North Carolina Press, 1941).

6. Paul Lazarsfeld, *Continuities in the Language of Social Research* (New York: Free Press, 1972), *Personal Influence; The Part Played by People in the Flow of Mass Communications* (New York: Free Press, 1964).

7. Melvin DeFleur and Sandra Ball-Rokeach, *Theories of Mass Communication* (New York: McKay, 1976).

8. Robert Merton, *Social Theory and Social Structure* (Glencoe, Illinois: Free Press, 1957).

9. Edmund Carpenter, *Explorations in Communication, an Anthology* (Boston: Beacon Press, 1960).

10. Marshall McLuhan, *The Gutenberg Galaxy: The Making of Typographic Man* (Toronto: University of Toronto Press, 1962); *The Medium is the Massage* (New York: Random House, 1967); *Understanding Media; The Extensions of Man* (New York: McGraw Hill, 1964).

11. Harold Innis, *Empire and Communications* (Toronto: University of Toronto Press, 1972).

12. Dwight Macdonald, *Against the American Grain* (New York: Random House, 1962).

14

THE FUTURE

As the present merges with the future, many of the same issues will remain. One of these is how the media, particularly television, will relate to the democratic process.

MEDIA RESPONSIBILITY

One area that has been carefully examined is the process of presidential nominations. The presidential nominating process begins long before the nominating conventions, and recently, television has been a major agenda setting force (those who receive exposure are the contenders). Candidates have been quick to adapt to this shift away from the former system, in which political bosses within parties made the initial decisions about who would run. The results of the new system have been perhaps too many candidates, too many primaries, and a lot of confusion about the real issues. The American Assembly on Presidential Nominations and the Media[1] recommends changes in the process. They say that the number of dates upon which presidential primaries can be conducted should be substantially reduced, and the intervals between primary dates should be lengthened beyond the typical one-week lapse. The media could not then concentrate all their coverage on a single, supposedly important state and instead would give the public fuller exposure to a wider array of voter reactions and candidate performances. The complexity of the political scene, crowded with candidates early in the campaign, could then be more accurately conveyed, in contrast to the media's current overly simplistic concentration on a single state's constituency. The restructuring of the primary system might diminish the concentration on the horse race aspect of the process—an exaggerated stress on the calculation of odds, which comes at the expense of attention to matters of substance

with long-range significance. Primaries punctuated by intervals for de-
liberation would enable the press and public to digest one primary's
results before confronting the next set of choices.

Changes in journalistic practices are desirable. There is a need for
highlighting the candidates' stands on issues, describing and analyz-
ing their records, and discovering and communicating their personality characteristics, which may affect their suitability for the presidency.
The following should be considered:[2]

1. Focusing more reports on comparisons of the candidates' positions on a single issue or set of issues, as distinguished from reports
which simply describe the point of view of a single candidate, without
the comparative dimension.

2. Using journalists with specialized knowledge in specific subject
matter areas to examine the candidates' issue stances. Rotating reporters among the candidates' campaigns (including that of an incumbent
President seeking renomination), to furnish a fresh perspective and to
guard against reporters acquiring vested interest in "their" candidate's
success.

3. Encouraging careful reporting and interpretation of the ways the
candidates are presenting themselves through campaign advertising
and through national and local news media.

4. Concentrating more journalistic resources on explorations of the
candidates' political and personal histories—allowing for the possibilities that human beings do change, but recognizing the probability of
consistency in handling future situations of a similar nature.

5. Comparing systematically the candidates' present pronouncements
with their previous statements and practices and calling them to account to explain to the public any discrepancies.

6. Strongly encouraging those journalists familiar with the candidates
and their campaigns to find ways to express—with all due care and
caution—their own judgments and observations about the candidates.

7. Describing and assessing the persons chosen by candidates to staff
their major campaign posts, with particular attention to the ideological
configurations they may represent.

8. Cooperating enthusiastically with efforts to facilitate comparisons
among candidates through such formats as debates and hearings, arranged by party, media, or interest group organizations.

Finally, there's the problem of timing. The tendency at present is for
the media to devote space and time to close examination of candidate
qualifications early in the nominating season—when, however, few
voters are motivated to pay attention to these reports. Later, when increasing numbers are interested, this information is subordinated to
more current and often less significant topics. The journalistic profession should devise ways to deliver the information needed when it is

needed. The quest for novel news, however, should not be allowed to detract from the public's overwhelming need for substantial and consistently developed political information.[3]

The dos and don'ts of good political reporting, however, are not always practical. Consider this case about honesty. Daniel Schorr, in his book *Clearing the Air,* tells of a luncheon in Paris at which William Paley, the founder of CBS, congratulated him on a documentary about East Germany. Its dramatic climax showed Walter Ulbricht, the East German Communist leader, upbraiding Schorr for his questioning and finally storming out of the room in full view of the camera. Paley said he admired the coolness with which Schorr sat there and looked at him while he was yelling. Schorr laughed and said the reverse shots were done in a conventional post-interview procedure after the subject had left the room. Paley had not known this and was furious. That very day Paley ordered staged reverses stopped, but his stern edict has since been relaxed as impractical.[4] Was this dishonesty? That's debatable. To resolve the problem, one would probably have to discuss intent and distortion. Did the reverse angles change the basic story?

RULES ABOUT TELEVISION BEHAVIOR

Rules about television behavior can be found in the CBS code of standards, which originated in memo form over the years and was gathered together in a manual in 1976. Some of the situations covered by the code:

Avoid interviews with victims of accidents or other tragedies or with their relatives. Exception: when they throw light on what happened or drive home a point which might help avoid future tragedies. Do not interview or attempt to interview a person who appears to be in a state of shock.

Riots: If, in your judgment, your presence is clearly inspiring, continuing or intensifying a dangerous, or potentially dangerous distur-

bance, cap your cameras and conceal your microphones regardless of what other news organizations may do. Avoid coverage of 1) self-designated leaders if they appear to represent only themselves or 2) any individuals or groups who are clearly performing. (Had these rules been in force, how different might the history of the 1960s have been?)

Terrorists: Except in the most compelling circumstances, and then only with the approval of the president of CBS news . . . there should be no live coverage of the terrorist/kidnapper since we may fall into the trap of providing an unedited platform for him.

Source: *Time Magazine*, December 5, 1977, p. 114.

In a business where crucial decisions must be made quickly, these are admirable distinctions between covering and sensationalizing the news.

FIGURE 14-1
M. A. Farber.

THE BATTLE OVER REPORTER'S PRIVILEGE

M. A. Farber, a reporter for *The New York Times,* sat for nearly six weeks in a cell block adjacent to a man who had allegedly murdered his mother and across from an accused German sodomist awaiting deportation. He was there for refusing to turn over to the court documents that he felt would prove that a man previously found not guilty was, in fact, guilty of murder.

In the mid-1960s, thirteen people died in a hospital in Oradell, N.J., under strange and unexplained circumstances. The local county investigation found nothing actionable in these deaths and dropped the case. Ten years later, acting on a tip, *The New York Times* assigned Farber to investigate the series of incidents again. His stories provoked the reopening of the case. Dr. Jascalevich was found innocent, but before the acquittal, the local judge hearing the case subpeonaed Farber, ordering him to deliver to the court all the documents on which he had based his story. He refused on the grounds that it would jeopardize his sources and that he'd given his word they would not be revealed. He was arrested and held in contempt.

If a reporter is to be made subject to a new jurisprudence that can compel him or her to become an official public informer, not only will the press suffer for it but so will the public good. The Law of Unintended Consequences has a dynamics of its own, and the willful refusal of the courts to understand how the American political system and the reporter's craft interlock may someday mark the Farber case as the beginning of a paradigm of Unintended Consequences.[5]

A reporter's highest function is to bring to public attention matters of common concern that should be thrust on the government's agenda for official action.

I once wrote a story about a famine in the Chinese province of Honan in which millions of people died. The story was printed in *Time* magazine and its publication saved countless lives. But not until now, writing this piece, have I told anyone that I came across the matter because friends in the United States Embassy in Chungking wanted someone to explore the story in the field. The embassy had received letters from American missionaries in the famine-struck area telling of a desolation and corruption concealed by censorship from the whole world. One of the young diplomats at the embassy called me in, simply put a batch of letters on the table between us, let me read—and said nothing. It was essential to conceal his name, for he was the key "leak." The "leak" was his way of appealing to American conscience beyond the bureaucratic channels of the State Department. Had I exposed him, he would probably have been purged at the time—in 1943—or later by John Foster Dulles or Joe McCarthy when they were blinding the State Department by cleansing it of alleged "Reds."[6]

The word leak in this connotation is positive, not negative. Journalism needs leaks. Maybe someday the process will have the dignity and importance it deserves.

If Farber had been compelled by imprisonment to name his sources, and to hand over his notes—all of which were only hearsay evidence—then the unintended consequence of his punishment could have reshaped American political history. Longer than anyone can remember, it has been accepted in American politics that a reporter's protection of his sources could not be violated. No law said so, no rulings said so; it was simply taken for granted.

> Neither the First nor the Sixth Amendment of the Constitution actually declares what the debaters have attempted to persuade us they say. The First Amendment says most briefly, "Congress shall make no law . . . abridging the freedom of speech, or of the press . . ." Around that curt phrase volumes of law have grown up; under its shelter television, publishing, cinema, pornography, polemic and poetry have all flourished; within its protection the American public has become better informed than any other.
>
> The Sixth Amendment has been similarly enlarged from its sparse phrases. It has been expanded in common talk to a Constitutional guarantee of "fair trial." Yet the phrase "fair trial" nowhere occurs in the Sixth Amendment. What is promised is simply "speedy and public trial"; the right of the accused to be confronted by the witnesses against him; and that the accused shall have "compulsory process for obtaining witnesses in his favor."[7]

The last phrase was expanded in the Farber case into what may become a dangerous precedent.

The press has done much wrong in the past ten years. Some reporters have tried to penetrate grand juries. Some have tried to provoke incidents. Some have become arrogant. But none has claimed that reporters are above the law. No law protects or should protect a reporter from being called to bear witness in an open court, and Farber did that. He responded for five days to every question, except those demanding that he divulge confidential sources or produce confidential notes.

The law holds that no wife can be forced to testify against her husband; no cleric against one who confesses; no doctors or psychiatrists against their patients. None of these privileges are written into the Constitution any more than a reporter's privilege to protect his informants from reprisal is. But they are part of the American way of life.

Claims of journalistic privilege have been met with skepticism, but not with outright rejection by the courts. The leading anti-press constitutional precedent is the Supreme Court's 1972 Branzburg decision, which rejected a journalist's privilege not to answer questions involving confidential sources before grand juries. In other cases, the court has upheld some forms of interference with the press's access to prejudicial information. It has admonished trial judges to prevent prejudicial statements to the press by counsel, witnesses, law enforcement officials, and even defendants. These decisions reflect the Burger Court's general approach to freedom of the press. It tends to stand firm against efforts to prohibit, punish, or compel publication, but also has upheld direct restrictions on the press's access to information, and where indirect inhibitions on news-gathering are at issue, the Court has not been sympathetic to press claims.[9] Obviously, the issue is not going to go away in the near future. The growing media web is demanding more news to feed the machine, and newsmakers will still want to keep secrets.

PRINT—UPS AND DOWNS

In late 1981, the book industry experienced a surprising surge in sales. The change is leading booksellers and publishers to think that their industry's year long recession may be over. Romances are extremely popular and young adult fiction is doing well. The resurgence is apparent even in hard-back fiction, which had been a particular trouble spot except for blockbuster novels. Nonfiction continues to keep pace with the surge of big books by big name novelists, but trade paperbacks also appear to be doing well and mass market paperbacks seem to be turning around after months of sluggish sales.

Theories abound as to why book sales are staging a comeback. One idea has it that customers are making multiple purchases. However, that would not explain why the top ten or twenty books are selling about double what they were a few months ago. Several publishers say the comeback reflects a growing confidence in the economy. Some bookstore owners say people are turning back to books because, despite ever higher prices, they are still a comparative entertainment bargain. The cost of a first run movie and a book are really not that far apart if the permanence of a book is taken into consideration. Other booksellers say the trend could be attributed to the lack of good movies and the baseball strike in the summer of 1981. Not everyone is convinced that the resurgence will last (in April, 1982, there were negative signs again), but whatever the reason, the industry is trying to exhibit a new found confidence.[10]

The same success cannot be said to have occurred for books with movie tie-ins. A few years ago, Bantam, Dell, Ballantine, and Warner Books were offering hundreds of thousands of dollars for screenplays they could turn into novels. This is not the case anymore. Today, the average price book publishers pay for a movie is $25,000. Recent box office successes such as *Bustin' Loose* and *The Four Seasons* never even got a nibble from publishers. In 1980, 80 percent of the major movies had book tie-ins. Today, publishers have painfully learned that it is the kind of movie rather than the success of the movie that motivates people to pay $2.50 for a volume of slightly more than 200 pages.

Love stories and comedies generally do poorly as novelizations, while horror and fantasy do well.[11] The most successful tie-in of 1982 was *E.T.*

David Rottman of Ballantine, however, is one editor who is not limiting his screenplay purchases to horror movies. "If a movie has some literary bent and you pay $25,000 for an intelligent, well-done book, you can do really well. We sold over 200,000 copies of *The Elephant Man.* That movie left a hunger in moviegoers for more information; no movie totally fleshes out a character like a book can."[12]

Most publishers are looking for well-written novelizations that can stand on their own as books. Christine Sparks, the novelizer of *The Elephant Man,* spent months researching the subject. Novelizers are no longer just studio hacks. There is a trend toward hiring authors who are already known to paperback readers to write novelizations. One of the biggest names in novelization, however, is not an author, but a producer. Random House reportedly paid George Lucas more than $1 million for a package of licensing rights to *The Empire Strikes Back,* including calendars, pop-up books, activity books, comic books, special effects books, and even a series of Hans Solo novels. There are already 900,000 copies of the novelization of Lucas's *Raiders of the Lost Ark* and such spin-offs as an illustrated film script and a book on the making of the movie are planned.[13] There is always the exception to the trend. Of course, major books are often made into successful pictures, but then, films are abbreviations of novels whereas novelizations are expansions of films. Expansion is probably the more difficult task.

If the future of novelization is cloudy, the danger of being in second place in the newspaper business is downright bleak. The demise of the *Philadelphia Bulletin* and the *Washington Star* are two recent examples. Newspaper analyst John Morton says that at least eleven major newspapers are in trouble and predicts that in the years to come there will be no second newspapers anywhere, with the possible exceptions of New York and Chicago.[14]

As the number of big city papers dwindles, the survivors become less partisan and become all things to all people.

> It is a tone curiously like that the Government imposed on television when parceling out its scarce and lucrative channels. "Equal time" and the "Fairness Doctrine" have narrow, legalistic application, but the public has extended these phrases to mean that the entire press should be a neutral, unbiased conduit of information. This notion of the press as a quasi-public utility would have enraged the domineering newspaper czars of earlier days. It might also have distressed the constitutional forefathers, who counted on a competitive free press to initiate robust, even unsporting debate.[15]

If newspapers are similar in tone and coverage, who needs to read a second paper to balance the first? Newspaper readership has been declining for years. Young people read fewer newspapers than their parents. The drop in circulation has been sharpest for the second paper, often a big city afternoon paper, which is particularly vulnerable because its best readers have fled to the suburbs where they read a suburban paper or watch the television news. Another cause of dying newspapers may be the loss of class identity. For example, there used to be papers aimed specifically at blue-collar workers. This group may have lost its specific point of view and therefore the need for a paper of its own.

To save remaining two paper markets, there would have to be changes along Madison Avenue. Leo Bogart, executive vice president of the Newspaper Advertising Bureau, says the second paper gets dropped from advertising budgets if the dominant paper reaches 60 percent of the market. Obviously, Madison Avenue does not see a difference in demographics between the two papers. If the American people really have become all alike and hold the same opinions, there are inherent dangers. If they are not already alike, the agenda set by the only paper in a city could eventually make them so, especially if the broadcast media are also presenting a single voice. Perhaps a lack of print sources can be balanced by more broadcast sources. "Equal Time" and the "Fairness Doctrine" are now being reconsidered by the Federal Communications Commission. They could be renounced, which could lead to a resurgence of multiple opinions on a broadcast station.

MEDIA CONGLOMERATES CONTINUE TO GROW

Peter A. Derow, former chairman and president of *Newsweek* has taken over the publication group of CBS. He is planning both to expand it and to make it more profitable. The publication group is divided into two areas: consumer publishing and educational and professional publishing. Recently CBS acquired *Family Weekly* and *American Photographer.* They were added to *Woman's Day, Field & Stream, Audio, Cycle World, Pick Up, Van & 4 WD, Road & Track, World Tennis,* and *Mechanix Illustrated.* Their educational and professional publishing division consists of W. B. Saunders, the world's largest medical publisher; Holt, Rinehart & Winston, which publishes educational texts as well as general interest books; and several smaller publishers of college and school books.

In addition to expansion in print, CBS is developing its own film operation again. Its first film, *Back Roads,* cost an estimated $7.5 million and has earned more than $12 million at the box office. CBS is considering establishing its own film distribution company. In addition, CBS is investing heavily in its Carrollton, Georgia, plant that is pressing video disks for the RCA Selecta Vision system, while at the same time trying to produce general programming for cable.

As television conglomerates are expanding in different media, so too are newspaper groups. Just as they were among the first to invest in television several decades ago, newspapers are now in the forefront of those who are sinking increasingly large sums into cable. Although Time Inc., Westinghouse, American Express, Warner Communications, and others also are buying extensively into cable, five of the nine all time largest cable acquisitions have been made by newspaper groups.

In moving into cable, newspaper publishers are hedging their bets. "Nobody's real sure what kind of competition cable will offer to the newspaper franchise," observed John Morton, a newspaper financial analyst. "Some people think they know, but nobody really knows. The newspaper companies want to be involved in the business so they'll be prepared."[16] Moreover, cable offers logical applications for the mountains of information constantly gathered by newspapers. Dozens of dailies have already leased cable channels through which to beam their news reports, and virtually every newspaper is studying such affiliations.

The *Los Angeles Times* became a cable operator back in 1969. It now beams service into 625,000 homes, ranking it seventh among all cable operators and the biggest cable presence among the newspaper groups. Another early starter was the Newhouse Group, the privately held empire that owns twenty-nine daily newspapers, the Condé Nast magazines, and the Random House book publishing company. It bought into the field in the late 1960s, and when its recent purchase of Vision Cable is completed, its subscriber base will reach 500,000, raising it to eighth among cable operators. Knight-Ridder Newspapers, the second biggest newspaper company, and Dow Jones & Company, publisher of *The Wall Street Journal,* came tantalizingly close to jointly buying UA-Columbia Cablevision before bowing out to United Artists Theater Circuit and Rogers' Cablesystems. The Gannett Company, the biggest newspaper group with eighty-three dailies, has shied away from cable, largely because of the steep prices. Cable systems have been getting between $700 and $1,000 a subscriber. Though it still owns no systems either, the Hearst Corporation is looking hard at cable.

An unsettled question is whether conflicts will crop up when there is common ownership of a newspaper and a cable system in the same community. No federal regulations bar such setups, though several states, among them Minnesota and Connecticut, have forbidden it. Times Mirror is locked in a court battle over a Connecticut order that it dispose of either two Connecticut cable franchises or *The Hartford Courant.* Another issue still up in the air is whether home information services will be subjected to regulation as television and radio are. And there is concern among newspaper groups about prospects like the electronic Yellow Pages from the American Telephone and Telegraph Company, which may siphon off their classified advertising.

BROADCASTING AND GOVERNMENT

Should broadcasters be freed from federal controls to make them more like newspapers? It is not a far-fetched idea. Broadcasting regulation under the present system has not worked very well. It has been cumbersome, uneven, and at times, unjust. Les Brown, writing in *The New York Times,* said he thinks that the FCC has been so protective of commercial broadcasting that it has created rules to retard the growth of cable and pay television, and a host of other new communications technologies just entering the marketplace—satellites, fiber optics, interactive cable, electronic data transmission, video disks, and home video recorders. One of government's chief justifications for broadcast regulation has been the scarcity of broadcast frequencies. But, that argument loses force with the abundance of channels of communication promised by the new technologies.

What about government involvement in public television? In 1978, *The New York Times* said that public broadcasting would get more federal funds, but not without some strings attached. In 1982, the question is whether the federal government will pull out of the funding business altogether. Such are the vagaries of public television. At one extreme, Congress is thrilled that public radio and television have found a significant audience at last. At the other extreme, they say that governments should not be involved in the broadcasting business at all. It is true that over the last several years the audience for public broadcasting has grown significantly and the industry might be able to support itself without federal aid, but only if it remains a favorite of corporate funders like Mobil and Exxon, and is allowed to have limited regular advertising. It is certain that the government should not be counted on to fund public broadcasting, and well-established fund raising auctions cannot do it all. Is there another alternative besides advertising? Probably not.

For years, broadcasters have belonged to one of the most exclusive clubs in the world, because the airways that carried television signals were limited. That's why the commercial television networks and the 600 local stations affiliated with them have just confronted each other again over the affiliates' right to a piece of lucrative evening prime time. The FCC's prime time access rule of 1970 that gave the stations the half hour from 7:30 to 8:00 P.M. or from 6:30 to 7:00 P.M. (CST) has just not worked.[18] The rule has not helped to create a more diversified line-up of shows. Of course, the affiliates want to hold on to their half hour. They grossed $585 million from it in 1980. They cite programs like "P.M. Magazine" as examples of how the rule has worked well. The local stations are not impressed with network plans for hour-long newscasts. But what it really comes down to is this: who is going to get all that money?

For those who are interested, there is an alternative to current commercial broadcasting and even cable—low power television. It began with a proposal to the FCC in 1980 for 139 additional television stations that could be "dropped in." The proposal is based on a technical decision. Engineers say that current licensees could use a narrower separation between assigned wavelengths. That would leave space for low power television with signals that cover twelve to fifteen mile areas, much like local newspapers. The price tag for constructing such a station is estimated at about $55,000, which would pay for building a 100-watt UHF station with a transmitter, a satellite earth station that allows reception and retransmissions of national or regional programming, and a transmitting antenna. Low power television makes neighborhood television a real possibility. Community groups, consumer groups, racial and ethnic groups, women's groups, and senior citizens could be heard on television.

The FCC also unveiled another new idea—micro stations. Micro stations can operate with power of one to ten watts and can cover an area of two miles. The low power stations are really adaptations of equipment that has been around for a long time but it is only recently that the FCC has encouraged applications. The original idea was to encourage local people to appear on television, but according to Rose Goldsen of Cornell University, the conglomerates already have gained control. A company called Neighborhood TV applied for 141 station licenses and all the stations will show the same programs, picking them up via satellite from a single station in Prescott, Arizona. The main earth station in Prescott sends up the program to a satellite and then the affiliated stations pick it up on their own earth stations. Allstate Insurance, a subsidiary of Sears Roebuck, owns this operation. The networks have gotten into the act, too, along with the NAB. The original idea of local and community control seems lost already.

THE WIRED SOCIETY

"I believe totally that man's lifestyle will change because of the new wired society," says Mike Dann,[19] once one of the most successful programmers in commercial television, and for most of the past decade a leading cable television consultant. "If we really are to have a better society, we simply have to stop wasting energy, crowding roads, performing services that are truly a waste of time. The bank lines are long enough. Cable affords us a much better world. We're right now in cable where we were in television at the beginning, when our idea of a television program was to televise radio. We really are just starting out. The full range of cable has hardly been touched."

Dann's vision of the future has been formed as he worked as a consultant to an ultimately unconsummated project to wire the city of Washington, D.C., as a teacher of a course at Yale called "The Wired Society," as developer of the Qube system for Warner Communications and as the initiator of a cultural channel for ABC Video Enterprises that recently began broadcasting over the Warner-Amex cable system.

In the Americas of the 1990s, says Dann, cable television will offer up to 220 different channels of services and entertainment. Most homes will be wired for cable, and, in addition to the cable console, most homes will have one or more video disk or video tape playback machines, several television sets with screens ranging in size from eight inches to eight feet, a facsimile machine, and a home computer.

Viewers may have dishes on the roofs that will allow them to receive directly from satellites as well. There will be some services on which advertising will be allowed and others for which there will be a monthly charge of as much as $50. Channels will be tailored to special interests: philatelists, bridge players, dieters, local community affairs people, computer games enthusiasts, and educational course takers. Viewers will use cable to order groceries and to pay bills. Fire and security alarm systems will use cable. Dann prophesies that the role in people's lives now captured by print media will be largely overtaken by cable. Newspapers, magazines, and books will adapt or die. Many will be printed in the home.[20] The future is already humming. For example, in 1982 every major radio network will virtually double its programming output and at least six new national networks will be on the airwaves. A major factor in network radio's renaissance is satellite distribution, a giant technological step that has vastly improved the sound quality of radio and made national networks a convenient, flexible, and economical method of programming.

CABLE'S COMPETITION

The FCC has allowed CBS to get a foot in the door of the cable television industry. The commission voted unanimously to allow CBS to own cable television systems, as long as they do not serve more than a total of 90,000 subscribers or 0.5 percent of the nation's cable television subscribers, whichever is less. About 25 percent of the 80 million U.S. households with television receive cable television, according to the National Cable Television Association.[21] The big question now is whether this is the first step by the FCC to eliminate the ban on network ownership of cable systems. Current FCC chairman, Mark Fowler, has said that he believes there should be full competition and that everyone should be allowed to compete in all the new technologies.[22]

CBS and the RCA Corporation have filed separate requests with the FCC to start services that would beam television programs from satellites directly to homes and apartments with small receiving antennas. The two communications giants and ten smaller companies met the FCC's deadline for direct broadcast proposals. The FCC will now have to decide which, if any, of the services to approve. It is expected to take into account a multinational conference scheduled for 1983 at which satellite frequencies will be divided among all nations wishing to use them.[23] These direct broadcast proposals would seem to offer competition to both cable television companies and local television stations by offering customers the option of obtaining their programming directly from a network.

The CBS plan proposed a system of satellites that would transmit three channels of high definition television—pictures twice as sharp as current television. One channel would be used to distribute programs to CBS's affiliate stations, which could then rebroadcast them.

TIME INC.—A MULTI-MEDIA PACKAGE

Time Inc. has discontinued its film operations and closed down *The Washington Star*. Although media critics were upset, Wall Street applauded. Time's $85 million investment in the *Star* over three-and-a-half years exceeded projections and Time-Life films had a pretax loss of almost $20 million in 1980. Time is moving its capital into video—spending in this area has increased from less than $50 million in 1976 to an estimated $300 million in 1981. About 60 percent of the 1981 capital budget was earmarked for the video group and the bulk of that was spent by American Television & Communications Corporation, Time's cable subsidiary.

ATC, which has 1.6 million subscribers, has more than 8,000 miles of cable to construct. Time is also in the bidding war for the remaining cable franchises around the country, but whether or not Time wins any of the remaining franchising battles, its video group will benefit from the cable explosion through its company Home Box Office Inc. Its pay TV programming service thrives. Alan P. Kassan, an analyst at First Manhattan Co., estimates that profits of Home Box jumped from $55 million in 1980 to $79 million in 1981. The cost of buying movies for the system are up, however, so profits may be squeezed in the future.

To assure itself enough channels to deliver new programming in the future, Time has agreed to buy six transponders—relay points on satellites for transmitting television signals—from Hughes Communications Inc. One of the transponders will be used for videotex, the technology used to transmit the printed word and graphics to the television screen.

The growth in Time's publishing arm is likely to be less dramatic. However, the country's largest magazine publisher and cable systems operator has started a new magazine to serve the nation's growing number of cable subscribers. Assigned to this project was the same team that brought out the highly successful *People* magazine—Richard B. Stolley, *People's* managing editor, and Richard J. Durrell, its publisher.

Source: *Business Week*, August 17, 1981, p. 107.

The other CBS channels would be use for subscription television and would carry entertainment and educational and commercial programming for use by customers, schools, hotels, and businesses.

RCA's request was more limited. It asked for use of satellites capable of transmitting six channels of television to home antennas, but it would not provide programming. It would rent the channels to other companies.[24]

Westinghouse also is expanding into cable television. Recovering from a decade of almost constant crises, the company is shifting away from the manufacture of equipment. When the FCC approved Westinghouse's acquisition of Teleprompter Corp., the second largest U.S. ca-

FIGURE 14–2 Ted
Turner (Cable News
Network)

ble television company, on June 30, 1981, the first step was taken. Teleprompters revenues, which hit about $240 million in 1981, will nearly double the size of Group W, the company's television, radio, and program production operation.[25]

NEW MEDIA ENTREPRENEURS

Ted Turner, the Atlanta entrepreneur who began the twenty-four hour Cable News Network in the spring of 1980, has started a second news network (headlines only) for cable systems. Under the name Cable News Network 2, it began operation in January, 1982, and competes with a similar service announced recently by ABC and Westinghouse. Conversely, ABC and Westinghouse also announced plans for their own second, in-depth news services aimed more directly at Turner's original Cable News Network, which includes features, talk shows, and longer news reports. That brings to four the number of news networks available via cable. Given that Turner's Cable News Network lost more than $1 million a month with the news arena to itself, the larger question is whether Turner can survive.[26]

Another entrepreneur who also takes risks is Charles Dolan. His privately held Cablevision has emerged as a maverick force in an industry increasingly dominated by large corporations. His service is novel: two nights a week of esoteric performing arts shows under the name "Bravo" and five nights a week of soft-core sex films in a package called "Escapade." The concept—brash, risky, inventive, and perhaps a bit ahead of its time—is fully consistent with the company's style.

In July, 1981, Cablevision won one of the nation's most sought after cable franchises, some 120,000 homes in affluent Fairfield County, Connecticut. It has also proven to be an aggressive bidder in the continuing competition for two of the largest remaining cable franchise plums—Boston and the New York City boroughs other than Manhattan.

The fifty-four-year-old Dolan, a pioneer in the cable industry, has parlayed a few Long Island franchises into a company that now serves 205,000 subscribers.

Cablevision's corporate structure and method of financing are unusual. Cablevision consists of a series of separate companies, each set up as a limited partnership. All are operated by Dolan, who receives about 40 percent of the equity. Thus, while his compensation has so far rarely exceeded $250,000 a year, his holdings are worth at least $80 million.

Dolan is always looking ahead. Cablevision is the only company bidding for the cable franchise in the Bronx, a borough considered economically hopeless by other companies. "I think its problems are probably exaggerated," Dolan says. "We're in this for the long haul, and I would guess that in five to ten years there will be some cycling and the Bronx will be regarded as a very valuable franchise." Besides, New York City officials have promised to give preference to companies

TED TURNER

On paper Turner has been dead several times—when he took over a failing billboard business, when he bought all but bankrupt television stations in Atlanta and Charlotte, North Carolina and when he started Cable News Network at a time when he wasn't sure how he would finance it.

Mike Dann, the ABC program advisor, tells anyone who will listen that Turner, challenged by corporate colossi like Westinghouse and ABC, will have to sell out—cheap.

Don't bet on it. Turner is used to living on the thin edge. Intense, arrogant, full of braggadocio, combative for the sheer hell of it—all the adjectives have been pulled out to describe this phenomenon and they all miss the mark. They are form. The substance is this: Ted Turner has made a career of taking on apparently impossible challenges and making spectacular successes of them against all odds.

A positive sign. Turner's first Nielsen survey of WTBS, his Atlanta "superstation," uncovered an audience at least 60% larger than Turner had been able to claim before. Now he can charge much higher advertising rates and considerably fatten his cash flow. (In 1975 Turner paid $750,000 for an earth station that carries his Atlanta Braves baseball team everywhere in North America at a fraction of the cost of laying cable.)

"Hell," says Turner, "the superstation alone will give us a cash flow of about $40 million to $50 million next year. Cable News is projected to earn around $10 million. So it's possible we could show a $60 million profit in 1982 after barely breaking even this year. When you consider that the NBC network only made $75 million last year, you see the potential."

His listener gets no chance to point out that cash flow has somehow become profit in midsentence. There is the little matter of interest, loan amortization, losses from his three sports teams of $7 million.

Source: *Forbes*, August 31, 1981, pp. 31–33.

that bid in more than one borough and Cablevision will not take the Bronx franchise unless it is given one of the other boroughs, too.[27]

Another media man to watch is Edward S. Rogers of Toronto, Canada. He wanted control of UA-Columbia Cablevision Inc. and its 450,000 U.S. subscribers badly enough to pledge his family's radio stations and extensive cable television interests for a loan to buy it. Late in May, 1981, Rogers bid $152 million for 51 percent of UA-Columbia, teaming with United Artists Theater Circuit Inc., in a $90-per-share bid that beat out an $80-per-share pitch made by Knight-Ridder and Dow Jones.

Rogers is moving into United States cable because it has fewer government regulations than Canada. UA-Columbia, for example, took in

$55 million in revenue last year from one third the subscriber base that brought Rogers's Cablesystems $70 million in revenues. The American company earned $4.8 million, more than three times the $1.4 million earnings of Rogers's cable operations.[28]

Two years ago, Timothy Flynn, a California-based cable consultant, wrote to RCA requesting space on Satcom 1, the company's new communications satellite. Because RCA must treat customers on a first-come, first-served basis, Flynn was awarded the right to a transponder—a device that transmits a television signal from a satellite. Flynn invested less than $250,000, and fourteen months later sold his space to Warner Amex Satellite Entertainment Co. for $5.5 million.

TUNING IN TO SATELLITE TV

In 1979, the Neiman-Marcus Christmas catalogue offered a backyard satellite earth station for $36,500. The dish-shaped antenna was an exotic plaything for the rich. No more. Prices for earth stations have fallen sharply, as low as $3,000, allowing home owners to pick up television satellite signals for programs such as movies, news, and sports that were formerly available only to cable television subscribers. An even bigger market consists of apartment complexes, hotels, etc.

If prices get low enough, could this spell the end of cable? Maybe.

The Microdyne Corp., a maker of earth stations for cable television and other users, has sold about 150 systems through distributors for home use in six months. Scientific Atlanta, a leading earth station maker, has sold some to the home market and the Heath Company is coming out with a do-it-yourself kit.

Those who see potential riches from the backyard antenna business point to a federal study indicating that 1.2 million American households in remote areas receive no television channels and that 4.6 million receive fewer than three channels.

Communications Satellite Corporation has proposed a service to start as early as 1985 that would broadcast three stations from satellites more powerful than the existing ones, and at a higher frequency, that would allow for home receiving dishes two and one half feet in diameter at a cost under $500.

Source: *Business Week*, June 29, 1981, p. 74.

As cable programming has increased, the demand for satellite time has intensified, and programmers are willing to pay millions of dollars in the scramble for broadcast rights. "It is a highly speculative business today, kind of like the gold rush," says Andy Setos, Warner Amex vice-president for engineering and operations. Another industry expert says, "Every cable programmer is negotiating like crazy to be sure he has good satellite space and has hedged his bets." This frenzied buying war has been created by a shortage of usable satellite space. There are currently nine domestic satellites in orbit—most with twenty-four transponders, all of which are occupied.[29]

Interestingly, despite the intense demand for space, satellite companies have been unable to participate in the profits made by middlemen such as Flynn, because the FCC monitors the amount that satellite companies can charge. But now, some companies are ready to challenge the FCC. Hughes Communications International Inc., a subsidiary of Hughes Aircraft Co., plans to launch Galaxy I at a cost of $100 million in 1983. Hughes is selling transponders and sources say the company has charged between $8 million and $15 million for each one. Time, Inc., has already said it will buy six, Westinghouse will buy four, and Times Mirror and Turner Broadcasting have snapped up two each.[30]

THE HOME INFORMATION REVOLUTION

The wired city of the future—where every home is linked in a communications grid that provides direct access to distant computer centers' large information banks—has long been the province of such authors as George Orwell and Alvin Toffler.

Now it is clear that videotex, the generic label applied to such home information retrieval systems, is no longer the stuff of science fiction. A giant home information industry is taking shape in the plans of hundreds of companies. By 1990, they are confident that videotex will be big business. This electronic cottage industry will fundamentally change the way people shop, bank, work, and communicate, since it will permit them to do all of these things without leaving their living rooms. On their video screens, they will be able to call up the news on any topic, as well as a wide variety of continuously updated information on subjects such as airline schedules and stock and commodity prices.

Several developments are now converging to launch this dream: the nation's telephone network is rapidly being upgraded to carry videotex data and more two-way cable television systems are being built. Transaction processing in financial services appears to be an item the public is willing to pay for right away. (A stumbling block in developing videotex has been the inability to identify services users would pay for.) That the public is becoming more receptive to such space age systems is indicated by the increased purchases of electronic products like computers. Most important, dozens of major corporations are now convinced that videotex could offer them their biggest potential for growth in the 1980s.[31]

Publishers like Dow Jones Co. and Knight-Ridder Newspapers Inc. see videotex opening new national markets for them by reusing the information that they already provide their readers. Financial institutions like Chemical Bank, American Express, and Merrill Lynch, Pierce, Fenner & Smith expect to use videotex immediately. Retailers ranging from Federated Department Stores Inc. to Sears, Roebuck and Company are testing videotex as a new distribution channel. Cable television operators see it as a way to win new cable franchises. Videotex will cause newspapers to change. Although no one seriously believes that newspapers will disappear, most industry watchers believe that videotex could make it difficult to recognize the newspapers of ten years from now. "I think the newspaper of the future is going to be smaller and it's going to have less detail," acknowledges Robert M. Johnson, vice-president and general manager of *The Columbus Dispatch.* Stock market listings, for example, will no longer be printed in the newspapers. As a result, newspapers are rushing to parlay their current information gathering an editing resources into a major role as information provider for the new videotex systems.

The concept of using cable in place of AT&T lines for transmitting videotex is a major reason why newspaper publishers like *The New York Times* and Times Mirror have acquired cable operations.

The telephone company, however, remains a major threat to most of the companies trying to move into the videotex market. It is in an ideal position to leverage its telephone network to perform all of the functions connected with the system. Because its phones are used an average of only about five minutes a day, there is plenty of time for adding videotex services. Thanks also to its strong expertise in computers and telephone switching, the phone company could easily run the centralized data banks of a videotex system; its Western Electric Company subsidiary currently is developing terminals for the home. It also has the base for information gathering in its staff that puts out the Yellow Pages, currently a $2.7 billion annual business. Furthermore, AT&T has blanket coverage of the U.S. market, whereas cable television has only 30 percent penetration. Only the television networks have as broad a reach as the phone company.[32] A major battle is shaping up.

CONCLUSION

Home information systems and home entertainment systems may be the wave of the future. Soon, news and research information may all come from videotex. Movies may be bought like records in the form of video disks or tape cassettes, and played at home. Sports events will come over pay television. Where there were once just 12 channels, soon there will be 200 available to the viewer. Video tape recorders will allow people to produce shows at home. Supermarket shopping, routine banking business, and other chores will be accomplished from the living room. A television conference will allow meetings between the home and the office or between offices.

It will be possible to exist without ever going outdoors. Will the public buy it? If they will, it will happen; but somehow the idea of rarely going outside seems a little claustrophobic. Why buy a video disk of a film if it will be seen only once? Isn't it fun to go out to a movie and see the picture on a larger screen with a better sound system and along with other people? Can watching a sports event on television ever be quite the same as watching it in person? How much information can be pumped into the home before the human beings living there suffer from information overload?

People may survive by interacting with machines more than they do with other people, but they will not be the same. Research in the field of communications is so weak, no one will know the results until people take a look at themselves twenty years from now.

New Directions

TRENDS IN THE '80s

■ Big city dailies will continue to die. The *New York Daily News* is already in trouble.

■ Cable television may become less important as satellite communication grows.

■ The news "leak" may become an acceptable form of journalism.

■ There will be a tremendous need for cable and satellite programming, but the money for it will be scarce.

■ Network television ratings will probably continue to drop.

■ Libel cases in journalism will continue to be a problem. In 1982, Mobil Oil President, William P. Tavoulareas, was awarded $2 million when a federal court jury concluded that The *Washington Post* libeled him in a 1979 article about his business relationship with his son.

ADDITIONAL READINGS

Branscomb, Anne W. *The First Amendment as a Shield or a Sword: An Integrated Look at Regulation of Multi-Media Ownership.* Santa Monica, Calif.: The Rand Paper Series, 1975.

The Carnegie Commission. *A Public Trust: The Report of the Carnegie Commission on the Future of Public Broadcasting.* New York: Bantam Books, 1979.

Kopkind, Andrew. "MacNeil/Lehrer's Class Act," *Columbia Journalism Review,* September/October, 1979.

NBC Corporate Planning. *Broadcasting: The Next Ten Years.* New York: National Broadcasting Company, 1977.

Owens, Bruce M.; Beebe, Jack N.; and Manning, Willard G. *Television Economics.* Lexington, Mass.: D.C. Heath, 1974.

FOOTNOTES

1. "Presidential Nominations and the Media," (Report of the American Assembly, Mt. Kisco, New York, May 11, 1979), p. 5.

2. Ibid., pp. 6-7.

3. Ibid., p. 7.

4. *Time Magazine*, December 5, 1977, p. 114.

5. Theodore H. White, "Why the Jailing of Farber Terrifies Me," *The New York Times Magazine*, November 26, 1978, p. 27.

6. Ibid., p. 72.

7. Ibid., p. 76.

8. Ibid., pp. 78, 80.

9. Benno C. Schmidt, Jr., "In the Matter of Free Press and Fair Trial," *New York Times*, July 30, 1978, p. E11.

10. *New York Times*, August 3, 1981, p. C11.

11. *New York Times*, July 21,1981, p. C7.

12. Ibid.

13. Ibid.

14. *Time Magazine*, September 14, 1981, p. 82.

15. Ibid.

16. *New York Times*, June 25,1981, p. D1.

17. Ibid., p. D17.

18. *Business Week*, August 31, 1981, p. 82.

19. *New York Times*, July 5, 1981, p. D1.

20. Ibid., p. D21

21. *Wall Street Journal,* August 5, 1981, p. 6.

22. Ibid.

23. *New York Times,* July 17, 1981, p. D4.

24. Ibid.

25. *Business Week,* August 31, 1981, p. 99.

26. *New York Times*, August 26, 1981.

27. *New York Times,* August 3, 1981, p. D7.

28. *Forbes*, July 6, 1981, p. 81.

29. *Business Week*, September 14, 1981, p. 89.

30. Ibid.

31. *Business Week*, June 29, 1981, p. 74.

32. Ibid., pp. 80, 83.

INDEX